A Short Introduction to the

Hebrew Bible

John J. Collins

Fortress Press

Minneapolis

A SHORT INTRODUCTION TO THE HEBREW BIBLE

Further materials on this volume can be found at fortresspress.com/collins.

Cover image: *Four Pithoi II*, acrylic on canvas, 2005, Carolyn Brunelle. Photo © 2007 Carolyn Brunelle.
Cover design: Josh Messner
Book design: Zan Ceeley, Trio Bookworks

Library of Congress Cataloging-in-Publication Data

Collins, John Joseph
 A short introduction to the Hebrew Bible / John J. Collins.
   p. cm.
 Includes bibliographical references and index.
 ISBN 978-0-8006-6207-3 (alk. paper)
 1. Bible. O.T.—Introductions. I. Collins, John Joseph
Introduction to the Hebrew Bible. II. Title.
 BS1140.3.C653 2007
 221.6'1—dc22

                                               2007008177

The paper used in this publication meets the minimum requirements of American National Standard for Information Sciences—Permanence of Paper for Printed Library Materials, ANSI Z329.48-1984.

Manufactured in the U.S.A.

14   13   9   10

A Short Introduction to the

Hebrew Bible

Contents

Part One The Torah/Pentateuch

Part Two The Deuteronomistic History

Part Three **Prophecy**

Part Four **The Writings**

List of Illustrations

Maps (*continued*)

Color Plates (following page 148)

Preface

This book is an abridgment edition of *Introduction to the Hebrew Bible with CD-ROM*, published by Fortress Press in 2004. The abridgment was achieved mainly by omitting elaborations and details. I have also omitted several minor prophets: Micah, Nahum, Zephaniah, Obadiah, and Habakkuk, and some of the deutero-canonical books (Tobit, Judith, Baruch). Some additional illustrations have been included, and also some short vignettes on topics of interest, scattered through the book. A companion website, available at fortresspress.com/collins, includes chapter summaries, study and research guides, materials for PowerPoint presentations, and other resources for teachers and students.

This book is written out of the experience of teaching introductory courses on the Old Testament or Hebrew Bible at several different institutions over thirty years. The students in these courses have included Catholic seminarians (at Mundelein Seminary and the University of Notre Dame), undergraduates (at DePaul, Notre Dame, and the University of Chicago), Master of Divinity students of all denominations (at Chicago and Yale), and Master of Arts students who, like the undergraduates, might have a religious commitment or might not. They have been predominantly Christians but have also included good numbers of Jews and Unitarians (especially at Chicago). Most of these students came to the courses with some knowledge of the Bible, but some were unencumbered by any previous knowledge of the subject. This introductory textbook is written to meet the needs of any or all such students. It presupposes a certain level of literacy, and some previous acquaintance with the Bible would definitely be helpful. It is intended, however, as a book for those who are beginning serious study rather than for experts. It is meant to be ecumenical, in the sense that it does not seek to impose any particular theological perspective, but to provide information and raise questions that should be relevant to any student, regardless of faith commitment. The information is largely drawn from the history, archaeology, and literature of the ancient Near East. The questions are primarily ethical and reflect the fact that people of different faith commitments continue to read these texts as scripture in the modern world.

The introduction is historical-critical in the sense that it emphasizes that the biblical text is the product of a particular time and place and is rooted in the culture of the ancient Near East. Since much of the Old Testament tells an ostensibly historical story, questions of historical accuracy must be addressed. In part, this is a matter of correlating the biblical account with evidence derived from archaeology and other historical sources. But it also leads to a discussion of the genre of the biblical text. The historylike appearance of biblical narrative should not be confused with historiography in the modern sense. Our best guide to the genre of biblical narrative is the corpus of literature from the ancient Near East that has been recovered over the last two hundred years.

This introduction, however, is not only historical in orientation. The primary importance of the Old Testament as scripture lies in its ethical implications. In some cases biblical material is ethically inspiring—the story of liberation from slavery in Egypt, the Ten Commandments, the preaching of the prophets on social justice. In other cases, however, it is repellent to modern sensibilities. The command to slaughter the Canaanites is the showcase example, but there are numerous issues relating to slaves, women, homosexuality, and the death penalty that are, at the very least, controversial in a modern context. In any of these cases, whether congenial to modern sensibilities or not, this introduction tries to use the biblical text as a springboard for raising issues of enduring importance. The text is not a source of answers to these issues, but rather a source of questions. Most students initially see the text through a filter of traditional interpretations. It is important to appreciate how these traditional interpretations arose, but also to ask how far they are grounded in the biblical text and whether other interpretations are possible.

Since this book is intended for students, I have tried to avoid entanglement in scholarly controversies. For this reason, there are no footnotes. Instead, each chapter is followed by suggestions for further reading. These suggestions point the student especially to commentaries and reference works that they can use as resources. Inevitably, the bibliographies are highly selective and consist primarily of books that I have found useful. Many other items could be listed with equal validity, but I hope that these suggestions will provide students with a reliable place to start. Since they are intended primarily for English-speaking students, they are limited to items that are available in English.

I would like to thank the staff at Fortress Press, particularly Neil Elliott and Josh Messner, James Pfeiffer, who suggested the abridgment, and anyone else who worked on the book. The chapter summaries were prepared in large part by Matthew Neujahr. The book is dedicated to the students of Yale Divinity School.

Abbreviations

AB   Anchor Bible

ABD   *Anchor Bible Dictionary*. Edited by D. N. Freedman. 6 vols. New York: Doubleday, 1992

ANET   *Ancient Near Eastern Texts Relating to the Old Testament*. Edited by J. B. Pritchard. 3d ed. Princeton: Princeton Univ. Press, 1969

AOTC   Abingdon Old Testament Commentaries

BAR   *Biblical Archaeology Review*

B.C.E.   Before the Common Era

BerO   Berit Olam

CC   Continental Commentaries

C.E.   Common Era

ConBOT   Coniectanea biblica: Old Testament series

FCB   Feminist Companion to the Bible

FOTL   Forms of the Old Testament Literature

GBS   Guides to Biblical Scholarship

HSM   Harvard Semitic Monographs

ICC   International Critical Commentary

JPS   Jewish Publication Society

JSOT   *Journal for the Study of the Old Testament*

JSOTSup   Journal for the Study of the Old Testament Supplement Series

LXX   Septuagint (Greek version)

MT   Masoretic text

NCB   New Century Bible

NIB   *New Interpreter's Bible*

NICOT   New International Commentary on the Old Testament

NRSV   New Revised Standard Version

OBT   Overtures to Biblical Theology

OTL   Old Testament Library

RSV   Revised Standard Version

SBL   Society of Biblical Literature

SBLDS   SBL Dissertation Series

SBLEJL   SBL Early Jewish Literature Series

SBLMS   SBL Monograph Series

SBLSymS   SBL Symposium Series

SBLWAW   SBL Writings from the Ancient World

VTE   Vassal Treaties of Esarhaddon

VTSup   Supplements to Vetus Testamentum

WBC   Word Biblical Commentary

Introduction

What Are the Hebrew Bible and Old Testament?

KEY POINTS

- **Hebrew Bible**: Law, Prophets, Writings (Torah, Nebiim, Ketibim = **TANAK**).
- **Protestant Old Testament**: same books, different order
- **Catholic Old Testament**: includes deuterocanonical or apocryphal books.
- **Septuagint (LXX)**: Greek Bible.
- **Vulgate**: Latin Bible, translated by Jerome.
- Gradual development of **canon**.
- **Dead Sea Scrolls**, discovered 1947–1956: oldest biblical manuscripts.
- **Biblical chronology**:
  Adam to the flood: 1,656 years, 10 generations (Genesis 5).
  The flood to Abraham: 290 years, 10 generations (Genesis 11).
  Abraham to the descent of Jacob and his family to Egypt: 290 years, 3 generations (Genesis 12–50).
  The sojourn in Egypt: 430 years, 3 generations (Exodus 12:40).
  The conquest of Canaan: 5 years.
  The Judges: 470 years.
  David and Solomon.

Divided kingdom:
—Israel (northern kingdom) survived 200 years;
—Judah (southern kingdom) survived 335 years.
Babylonian exile.
The Postexilic or Second Temple period.
- **Modern chronology**:
1250 B.C.E: Exodus
950: Solomon
722: Destruction of northern kingdom
586: Destruction of Jerusalem. Babylonian exile
539: Restoration
- **Methods in Biblical Study**:
  Source criticism
  Form criticism
  Redaction criticism
  Archaeology
  Literary criticism
  Sociological approaches

The writings that make up the Hebrew Bible or the Christian Old Testament are by any reckoning among the most influential writings in Western history. In part, their influence may be ascribed to their literary quality, but mainly it derives from the fact that they are regarded as sacred scripture by Jews and Christians and are viewed as authoritative in a way that other literary classics are not. The idea of sacred Scripture, however, is by no means a clear one, and it means very different things to different people. Some conservative Christians regard the Bible as the inspired word of God, verbally inerrant in all its details. At the liberal end of the spectrum, others regard it only as a witness to the foundational stages of Western religion.

1

The Different Canons
of Scripture

The Hebrew Bible and the Old Testament are not quite the same thing.

The *Hebrew Bible* is a collection of twenty-four books in three divisions: the Law *(Tōrāh)*, the Prophets *(Nᵉbi'im)*, and the Writings *(Kᵉtûbim)*, sometimes referred to by the acronym Tanak.

The Torah consists of five books: Genesis, Exodus, Leviticus, Numbers, and Deuteronomy (traditionally, the books of Moses).

The Prophets are divided into the four books of the Former Prophets (Joshua, Judges, Samuel, and Kings; 1 and 2 Samuel and 1 and 2 Kings are each counted as one book) and the four of the Latter Prophets (Isaiah, Jeremiah, Ezekiel, and the Twelve; the twelve Minor Prophets [Hosea, Joel, Amos, Obadiah, Jonah, Micah, Nahum, Habakkuk, Zephaniah, Haggai, Zechariah, Malachi] are counted as one book).

The Writings consist of eleven books: Psalms, Proverbs, Job, Song of Songs (or Canticles), Ruth, Lamentations, Qoheleth (or Ecclesiastes), Esther, Daniel, Ezra-Nehemiah (as one book), and Chronicles (1 and 2 Chronicles as one book).

The *Christian Old Testament* is so called in contrast to the New Testament, with the implication that the Old Testament is in some sense superseded by the New. There are significant differences, however, within the Christian churches as to the books that make up the Old Testament.

The *Protestant Old Testament* has the same content as the Hebrew Bible but arranges the books differently. The first five books are the same but are called the Pentateuch rather than the Torah. Samuel, Kings, Ezra-Nehemiah, and Chronicles are each counted as two books,

and the Minor Prophets as twelve, yielding a total of thirty-nine books. The Former Prophets are regarded as historical books and grouped with Chronicles and Ezra-Nehemiah. Daniel is counted as a prophetic book. The (Latter) Prophets are moved to the end of the collection, so as to point forward to the New Testament.

The *Roman Catholic canon* contains several books that are not in the Hebrew Bible or the Protestant Old Testament: Tobit, Judith, Wisdom of Solomon, Ecclesiasticus (or the Wisdom of Jesus, son of Sirach = Ben Sira), Baruch, Letter of Jeremiah (= Baruch 6), 1 and 2 Maccabees. Furthermore, the books of Daniel and Esther contain passages that are not found in the Hebrew Bible. In the case of Daniel, these are the Prayer of Azariah and the Song of the Three Young Men, which are inserted in Daniel 3, and the stories of Susanna and Bel and the Dragon.

The additional books are called Apocrypha (literally, "hidden away") in Protestant terminology. Catholics often refer to them as "deuterocanonical" or "secondarily canonical" books, in recognition of the fact that they are not found in the Hebrew Bible.

Why Are There Different Canons
of Scripture?

The *Hebrew Bible* took shape over several hundred years and attained its final form only in the first century C.E.

The *Torah* may have been substantially complete in the fifth century B.C.E., but there were still some additions or modifications later than that.

The *Prophets* formed a recognized category in the second century B.C.E. We find references to the Torah and the Prophets in the second century B.C.E. in the book of Ben Sira (Ecclesiasticus) and again in the Dead Sea Scrolls (in a document known as 4QMMT). The book of Daniel, which was composed about 164 B.C.E., is not included in the Prophets in the Hebrew Bible, and this may indicate that the collection of the Prophets was already fixed.

The *Writings*: The preface to the book of Ben Sira also mentions other writings that were regarded as authoritative, but there was no definitive list of these before the first century C.E. Most references to the Jewish Scriptures in the writings of this period (including references in the New Testament) speak only of "the Law and the Prophets." The Psalms are sometimes added as a third category. The first references to a fixed number of authoritative Hebrew writings are found toward the end of the first century C.E. The Jewish historian Josephus gives the number as twenty-two, while the Jewish apocalypse of *4 Ezra* (= 2 Esdras 3–14) speaks of twenty-four. It is possible that both had the same books in mind but that Josephus combined some books (Judges-Ruth and Jeremiah-Lamentations) that were counted separately in *4 Ezra*.

The fixing of the Hebrew canon is often associated with the so-called Council of Jamnia, the discussions of an authoritative group of rabbis after the fall of Jerusalem in 70 C.E. It is misleading, however, to speak of a "Council" of Jamnia, since it suggests a meeting like the ecumenical councils of the Christian church. The rabbis debated the status of some books (Qoheleth and Song of Songs), but there is no evidence that they proclaimed a formal list of Scriptures. Nonetheless, it is at this time (70–100 C.E.) that we first find references to a fixed number of authoritative books.

The books that were included in the Hebrew Bible were only a small selection from the religious writings that were current in Judaism. A larger selection was preserved in the Greek Scriptures that were taken over by the early Christians but had been current in Jewish communities outside Israel, especially in Alexandria in Egypt. According to legend, the Torah had been translated into Greek at the request of Ptolemy II Philadelphus, king of Egypt, in the first half of the third century B.C.E., by seventy-two elders. The translation became known as the Septuagint or LXX ("Septuagint" means "seventy"). The name was eventually extended to cover the whole collection of Greek Scriptures. This larger collection included translations of some books that were written in Hebrew (e.g., the book of Ben Sira, 1 Maccabees) and also some books that were composed in Greek (2 Maccabees, Wisdom of Solomon). The Jews of Alexandria did not set a limit to the number of the sacred writings. The Jewish community in Alexandria was virtually wiped out in the early second century C.E. Christians who took over the Greek Scriptures of the Jews inherited a larger and more fluid collection than the Hebrew Bible. There is still considerable variation among the lists of Old Testament books cited by the church fathers centuries later.

When Jerome translated the Bible into Latin about 400 C.E., he based his translation on the Hebrew. He also translated the books that were not found in the Hebrew but accorded them lesser status. His translation, known as the Vulgate, was very influential, but nonetheless the Christian church continued to accept the larger Greek canon down through the Middle Ages. At the time of the Reformation, Martin Luther advocated a return to the Hebrew canon, although he also translated the Apocrypha. In reaction to Luther, the Roman Catholic Church defined its larger canon at the Council of Trent in the mid-sixteenth century.

It should be apparent from this discussion that the list of books that make up the

Canons of the Hebrew Bible and Old Testament

Hebrew Bible	Protestant Old Testament	
Torah	**Pentateuch**	**Prophets**
Genesis	Genesis	Isaiah
Exodus	Exodus	Jeremiah
Leviticus	Leviticus	Lamentations
Numbers	Numbers	Ezekiel
Deuteronomy	Deuteronomy	Daniel
		Hosea
Prophets (Former)	**Historical Books**	Joel
Joshua	Joshua	Amos
Judges	Judges	Obadiah
Samuel (1 and 2)	Ruth	Jonah
Kings (1 and 2)	1 Samuel	Micah
	2 Samuel	Nahum
Prophets (Latter)	1 Kings	Habakkuk
Isaiah	2 Kings	Zephaniah
Jeremiah	1 Chronicles	Haggai
Ezekiel	2 Chronicles	Zechariah
Minor Prophets	Ezra	Malachi
("The Twelve"):	Nehemiah	
Hosea, Joel, Amos,	Esther	**Apocrypha**
Obadiah, Jonah,		1 Esdras
Micah, Nahum,	**Poetry/Wisdom**	2 Esdras
Habakkuk,	Job	Tobit
Zephaniah, Haggai,	Psalms	Judith
Zechariah,	Proverbs	Additions to Esther
Malachi	Ecclesiastes	Wisdom of Solomon
	(Qoheleth)	Ecclesiasticus
Writings	Song of Solomon	(Wisdom of Sirach)
Psalms	(Songs)	Baruch
Proverbs		Letter of Jeremiah
Job		Prayer of Azariah
Song of Songs		and Song of the
Ruth		Three Young Men
Lamentations		Susanna
Qoheleth		Bel and the Dragon
(Ecclesiastes)		Prayer of Manasseh
Esther		1 Maccabees
Daniel		2 Maccabees
Ezra-Nehemiah		
Chronicles (1 and 2)		

Canons of the Hebrew Bible and Old Testament (cont.)

Roman Catholic Old Testament

Pentateuch

Genesis
Exodus
Leviticus
Numbers
Deuteronomy

Historical Books

Joshua
Judges
Ruth
1 Samuel
2 Samuel
1 Kings
2 Kings
1 Chronicles
2 Chronicles
Ezra (Greek and
    Russian Orthodox
    Bibles also include
    1 Esdras, and Russian
    Orthodox includes
    2 Esdras)
Nehemiah
Tobit
Judith
Esther (with additions)
1 Maccabees
2 Maccabees (Greek
    and Russian
    Orthodox Bibles
    include 3 Maccabees)

Poetry/Wisdom

Job
Psalms (Greek and
    Russian Orthodox
    Bibles include
    Psalm 151 and Prayer
    of Manasseh)
Proverbs
Ecclesiastes
(Qoheleth)
Song of Solomon
    (Songs)
Wisdom of Solomon
Ecclesiasticus
    (Wisdom of Sirach)

Prophets

Isaiah
Jeremiah
Lamentations
Baruch (includes
    Letter of Jeremiah)
Ezekiel
Daniel (with
    additions)
Hosea
Joel
Amos
Obadiah
Jonah
Micah
Nahum
Habakkuk
Zephaniah
Haggai
Zechariah
Malachi

Hebrew Bible and the Christian Old Testament emerged gradually over time. The various canons were eventually determined by the decisions of religious communities. Christian theology has often drawn a sharp line between Scripture and tradition, but in fact Scripture itself is a product of tradition. Its content and shape are subject to the decisions of religious authorities.

The Text of the Bible

Modern English translations of the Bible are based on the printed editions of the Hebrew Bible and the principal ancient translations (especially Greek and Latin). These printed editions are themselves based on ancient manuscripts. In the case of the Hebrew Bible, the most important manuscripts date from the tenth and eleventh centuries c.e., almost a thousand years after the canon of the Hebrew Bible was fixed. The text found in these manuscripts is called the Masoretic text, or MT. The discovery of the Dead Sea Scrolls in caves near Qumran, south of Jericho, beginning in 1947, brought to light manuscripts of all biblical books, except Esther and Nehemiah, that are more than a thousand years older than these manuscripts. The oldest of these scrolls date

from the third century b.c.e. Many of these texts agree with the MT, but some differ and are closer to the Greek.

There are fragments of Greek biblical manuscripts from the second century b.c.e. on. The oldest complete manuscripts date from the fourth century c.e. The Greek translations were generally very literal and reflected the Hebrew text closely. Nonetheless, in many cases they differed significantly from the MT. The books of Jeremiah and Job are much shorter in the Greek than in the Hebrew. The Dead Sea Scrolls contain Hebrew texts of Jeremiah that are very close to the Greek, although other copies agree with the MT.

Fig. 0.1. A few lines of the Hebrew Bible (from Isaiah). Israel Museum, Jerusalem. Photo: © Erich Lessing / Art Resource.

The Dead Sea Scrolls

In 1947, ancient Hebrew scrolls were found in a cave near the site of Qumran, on the shore of the Dead Sea, south of Jericho. These included a copy of the book of Isaiah that proved to be 1,000 years older than than the oldest extant Hebrew biblical manuscripts. Over the next decade, many more scrolls came to light, fragments of more than 800 manuscripts in all. Some of these scrolls describe a quasi-monastic sectarian community that is thought to have lived on the site of Qumran. Some of the scrolls

continues on next page

continues from previous page

deal with matters of legal interpretation, on which the sect disagreed with the rest of Judaism. Some provide the earliest formal commentaries on biblical texts. Others speak of a coming war between Sons of Light and Sons of Darkness or refer to the expectation of messianic figures. These scrolls are important evidence for Judaism in the century or so before the rise of Christianity. They provide evidence of some Jewish trends that were taken up in Christianity and others that were developed in rabbinic Judaism.

More than 200 manuscripts are fragments of biblical books. These are by far the oldest biblical manuscripts that we have. They include fragments of every book in the Hebrew Bible except Esther and Nehemiah. On the whole, the Dead Sea Scrolls show that the text now printed in our Hebrew Bibles (the Masoretic text) had taken shape before the time of Jesus. But they also show some interesting variations. In some cases, Hebrew manuscripts found at Qumran agree with the Greek Bible (the Septuagint, LXX). For example, the Masoretic text says that 70 of Jacob's descendants went with him to Egypt. The LXX and a text of Exodus found in Cave 4 at Qumran say 75. A more significant variation occurs at Deut 32:8, where the Masoretic text says that God divided the nations according to the number of the sons of Israel. Scholars had long suspected that the Greek, which reads either "angels of God" or "sons of God," was correct. A manuscript from Qumran preserves the reading "sons of God." In the story of David and Goliath, the Masoretic text gives Goliath's height as six cubits and a span, or about nine feet nine inches. The Greek measures him at four cubits and a span (about six feet nine inches). A manuscript from Qumran supports the Greek. The Greek translation was made long before the scrolls containing the Masoretic text were copied, and it sometimes contains superior readings.

The differences in some books are more far-reaching still. The Greek text of Jeremiah is about one-eighth shorter than the Masoretic Hebrew. Both forms of the text are found in the scrolls. A scroll containing psalms from Qumran arranges the last part of the psalter in a different order from the Masoretic Bible and includes an extra psalm that is also found in the Greek.

All of this provides a rare glimpse of the process by which the text of the Bible was formed. Few of the variations involve matters of major importance, but they teach us to be wary of any claims based on the literal words of the Bible. Often these words exist in more than one form.

Chronology
Approximate dates implied in Bible for early history

4000 B.C.E.	Creation
2400	Flood
2100	Abraham
1875	Descent into Egypt
1445	Exodus
1000	David

It now seems likely that the differences between the Greek and the Hebrew texts were not due to the translators but reflect the fact that the Greek was based on a shorter Hebrew text. This is also true in 1 Samuel 16–18 and in a number of other cases. There were different forms of the Hebrew text in circulation in the third, second, and first centuries B.C.E. In some cases, the Greek may preserve an older form of the text than the Hebrew. For example, the shorter form of Jeremiah is likely to be older than the form preserved in the Hebrew Bible.

In light of this, it makes little sense to speak of verbal inerrancy in connection with the biblical text. In many cases we cannot be sure what the exact words of the Bible should be. This is not to say that the wording of the Bible is unreliable. The Dead Sea Scrolls have shown that there is, on the whole, an amazing degree of continuity in the way the text has been copied over thousands of years. But even a casual comparison of a few current English Bibles should make clear that there are many areas of uncertainty in the biblical text. We do not have a perfect copy of the original text. We only have copies made centuries after the books were originally composed, and these copies often differ among themselves.

The Bible and History

The Bible is a product of history. It took shape over time, and its content and even its wording changed in the process.

The Bible is also immersed in history in another way. Much of it tells the story about the people Israel that has at least the appearance of a historical narrative. For most of Jewish and Christian history there has been an uncritical assumption that this story is historically true. In the last 200 years, however, other information about the ancient world has come to light, through archaeological exploration and through the recovery of ancient literature. This information is often at variance with the account given in the Bible.

Biblical Chronology

The following outline of history emerges from data in the biblical text:

Adam to the flood: 1,656 years, 10 generations (Genesis 5)

The flood to Abraham, 290 years, 10 generations (Genesis 11)

Abraham to the descent of Jacob and his family to Egypt: 290 years, 3 generations (Genesis 12–50)

The sojourn in Egypt: 430 years, 3 generations (Exod 12:40)

The conquest of Canaan: 5 years

The Judges: 470 years

Transition period under Saul and David

According to 1 Kgs 6:1, Solomon began to build the temple in Jerusalem 480 years after the exodus. This figure is incompatible with the number of years assigned to the Judges.

In the generation after Solomon, the kingdom was divided in two:

Israel (the northern kingdom) survived 200 years.

Judah (the southern kingdom) survived 335 years.

Then came the Babylonian exile, followed by the postexilic or Second Temple period.

The destructions of northern Israel and its capital, Samaria, and of Judah and its capital, Jerusalem, allow us to correlate the history of Israel with the general history of the Near East, since these events are also recorded in Assyrian and Babylonian records. From these records we get the following dates:

722 B.C.E.: The fall of Samaria

597 B.C.E.: First capture of Jerusalem by the Babylonians

586 B.C.E.: Second capture of Jerusalem, the destruction of the temple, and the beginning of the Babylonian exile.

If we work back from the dates of the destructions and add up the years of the kings of Israel and Judah, we arrive at the following dates:

About 950 B.C.E.: Solomon

About 1450 B.C.E.: The exodus

About 1876 B.C.E.: The descent of Jacob and his family into Egypt

About 2100 B.C.E.: Abraham

The seventeenth-century Irish Anglican bishop James Ussher famously calculated the date of creation as 4004 B.C.E.

Modern scholarship has generally accepted the biblical chronology of the period of the monarchy, since it can be correlated with nonbiblical sources at several points. The dates for the exodus and the patriarchs, however, are viewed with great skepticism. The life spans of the patriarchs are unrealistic, ranging from 110 to 175 years. The 430 years in Egypt are supposed to cover only three generations. Most scholars place the exodus about 1250 B.C.E., but many now question whether we can claim any historical knowledge about the patriarchs or even the exodus.

Both the biblical record and modern scholarship place the emergence of Israel as a people in the second half of the second millennium B.C.E. Modern reconstructions favor the last quarter of that millennium, roughly 1250–1000 B.C.E. The biblical dates put it about two centuries earlier.

One implication of this chronological survey is that Israel was a late arrival on the stage of Near Eastern history. The great civilizations of Egypt and Mesopotamia had already flourished for a millennium and a half before the tribes of Israel appeared on the scene.

A second implication is that there is a gap of several centuries between the date when the biblical books were written and the events that they claim to describe. Traditionally, the books of the Torah were supposed to be works of Moses, but it has long been clear that Moses could not have been their author. It now seems clear that the entire Hebrew Bible received its final shape in the postexilic, or Second Temple period, long after the events it describes.

Modern Chronology

The historical value of the stories of the patriarchs is uncertain.
Modern scholars have often proposed a date of 1800 B.C.E. for Abraham.

1250 B.C.E. (approx.)	Exodus from Egypt (disputed).
1250–1000	Emergence of Israel in the highlands of Canaan.
1000–960 (approx.)	King David. Beginning of monarchy in Jerusalem (disputed).
960–922 (approx.)	King Solomon. Building of Jerusalem temple (disputed).
922	Division of kingdom: Israel in the north, Judah in the south.
722/721	Destruction of Samaria, capital of Israel, by the Assyrians. End of kingdom of Israel.
621	Reform of Jerusalem cult by King Josiah. Promulgation of "the book of the law" (some form of Deuteronomy).
597	Capture of Jerusalem by Babylonians. Deportation of king and nobles to Babylon.
586	Destruction of Jerusalem by Babylonians. More extensive deportations. Beginning of Babylonian exile.
539	Conquest of Babylon by Cyrus of Persia. Jewish exiles allowed to return to Jerusalem. End of exile. Judah becomes a province of Persia.
520–515	Rebuilding of Jerusalem Temple.
458	Ezra sent from Babylon to Jerusalem with a copy of the Law.
336–323	Alexander the Great conquers the Persian Empire.
312–198	Judea controlled by the Ptolemies of Egypt (a Greek dynasty, founded by one of Alexander's generals).
198	Jerusalem conquered by the Seleucids of Syria (also a Greek dynasty).
168/167	Persecution of Jews in Jerusalem by Antiochus IV Epiphanes, king of Syria. Maccabean revolt.
63	Conquest of Jerusalem by Roman general Pompey.
66–70 C.E.	First Jewish revolt against Rome. Destruction of Jerusalem Temple.
132–135 C.E.	Second Jewish revolt under Bar Kochba. Jerusalem rebuilt as Aelia Capitolina, with a temple to Jupiter Capitolinus.

Chronology of Modern Biblical Scholarship

1735	Jean Astruc observes multiple names for the divinity in the Pentateuch.
1805	W. M. L. de Wette dates Deuteronomy later than the rest of the Pentateuch.
1822	Jean-François Champollion deciphers Egyptian hieroglyphics for the first time.
1860s	Karl Heinrich Graf and Abraham Kuenen establish a chronological order for the various "sources" in the Pentateuch: (J, E, D, P).
1870s	Discovery of great works of Akkadian literature, such as the creation story *Enuma Elish* and the Gilgamesh epic.
1878	Julius Wellhausen, in *Prolegmonena to the History of Israel*, presents his classic study of the Documentary Hypothesis.
1890–1920	Hermann Gunkel pioneers form criticism, which examines the literary genre of shorter biblical passages and their *Sitz im Leben* (social location).
1920s–1930s	Discovery of Canaanite texts at Ugarit (1929) and the efforts of W. F. Albright to confirm the historical accuracy of the Bible through archaeology.
Mid-20th c.	Gerhard von Rad and Martin Noth examine the editorial history of biblical texts through redaction criticism.
	American scholarship dominated by Albright and his students.
	John Bright's *History of Israel* (1959) provides synthesis of biblical data and ancient Near Eastern history.
	Biblical Theology Movement, emphasizing the "acts of God in history" typified by archaeologist G. Ernest Wright.
1947–54	Discovery of Dead Sea Scrolls at Qumran.
1960s–present	Biblical scholarship characterized by a multiplicity of approaches, including study of religion and literature of Israel in light of Near Eastern, especially Ugaritic, traditions (F. M. Cross); sociological (N. K. Gottwald), literary (R. Alter), feminist/literary (P. Trible) approaches; canonical approach to biblical theology (B. S. Childs); revisionist Pentateuchal studies; questioning traditional sources (see overview by E. W. Nicholson); revisionist approaches to Israelite history (see I. Finkelstein and N. A. Silberman).

Methods in Biblical Study

Most of the books that make up the Hebrew Bible were composed in several stages over many centuries. Consequently there are many gaps and inconsistencies in the biblical text, and it seems to reflect several different historical settings.

The history of biblical scholarship is in large part a sequence of attempts to come to grips with the composite character of the biblical text:

1. Source Criticism. In the nineteenth century "literary criticism" of the Bible was understood primarily as the separation of sources (source criticism), especially in the case of the Pentateuch. This phase of biblical scholarship found its classic expression in the work of the German scholar Julius Wellhausen (1844–1918) in the 1870s and 1880s, and it remains important today.

2. Form Criticism. A reaction against this kind of source criticism appeared in the work of another German scholar, Hermann Gunkel (1862–1932). Form criticism focuses on the smaller units that make up the biblical text, such as the individual stories in Genesis. Gunkel drew attention to the importance of literary form or genre, and to the importance of social location (the *Sitz im Leben*) for the meaning of a text. Gunkel also made extensive use of newly available Babylonian literature for comparison with the biblical material.

3. Redaction Criticism. One disadvantage of form criticism was that it tended to break up the biblical text into small fragments. In the mid-twentieth century, a reaction against this fragmentation arose in the form of redaction criticism. Here the focus was on the way in which the smaller units were combined by an editor, who imposed his own theological agenda on the material. The classic works of redaction criticism were again by German scholars, Gerhard von Rad (1901–1971) and Martin Noth (1902–1968). Redaction criticism showed the beginnings of a shift of interest that has continued in more recent scholarship, placing the main emphasis on the later rather than on the earlier forms of the text.

4. Archaeology. The scholarship mentioned thus far all developed in Germany, where the most influential biblical criticism developed in the nineteenth and early twentieth centuries. A different tradition of scholarship developed in North America, which attached great importance to archaeology as a source of independent confirmation of the biblical text. Archaeological discoveries could also help to fill out the context of the biblical material. The dominant figure in North American scholarship through the first half of the twentieth century was W. F. Albright (1891–1971). Albright also made extensive use of the literature of the ancient Near East as the context within which the Bible should be understood. Albright's view of the history of Israel found classic expression in the work of his student John Bright (1908–1995).

In Albright's lifetime, archaeology was believed to support the historicity of the biblical account (not necessarily in all its details), although there were some troubling discrepancies (for example, archaeologists found no evidence of the destruction of a walled city at Jericho in the time of Joshua). In the last quarter of the century, however, the tide has turned on this subject. Discrepancies between the archaeological record and the biblical narrative are now seen to outweigh the points of convergence.

5. Current Methods. At the dawn of the twenty-first century, biblical scholarship is characterized by a diversity of methods. Here I will comment only on two broad trends, the

rise of literary criticism and the influence of sociological methods.

a. **Literary Criticism.** The Bible is literature, whatever else it may be, and any serious biblical study must have a literary component. Literary scholarship, however, is of many kinds. Beginning in the 1960s, literary criticism of the Bible was heavily influenced by a movement called "New Criticism" in the study of English literature. New Criticism was a formalistic movement that held that the meaning of a text can be found through close examination of the text itself, without extensive research into questions of social, historical, and literary context. The attraction of this method was that it directed attention to the text itself. Nonetheless, it has obvious limitations insofar as it leaves out of account factors that may help to clarify and explain the text. In general literary studies, a reaction against the formalism of New Criticism has arisen in a movement called "New Historicism," which appreciates the importance of contextual information while still maintaining its focus on the literary text.

Another consequence of the rise of literary criticism has been increased attention to the final form of biblical books. On the whole, this has been a positive development. We should bear in mind, however, that the books of the Bible are not governed by the same literary conventions as a modern novel or treatise. In many cases they are loose compilations and the conventional book divisions are not always reliable guides to literary coherence. There is more than one way to read such literature. If we are to appreciate the "composite artistry" of biblical literature, then the final form of the text cannot be the only focus. Questions of genre and literary conventions are fundamental, but we are dealing with ancient genres and conventions, not those of modern literature.

b. **Sociological approaches.** The second major trend in recent biblical studies is the increased use of sociological methods. These methods also vary. They may be viewed as an extension of traditional historical criticism insofar as they view the text as a reflection of historical situations. Perhaps the most fundamental contribution of sociological theory to biblical studies, however, is the realization that interpretation is not objective and neutral but serves human interests and is shaped by them. On the one hand, the biblical texts themselves reflect the ideological interests of their authors. This insight follows naturally enough from the form-critical insistence on the importance of the *Sitz im Leben*. On the other hand, the modern interpreter also has a social location. Feminist scholarship has repeatedly pointed out male patriarchal assumptions in biblical scholarship and has made little secret of its own agenda and commitments. Jewish scholars have pointed out that Christian interpretations are often colored by theological assumptions. But no one is exempt from presuppositions and special interests. One of the clearest gains of recent "postmodern" scholarship has been the increased attention to figures and interests that are either marginal in the biblical text or have been marginalized in previous scholarship. Feminist scholarship has led the way in this regard.

The Approach of This Introduction

This introduction builds on the tradition of historical-critical scholarship. I view the text in its historical context, relating it where possible to the history of the time and respecting the ancient literary conventions.

Placing the Bible in its historical context is not, however, an end in itself. For most readers of the Bible, this is not only a document of ancient history but also in some way a guide for modern living. The responsible use of the Bible must begin by acknowledging that these books were not written with our modern situations in mind, and are informed by the assumptions of an ancient culture remote from our own. To understand the Bible in its historical context is first of all to appreciate what an alien book it is. But no great literature is completely alien. There are always analogies between the ancient world and our own. Biblical laws and the prophetic preaching repeatedly raise issues that still confront us in modern society. The Bible does not provide ready answers to these problems, but it provides occasions and examples to enable us to think about them and grapple with them.

Further Reading

Formation of the Canon

Collins, John J. "Before the Canon: Scriptures in Second Temple Judaism," in *Old Testament Interpretation—Past, Present, and Future: Essays in Honor of Gene M. Tucker*, ed. J. L. Mays, D. L. Petersen, and K. H. Richards, 225–41. Nashville: Abingdon, 1995.

Biblical Chronology

Finkelstein, Israel, and Neil Asher Silberman. *The Bible Unearthed: Archaeology's New Vision of Ancient Israel and the Origin of Its Sacred Texts*. New York: Free Press, 2001.

Methods in Biblical Scholarship

Barton, John. *Reading the Old Testament*. Rev. ed. Louisville: Westminster, 1996.
———, ed. *The Cambridge Companion to Biblical Interpretation*. Cambridge: Cambridge Univ. Press, 1998.
McKenzie, Steven L., and Stephen R. Haynes. *To Each Its Own Meaning: An Introduction to Biblical Criticisms and Their Application*. Louisville: Westminster, 1993.

1

The Near Eastern Context

KEY POINTS

- **Canaan** between **Egypt** and **Mesopotamia** (Assyria and Babylon).
- **Hittites** to the north.
- **Mesopotamian myths** about **creation** and early humanity are:
  —**Atrahasis**, an account of creation and the flood sharing many points of contact with the biblical story of Noah
  —**Gilgamesh**, the story of a legendary hero, including a version of the flood story
  —**Enuma Elish**, the creation of the world following the defeat of the primordial sea monster
- The gods of Near Eastern myth are **anthropomorphic**.

- **Canaanite myths** known from **Ugaritic** texts.
- **Canaanite gods**: **El** (whose name is the Hebrew word "god") and **Baal**. The major work recounting their deeds is known as the **Baal Cycle**.
- **Egyptian creation stories** have far **less emphasis on conflict** among gods than do those of Canaan and Mesopotamia.
- An important event in Egyptian religion was the focus of worship on one god alone, the sun-god Re (or Aten), instituted by Pharaoh **Akhenaten**.

Early History of the Near East

Life in the ancient Near East can be traced back thousands of years. There was a settlement at Jericho as early as the eighth millennium B.C.E., and village life developed throughout the Near East in the Neolithic period (8000–4000). With the coming of the Early Bronze Age (3200–2200), the first great civilizations emerged in proximity to the great rivers of the region, the Nile in Egypt, and the Tigris and Euphrates that define Mesopotamia (literally, the land "between the rivers") in modern Iraq.

The Sumerians developed the earliest known writing system around 3200 B.C.E., a system of wedge-shaped signs, called cuneiform, inscribed on clay tablets. About 2300 B.C.E. the Sumerians were conquered by Sargon of Akkad. His successors ruled for almost 200 years, but the Akkadian language remained the main one for Mesopotamian literature for 2,000 years.

Babylon rose to power under Hammurabi (18th century B.C.E.), who was famous for a code of laws. Babylon only became dominant again a thousand years later, under Nebuchadnezzar, the conqueror of Jerusalem in the early 6th century B.C.E.

Fig. 1.1. The stele of Hammurabi, eighteenth century B.C.E. Louve, Paris. Photo: © Erich Lessing / Art Resource, N.Y.

Assyria attained its greatest power first in the Middle Assyrian period in the thirteenth and twelfth centuries and then especially in the Neo-Assyrian period in the ninth and eighth centuries B.C.E.

Egyptian civilization is almost as old as that of Sumer. A form of writing known as hieroglyphics first appeared around 3100 B.C.E. Many of the great pyramids were constructed during the Old Kingdom (2700–2160). The Middle Kingdom extended from 2033 to 1648. For about a century in the middle of the second millennium (1648–1540), Egypt was ruled by foreigners from Asia known as the Hyksos, who were eventually driven out. The New Kingdom followed. Egypt ruled over Canaan, the region where Israel would emerge, for much of this period.

In the mid-fourteenth century, Pharaoh Amenophis IV abandoned the traditional worship of the god Amun and devoted himself to the worship of the sun and the solar disk (Aten). He changed his name to Akhenaten and moved his capital to Amarna. This is therefore known as the Amarna period. It is important because of the monotheistic character of Akhenaten's devotion, but also because of a hoard of tablets from this period (the Amarna letters) that give information about the state of affairs in Canaan. After Akhenaten's death, his successor, Tutankhamun, departed from Amarna and reverted to the cult of Amun.

In this period, the main challenge to Egyptian power in Asia came from the Hittites, a people who lived in Anatolia or modern Turkey.

Canaan lay between Egypt and Mesopotamia; it comprised modern Palestine/Israel, Jordan, Lebanon, and part of Syria. It was a loose configuration of city-states. Later, in the first millennium, the Canaanites in the coastal

Chronology of Ancient Near Eastern History

Early Bronze Age 3200–2200 B.C.E.	Middle Bronze Age 2200–1550 B.C.E.	Late Bronze Age 1550–1200 B.C.E.
Egypt	**Egypt**	**Egypt**
From 3100 B.C.E. Hieroglyphic writing	2160–2106 B.C.E. First Intermediate Period	1540–1069 B.C.E. New Kingdom
2700–2160 B.C.E. Old Kingdom Age of the Pyramids	2033–1648 B.C.E. Middle Kingdom	Ca. 1350 B.C.E. Amarna Period / Akhenaten
	1648–1540 B.C.E. Second Intermediate Period Hyksos rule in Egypt	1279–1213 B.C.E. Reign of Ramesses II
Mesopotamia 3200 B.C.E. Sumerians develop first known writing system	**Mesopotamia** 18th century B.C.E. Rise of Babylon under Hammurabi Assyrian kingdom becomes an established power	**Mesopotamia** 1124 B.C.E. Elevation of Marduk under Nebuchadnezzar
2300 B.C.E. Sumerian city-states (Uruk, Lagash, Umma) Sargon of Akkad conquers the Sumerians		**Canaan** 14th century B.C.E. Kingdom at Ugarit

cities of Tyre, Sidon, and Byblos were known as Phoenicians. The biblical texts sometimes use the designation "Amorite" as a variant for "Canaanite."

From the twelfth century on, the people of northern Syria were called Arameans. These were not a unified people but included several small kingdoms.

The Philistines were sea people who came to Canaan from the Aegean. Their origin remains obscure. They were defeated by Egypt about 1190 B.C.E., but they then settled in the coastal towns of Palestine, including Ashkelon, Gaza, and Ashdod. The history of the Philistines parallels that of Israel to a great degree.

The Modern Rediscovery of the Ancient Near East

The modern recovery of the ancient Near East began with Napoleon's expedition to Egypt in 1798–1802 and the discovery of the Rosetta Stone. Since the same text was written in both Greek and Egyptian, it became

Fig. 1.2. King Akhenaten and Queen Nefertiti standing with offerings for the sun-god Aten. Relief from Amarna, Egypt, 1350 B.C.E. Egyptian Museum, Cairo. Photo: © Erich Lessing / Art Resource, N.Y.

possible in 1822 to decipher hieroglyphics for the first time.

The first explorations of Assyrian sites (Nineveh, Khorsabad) were carried out in the 1840s. The key to the decipherment of Akkadian was provided by an inscription by Persian king Darius on the rock of Behistun in Persia, in Old Persian, Elamite, and Akkadian. In the 1870s the great works of Akkadian literature, such as the creation story *Enuma Elish* and the Gilgamesh Epic were discovered and first translated. The Babylonian flood story, which was contained in the Epic of Gilgamesh, caused a sensation because of its similarity to the story of Noah and the ark.

Other major discoveries followed in the late nineteenth and early twentieth centuries, among them: The Amarna letters, noted above, discovered in 1887; the Ugaritic tablets (fourteenth century B.C.E.), found on the Mediterranean coast in northern Syria in 1929; the Mari tablets (mostly from the eighteenth century B.C.E.), at Mari on the Euphrates, beginning in 1933; the Ebla tablets (third millennium B.C.E.), from Tell Mardikh, near Aleppo in northwestern Syria, discovered beginning in 1964; and tablets from Emar (modern Meskene, in Syria), uncovered in the mid-1970s.

Ancient Near East

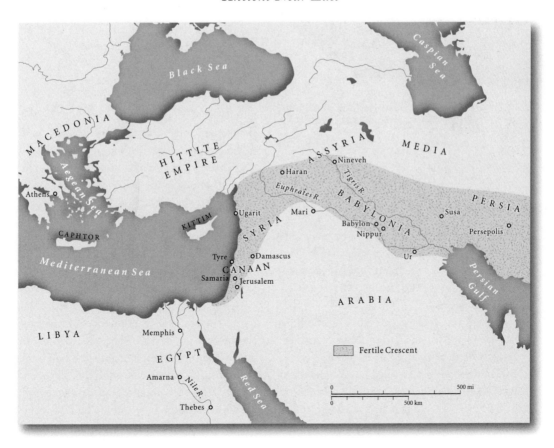

1.3. The Rosetta Stone, inscribed in hieroglyphic, demotic (late, popular Egyptian), and Greek. British Museum, London. Photo: © HIP / Art Resource, N.Y.

Aspects
of Near Eastern Religion

The worship of gods and goddesses was a significant part of life in the ancient Near East. Religion was not standardized and systematized. Each city-state had its own cult of its chief god or goddess.

There was, however, a corpus of literature that circulated widely in the ancient Near East. As part of their training in Akkadian, scribes had to copy out a prescribed body of standard texts. Consequently, some works (e.g., the Epic of Gilgamesh) could be found at widely differ-

ent locations at diverse dates. Modern scholars often refer to such texts as "canonical," but it is important to bear in mind that the "canon" or standard that they established was literary and that it did not involve orthodoxy in religious belief.

We may get an impression of the Mesopotamian view of the world by considering some of the myths or stories about the origin of the world and of humanity. The word "myth" is derived from the Greek *mythos*, or story, but is used especially for sacred stories or traditional stories deemed to have religious import. In modern English usage, "myth" is often opposed to factual truth, but this is unfortunate, as it makes it difficult to take myths seriously. The ancient myths are serious but imaginative attempts to explain life in this world. Two Akkadian creation myths stand out because of their length and wide distribution. These are the myth of Atrahasis and *Enuma Elish*.

Atrahasis

Atrahasis is most fully preserved in an Old Babylonian version from about 1700 B.C.E. It was copied for at least a thousand years.

The story begins at a point before the creation of humankind, "when the gods instead of man did the work, bore the loads." When the gods cast lots and divided the world, Anu took the sky, Enlil the earth, and Enki the waters below the earth. The labor of agriculture was imposed on a class of gods called the Igigu. The first section of the myth deals with the rebellion of these worker gods, which led to the creation of humanity by Enki and the mother goddess, "to bear the load of the gods." They slaughtered "a god who had intelligence" and mixed clay with his flesh and blood. After six hundred years the people became too numerous, and a plague was sent to reduce humanity. At this point, Atrahasis ("the very wise") emerged and averted the plague by the advice of Enki. Enlil made a number of similar attempts to reduce humanity at six-hundred-year intervals, but each time Enki instructed Atrahasis and the danger was averted. Finally, the gods sent a flood to wipe humanity off the face of the earth. Enki instructed Atrahasis to build a boat that was big enough to ride out the deluge. Atrahasis took his family and livestock on board. The flood lasted seven days and seven nights and wiped out the rest of humanity. The gods, other than Enlil, were horrified at the destruction, but they were mainly affected by the fact that they were deprived of their offerings. When the flood subsided, Atrahasis made an offering in thanksgiving. When the gods smelled the odor, "they gathered like flies over the offering." In the end, the gods devised a new scheme for population control. Some women would be barren, some children would die at birth, and some categories of priestesses would not bear children at all.

The gods are anthropomorphic, conceived and portrayed in the likeness of human beings. There is a whole society of gods, analogous to a human society. Especially important is the role of the council of the gods, where the gods deliberate and arrive at decisions. These gods are not fully in control of events. Rather, they react to crises as they develop. Moreover, they are not the guardians of a moral order. The crises develop for various reasons: overwork in the case of the Igigu, overpopulation in the case of humanity. The actions that lead to the crises are not necessarily wrong or sinful. The gods react differently to these crises, and the eventual solutions are reached by compromise. While Enki frustrates the designs of Enlil, in the end they arrive at a balance of forces rather than the dominance of any one god.

Enuma Elish

The *Enuma Elish* was composed some centuries later than Atrahasis, probably in the reign of Nebuchadnezzar I of Babylon (1125–1104 B.C.E.), when Marduk became the chief god of Babylon. It was widely copied. It was recited on the fourth day of the New Year's festival, the Akitu. It was still copied in the Hellenistic period in the third century B.C.E.

> When skies above were not yet named
> Nor earth below pronounced by name,
> Apsu, the first one, their begetter
> And maker Tiamat, who bore them all,
> Had mixed their waters together
> But had not formed pastures, nor discovered reed-beds;
> When yet no gods were manifest,
> Nor names pronounced nor destinies decreed,
> Then gods were born within them.
>
> —Enuma Elish, trans. S. Dalley, *Myths from Mesopotamia*, 233.

The *Enuma Elish* begins at an earlier point in primordial time than does the Atrahasis story. In the beginning, there was only the primordial pair, Apsu and Tiamat. The *theogony* (begetting of the gods) comes before the creation of humanity. Here it is the young gods who create a tumult. Finally, Apsu, with his counselor Mummu, goes to Tiamat and proposes that the young gods be eliminated. The young gods, however, learn of the plot because of the wisdom of Ea. Ea then devises a spell, puts Apsu to sleep, and slays him. He sets up his dwelling on top of Apsu. There he begets new gods, Bel and Marduk. Tiamat then prepares for battle. Ea urges Marduk to come forward. Marduk agrees to fight Tiamat on condition that his word should be law. The gods accept and proclaim him king.

Marduk then defeats Tiamat in battle. He cuts the corpse of Tiamat in two, puts up half of it to make the sky and arranges her waters so that they cannot escape. He then proceeds to establish the constellations of the stars as stations for the gods. He has Ea create humankind from the blood of Qingu, an ally of Tiamat, to do the work of the gods. Finally, he gives the command to create Babylon. The gods labor for a year to construct Babylon and the temple Esagila. On its completion, Marduk invites them to a banquet in the temple. The myth ends with a lengthy litany of the names and praises of Marduk.

The *Enuma Elish* celebrates the exaltation of Marduk, god of Babylon, to kingship among the gods. Tiamat is a complex and fascinating figure. She is Mother Nature, at one point concerned for the survival of her offspring, at another ready to devour them. She is not evil; indeed, she is only slowly provoked to rage. But since she is a threat to the lives of the young gods, she must be destroyed. If life is to flourish on earth, nature must be subdued.

The story has a clear formula for establishing a successful society. Faced with the threat of Tiamat, the gods realize that they need to unite behind the strong leadership of a king. The kingship of Marduk among the gods carries a strong implication that kingship is also necessary in human society. There is a clear symmetry between the king and his palace and the god and his temple. The myth can easily be read as a story composed to legitimate the rise of monarchy. But a story like this has many meanings, and we should not try to reduce it to a simple political message.

The Epic of Gilgamesh

The Epic of Gilgamesh is one of the most remarkable works that has come down to us from antiquity. This work is called an epic rather than a myth because the main characters are human, although gods and goddesses also intervene in the action. Gilgamesh was regarded in antiquity as a historical character. He may have lived in the third millennium.

According to the epic, Gilgamesh, king of Uruk, was two-thirds divine and one-third mortal. He would not leave young women alone, and the gods often heard their complaints. Eventually the gods created someone to be a match for him, a primitive man named Enkidu, who lived with the beasts on the steppe but was tamed by a harlot. She tells him, after sex, that he is wise and has become like a god. Enkidu goes to Uruk, where he becomes a well-matched companion for Gilgamesh. He puts on clothes and learns to eat and drink in the human fashion.

Together, Gilgamesh and Enkidu undertake great adventures. They kill Humbaba, the giant of the forest. When they return to Uruk, Gilgamesh is so resplendent that the goddess Ishtar becomes enamored of him and proposes marriage. Gilgamesh, however, insults her by recalling the misfortunes that have befallen her former lovers. Ishtar persuades Anu, the god of heaven, to give her the Bull of Heaven to punish Gilgamesh and Uruk. But Enkidu subdues the bull and Gilgamesh kills it.

By killing Humbaba and the Bull of Heaven, Gilgamesh and Enkidu win fame in Uruk, but they incur the displeasure of the gods. It is decreed that one of them must die, and the sentence falls on Enkidu, who learns of his fate in a dream. When Enkidu dies, Gilgamesh mourns bitterly: "Shall I die too? Am I not like Enkidu?" He decides to visit Utnapishtim, the flood hero (the counterpart of Atrahasis in the Atrahasis story), who was granted eternal life and now lives far away at the ends of the earth. The journey takes Gilgamesh into the mountain in the west where the sun sets, through a dark tunnel to the sunrise at the other side. He comes to the shore of the sea that circles the earth, where he finds an inn kept by an alewife, Siduri. He tells her his story and asks for directions. She sees that his quest is hopeless:

> Gilgamesh, where do you roam?
> You will not find the eternal life you seek.
> When the gods created mankind
> They appointed death for mankind,
> Kept eternal life in their own hands.
> So, Gilgamesh, let your stomach be full,
> Day and night enjoy yourself in every way...
> This is the work [of the living].
> (Old Babylonian Version; Dalley, *Myths*, 150)

She directs him to Urshanabi, boatman of Utnapishtim. Gilgamesh prevails on the boatman to ferry him over to Utnapishtim, who tells him the story of the flood. Before Gilgamesh sets out on his return journey, Utnapishtim tells him about a plant that has the power to rejuvenate or make the old young again. Gilgamesh dives and brings up the plant. On the way back, however, he stops to bathe in a pool, and while he is doing so a snake carries off the plant. At this point Gilgamesh becomes resigned. When they return to Uruk, he displays the walls of Uruk to Urshanabi, with the implication that the city walls have a permanence that is denied to human beings, even to heroes.

The story of Gilgamesh needs little commentary. It is a poignant reflection on human mortality that belongs to the classics of world literature. In contrast to what we find in the Bible, morality is not a consideration in this story. The exploits of Gilgamesh and Enkidu are neither good nor bad. They win fame for the heroes, but they also bring about their fall. There is a nice appreciation of both the curses and the blessings that attend the harlot. The gods are sometimes capricious (especially Ishtar), sometimes reasonable (Shamash). In the end, however, death is the great leveler of humanity. As Utnapishtim remarks, death is inevitable for Gilgamesh as for the fool.

The Role of Goddesses

The role of Ishtar draws attention to an aspect of Near Eastern religion that contrasts with the Hebrew Bible. Goddesses figure in the stories beside the gods. In general, goddesses declined in importance in the second millennium. One goddess who did not decline was Ishtar, who was associated with fertility in all its aspects. She is the goddess of thunderstorms and rain; she is also the goddess of battle. Above all, she was the goddess of sexual attraction. She was also associated with the morning star. She is most probably the goddess venerated as the "queen of heaven" (Jer 44:17, 19).

Canaanite Mythology

Our sources for Canaanite mythology are much less extensive than those for Mesopotamia. Until the discovery of the tablets at Ugarit in 1929, we were dependent on the polemical accounts of Canaanite religion in the Bible and some information in Greek sources. The gods that appear in the Ugaritic tablets (El, Baal, Anat, etc.) are the same deities that figure in the Hebrew Bible. The Ugaritic texts are the best representatives we have of Canaanite religion in the second half of the first millennium. Different myths, or different forms of these myths, may have circulated in other locations.

In the Ugaritic pantheon, El was king and father of the gods. His decree is wise and his wisdom eternal. The word *El* is familiar from Hebrew, where it is both the common noun for "god" and a designation for the God of Israel (YHWH). El is said to live in a tent on a mountain that is the source of two rivers. He presides over assemblies of "the sons of El," the council of the gods.

By the time the Ugaritic myths were composed, however, El's position among the gods was largely ceremonial. In the Baal cycle of myths, Baal emerges as the dominant figure, although his claim to rule is still challenged by Yamm (Sea) and Mot (Death). Three goddesses figure prominently in the stories: Asherah, wife of El; Anat, sister and wife of Baal; and Astarte, who is the least prominent of the three.

The Baal Cycle from Ugarit resembles *Enuma Elish* insofar as it describes a conflict among the gods that ends in the establishment of a king (in this case, Baal). The Ugaritic text does not discuss the creation of the world, but it can be read as an account of how things came to be the way they are. The first episode of the myth begins when Yamm (Sea) demands that the assembly of the gods surrender Baal into his power. The gods are intimidated by the violent approach of the messengers, and El agrees to hand Baal over. Baal, however, refuses to submit. Instead, he gets two clubs and smashes Sea on the skull and kills him. Another passage in the myth says that Baal finished off Lotan, the fleeing serpent, the seven-headed monster. This is probably another way of referring to the same victory. Lotan appears in the Bible as Leviathan (Isa 27:1; Job 3:8; 41:1; Pss 74:13-14; 104:26).

A second episode of the myth begins with the construction of Baal's house and a celebratory banquet. The third episode presents a more serious challenge to Baal, on the part of Mot, or Death. Baal is terrified and declares that he is Mot's servant forever. The story vividly describes how Death swallows Baal. Eventually, Baal is rescued by his sister Anat, who splits Death with a sword. Baal then returns to life, and the heavens rain down oil, and the wadis (or gullies) run with honey. Finally, there is a tussle between Baal and Mot.

> One lip to the earth, one lip to the heavens;
> he stretches his tongue to the stars.
> Baal must enter inside him;
> He must go down into his mouth,
> Like an olive cake, the earth's produce, the fruit of the trees.
> —Coogan, Stories, 107.

While the Baal cycle has much in common with *Enuma Elish*, it does not seem to have the same political implications. Rather, it seems to reflect the seasonal changes, at least in the struggle of Baal and Mot. When Baal dies, there is no rain, and the fields are dry. When he comes back to life, the rain comes again. This story is not concerned with morality. Mot is not evil; he is just a power that must be given his due. In the end there is some equilibrium between Baal and Mot. A striking feature of the Canaanite mythology is the violence of the goddess Anat, who not only dismembers Death but also berates the high god El on occasion and threatens to smash his skull if he does not comply with her wishes.

Baal's victory over the Sea is more decisive. We may imagine that the image of a monster with seven heads was suggested by the waves of the sea, beating against the Mediterranean coast. Both Sea and Death may be considered chaos monsters: they are forces that threaten the survival of life. In this they resemble Tiamat in the Babylonian myth. Baal, like

---

Akhenaten

About 1350 B.C.E. there was a religious revolution in Egypt. The pharaoh Amenhotep IV came to the throne about 1353 B.C.E. In the fifth year of his reign, he moved his court to Amarna in Middle Egypt and built a new capital. He concentrated all worship on the god Aten, the solar disk. The temples of other gods were closed. The pharaoh directed special fury against the cult of Amun, widely regarded as the most powerful god in Egypt. Amun's name was hacked from the temples, and his priests were sent to the stone quarries. In effect, only Aten could be worshiped. Akhenaten has been called "the first individual in history," and "the first monotheist," but it does not seem that he denied the existence of other gods. The pharaoh is shown on surviving portraits and statues as misshapen. He had a long head and chin, female breasts and hips, spindly arms and legs, and a protruding belly. But he claimed to be the only true interpreter of Akhenaten. The Great Hymn to Aten says, "There is no other who truly knows you but your son Akhenaten."

Akhenaten reigned for less than twenty years. After his death, his successors reverted to the worship of Amun. Tutankhaten, the famous boy king, the treasures of whose tomb have dazzled Western museums, changed his name to Tutankhamun. Atenism was dismissed as a heresy, a short-lived aberration.

People have always wondered, however, whether Akhenaten's singular devotion to the sun disk might not have influenced in some way the monotheistic religion associated with the name of Moses, who was, after all an Egyptian. In modern times, this suspicion was given currency by Sigmund Freud, in his book Moses and Monotheism. But Israelite religion as it developed was very different from the cult of Aten.

Marduk, is a god who protects life, but Baal has much stronger overtones of fertility.

All the characters in the Baal myth are gods or goddesses. But the Canaanites also had stories with human heroes. One such story tells of a man named Danel, who had no son and besought one from the gods. He is given a son named Aqhat, who has a wonderful bow that attracts the attention of the goddess Anat. She offers Aqhat gold and silver for the bow, and when he refuses, she offers him immortal-ity. Aqhat refuses to believe that this is possible and goes on to insult Anat, who has him killed in revenge by a vulture. Danel then puts a curse on nature. Aqhat's sister Paqhat sets out to avenge him, but the end of the story is lost.

Another cycle of stories from Ugarit tells the tale of a king named Keret or Kirta, who, like Job, saw his numerous family destroyed. The gods grant him a new family, but he is afflicted by illness and has to contend with a challenge to his rule by his son. The latter episode recalls the revolt of David's son Absalom in 2 Samuel.

Egyptian Religion

As in Mesopotamia and Canaan, religion in ancient Egypt was subject to local variations. The Old Kingdom, in the second half of the third millennium B.C.E., had its capital at Memphis. The preeminent god was the creator-god Ptah. The priests of Heliopolis, however, exalted the god Atum as creator. The New Kingdom, in the second half of the second millennium, had its capital at Thebes in Middle Egypt, and here the god Amun came to prominence and was linked with the sun-god Re. Several different gods appear as creators in Egyptian myths—Ptah, Re, Atum, Amun, Khnum—but there is only one creator in any given myth. The sun-god Re was universally worshiped and appears in almost every creation myth, although his role varies. The process of creation also varied. In the theology of Heliopolis, the sun-god emerged from the abyss on a primal mound and created the first pair of deities by masturbation or spittle. The god Ptah was said to conceive in his heart the things he wanted to create and bring them into existence by uttering a word. The god Khnum was a potter-god, who fashioned human beings as a potter fashions clay. The models of creation by a word and of fashioning like a potter appear in the Bible, but on the whole the Bible is much closer to the idiom of the Canaanite and Mesopotamian myths than to the Egyptian.

The Egyptian creation stories place less emphasis on conflict than *Enuma Elish* or the Baal myth. The main mythical conflict in Egyptian tradition was the conflict of Horus and Seth. Seth is the symbol of chaos and evil (the Greeks identified him with Typhon). He murders his brother and rival, Osiris. Isis, widow and sister of Osiris, recovers his body and conceives his son Horus. Horus engages in many struggles with Seth and eventually defeats him. The pharaoh was regarded as the living Horus and after death was identified with Osiris. Osiris became the king of the dead and symbolized the hope for eternal life.

One of the most striking features of ancient Egyptian culture was the pervasive belief in life after death. It is to this belief that we owe the pyramids. Many of the artifacts that stock the Egyptian section of modern museums were discovered in tombs, where they had been buried as provisions for the deceased in the afterlife. There is a considerable corpus of Egyptian literature that deals in some way with death and the afterlife. The most ancient corpus of Egyptian religious texts are the Pyramid texts, spells for the protection of the deceased inscribed on the inside walls of the pyramids. In the Middle Kingdom, such spells were inscribed on the panels of wooden coffins, and are called the Coffin texts. In the New Kingdom many of these spells appear on papyrus scrolls in Books of the Dead.

One episode in the history of Egyptian religion may be relevant to the development of monotheism in Israel. This was the religious reform of Pharaoh Amenophis IV, also known as Akhenaten (ca. 1350 B.C.E.). This pharaoh broke with the traditional cult of Amun at Thebes. He moved his capital to Amarna or Akhetaten, farther north on the Nile, and concentrated worship on one god alone, Aten, the solar disk. (This period is known as the Amarna period. It is also famous for the Amarna letters, sent to the pharaoh by his vassals in Canaan, describing conditions there.) Akhenaten focused all worship on Aten, identified with Re, the sun-god, who had given birth to himself and was beyond compare. He was supreme and all-powerful, the creator and sustainer of the universe. Scholars dispute whether this cult is properly described as monotheistic. It is not clear that Akhenaten denied the existence of other gods. But it certainly came closer to monotheism than any other cult in the Near East before the rise of Israel. Akhenaten died in the seventeenth year of his rule. After his death, his successor, Tutankhaten, changed his name to Tutankhamun and moved the royal residence from Amarna to the ancient site of Memphis, south of modern Cairo. Akhenaten's monuments were destroyed or concealed, and the royal cult returned to the old ways.

Conclusion

The material reviewed in this chapter is meant to give an impression of the world of the second millennium B.C.E. and the ways in which people imagined gods and goddesses. The Bible claims that Moses received a new revelation, but even a new revelation was of necessity expressed in language and imagery that was already current. The Hebrew language was a Canaanite dialect, and Canaanite was a Semitic language, like Akkadian. Israelite religion, too, did not emerge in a vacuum. Its novel aspects came into being as modifications of beliefs and practices that had been current for centuries. The Hebrew language uses the word *El* for God, and the term inevitably carried with it associations of the Canaanite high god. The biblical creation stories draw motifs from the myths of Atrahasis and *Enuma Elish* and from the epic of Gilgamesh. In short, much of the language

and imagery of the Bible was culture specific and was deeply imbedded in the traditions of the Near East.

Further Reading

History

Mieroop, M. van de. *A History of the Ancient Near East*. Oxford: Blackwell, 2004.

Texts

Dalley, Stephanie. *Myths from Mesopotamia*. Oxford: Oxford Univ. Press, 1989.

Foster, Benjamin R. *From Distant Days: Myths, Tales and Poetry of Ancient Mesopotamia*. Bethesda, Md.: CDL, 1995.

Lichtheim, Miriam. *Ancient Egyptian Literature*. 3 vols. Berkeley: Univ. of California Press, 1975–80.

Coogan, Michael D. *Stories from Ancient Canaan*. Philadelphia: Westminster, 1978.

Pritchard, James B., ed. *Ancient Near Eastern Texts*. 3rd ed. Princeton: Princeton Univ. Press, 1969.

Articles

Freedman, David Noel, ed. *Anchor Bible Dictionary*. 6 vols. New York: Doubleday, 1992.

Meyers, Eric M., ed. *The Oxford Encyclopedia of Archaeology in the Near East*. 5 vols. Oxford: Oxford Univ. Press, 1997.

Sasson, Jack M., ed. *Civilizations of the Ancient Near East*. 4 vols. New York: Scribners, 1995.

2

The Nature of the
Pentateuchal Narrative

KEY POINTS

- The first five books of the Bible, the **Torah** or **Pentateuch**: Genesis, Exodus, Leviticus, Numbers, and Deuteronomy (**books of Moses**).
- **The Documentary Hypothesis**: Pentateuch a combination of **four major sources**:
  —**The Yahwist, or J,** includes many of the well-known tales of Genesis and Exodus (including the story of Adam and Eve) and is associated with Judah and the south; it is possibly as early as the 9th century B.C.E.
  —**The Elohist, or E,** is dated slightly later than J; this source has particular associations with the northern tribes of Israel.
  —**The Deuteronomist, or D,** basically Deuteronomy. Connected to the reforms of King Josiah of Judah in the 7th century B.C.E.

- —**The Priestly source, or P,** an exilic or postexilic composition largely concerned with issues of ritual practice; it is easy to identify by its dry, formulaic style. Includes a distinct source **H, the Holiness Code,** in Lev 17–26.
- J refers to the God of Israel by **the divine name Yahweh** (German Jahweh) in Genesis. E and P refer to him by the Hebrew word Elohim, meaning "God," until the exodus.
- **Julius Welhausen** formulated the classic form of the Documunetary Hypothesis at the end of the 19th century.
- **Recent critics of Documentary Hypothesis**: Rendtorff, Blum
- **Final editing** of Pentateuch no earlier than the postexilic period

Mosaic Authorship

The first five books of the Bible (Genesis, Exodus, Leviticus, Numbers, and Deuteronomy; collectively known as the Pentateuch) tell the story from creation to the death of Moses. These books are traditionally known as the Torah and as the books of Moses. The Torah is commonly, but not quite accurately, translated as "Law." Much of the Pentateuch is a presentation of laws, but Genesis and the first half of Exodus consist of narratives.

The problematic nature of Mosaic authorship was noticed at least as early as the Middle Ages. The medieval Jewish scholar Ibn Ezra (twelfth century) noted that Gen 12:6, "the Canaanites were then in the land," must have been written at a later time, when this was no longer the case. Similarly, Gen 36:31, which refers to "the kings who reigned in the land of Edom, before any king reigned over the Israelites," must have been written after the establishment of the monarchy. Others noted that Moses could not have written the account of his own death at the end of Deuteronomy. Attention was gradually drawn to various repetitions and contradictions that suggested that the Torah was not the work of any one author but was rather a compilation long after the time of Moses. Such observations proliferated in the wake of the Reformation, when the Bible was subjected to a new level of scrutiny.

A major advance in the study of the Pentateuch is credited to Jean Astruc, a convert to Catholicism who became private physician to King Louis XV. In 1735, Astruc observed that in some passages God is called by the general Hebrew word for God, *Elohim,* while in others he is called by the proper name Yahweh. (It is often written without vowels, YHWH, so as not to profane the name by pronouncing it. Jewish tradition substitutes the word *Adonai,* "the LORD." The mongrel form "Jehovah" is a combination of the consonants of YHWH, or JHVH, with the vowels of *Adonai.*) Astruc supposed that different source documents had been woven together in the composition of Genesis.

Astruc's observation was gradually developed into a theory of the composition of the entire Pentateuch. The book of Deuteronomy was recognized as a distinct source. A distinction was made between passages that refer to God as Elohim. Some of these (e.g., Gen 1:1—2:4a, and various passages dealing with genealogies) were recognized as part of a Priestly source (P) that is represented extensively in Leviticus. The remaining narrative material was seen as a combination of a Yahwistic source (J, following the German spelling Jahweh) and an Elohistic one (E). From the 1860s, P was viewed as the latest (or next to latest) document, and the order was established as J, E, D, P (or J, E, P, D). The theory received its classic formulation from Julius Wellhausen in the 1870s and 1880s.

The Documentary Hypothesis, the view that the Pentateuch is a combination of (at least) four different documents, enjoyed the status of scholarly orthodoxy for about a century. Many variations of the theory were proposed, but the four-source theory was by far the dominant view. Only in the last quarter of the twentieth century has it come to be widely questioned. Before we can evaluate these objections, however, we need to appreciate the observations on which the hypothesis was based.

Indications of Multiple Authorship

In Exod 6:2-3: "God also spoke to Moses and said to him: "I am YHWH. I appeared to Abraham, Isaac, and Jacob as El Shaddai, but by my name YHWH I did not make myself known to them." Yet in Gen 4:26 people began to call upon the name of YHWH in the time of Enosh, grandson of Adam. God is often called YHWH in his dealings with the patriarchs, especially with Abraham. It is apparent, then, that Exod 6:2 comes from a different source than these passages in Genesis.

The variation in divine names is by no means the only criterion. In numerous cases we have doublets, or variant forms of the same story. The account of creation in Gen 1:1—2:3 is quite different from the story of Adam and Eve. Two versions of the flood story are intertwined in Genesis 6–9. Abraham identifies his wife Sarah as his sister to a foreign king in two separate stories (in chaps. 12 and 20). In a third story, Isaac identifies his wife Rebekah as his sister (chap. 26). There are two accounts of God's covenant with Abraham (chaps. 15 and 17), two accounts of Abraham's dealings with Hagar and

Ishmael (chaps. 16 and 21), two accounts of the naming of Beersheba (chaps. 21 and 26). There are variant accounts of the crossing of the Red Sea in Exodus 14–15 and different accounts of the revelation of the commandments in Exodus 19–20 and in Deuteronomy. The mountain of the revelation is variously named Sinai or Horeb. The Decalogue (Ten Commandments) is given three times, with some variations (Exod 20:1-17; 34:10-28; Deut 5:6-18). The list of forbidden animals is given twice (Leviticus 11 and Deuteronomy 14). Many further examples could be given.

The argument that these duplications result from the combination of different documents can be well illustrated from the story of the flood, where J and P versions of the story can be separated. The two versions have not been preserved in full. Noah is never instructed to build the ark in J. But the outline of the two stories is clear. In one account Noah takes only one pair of animals into the ark. In the other he takes seven pairs. In one account the flood lasts 150 days, in the other, 40 days and 40 nights. Moreover, these two accounts can be aligned with strands or sources elsewhere in Genesis. There are clear links between the Priestly version and the Priestly account of creation in Gen 1:1—2:3, typified by the command to be fruitful and multiply. The anthropomorphic character of God in the J account (he regrets that he made humankind and is pleased by the odor of sacrifice) is typical of the J source.

The Flood Story in Genesis 6–9

J, the Yahwist	P, the Priestly source
6:5-8	6:9-22
7:1-5	7:6-16a
7:16b-23	7:24—8:5
8:6-12	8:13-19
8:20-22	9:1-19

The example of the flood should suffice to show that sources are combined in the Pentateuch at least in some cases. It also shows that it is possible to line up consistent features of these sources in different passages. Proponents of the Documentary Hypothesis insist that consistent profiles can be established for each of the four sources, with strands that run through several biblical books.

Profiles of the Sources

The Priestly document is the easiest source to recognize. The dry, formulaic style is familiar from the account of creation in Genesis 1. God said, "Let there be light," and there was light. It is marked by a strong interest in genealogies, in dates, and in ritual observance (the Creator observes the Sabbath by resting on the seventh day). The book of Leviticus is quintessential Priestly material, as is the description of the tabernacle in Exodus 25–31 and 35–40. In P, history is punctuated by a series of covenants, with Noah, Abraham, and finally Moses. P has no angels, dreams, or talking animals. There is little dispute about the identification of P, although its date remains very controversial. I shall examine this strand of the Pentateuch in more detail in chapter 7.

> P: "Then God said, 'Let there be light'; and there was light."
> —Genesis 1:3

The D source is also relatively unproblematic. It is found primarily in the book of Deuteronomy, although some scholars now try to identify Deuteronomic passages also in Genesis and Exodus. There are a few independent passages in Deuteronomy 32–34, but the main body of the book constitutes the basic D corpus. This material is written in a distinctive style. YHWH is said to love Israel, and Israel is commanded to love YHWH "with all your heart and soul," to listen to his voice, and to do what is right in his sight. YHWH brought Israel out of Egypt "with a strong hand and an outstretched arm." The central theme in Deuteronomy is the covenant, and its most distinctive commandment is that it forbids sacrifice outside of the central sanctuary. Since the work of W. M. L. de Wette at the beginning of the nineteenth century, Deuteronomy has been associated with the reform of King Josiah in 621 B.C.E. Deuteronomy is also the subject of chapter 8 below.

D: "You shall love the LORD your God with all your heart, and with all your soul, and with all your might."
—Deuteronomy 6:5

The most problematic part of the Documentary Hypothesis is the distinction between the narrative sources, J and E. The distinction emerges clearly in three doublets in Genesis: Gen 12:10-21 (J), with its parallel in 20:1-18 (E; the wife-sister motif); 16:4-14 (J) and parallel in 21:8-21 (E; Hagar and Ishmael); and 26:26-33 (J) and parallel in 21:22-34 (E; controversy at Beersheba). The E versions use the name Elohim for God and associate revelation with dreams. They reflect on problems of guilt and innocence and emphasize the "fear of God." E has no primeval history; it begins with Abraham in Genesis 15. Abraham is called a prophet in 20:7 and is said to receive revelations in visions and dreams. Jacob and Joseph also receive revelations in dreams. The call of Moses closely resembles the call of prophets in the later books.

The J source is more colorful. It is familiar from the story of Adam and Eve, with its anthropomorphic God and talking snake. God is described in very human terms. He walks in the garden, regrets that he made humanity, is pleased by the odor of sacrifice, and gets angry. Abraham argues directly with YHWH over the fate of Sodom, and the deity is also represented by "the angel of the LORD" who appears on earth. The call of Abraham in Genesis 12 and the covenant with Abraham in Genesis 15 are ascribed to J. The theme of promise and fulfillment is prominent in this strand. Abraham is told that in him all the families of the earth will be blessed (Gen 12:3).

J: "Then they heard the sound of the LORD God walking in the garden at the time of the evening breeze."
—Genesis 3:8

While J and E are clearly distinguished in some passages, they are more difficult to disentangle in others. The narratives of the sacrifice of Isaac in Genesis 22 and of Jacob's dream at Bethel in Genesis 28 are mainly E stories, but they also mention YHWH. It is possible that different forms of the stories were spliced together. The story of the burning bush in Exodus 3 is especially difficult. Moses was guarding the flock of his father-in-law, Jethro, when he came "to Horeb, the mountain of God (Elohim). There the angel of YHWH appeared to him in a flame of fire out of a bush. . . . When YHWH saw that he had turned aside, God (Elohim) called to him out of the bush." It is possible to explain this passage as the close intersplicing of J and E narratives, but we must assume that the editor took half a verse from one source and the other half from the other. Some scholars prefer to speak of JE, without attempting to separate the sources. The distinction between J and E becomes even more elusive in the book of Exodus, after the revelation of the name YHWH to Moses, and only scattered verses there are ascribed to the Elohist with any confidence. Some scholars dispute whether E ever existed as a distinct, coherent source, while granting that J incorporated fragmentary E traditions.

E: "Then God said to him in a dream...."
—Genesis 20:6

"Moses was keeping the flock of his father-in-law Jethro, the priest of Midian; he led his flock beyond the wilderness and came to **Horeb, the mountain of God**. There the angel of the Lord appeared to him in a flame of fire out of a bush; he looked, and the bush was blazing, yet it was not consumed. Then Moses said, 'I must turn aside and look at this great sight, and see why the bush is not burned up.' When the Lord saw that he had turned aside to see, **God called to him** out of the bush...."
—Exodus 3:1-4
(**bold** = E; italics = J)

Dating the Sources

Once it became clear that the Pentateuch was not written by Moses, the dates of its various parts became matters of speculation. One fairly firm point of reference is provided by the date of Deuteronomy. Deuteronomy 12 restricts sacrificial worship to the one "place that YHWH your God will choose," and calls for the destruction of all the places of worship at the "high places." Yet there were still multiple sacrificial sites after Moses, according to the books of Joshua, Judges, and Samuel. Lead-

ers of Israel (Samuel, in 1 Samuel 7; Elijah in 1 Kings 18) build altars and offer sacrifices at various locations. Even prophets such as Amos, who are very critical of cultic practices, never mention a law forbidding worship at more than one place. We only know of two attempts to centralize the Israelite cult. The first was by King Hezekiah, at the end of the eighth century (2 Kings 18), and the second was by his great-grandson, Josiah, in 621 B.C.E., roughly a century later (2 Kings 22). Only Josiah's reform was based on a written law—the "book of the Torah" that had just been found in the temple. It appears that the law of centralization was an innovation of Josiah, and that the "book of the Torah" was Deuteronomy, or at least parts of it. This datum provides a fixed point for the dating of biblical narratives and laws. Texts that allow or endorse worship at multiple sanctuaries are probably older than the time of Josiah. Those that reflect knowledge of this law are presumably later.

Until recent years, most scholars have assumed that the narratives ascribed to J and E are pre-Josianic. Julius Wellhausen put J in the ninth century, E in the eighth, D in the seventh, and P in the sixth or fifth, but he paid little attention to the dates of J and E. His main argument was that P was later than D. This argument was controversial and remains so more than a century later. I will consider it in detail in chapter 8 when I discuss the relation between P and D.

Gerhard von Rad popularized the view that J should be associated with the reign of Solomon, which he held to be a time of enlightenment. It is widely agreed that J originated in Judah, in the southern part of Israel. Abraham is associated with Hebron, a village near Jerusalem. There are analogies between J's account of Abraham and the story of David. Both are associated with Hebron (David was crowned king there) and both are given covenants that require only that they be faithful to their God. Both Abraham and Isaac are associated with the cult at Beersheba, in southern Judah. Judah is especially prominent among the sons of Jacob. Only J includes the long story from the life of Judah found in Genesis 38, which ends in the birth of Perez, the supposed ancestor of David and the kings of Judah. Judah is said to save Joseph from the older brothers who plan to kill him. In the J account of the covenant with Abraham in Genesis 15, God promises that Abraham's descendants will rule over the land "from the river of Egypt to the river Euphrates." It has been claimed that these were the bounds of the kingdom of David and Solomon, although recent historians have been very skeptical about this claim. In von Rad's view, the Yahwist was a court historian, who wrote to explain how a people that had been slaves in Egypt became a kingdom. The Solomonic empire was the fulfillment of a promise made to Abraham centuries earlier.

Von Rad's hypothesis has not stood the test of time. On the one hand, scholars have been increasingly troubled by the lack of any evidence outside the Bible for the glory of Solomon. On the other hand, even if Solomon's empire extended from the river of Egypt to the river Euphrates, at most this would mean that Genesis 15 was written no earlier than the time of Solomon. It would not guarantee a Solomonic date.

The Elohistic source has usually been dated a little later than J, on the assumption that it was created as a northern alternative account of the prehistory of Israel, after the separation of the northern kingdom (Israel) from Judah after the death of Solomon. There are good reasons to associate the E source with the northern kingdom. In Genesis 28 Jacob names the place where he has a dream Bethel, the "house

of God." Bethel was one of the state temples of the northern kingdom set up by Jeroboam I, the secessionist king. Jeroboam also built the city of Peniel, which is the site of a struggle between Jacob and God or an angel in Genesis 32. In the E story of Joseph, it is Reuben, rather than Judah, who saves Joseph from his brothers. There is a close analogy between the forced labor imposed on the Israelites in Egypt in Exodus 1 and the labor draft, imposed by Solomon and his son Rehoboam, which led to the revolt of the northern tribes. Some stories in the E source are critical of Aaron, the supposed ancestor of the Jerusalem priests. It is plausible, then, that E was composed in the northern kingdom. The prominence of the Arameans in the Jacob story may suggest a date in the ninth century or early eighth century, when the Arameans were the most significant foreign power in relation to Israel. J is generally thought to be slightly older, but the evidence is not conclusive.

The two narrative sources were probably combined after the fall of the northern kingdom in 722, when many refugees from the north fled to Jerusalem, and the size of the city was greatly expanded. Neither J nor E shows any awareness of the Deuteronomic prohibition of worship outside of the central sanctuary in Jerusalem. It is most probable, then, that these sources were compiled and combined before the reform of King Josiah in the late seventh century B.C.E., although some additions could still have been made later.

Criticism of the Documentary Hypothesis

In the last quarter of the twentieth century, many of the established certainties of the Documentary Hypothesis were called into question. It has been argued that the migration of Abraham would make best sense in the period after the Babylonian exile, when Jewish exiles in fact returned from Babylon to Israel. Abraham is not described as a returning exile, however, and so the analogy is imperfect. Nonetheless, the early chapters of Genesis (both J and P sources) show extensive points of contact with Mesopotamia, and these contacts can be explained more easily in the exilic period or later than in the early monarchy. The story of Adam and Eve is never cited in the preexilic prophets and becomes prominent only in the Hellenistic period. This does not prove that the J source was written late, but it does create some misgivings about the supposedly early date of the J strand of Genesis. It may be that the primeval history in Genesis 1–11, where most of the Babylonian analogies are found, was a late addition to the J source.

A different line of critique was developed by Rolf Rendtorff, a student of von Rad. Rendtorff noted that Gunkel, the founder of form criticism, treated the stories of Genesis as discrete units, akin to folklore, and paid little attention to the major sources, although he did not deny their existence. Martin Noth, a contemporary of von Rad, analyzed the Pentateuch in terms of five major themes, which both J and E formulated in their different ways. Implicit in Noth's analysis was the insight that the patriarchal stories are different in kind from the story of the exodus, even if one recognizes J and E strands in both. For most readers, the differences between these blocks or themes are more obvious and more significant than the difference between J and E.

Rendtorff went further than Noth and questioned the entire validity of the J and E sources. His student Erhard Blum has proposed an elaborate alternative to the Documentary Hypothesis. Abandoning J and E, Blum finds two main stages in the composition of the Pentateuch. The first he calls the "D-Komposition" (K^D), which was the work of editors from the Deuteronomistic tradition. He dates this composition to the generation after the Babylonian exile. The second stage is the "P-Komposition" (K^P), the work of Priestly writers who edited K^D, and so worked even later. This is not to suggest that all of the pentateuchal narratives are as late as the exile. The authors of K^D inherited two main documents. One was an edition of Genesis 12–50. The second was a "Life of Moses," which had been composed some time after the fall of the northern kingdom. Both stories incorporated elements from the early monarchy. There have been several other proposals along the lines of Blum's work, but differing in details.

Perhaps the main issue raised by the work of Rendtorff and Blum is whether the composition of the pentateuchal narratives can be ascribed to Deuteronomistic editors, no earlier than the Babylonian exile. There is an obvious problem with this thesis. The signature element of Deuteronomy was the insistence that sacrifice should be offered only at the central sanctuary in Jerusalem. Yet much of Genesis consists of stories of the founding of other cult sites, including the northern sanctuary of Bethel, by the patriarchs. Such stories could only lend legitimacy to the sanctuaries that were condemned to destruction in Deuteronomy. Blum allows that the narratives of Genesis 12–50 had already been put together before the exile, but it is still difficult to see why Deuteronomistic editors would let so much of this material stand. It is surely more plausible that the pentateuchal narrative was already established and authoritative before Deuteronomy was added. Also, Blum's argument does not do justice to the clear distinction between J and E in the patriarchal stories noted above. It remains likely that J and E were composed, and probably also combined, before the Deuteronomic reform, although some material in the primeval history may have been added later.

The recent debates about the Pentateuch show that the reconstruction of earlier forms of the biblical text is a highly speculative enterprise. Perhaps the main lesson to be retained is that these texts are indeed composite and incorporate layers from different eras. The biblical text is not a consistent systematic treatise. Rather, it is a collection of traditional materials that places different viewpoints in dialogue with one another and offers the reader a range of points of view.

The Pentateuch cannot have reached its present form earlier than the postexilic period. There is good evidence that the Priestly strand was added as an editorial layer. It provides the opening chapter of Genesis and connects the narrative with its genealogies and dating formulae. It is not apparent that there ever was a coherent Priestly narrative about the patriarchs. We shall also see that some elements in the Priestly strand were added quite late, long after the Babylonian exile. Nonetheless, it is not clear whether Priestly or Deuteronomic editors should be credited with establishing the shape of the Pentateuch as we have it. The evidence for Priestly editing of Genesis and Exodus is much clearer than that for Deuteronomic editing. This suggests that the first four books of the Pentateuch were edited by Priestly writers before Deuteronomy was added. The fact that Deuteronomy stands as the last book of the Pentateuch gives the impression that it was added last. There were certainly some Deuteronomic additions in the earlier books, but their extent remains in dispute. Ultimately there is much to be said for the view that the Pentateuch as it stands is a compromise document, in which Priestly and Deuteronomic theologies were presented side by side without any clear indication that one should take precedence.

In the following chapters I do not attempt to extrapolate theologies of J or E to any significant degree. P and D, in contrast, correspond to well-defined blocks of text and present clear and well-developed theologies. These sources will accordingly be treated in separate chapters.

Further Reading

Campbell, Antony R., and Mark A. O'Brien. *Sources of the Pentateuch: Texts, Introductions, and Annotations.* Minneapolis: Fortress Press, 1993.

Dozeman, Thomas B., and Konrad Schmid. *A Farewell to the Yahwist? The Composition of the Pentateuch in Recent European Interpretation.* SBLSym 34. Atlanta: Society of Biblical Literature, 2006.

Friedman, Richard E. *The Bible with Sources Revealed.* San Francisco: HarperSanFrancisco, 2003.

Nicholson, Ernest. *The Pentateuch in the Twentieth Century: The Legacy of Julius Wellhausen.* Oxford: Clarendon, 1998.

3

The Primeval History

KEY POINTS

- **Genesis 1–11**: creation through the flood = the primeval history.
- **Adam and Eve in Genesis 2–3**: J source.
- **Adam** = the generic Hebrew word for "human."
- Transition to a state of self-consciousness and consciousness of death are paralleled in the **Epic of Gilgamesh**.
- **Eve is not the primary culprit in the Hebrew story.**

- **The P creation account** in Genesis 1 supplements the J account.
- Genesis 6:1-4: the **Sons of God** who descended to earth.
- **The P flood story**: exact numbers, measurements, and calculations.
- **Covenant with Noah, or Noahide** laws: applies to all humanity.

The primeval history, in Genesis 1–11, is woven from the J and P strands. The contrast is clearly evident in the two accounts of creation—the ritualistic Priestly account in Genesis 1 and the colorful Yahwistic account in chapters 2 and 3. P is responsible for the genealogy in chapter 5, for one strand of the flood story, and for the genealogies of Noah's sons in Genesis 10 and 11. I shall begin with the J account and then consider how it has been shaped by the Priestly editors.

Adam and Eve

The J account begins with the story of Adam and Eve. There is surprisingly little reference to this story in the remainder of the Hebrew Bible. Ezekiel 28:13-16 alludes to a figure who is driven out of "Eden, the garden of God," by a cherub, but it is not clear that he had the same story in mind. For clear allusions to Adam and Eve we have to wait until Ben Sira, in the early second century B.C.E., and the Dead Sea Scrolls.

The Creation of Humanity

The story focuses on the creation of humanity. The man ('ādām is the generic Hebrew word for human being) is made from the dust of the ground and animated by the breath of life. In the Babylonian myth of Atrahasis, humanity is also made from clay, mixed in that case with the flesh and blood of a slain god. In the Atrahasis story humanity was created to do agricultural work for the gods. In Genesis the first human being is also charged with the keeping of the garden, but the task does not appear very onerous.

Two trees are singled out in this garden: the tree of life in the middle of the garden, and the tree of the knowledge of good and evil. (The precise meaning of "the knowledge of good and evil" is disputed. It may mean "universal knowledge" or it may mean the power of discernment between good and evil—cf. Isa 7:15-16.) Symmetry would lead us to expect that if one tree is the tree of life, the corresponding one should be the tree of death and, sure enough, Adam is told that if he eats of it he shall die. The plot of the story hinges on the idea that God does not want humanity to eat from the tree of knowledge. Adam is not initially forbidden to eat from the tree of life.

The plot is complicated when the Creator decrees that "it is not good that the man should be alone." (In the Atrahasis myth human beings were created in pairs, and in the Priestly account of creation in Genesis 1 they were created male and female.) In the J account the man is allowed to choose his mate and to name all the beasts, none of which is a fit partner for him. The Creator proceeds by a process of trial and error and engages in unsuccessful experiments. This is also the way creation is imagined in Atrahasis.

Adam finds a partner in the woman who is taken from his rib. Whether this implies the subordination of woman to man is a matter of heated dispute. For two thousand years, the implication of subordination was thought to be obvious. So Paul writes, "Man was not made from woman, but woman from man. Neither was man created for the sake of woman, but woman for the sake of man" (1 Cor 11:8-9; cf. 1 Tim 2:13, which forbids women to teach or have authority over men, because "Adam was formed first"). Even Paul recognized the anomaly of this claim. He added that though woman came from man, "so man comes through woman, and all things come from God" (1 Cor 11:12). Nonetheless, the reversal of the natural order of birth, by having the woman taken from the man's body, suggests an order. In the ancient (and modern) Near East, it was assumed that females should defer to males. But to speak of subordination here is too strong. Genesis emphasizes the closeness of the man and woman: "This at last is bone of my bones and flesh of my flesh. . . . Therefore a man leaves his father and his mother and clings to his wife, and they become one flesh" (Gen 2:23-24).

Fig. 3.1. Adam and Eve. Bas-relief from a sarcophagus. Museo Civico, Velletri, Italy. Photo: © Erich Lessing / Art Resource, N.Y.

Man and wife were naked and not ashamed. This notice alerts us to the sexual overtones of the story. Some interpreters even hold that the "knowledge of good and evil" refers to sexual initiation. Immediately after their expulsion from Eden, we are told that Adam "knew his wife, Eve, and she conceived and bore Cain" (Gen 4:1). The verb "to know" often refers to sexual relations in biblical idiom. Genesis does not say explicitly that Adam "knew" his wife in the garden. Nonetheless, the motif of the forbidden fruit in Genesis 3 has always lent itself to a sexual interpretation. More fundamentally, however, the nudity of Adam and Eve symbolizes their initial innocence and lack of self-awareness—a state in which human beings are not different from animals. By the end of the story they will have put on clothes and become human, for better or worse.

The Serpent

Genesis 3:1 introduces another character. In later tradition, the serpent would be identified as Satan, or the devil. According to the Wisdom of Solomon, death entered the world "by the envy of the devil" (Wis 2:24). The book of Revelation refers to "the ancient serpent, who is called the Devil and Satan, the deceiver of the whole world" (Rev 12:9). The figure of the devil is a latecomer on the biblical scene. When Satan appears in the Hebrew Bible (in the book of Job, and again in Chronicles and Zechariah), he is not yet quite "the devil"; in Job he appears among "the sons of God" in the heavenly court. Talking animals are a standard device in the literary genre of the fable, which was developed most famously by the Greek writer Aesop. The appearance of a talking snake should alert even the most unsophisticated reader to the fictional nature of the story. The snake articulates the voice of temptation, but it is not yet the devil or Satan.

The Knowledge of Good and Evil

The snake leads the human couple to question the divine prohibition against eating from the tree of the knowledge of good and evil. So the woman, and then Adam, takes and eats. Then "the eyes of both were opened." The "knowledge of good and evil" that they attain does not make them like gods, but it does give them self-awareness.

At this point, light can be shed on the story of Adam and Eve by the Epic of Gilgamesh. When Enkidu, the companion of Gilgamesh, is first introduced, he roams with the wild beasts until he is tamed by a harlot. When he returns to the beasts, they run off, and he cannot keep pace with them as before. The harlot tells him: "You have become [profound], Enkidu. You have become like a god!" She teaches him to eat human food and drink strong drink. Then he puts on clothes and becomes human. On the one hand, his encounter with the harlot leads to loss of his natural strength but, on the other hand, he becomes wise like a god, or at least like a human being.

Adam is told that his death is the direct result of eating from the tree of knowledge. Enkidu's fate is not the direct result of his encounter with the harlot. There is nonetheless an analogy between the two. Both characters make the transition to self-consciousness and become conscious of death. Both aspire to being wise like the gods, but when their eyes are opened, all they discover is that they are naked and that they will die.

In the Babylonian story, Enkidu's action and its results are mixed. He has to confront death, but he also gains a richness of life unknown to the animals. The evaluation of Adam's action is more severe. First, God curses the snake. Then he tells the woman that he will greatly increase her pain in childbearing. Yet

The Sons of God

The story of the sons of God in Genesis 6 was developed in later tradition to become another way of explaining the origin of evil. In Genesis there is no explicit connection between the descent of the sons of God and the flood, and it is not even clear that what they did was wrong, although that may well be implied. In the Book of the Watchers, in 1 Enoch, however, they are said to conspire in full awareness of their transgression. Fragments of the story survive in Aramaic in the Dead Sea Scrolls, and the full text of 1 Enoch is preserved in Ethiopic. The book was written in the third or early second century B.C.E. According to this elaboration of the biblical text, the Watchers, or fallen angels, not only seduced human women and begat giants, but led humans astray by revealing to them all sorts of knowledge, from astrology to the art of making up the eyes. They also introduced weapons on earth. Consequently there was a rise in violence and fornication. Eventually the Lord intervened to purge the earth with the flood. The spirits that came forth from the giants, however, remained on earth as evil spirits. According to the book of Jubilees, which was written some time after the Book of the Watchers, Noah asked the Lord to imprison all these spirits. Mastema, or Satan, however, besought the Lord to allow one tenth of them to remain on earth so that he could do his job of leading people into temptation.

In later tradition, the rebellion of the angels in heaven was combined with an older myth about Lucifer the son of Dawn, which is reflected, although it is not told in full, in Isaiah 14. It was this form of the story that was used by John Milton in Paradise Lost and became the popular story of the origin of Satan or the devil.

"your desire shall be for your husband, and he shall rule over you" (3:16). Finally, the man is told that the ground is cursed because of him: "By the sweat of your face you shall eat bread until you return to the ground, for out of it you were taken. For you are dust, and to dust you shall return" (3:19). God then expels Adam and Eve from the garden, lest they put forth their hands and eat from the tree of life and live forever.

Disobedience and Fall

The story of Adam and Eve is known in Christian theology as the fall, and it is assumed that the human condition, subject to suffering and death, is due to the sin of Adam. The narrative can still be read, like that of Enkidu, as a story of the transition from a prehuman to a human state. But unlike the Babylonian story, Genesis judges this transition negatively. Even though no words meaning "sin" or "punishment" are used in the story, it is quite clear that the conditions in which men and women must henceforth live are punishment for disobedience.

These conditions are described in Gen 3:14-19. The nature of these passages can be seen clearly in the words addressed to the snake: "Upon your belly you shall go, and dust you shall eat all the days of your life." Snakes do not in fact eat dust. What we have here is an etiology—a story that is told to explain the cause of something.

God's words to the woman likewise reflect the author's view of the female condition. There is pain in childbearing and subordination to a husband who "will rule over you." This condition is not the original design of creation. It is a mistake to read this passage as the normative expression of God's will for women. In that case, one would also have to conclude that it is God's will that snakes eat dust and that men earn their bread by the sweat of their brow. God's words to the woman simply reflect the common experience of women in ancient Israel.

God's judgment recalls the words of the alewife Siduri in the Epic of Gilgamesh: "You will not find the eternal life you seek. When the gods created mankind they appointed death for mankind, kept eternal life in their own hands." There is no hint here of any possibility of meaningful life after death. (The common assumption in the Hebrew Bible was that after death all people, good and bad, went to the shadowy underworld, Sheol, the counterpart of the Greek Hades.) Where the Babylonian epic simply presents this situation as a matter of fact, Genesis lays the blame on human beings. In part, the problem is disobedience to the divine command. More broadly, the problem is human overreaching. Like the heroes of Greek tragedy, Adam and Eve are guilty of

hubris in their desire to be like God. Human beings should know their place and stay in it.

Theological Misconceptions

More than most stories, these chapters of Genesis have been overlaid with theological interpretations that have little basis in the Hebrew text. Since the time of St. Augustine, Christian theology has maintained the doctrine of original sin—the belief that human beings after Adam are born in a state of sin. There is a partial basis for this idea in the New Testament, where St. Paul asserts that "one man's trespass led to condemnation for all" and "by the one man's disobedience the many were made sinners" (Rom 5:18-19). In the first century c.e., when Paul wrote, there was some debate in Judaism about the significance of Adam's disobedience. This debate is reflected in apocalyptic writings from the end of that century. In *4 Ezra* 7:48 [118] Ezra asks, "O Adam, what have you done? For though it was you who sinned, the fall was not yours alone, but ours also who are your descendants." In the nearly contemporary apocalypse known as *2 (Syriac) Baruch*, Baruch rejects this sentiment and takes a position that is more typical of Jewish tradition: "Adam was responsible for himself only; each one of us is his own Adam" (*2 Bar.* 54:15, 19).

Equally unfounded is the view that the responsibility for sin lay with Eve rather than with Adam. The earliest occurrence of this idea is found in Ben Sira in the early second century b.c.e.: "From a woman sin had its beginning, and because of her we all die" (Sir 25:24). It is repeated in the New Testament in 1 Tim 2:14: "Adam was not deceived, but the woman was deceived and became a transgressor." One may reasonably infer from the text of Genesis that the serpent approached Eve first because she was weaker, but Adam still bears the primary responsibility. Only after they have both eaten are their eyes opened. Adam and Eve both suffer the consequences.

The Priestly Creation Story

The Priestly account of creation now forms the opening chapter of the Bible. The opening verse (Gen 1:1) is majestic in its simplicity: "In the beginning, God created the heavens and the earth." Originally, the Hebrew was written without vowels. The vowels were added later as points above and below the consonants. If the Hebrew is pointed slightly differently, the verse can be translated as: "In the beginning, when God created the heavens and the earth. . . ." The Babylonian creation myth, *Enuma Elish*, similarly begins with a temporal clause. (There is another possible reflection of the Babylonian myth in Gen 1:2. The Hebrew word for "the deep" [*tĕhôm*] is a cognate of the name of the Babylonian monster Tiamat in *Enuma Elish*.) If the opening words are translated as a temporal clause, it is clear that we are not speaking of creation out of nothing. Already when God set about creating the heavens and the earth, there was a formless void (*tōhû wābōhû*), and the wind or spirit of God was hovering over the waters. God proceeds to bring order out of chaos simply by uttering commands. There were precedents for creation by divine word in Egyptian mythology, but there is clear contrast here with Genesis 2 and with the creation mythologies of Mesopotamia. The God of the Priestly writers is more exalted than the God of J.

The creation is arranged in seven days. Human beings are created on the sixth day. While humankind is designated by the masculine word *'ādām*, both male and female are explicitly created in the image of God. In the

---

> **The Priestly Creation Account**
>
> 1. Light . . . light/darkness . . . "good"
> 2. Firmament . . . lower/upper waters
> 3. Dry land . . . water/dry land . . . earth sprouts vegetation
> 4. Sun, moon, stars . . . day/night . . . "good"
> 5. Water and air creatures . . . "good"
> 6. Land creatures, including humans. Humans given dominion . . . "very good"
> 7. God rests

---

ancient Near East, images were very important for worship, as they made the presence of the divinity manifest to the worshipers. No such images were used in the cult of YHWH. Instead, the presence of God was made manifest in human beings. This account of creation, then, attributes great dignity to human beings, both male and female. Moreover, humanity is given dominion over the rest of creation. From a modern perspective, however, human sovereignty over creation has not always been a blessing, but has often been abused. Genesis 1 only allows for vegetarian food. Only after the flood would provision be made for eating meat.

One other commandment is given to humanity in Genesis 1: to increase and multiply. The Priestly account of creation affirms human sexuality and seems to rule out at the outset an ethic of abstinence and asceticism. This point is important, as the purity rules in Leviticus might suggest a rather negative view of sexuality.

The most striking thing about the Priestly creation account is its positive tone. Everything is very good. The origin of sin and evil is not addressed. It is likely, however, that the editor who placed this account at the beginning of Genesis presupposed the Yahwist creation account of Genesis 2–3. The Priestly account is not the whole story. Rather, it supplements the Yahwist account and is meant to forestall a negative interpretation of the human situation, which might be derived from Genesis 3.

If this is correct, then the Priestly account must have been composed after the Yahwist account. There is nothing in this passage to indicate a more precise date. There is a possible allusion to Gen 1:2 in the prophet Jeremiah at 4:23: "I looked on the earth, and lo, it was waste and void." Jeremiah prophesied during the Babylonian crisis, around 600 B.C.E. But Jeremiah is not necessarily referring to the text of Genesis as we know it. The idea that the earth was "waste and void" before YHWH created it may have been current before it was incorporated into the Priestly account of creation.

Genesis 4–11

The Sons of God

The brief notice about "the sons of God" (that is, gods, or heavenly beings) in Gen 6:1-4 is difficult to assign to a source. (The statement in v. 3, where YHWH limits the span of human life, is not necessarily part of the story about the sons of God [*Elohim*].) The episode of the sons of God seems to be a fragment of a polytheistic myth. In itself, the report in Gen 6:1-4 passes no judgment on either the "sons of God" or the Nephilim ("fallen ones"), except to note that the latter were famous. This episode is followed, however, by the statement that YHWH saw that the wickedness of humankind was great on the earth; this leads to the flood. It may be that the Yahwist intended to imply a connection. In the Book of the Watchers (*1 Enoch* 1–36), an apocalyptic work written in

Aramaic in the third or early second century B.C.E., the sons of God become "the Watchers," angelic beings who descend to earth in an act of rebellion. They beget giants who cause havoc. Eventually the flood is sent to cleanse the earth. The myth of the fallen angels had a long life in Western tradition and received a classic expression in John Milton's epic, *Paradise Lost*. The biblical text contains only the germ of this myth. The Yahwist located responsibility for sin in the actions of human beings rather than in those of fallen angels.

The Flood

According to Gen 6:5, the wickedness of humankind is due to the fact that "every inclination of the thoughts of their hearts was only evil continually." We get the impression of an experiment gone awry: "The Lord was sorry that he made humankind on the earth." In this respect, the Genesis account resembles the Babylonian myth of Atrahasis, where the gods try various means to wipe out humanity, including, finally, a flood. Genesis dispenses with the attempts to destroy humanity by disease and goes directly to the flood. It is characteristic of Genesis that the problem is wickedness rather than population or noise control. In the end, YHWH reacts more generously than his Babylonian counterparts. Humanity is not entirely to blame, "for the inclination of the human heart is evil from youth," and so YHWH resolves that he will never again try to destroy it.

The Priestly account of the flood is characterized by precise detail. Noah is given specific measurements for the ark. Only one pair of each kind of animal is taken, reflecting the Priestly preference for binary opposites. Events are dated precisely. The flood occurs in the six hundredth year of Noah's life. He emerges from the ark in his six hundred and first year, in the second month, on the twenty-seventh day of the month. Like the first human beings in the creation story, he is given dominion over the earth and commanded to increase and multiply. Henceforth, humanity is allowed to eat meat: "Every moving thing that lives shall be food for you" (9:3). There is a restriction, however: "only you shall not eat flesh with its life, that is, its blood" (Gen 9:4). Moreover, the fact that humanity is made in the image of God is cited as reason to refrain from murder (9:6).

Perhaps the most important detail in the Priestly account of the flood is the covenant that God concludes with Noah at its end. God undertakes not to destroy the earth by flood again, and sets the rainbow in the sky as a sign of this promise. The covenant is usually understood to include the commandment to Noah not to eat flesh with the blood in it. In Jewish tradition, the "Noachian laws" were expanded and were understood to apply also to Gentiles. Typically, they included prohibitions of idolatry, cursing God, cursing judges, murder, incest and adultery, robbery, and the eating of meat with the blood. Gentiles who observed these laws could be regarded as righteous. The Priestly theology was primarily concerned with God's commandments to Israel, but it also recognized that God's creation includes all humanity.

The Priestly Genealogies

The Priestly editors of these narratives tried to integrate them into an unfolding history by inserting genealogies. These genealogies are fictional, but they served to bring a sense of order to the diversity of human society, and they also helped to keep the biblical focus on the story of Israel in perspective. Even the Gentiles, in all their ethnic variations, were made in the image of God.

Further Reading

Commentaries

Fretheim, Terence E. "Genesis." In *NIB* 1:319–426.

Rad, Gerhard von. *Genesis*. Trans. J. H. Marks. OTL. Philadelphia: Westminster, 1972.

Westermann, Claus. *Genesis 1–11: A Commentary*. Trans. J. J. Scullion. CC. Minneapolis: Augsburg, 1984.

Other Studies

Barr, James. *The Garden of Eden and the Hope of Immortality*. Minneapolis: Fortress Press, 1992.

Trible, Phyllis. *God and the Rhetoric of Sexuality*. OBT. Philadelphia: Fortress Press, 1978.

4

The Patriarchs

KEY POINTS

- **No independent, nonbiblical evidence** for Abraham and the other patriarchs.
- **Hermann Gunkel**, a German scholar of the late 19th and early 20th centuries, identified several types of stories or legends contained in the patriarchal narratives:
  —**Etiological legends** claim to explain the cause or origin of a phenomenon (e.g., the story of Lot's wife explains the origin of a pillar of salt).
  —**Ethnological legends** explain the origin of a people or of their customs (the story of Cain explains why Kenites are itinerant).
  —**Etymological legends** explain the origin of names (there are two accounts of the origin of the name of Beersheba: Gen 21:31; 26:33).
  —**Ceremonial legends** explain the origin of a ritual (e.g., the story of the Passover; the origin of circumcision).
- The association of certain patriarchs with specific holy places gave legitimacy to **shrines at those locations later on** (e.g., Abraham's association with Hebron and Jerusalem; Jacob with Bethel).
- Both J and P cast God's promise to Abraham in the form of a **covenant**.
- **Trickery and deception** appear as a theme throughout the narratives, particularly in the narratives about Jacob and in the story of Judah and Tamar.
- Genesis closes with the story of **Joseph** (J and partly E). Not composed as early as older scholarship suggests.
- In literary terms, the Joseph story is most like the books of Ruth and Esther or the court narratives in the book of Daniel.

A new phase in biblical history is ushered in with Abram. (His name is changed to Abraham in Gen 17:5; his wife, Sarai, becomes Sarah in 17:15.) Abram is first introduced in a genealogical list in chapter 11 (P). In 11:31, he departs from "Ur of the Chaldeans," "to go into the land of Canaan," but settles in Haran on the way. Haran was a major city in northwestern Mesopotamia, on a tributary of the Euphra-

tes. The area is also called Aram-Naharaim (Aram or Syria of the two rivers). Ur was a famous and ancient city in southern Mesopotamia that flourished in the third millennium B.C.E. It could be called "Ur of the Chaldeans" only after the rise of the Neo-Babylonian Empire, in the late seventh century B.C.E. The reference to Ur of the Chaldeans can be no older than the Babylonian exile.

Aspects
of the Patriarchal Stories

The Patriarchs and History

As noted in the introduction, the internal chronology of the Bible suggests a date around 2100 B.C.E. for Abraham and a time around 1876 for the descent of his grandson Jacob into Egypt with his family. Only extremely conservative scholars would now take these dates at face value, but many have tried to set the stories of Genesis against the background of the second millennium. Some have suggested that King Amraphel of Shinar, mentioned in Gen 14:1, was the famous Hammurabi of Babylon (1850–1800 B.C.E.), but there is no basis for the identification. There were population movements in the early second millennium involving "Amorites" or "westerners" (from a Babylonian perspective), but Abraham is not associated with any larger group. The kind of society described in Genesis is "dimorphic" (twofold) because it involves both nomads and a settled population. Such a society is also reflected in tablets from Mari on the Euphrates, which flourished around the time of Hammurabi. But this kind

The World of the Patriarchs

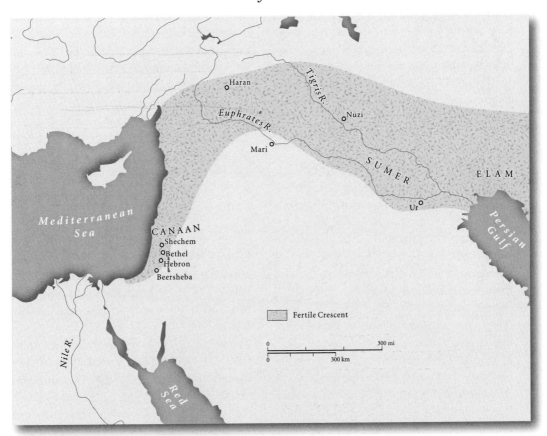

of society has persisted in the Near East down to modern times. Second millennium parallels to biblical laws and customs are likewise inconclusive, since the same customs persisted for centuries.

There is no positive evidence to set the patriarchs in the early or middle part of the second millennium. Several considerations tell against such an early background. The Philistines, who are mentioned in Gen 21:32-34; 26:1, 8, 14-15, were one of the Sea Peoples who invaded the coastal plain in the twelfth century and gave their name to "Palestine." The Arameans, who figure especially in the Jacob stories, are attested only from the end of the second millennium (eleventh century). The earliest mention of the camel as a domesticated animal dates only from the eleventh century, and its use became common only some centuries later. Archaeological evidence suggests that Beersheba was not settled before the twelfth century. It is unlikely that these stories originated earlier than the end of the second millennium B.C.E.

The Patriarchal Stories as Legends

The stories of Genesis do not lend themselves to historical analysis. As Hermann Gunkel saw clearly, they are not history but legend. Legend is originally oral tradition and gives rise to variants of the same tales. History treats great public occurrences, while legend deals with more personal and private matters. Even when legends concern matters of great historical import, they still tend to focus on the personal. The clearest criterion of legend, wrote Gunkel, is that it frequently reports things that are incredible. It is poetry rather than prose, and a different sort of plausibility applies. As poetry, legend aims to please, to elevate, to inspire, and to move. It does not necessarily tell "what actually happened" in a way that would satisfy a modern historian.

Gunkel went on to distinguish several kinds of legends in Genesis. Etiological legends claim to explain the cause or origin of a phenomenon (e.g., the story of Lot's wife explains the origin of a pillar of salt). Ethnological legends explain the origin of a people or of their customs (the story of Cain explains why Kenites are itinerant).

Etymological legends explain the origin of names (there are two accounts of the origin of the name of Beersheba: Gen 21:31; 26:33). Ceremonial legends explain the origin of a ritual (e.g., the story of the Passover; the origin of circumcision).

Gunkel did not rule out the possibility that historical memories might be preserved in such legends, but he changed the focus of inquiry, from the events behind the text to the function of the story and its setting in life (*Sitz im Leben*). His question was, why, and in what kind of setting, was this story told? Many stories were presumably told in a cultic setting— for example, to explain why Bethel was a holy place (Genesis 28)—but some may have been told simply for entertainment.

Patriarchal Religion

Abraham has a personal relationship with a God who makes promises to him and protects him. Isaac is guided by "the God of your father Abraham" (26:24). Jacob has a revelation from "the God of Abraham, your father, and the God of Isaac" (28:13). God tells Abraham, "I am your shield" (15:1). Jacob swears by "the Fear of Isaac" (31:53; cf. 31:42). We read of the Mighty One (or Bull) of Jacob (49:24). The protection of this God follows the patriarchs wherever they go. This form of worship is especially well suited for nomadic or migratory tribes.

But the patriarchs also worship God in specific places, as manifestations of the God El. *El* was the common Hebrew word for "god," but it was also the name of the high god in the Canaanite myths from Ugarit. In Genesis 14, Abraham gives a tithe to Melchizedek, king of Salem (Jerusalem), priest of El Elyon (God Most High). By so doing he recognizes, and lends legitimacy to, an established Canaanite cult. El and YHWH are recognized as one and the same god in biblical religion. According to the Elohist and Priestly strands of the Pentateuch, the name YHWH was not revealed until Exodus, and so the patriarchs worshiped El in his various manifestations. In contrast, the Canaanite god Baal is not mentioned at all in Genesis, and the patriarchs are never said to worship a goddess.

The patriarchs encounter El under different names and in different manifestations. He can be called El-Roi (16:13), or El Shaddai (17:1; 28:3; et al.). In Genesis 28 Jacob has a dream, in which he sees a ladder going up to heaven and the angels of God going up and down on it. When he awakes, he declares, "Surely the LORD is in this place—and I did not know it!" (28:16), and so he names it Bethel, the house of God. He has another encounter with divinity in Genesis 32, at the ford of the Jabbok. Jacob names the place "Peniel," or "Penuel," "for I have seen God face to face, and yet my life is preserved" (v. 30). All these manifestations are regarded as different revelations of the same god.

There is a striking discrepancy between the manner of worship practiced by the patriarchs and what is commanded later in the Bible. Wherever the patriarchs go, they build altars to the Lord. Abram builds an altar by the oak of Mamre and again between Bethel and Ai. Later he plants a tamarisk tree at Beersheba and there calls on the name of the Lord. Isaac builds an altar in Beersheba, and Jacob at Bethel and Shechem. At Bethel, Jacob takes the stone he had used as a pillow and sets it up as a pillar. Later, in Deuteronomy 12, Israel is commanded to restrict sacrificial worship to the one "place that the LORD your God will choose" (v. 5). Then: "you must demolish completely all the places where the nations whom you are about to dispossess served their gods. . . . Break down their altars, smash their pillars, burn their sacred poles with fire, and hew down the idols of their gods" (vv. 2-3).

Deuteronomic law did not apply to the patriarchs, who were supposed to have lived before Moses. Nonetheless, the association of the patriarchs with a given shrine gave it legitimacy. In Genesis 14, Abraham accepts a blessing from Melchizedek, king of Salem, and gives him a tithe. Salem, or Jerusalem, was an old Canaanite city, with its own religious traditions. Since Abraham acted respectfully toward Melchizedek, however, it was all right for later Israelites or Judeans to worship there. In Psalm 110 the king of Judah is told, "You are a priest forever according to the order of Melchizedek." Melchizedek, king and priest of El Elyon, was an ancestor of whom one could be proud.

Jerusalem, of course, was later regarded as the place that the Lord had chosen. In the books of Kings, and sometimes in the prophets, great scorn is poured on the rival sanctuary of Bethel, which was one of two state temples erected by King Jeroboam I, when the northern kingdom of Israel seceded from Jerusalem (1 Kgs 12:25-33; the other one was at Dan, on the northern border of Israel). Yet in Genesis 28 we read how Jacob discovered that Bethel was "none other than the house of God and gate of heaven" (28:17). This would seem to establish that Bethel was a holy place, and so lend credibility to Jeroboam's sanctuary. Jeroboam is also said to build Penuel (1 Kgs 12:25), the scene of Jacob's encounter with God (or an angel) in Genesis 32. Here again the Elohist may have been giving support to Jeroboam's actions by associating his sites with the patriarch Jacob.

It is at least clear that the stories of Genesis were not the work of the Deuteronomistic school, which insisted on the centralization of the cult. The religion of the patriarchs was the kind of observance that the Deuteronomists sought to suppress. The stories about the patriarchs must have been established too well for the Deuteronomists to repudiate them. It is reasonable then to conclude that Genesis reflects a form of popular, family religion that flourished before the Deuteronomic reform. One cannot, however, take these stories as a reliable or full account of Israelite religion in any period.

The Abraham Cycle

The Theme of the Promise

The J account of Abraham begins in Genesis 12. YHWH commands the patriarch, "Go forth from your country and your kindred and your father's house to the land that I will show you." This passage introduces the theme of the promise to the fathers, which runs through Genesis and is arguably the unifying theme of the Pentateuch. There are no strings attached to the promise. All Abraham has to do is trust in YHWH and obey the command to move.

Both J and P provide a more formal account of the promise to Abraham, casting it in the form of a covenant. The J account is found in Genesis 15. The point of departure is provided by Abraham's desire for an heir and his distress over being childless. He is told to "look toward heaven and count the stars, if you are able to count them . . . so shall your descendants be." This promise is formalized in a covenant. The Lord promises that he will give this land to Abraham's descendants, from the river of Egypt to the great river, the river Euphrates.

The kind of covenant involved here is quite different from that which God makes with Moses and Israel at Mount Sinai. In the latter case, there is a law attached, and the benefits of the covenant are contingent on keeping the law. The covenant with Abraham is really a grant—an unconditional promise. A similar covenant is made with David in 2 Samuel 7. All that is required of Abraham, or of David, is that they trust in the promise. The Priestly account of God's covenant with Abraham, which is found in Genesis 17, introduces another requirement—every male among the descendants of Abraham must be circumcised.

The statement in Gen 15:6, "And he [Abraham] believed in the Lord, and the Lord reckoned it to him as righteousness," has played an important and controversial role in Christian theology. It is cited by Paul in Gal 3:6. Paul argues that since Abraham is also told that all the peoples of the earth will be blessed in him (Gen 12:3), this shows that Gentiles can be justified by faith, not by the law. This argument later played a fundamental role in the theology of Martin Luther. There is no contrast between faith and law implied in Genesis (although it is true that there is no requirement of legal observance). Faith here is trust in the promise. In Jewish interpretation, the key element is that the promise relates to possession of the land. The promise to Abraham is seen as the original charter for possession of the land of Israel. The extent of the land, from the Nile to the Euphrates, far exceeds the territory over which the kingdoms of Israel and Judah would later rule.

Tales of Deception

Abraham's actions are not always exemplary. On two occasions (Gen 12:10-20; 20:1-7), he passes off his wife as his sister. A very similar story is told about Isaac in Gen 26:6-11. Genesis 12:10-20 and 26:6-11 are usually assigned to the J source, while Gen 20:1-7 is from E. The similarity between the stories suggests a background in oral tradition, where essentially the same story is transferred easily from one character to another. The stories are not simple retellings, however, but ring some changes: for example, Gen 20:1-7 is careful to note that Abimelech had not touched Sarah.

Fathers and Sons

Another set of issues is raised in the Abraham cycle by the question of an heir who should inherit the promise. Abraham has a child, Ishmael, by Hagar, Sarah's slave girl. There is an ethnographic aspect to the story: Ishmael becomes the ancestor of a desert tribe. Like the story of Jacob and Esau, the account of Ishmael explains how Israel was defined over against its neighbors.

The story of Hagar is told twice, with variations, in Genesis 16 (J) and 21 (E). In the J account, the conflict between Hagar and Sarai arises when Hagar becomes pregnant and looks on Sarai with contempt. Abram makes no attempt to defend her but allows Sarai to do as she pleases, so that Hagar has to flee. The angel of the Lord intervenes and persuades Hagar to return by promising that her son will have plentiful offspring. But Hagar is also told to submit to her mistress. We are left in no doubt about Sarai's greater importance in the eyes of the Lord. Abram does not come off well in this story, but, typically, he is not censured in the text.

The E account locates the conflict later, after Isaac is born and weaned. In this case Sarah's harshness to Hagar has less justification: she is jealous for her son. Abraham is distressed, but God tells him that Sarah is right, and that through Isaac the promise will be transmitted. He then sends Hagar and her child off into the wilderness. The plight of mother and child in the desert anticipates the later wandering of Israel and that of the prophet Elijah. In each case God comes to the rescue. This time there is no reason for Hagar or Ishmael to return to Abraham, but God causes the boy to prosper. Here again the idea of divine election seems to take priority over human compassion. The story seems to champion ethnocentrism by suggesting that those who do not belong to the chosen people can be sent away. We shall meet a chilling application of the same principle much later in the book of Ezra.

The crowning episode in the narratives about Abraham's heirs is the sacrifice of Isaac in Genesis 22. The basic story, 22:1-14, 19, is generally ascribed to E. There are some problems with the source-critical division, since "the angel of YHWH" is mentioned in v. 11, and v. 14 explains the name Moriah by the phrase "YHWH will see." Evidently, the story has been reworked by different hands.

The opening verse is exceptional among the stories of Genesis in offering an explicit key to interpretation: "God tested Abraham." While the reader is told in advance that this is a test, Abraham is not. To appreciate the force of the story, the awfulness of the command must be taken fully seriously.

Another key to the story is provided by the theme of providence. Abraham tells Isaac that "God himself will provide a lamb for the burnt offering" (v. 8). At this point in the story, this is an understandable attempt to dodge the awful truth, but it is more prophetic than

Abraham knows. When the angel of the Lord intervenes, Abraham names the place "the Lord will provide."

The fascination of the story, however, lies in the command to Abraham to sacrifice his only legitimate son. Child sacrifice was practiced in ancient Israel. Kings of Judah (Ahaz in the eighth century, 2 Kgs 16:3, and Manasseh in the seventh century, 2 Kgs 21:6) made their sons "pass through fire," that is, offered them as burnt offerings. There was an installation called the Topheth in Ge (valley) Hinnom outside Jerusalem, where children were burned as victims (hence the name Gehenna for hell in New Testament times). King Josiah destroyed the Topheth in the reform of 621 B.C.E., allegedly so that "no one would make

a son or a daughter pass through fire as an offering to Molech" (2 Kgs 23:10). Molech is usually taken to be a Canaanite god, but there is evidence that child sacrifice was also practiced in the name of YHWH. In Micah 6:6-8, a Yahwistic worshiper ponders: "Shall I give my firstborn for my transgression, the fruit of my body for the sin of my soul?" Micah replies that God requires only justice and kindness, but the question shows that a worshiper of YHWH could contemplate child sacrifice in the eighth century B.C.E. Moreover, child sacrifice appears to be commanded in Exod 22:28-29: "The firstborn of your sons you shall give to me. You shall do the same with your oxen and with your sheep: seven days it shall remain with its mother; on the eighth you shall give

The Binding of Isaac

The divine command to Abraham to offer up his son as a sacrifice was troubling to people already in antiquity. In the book of Jubilees, in the second century B.C.E., it is Mastema, or Satan, who suggests to the Lord that he tempt Abraham in this way (just as Satan induced the Lord to tempt Job, see below chapter 25). Later, in the Targums (Aramaic paraphrases of the Bible, of uncertain date, but probably from the Common Era), we are told that Isaac was a willing victim, who urged his father to bind him properly, lest he struggle and make the sacrifice unworthy. Thus the incident becomes known as "the binding of Isaac," or Akedah (from the Hebrew verb, to bind). Later Targums say that the lamb was chosen as a sacrificial victim to recall "the merit of one man who was bound upon a mountain as a lamb for a burnt offering." At a later time, God would have exterminated Israel if he had not recalled the Akedah. So the sacrifice of Isaac became a source of merits for Israel.

There is an obvious analogy between the willing sacrifice of Isaac and the Christian understanding of the death of Jesus. Some scholars have thought that the Jewish tradition influenced the New Testament, but the motifs of Isaac's willingness and of the merit of his sacrifice are not attested before the end of the first century C.E. It is possible that the tradition developed as a Jewish response to Christianity.

it to me" (Hebrew, v. 28; English, v. 29). This commandment is modified in Exod 34:19-20, which likewise says that "all that first opens the womb is mine," but adds, "all the firstborn of your sons you shall redeem." Underlying this commandment is the conviction that all life is from God, and that God's right to the firstborn must be acknowledged in order to ensure future fertility. We should expect that human firstborn sons were normally redeemed, as commanded in Exodus 34, but it is remarkable that the commandment in Exodus 22 is left on the books. YHWH is also said to have commanded human sacrifice in Ezek 20:25-26, about the time of the Babylonian exile. The polemic against child sacrifice in Deuteronomy and Jeremiah would not have been necessary if the practice were not current.

Unlike Deuteronomy and Jeremiah, Genesis 22 does not condemn child sacrifice or polemicize against it. On the contrary, Abraham is praised for his willingness to carry it out. He does not have to go through with it, but that may be an exceptional case. In Judges 11, Jephthah makes a vow to the Lord that if he is victorious in battle he will sacrifice "whoever comes out of the doors of my house to meet me." He is greeted by his only daughter. He expresses more grief than does Abraham, and is no less steadfast in fulfilling his vow. Modern commentators often fault Jephthah, since, unlike Abraham, he brought his misfortune on himself by a rash vow. But the Bible does not pronounce his vow rash, or pass judgment on him at all. (The New Testament in Heb 11:32-34 proclaims him, like Abraham, a hero of faith.) In this case there is no ram in the bushes. The Lord does not always provide a substitute.

The story of Abraham and Isaac continues to fascinate philosophers and theologians down to modern times. Danish philosopher Søren Kierkegaard reasoned that Abraham could only be justified by "the teleological suspension of the ethical"—the idea that ethical standards do not apply to a divine command. Immanuel Kant offered a more penetrating critique. For Kant, the problem was how one can know whether such a command comes from God in the first place. This is, of course, a modern critique, which arises in a world where God is not thought to speak to people on a daily basis, and where claims of divine revelation are regarded as problematic. We shall find, however, that such a critique is not as foreign to the Bible as we might suppose.

The Jacob Cycle

Jacob the Trickster

Deception is a minor theme in the Abraham cycle, but it figures more prominently in the stories of Jacob. A prime example is presented by the story of Jacob and Esau in Genesis 27. The context is the rivalry between the two brothers that began already in the womb. Jacob deceives his aging, blind father and, with the connivance of his mother, steals the blessing meant for his brother. His father Isaac cannot revoke the blessing. The story is told in exquisite detail, and no moral judgments are made. One is left to marvel at the strange way in which the blessing is transmitted.

Jacob's character changes somewhat as he ages. In Genesis 34, Shechem rapes Jacob's daughter, Dinah, but then is willing to marry her (cf. Deut 22:28). Jacob's sons trick the Shechemites by requiring them to get circumcised and then attacking them while they are sore. Jacob, however, reproaches them: "You have brought trouble on me by making me odious to the inhabitants of the land." The sons protest that their action was required by honor. The story leaves the issue open. There is more than one side to a question.

Judah and Tamar

Another fine case of moral ambiguity is found in Genesis 38 (Judah and Tamar). In one respect, it is a genealogical tale; it explains how King David was descended from Judah. Mainly, however, it is a morality tale on the dangers of double standards and moral absolutes.

The story begins with Judah's marriage to a Canaanite woman. This is not condemned in the text, but it goes against the practice of the patriarchs. When their son Er dies, his brother Onan is expected to "go in" to his widow, Tamar, to raise up offspring to him. (This is known as the levirate law and is spelled out in Deut 25:5-10.) When Onan shirks his duty, he too dies. Judah then tells Tamar to wait until his youngest son, Shelah, has grown up, but he does not give her to him in marriage. Tamar then takes the initiative. She dresses like a prostitute, covering her face, and waits for Judah by the roadside when he is at a sheepshearing. There is no implication that Judah does anything extraordinary when he hires a prostitute. He promises a kid from the flock as payment, but she prudently secures pledges from him. When he sends the kid, there is no prostitute there. Only at this point does Judah show embarrassment, fearing that he may be a laughingstock. When Tamar is found to be pregnant, however, Judah suddenly becomes a pillar of rectitude: "Bring her out; let her be burned." (In Deut 22:24 the penalty for fornication is death by stoning. Burning is demanded only in the story of Tamar.) When he sees the pledges, however, he quickly acknowledges that "she is more in the right than I, since I did not give her to my son Shelah." There is no suggestion that Judah should be punished for his action, but the pas-

sage is unique in Genesis for its explicit admission that a patriarch was in the wrong. There is also a recognition here of the relativity of law—Tamar's actions are justified because she is pursuing a greater good, the continuation of her husband's line. In fact, one of her twin sons, Perez, becomes the ancestor of King David. An act of deception and prostitution becomes a pivotal link in the transmission of the divine promise. Such is the irony of history.

The Joseph Story

The story of Judah and Tamar is integrated into the longer and more complex story of Joseph, which provides the richest illustration in Genesis of the irony of history and mystery of providence. The Joseph story is a novella, a superb example of early prose fiction. The story is usually attributed to the Yahwist (J) with some passages assigned to the Elohist (E). The brothers of Joseph appear as sons of Israel (J) or sons of Jacob (E). First Reuben intervenes to save Joseph's life (E), then Judah intervenes (J). He is variously said to be sold in Egypt by the Midianites (37:36) or by the Ishmaelites (39:1). Joseph says that his brothers sold him into Egypt (Gen 45:4).

The story unfolds through a roller coaster of plot twists. Joseph incurs the hatred of his brothers because he is his father's favorite, and he exacerbates the situation by telling a dream in which his parents and brothers bow down to him. The brothers want to murder him, but they sell him instead. The brothers then dip Joseph's robe in blood and present it to Jacob as evidence of Joseph's death. This cruel deception echoes Jacob's own deception of his blind father, Isaac.

Joseph experiences the transition from captivity to power not once but twice. First, he is overseer of his master's house, but his master's wife tries to seduce him, and then accuses him, and has him thrown in prison. He rises again because of his God-given ability to interpret dreams, and now he is placed in authority over all Egypt. He distinguishes himself by storing grain in anticipation of a time of famine. When there is famine in the land of Canaan, his brothers come and fulfill his prophecy by bowing down before him, in ignorance of his identity. Joseph tests his brothers, especially with respect to their feelings for their youngest brother, Benjamin, adding to Jacob's distress in the process. In the end, however, he discloses his identity (45:1-3). He does not reproach his brothers for selling him into Egypt, because it was providential. But Joseph is also responsible for causing Jacob and his whole family to go down into Egypt and settle there, as shepherds. Moreover, Joseph is credited with centralizing wealth in the hands of the pharaoh and bringing the people into a state of slavery (47:20-21). Even as Joseph saved his family from famine, he set the stage for their future oppression. But that oppression, in turn, would be the occasion of their greatest deliverance.

Many scholars have tried to find a kernel of history in the Joseph story. There was a time (ca. 1750–1550 B.C.E.) when people from Syria, known as the Hyksos, ruled Egypt. We shall consider the story further in connection with the exodus. The career of Joseph, however, bears little resemblance to anything we know of Hyksos rule in Egypt. The Hyksos were a hostile invading force, while Joseph was throughout the faithful servant of Pharaoh, and his people settle peacefully in Goshen.

The Joseph story has several facets. It is entertaining. We have many such stories from ancient Egypt. Compare also the biblical books of Ruth and Esther. It also has a clear theological theme, illustrating the role of divine providence. The character of Joseph has an exemplary quality that was often emphasized in later Jewish tradition. In the edition of the Pentateuch, the story forms a bridge from the patriarchal narratives to the exodus, by explaining how the Israelites came to be in Egypt.

The Joseph story is unlikely to have been composed as early as the reign of Solomon, as earlier scholars had supposed. The theme of the wise courtier, of which Joseph is the prototype, is especially popular in late Hebrew literature (in the books of Esther and Daniel). It is noteworthy that the heroes of all these stories are Israelites or Jews in the service of foreign kings. Many Jews in fact rose to prominence in the service of foreign kings in the period after the Babylonian exile.

The book of Genesis concludes with the deaths of Jacob and Joseph. Before his death, Jacob blesses his sons. The Blessing of Jacob is an old poem, and it includes an important early list of the twelve tribes. The comment on Simeon and Levi is no blessing: they are condemned as men of violence, presumably because of the sack of Shechem, and doomed to be scattered in Israel. In contrast, Judah is promised a scepter that will never depart from him. The blessing presumably reflects a Judean perspective, even though it affirms an inclusive view of Israel as embracing all twelve tribes.

The Priestly Edition of the Patriarchal Stories

The Priestly source can be detected only in a few places in the patriarchal narratives. Abram is first introduced in a genealogy (P) in Genesis 11, and we are informed that he was seventy-five years old when he departed from Haran in 12:4. The most significant Priestly addition to the Abraham stories is the account of the covenant with Abraham in Genesis 17, which requires circumcision. The practice is attested in the Near East long before the rise of Israel. There is no reason to doubt that Israelites practiced it from very early times, but it cannot have been a distinctive marker in early Israel. From the time of the Babylonian exile on, however, it becomes a marker of Jewish identity. The Priestly account of the covenant with Abraham is unlikely to be older than the Babylonian exile. It is characteristic of the Priestly source that the covenant is identified so closely with a ritual requirement. The association has survived down to modern times. The colloquial Yiddish word for circumcision is *bris,* a modification of the Hebrew word for covenant, *b'rit.*

Elsewhere in Genesis 12–50 the Priestly source is found primarily in genealogical lists (31:22-26; 36:1-14; 46:6-27).

Further Reading

Commentaries

Fretheim, Terence E. "The Book of Genesis." In *NIB* 1:321–673.

Rad, Gerhard von. *Genesis.* Trans. J. H. Marks. OTL. Philadelphia: Westminster, 1972.

Westermann, Claus. *Genesis 12–36: A Commentary.* Trans. J. J. Scullion. CC. Minneapolis: Augsburg: 1985.

———. *Genesis 37–50.* Trans. J. J. Scullion. CC. Minneapolis: Augsburg, 1986.

Other Studies

Alter, Robert. *The Art of Biblical Narrative.* New York: Basic Books, 1981.

Gunkel, Hermann. *The Legends of Genesis.* Trans. W. H. Carruth. New York: Schocken, 1964.

Hendel, Ronald S. *Remembering Abraham: Culture, Memory, and History in the Hebrew Bible.* New York: Oxford, 2005.

McCarter, P. Kyle. "The Patriarchal Age." In *Ancient Israel: A Short History from Abraham to the Roman Destruction of the Temple,* ed. H. Shanks, 1–29. Washington, D.C.: Biblical Archaeology Society, 1988.

Trible, Phyllis. *Texts of Terror: Literary-Feminist Readings of Biblical Narratives.* OBT. Philadelphia: Fortress Press, 1984.

Joseph Gen 50:20

You intended to harm me, but God intended it for good to accomplish what is now being done, the saving of many lives

5

The Exodus from Egypt

KEY POINTS

- J and E are more difficult to distinguish in Exodus than in Genesis.
- There is **no archaeological or other nonbiblical evidence** supporting the story of the exodus; however, it is likely that **some historical memory** of people enslaved in Egypt underlies the tale.
- Two major themes:
  —**The revelation of YHWH**
  —**Liberation from slavery**
- P: **Passover** prior to leaving Egypt.
- Oldest account of crossing of the sea is **poetic** and **mythological** (Exodus 15). Later supplemented by **prose narrative** (Exodus 14).
- Exodus story became the **founding myth** of Israel (especially in the northern kingdom) and of later Judaism.

The exodus is the most celebrated event in the entire Hebrew Bible and the event that is most important for the later identity of Israel and of Judaism. The story is told primarily in the first half of the book, proceeding from slavery in Egypt to the revelation at Mount Sinai in chapter 19.

It is much more difficult to distinguish the J and E sources in Exodus than it was in Genesis. Most analyses ascribe only scattered verses to E. After Exodus 6, all sources use the proper divine name YHWH for God. P is prominent in Exodus. It includes the revelation of the divine name (chap. 6), the account of the Passover (chap. 12), the crossing of the sea (chap. 14), the instructions for the tabernacle (chaps. 25–31) and the account of its construction (chaps. 35–40).

Exodus as History

The exodus is not attested in any ancient nonbiblical source. The Egyptians kept tight control over their eastern border and kept careful records. If a large group of Israelites had departed, we should expect some mention of it. For an Egyptian account of the origin of Israel we have to wait until the Hellenistic era, when a priest named Manetho wrote a history of Egypt in Greek. Manetho claimed that Jerusalem was built "in the land now called Judea" by the Hyksos, after they were expelled from Egypt. Moses, according to this account, was the leader of a rebellion of lepers in Egypt, who got help from these Hyksos. Manetho probably did not invent this story. Another Hellenistic writer, Hecataeus of Abdera, also

Exodus

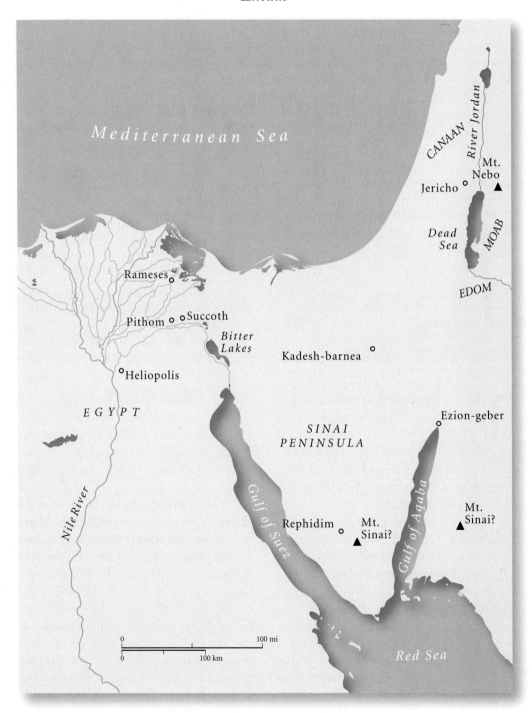

says that Jerusalem was built by people led by Moses, who had been driven out of Egypt. There was a strong folk memory in Egypt of the Hyksos as the hated foreigners from Asia who had once ruled the country. But the idea that Jerusalem had been built by these people is probably a late guess; it provided Egyptians with an explanation of the origin of the strange people just beyond their borders. It is unlikely that Manetho had any reliable tradition about the origin of Israel.

> The Hyksos were people of Syrian origin who ruled Egypt for a time and were driven out of Egypt ca. 1530 B.C.E.

The biblical account offers few specific details that might be corroborated by external evidence. The pharaoh is never named. Exodus 1 mentions the building of the cities Pithom and Rameses. Rameses (Pi-Ramesse) was built on the site of the old Hyksos capital of Avaris in the time of Ramesses II (1304–1237 B.C.E.). The location of Pithom (Per-Atum) is uncertain. One of the possible sites was also rebuilt at that time. Because of this, most scholars have favored a date around 1250 B.C.E. for the exodus. (The internal biblical evidence gives a date of 1450 B.C.E.). All we can really say, however, is that the biblical account was written at some time after the building of Pi-Ramesse and Per-Atum, and possibly that the author was aware of some tradition associating Semitic laborers with these sites. If the story of the exodus has any historical basis, then the thirteenth century B.C.E. provides the most plausible backdrop.

The existence of Semitic slaves in Egypt in the late second millennium is well attested. Habiru or ʿApiru (Hebrews?) worked on the construction of the capital city of Ramesses II. Papyri show that access to Egypt was tightly controlled in the thirteenth century B.C.E. One papyrus records the passage into Egypt of an entire tribe during a drought. Another reports the pursuit of runaway slaves who had escaped to the desert. It has been suggested that the story of the plagues contains a reminiscence of an epidemic in the mid-fourteenth century that is referred to as "the Asiatic illness" (compare the story of the lepers in Manetho). While parallels such as these suggest that there is a certain amount of Egyptian "local color" in the story, they fall far short of establishing the historicity of the exodus.

Other considerations must be weighed against these elements of local color. The consensus of archaeologists is that the material culture of early Israel, in the central highlands of Palestine, was essentially Canaanite. If there was an exodus from Egypt, then, it must have been on a small scale. Indeed, the claim in Exod 12:37 that about six hundred thousand men, in addition to children, came out of Egypt is hyperbolic in any case. Some scholars now suppose that the biblical account may have "telescoped" several small exoduses, which took place over centuries.

Further, the genre of the stories in Exodus is legendary and folkloristic. The story is replete with miraculous incidents, from the rescue of Moses from the Nile, to the burning bush, to the contest with the magicians of Egypt, to the crossing of the sea. The story of the baby Moses found in the bulrushes is a common folkloric motif. A similar story was told of King Sargon of Akkad (ca. 2300 B.C.E.). The final edition of the book of Exodus is no earlier than the Babylonian exile, some seven hundred years after the events it describes. It is not an exercise in historiography, even by ancient standards, as can be seen readily from the differences in style between the book of Exodus and the books of Kings.

Nonetheless, it seems likely that some historical memories underlie the tradition of the exodus. The name Moses is of Egyptian origin. The word means "child," and it normally occurs as an element in a longer name, which begins with the name of a god, such as Ptah-mose, Ra-mose, or Thut-mose. It is unlikely that a people would claim that it had experienced the shameful condition of slavery if there were no historical basis for it.

The memory of the exodus seems to have been especially important in the hill country of Ephraim. When Jeroboam I led the revolt of the northern tribes against Rehoboam, son of Solomon, he allegedly set up golden calves in Bethel and Dan and told the people, "These are your gods who brought you up out of the land of Egypt" (1 Kgs 12:28). There is also a parallel between the career of Jeroboam and the beginning of the book of Exodus. Jeroboam was in charge of the forced labor of the house of Joseph under Solomon (1 Kgs 11:28). He rebelled and had to flee to Egypt, but he came up from Egypt after Solomon's death. Moses also encounters a situation of forced labor and has to flee when he kills an Egyptian. The motif of forced labor, then, had special resonance in the time of Jeroboam. It is clear from the prophets Amos and Hosea that the exodus was celebrated at Bethel during the period of the monarchy. The exodus has been described as the "charter myth" of the northern kingdom of Israel. In contrast, it does not figure prominently in the southern prophets, such as Isaiah of Jerusalem. Also, there are surprisingly few references to the exodus in the books of Judges and Samuel. Jeroboam would not have taken the exodus as his "charter myth" if there were not already a tradition about it, but the story may not have been as prominent in the life of Israel in the period before the monarchy as it later became.

The Revelation of YHWH

There are two major themes in the story of the exodus: the revelation of YHWH and the liberation from slavery. These themes appear to have been originally independent of each other. Several old poetic passages speak of YHWH as the divine warrior who marches out from Mount Sinai, or from some other location in the region south of Israel (Deut 33:2; Judg 5:4-5; Ps 68:7-8). These passages do not speak of an exodus from Egypt. Conversely, the events at Sinai are usually passed over in summaries of the early history of Israel (Deut 26:5-9; Josh 24:2-13). In the poetic passages, Sinai appears to be located south of Israel, in the region of Edom or Midian. It appears that YHWH was associated with a mountain in Midian even before the exodus, and this tradition is also reflected in the story of the burning bush in Exodus 3–4. The oldest poetic passages do not mention the giving of the law in connection with Sinai. In the Elohistic and Deuteronomistic traditions, the mountain where the law is revealed is called Horeb, which means "wilderness"—and may be understood as an unspecified mountain in the wilderness. It appears that the book of Exodus draws on various old traditions, but it is difficult to say with any confidence when these traditions were combined.

The Burning Bush

There are two revelations on a mountain in Exodus, first in Exodus 3–4 and then in Exodus 19–34. In the first episode, the mountain is called "Horeb, the mountain of God," but the Hebrew word for "bush" (*sᵉneh*) is wordplay on Sinai. The mountain is located in Midian, which was east of the Gulf of Aqaba. The traditional site identified with Mount Sinai, in contrast, is Jebel Musa, in the Sinai peninsula, west of the Gulf of Aqaba. The context of the stories in Exodus would seem to require a location close to Egypt, so in the Sinai Peninsula rather than further east, but the association of Sinai with Midian and Edom requires the location east of Aqaba. It may be that the theophanies at Sinai were not originally part of the exodus story.

In Exod 3:13-14, when Moses asks for God's name, he is told "I AM WHO I AM" (Hebrew *'ehyeh 'ašer 'ehyeh*). The Greek translators of the Bible rendered this passage as *eimi ho ōn*, "I am the one who is." Beginning with Philo of Alexandria, around the time of Christ, countless generations of theologians argued that the God revealed to Moses was identical with absolute Being, as understood in Greek philosophy. The Greek translation became the foundation for a theology that assumed that Greek philosophy and biblical revelation were speaking about the same thing. Historically it is impossible to find this meaning in the Hebrew text. Hebrew simply did not have a concept of Being. The actual meaning of the Hebrew phrase is enigmatic. The Hebrew name for the God of Israel, Yahweh, can be understood as a form of the verb "to be"—specifically the causative (Hiphil) third person singular imperfect: "He causes to be." "The Lord of hosts" (YHWH Sabaoth) may mean "he causes the hosts (of heaven) to be" or "creator of the hosts." Whether the name was originally understood as a verbal form, however, is uncertain. It often appears in Hebrew names in the form *yahu* or *yaho*. In Exodus 3 the association with the verb "to be" is assumed. The phrase "I AM WHO I AM" in effect changes the verbal form to the first person. The phrase may be taken as a refusal to divulge the divine name. Jewish tradition is reluctant to pronounce the divine name. Rather, it substitutes *Adonai*, "the Lord," or *HaShem*, "the name." But elsewhere in Exodus the name YHWH is used freely, and it is explicitly

revealed in the Priestly passage in Exodus 6. It may be that the passage is only an attempt to put the divine name YHWH, understood as a form of the verb "to be," in the first person.

Exodus 3 goes on to give a fuller explanation of the identity of the Deity. He is the God of Abraham, Isaac, and Jacob. The key element, however, is what he promises to do in the future: "I will bring you up out of the misery of Egypt to the land of the Canaanites," in effect fulfilling the promise to Abraham in Genesis 15. The Deity is motivated by the suffering of Israel (Exod 3:7-8). YHWH may already have been worshiped in Midian as a god who appeared in fire on the mountain, but henceforth he would be worshiped as the God who delivered the Israelites from Egypt.

Exodus 6 contains a parallel account of the revelation of the divine name, from the Priestly source. Here Moses is told explicitly: "I am YHWH. I appeared to Abraham, Isaac, and Jacob as God Almighty, but by my name YHWH I did not make myself known to them" (6:2). For the Priestly tradition, as for the Elohist, this God was not known to the patriarchs as YHWH. The passage goes on to link the revelation of the name with the promise of liberation from slavery in Egypt. There is an obvious sociopolitical dimension to this liberation. But it also involves a religious commitment: "I will take you as my people, and I will be your God" (6:7). The Israelites will no longer serve the Egyptians but will serve YHWH instead.

The Liberation from Egypt

The Plagues

The plagues affect not only Pharaoh and the taskmasters but especially the common Egyptians, who also labored under Pharaoh. The most chilling plague is the slaughter of the firstborn. Exodus appreciates the depth of grief to which this gives rise, but in the end there is little sympathy for the Egyptians. Underlying this episode is the claim made in Exod 4:22-23 (J): "Israel is my firstborn son. I said to you, 'Let my son go that he may worship me.' But you refused to let him go; now I will kill your firstborn son." The notion that Israel is the son of God is an important one. In the present context it implies a stark claim of divine election that makes the Egyptians expendable.

The hardening of Pharaoh's heart serves to justify the punishments that follow. Pharaoh is held responsible for his hard heart, even though it was the Lord who hardened it. In much of the Hebrew Bible the Lord is responsible for everything, good and bad, but this in no way lessens human responsibility.

The Passover

Before the Israelites depart from Egypt, they celebrate the Passover. This celebration is found only in the Priestly source. Just as P grounded the Sabbath in the story of creation, so it grounds the Passover in the story of the exodus. The Passover was probably originally a rite of spring, practiced by shepherds. In early Israel, it was a family festival. It is not included in the pilgrimage feasts in the oldest cultic calendars, in Exodus 23 and 34. It was also distinct from the Festival of Unleavened Bread. The celebration was changed by the reform of King Josiah

---

The Passover Night

The night of the Passover has special significance in both Jewish and Christian tradition. According to the Targum on Exodus:

> There are four nights that are written in the Book of Records. The first night was when the Lord revealed himself to the world in order to create it. . . . The second night was when the Lord revealed himself to Abraham . . . and Isaac was thirty-seven years old when he was offered on the altar; the heavens bowed down and Isaac saw their perfections . . . and He called it the second night. The third was when the Lord was revealed to the Egyptians at midnight, and His hand killed the Egyptians' first-born but His right hand protected the firstborn of Israel . . . and He called it the third night. The fourth night is when the world will finish the period until its redemption . . . this is the night of the Passover for the name of the Lord, a night of watching, for it is already established for the redemption of all Israel's generations.

The Christian typology can be illustrated from the Syrian father Aphrahat: "At Passover, the Jews escaped the slavery of Pharaoh; we (Christians) were liberated from Satan's thrall on the day of the crucifixion. They sacrificed a lamb and were saved from the destroyer by his blood. We were saved from the corrupt deeds which we had done by the blood of the beloved Son."

in 621 B.C.E. into a pilgrimage festival, to be celebrated at the central sanctuary (Jerusalem) and was combined with the Festival of Unleavened Bread. It is also combined with Unleavened Bread in Exodus 12. Whether the Exodus account assumes that it is celebrated at a central shrine is more difficult to determine. The story is set in Egypt, long before there was a temple of YHWH in Jerusalem. It would have been anachronistic to speak of a pilgrimage to a central shrine. What Exodus says is that the paschal lamb must be sacrificed by "the whole congregation of the assembly of Israel" (Exod 12:6). This formulation seems to imply that it is not just a family festival, although each family takes its own lamb, but is a collective celebration of the assembled people. I shall return to this issue in discussing the relationship between P and D.

The Crossing of the Sea

The story of the exodus reaches its climax in the crossing of the sea. The sea in question is called the *Yam Sûp*. The conventional translation, "Red Sea," derives from the LXX. The Red Sea is the body of water between Africa and the Arabian peninsula, ranging in width from 100 to 175 miles, which splits at its northern end into two gulfs, the Gulf of Suez (20–30 miles wide) between Egypt and the Sinai Peninsula, and the Gulf of Aqaba (east of the Sinai Peninsula, 10–20 miles wide). The Hebrew expression *Yam Sûp* is used several times in the Bible to refer to the Gulf of Aqaba and may refer to the Gulf of Suez on a few occasions The Hebrew word *sûp*, however, does not literally mean "red" but "reed," and some scholars have suggested that the site of the exodus was not a great sea but a reedy marsh or lake. It is difficult to see why the Israelites would go toward the Gulf of Suez, still less the Gulf of Aqaba.

For this reason, many people have found the suggestion of "the Sea of Reeds" attractive. The situation is further complicated by the fact that the sea of the exodus seems to be distinguished from the *Yam Sûp* in Num 33:8-10.

Exodus 15:4 says that Pharaoh's officers were sunk in the *Yam Sûp*. Exodus 15:1-18 is a hymn, which is generally believed to contain some of the oldest poetry in the Bible. The basic hymn is found in 15:1-12, 18. Verses 13-17 are a later expansion, and change the focus from the victory over Pharaoh to the triumphal march of Israel into the Promised Land. The hymn does not actually speak of people crossing through the sea, and it makes no mention of dry land. The central theme is how YHWH, the Lord, cast Pharaoh and his army into the depths of the sea. It is important to remember, however, that this is a hymn, not a ballad, and that its purpose is to praise God, not to describe a historical event. The imagery of sinking in water is used elsewhere in Hebrew poetry as a metaphor for a situation of distress (e.g., Psalm 69). A psalm found in Jonah 2 says: "The waters closed in over me; weeds [Hebrew *sûp*] were wrapped around my head at the roots of the mountains." (Jonah is supposedly in the belly of the whale, but the psalm was not composed for that context.) In these cases, sinking in the depths is not a description of a physical condition, but simply a metaphor for distress. By analogy, to say that Pharaoh and his army sank in the depths is a metaphorical way of saying that they were completely destroyed. We do not actually know whether the hymn was composed to celebrate the exodus. It may have been a celebration of the withdrawal of Egypt from Canaan, or it may have had a specific battle in mind. It is poetic language, and it does not lend itself to the reconstruction of historical events.

The biblical prose writers, however, wanted to describe the overthrow of Pharaoh in more specific terms. The account in Exodus 14 is largely from P, but a J account can be reconstructed, according to which the Lord drove back the sea by an east wind and caused the Egyptians to panic. At dawn the sea returned to its normal depth and he threw the Egyptians into it. We are left with the impression of a tidal wave, which returned and engulfed the Egyptians. One can imagine how this account might have been inferred from the poetry of Exodus 15.

The Priestly account adds further embellishment to the story. Moses is told to stretch out his hand over the sea so that the waters are divided (cf. Gen 1:6-10, where God separates the waters and gathers the waters under the sky in one place so that dry land appears). The Israelites pass through, but then Moses again stretches out his hand and causes the waters to return on the pursuing Egyptians. This vivid account should not be viewed as a historical memory but as one of a series of imaginative attempts to give concrete expression to the belief that YHWH had rescued his people and overthrown the Egyptians.

The sea imagery continued to exercise a powerful effect on the religious imagination of ancient Israel. Other ancient Near Eastern peoples had stories of combat between a god and the sea or a sea monster. The Ugaritic myth of Baal and Yamm is the one closest to the context of Israel. In the biblical psalms, too, we often find that YHWH is said to do battle with the sea. In Psalm 114 the sea looked and fled before the Lord. In Psalm 77 the waters were afraid, in view of the thunder and lightning of the Lord, as he led his people. One of the most vivid passages is found in Isa 51:9-11, where the prophet asks: "Was it not you who cut Rahab in pieces, who pierced the dragon?

Was it not you who dried up the sea, the waters of the great deep, who made the depths of the sea a way for the redeemed to pass over?" Rahab and the dragon were sea monsters, supposedly defeated and slain by YHWH in the process of creation (although this story is never narrated in the Bible). The exodus was an event of the same type, in effect, the creation myth of Israel. The prophets imagined a new exodus, as a way in which Israel might start over and renew its relationship with its God. This motif becomes especially important after the Babylonian exile, either in the form of return from exile or of a final, eschatological deliverance.

Exodus 15 declares "YHWH is a warrior, YHWH is his name!" The idea that gods are warriors was a common one in the ancient Near East. A major reason why the early Israelites worshiped YHWH was that they believed that he was a powerful warrior who could help them defeat their enemies. Implicit in this image of God is a view of life as an arena of constant conflict. Exodus makes no pretense that we should love our enemies. Some people in the modern world may find the violence of such imagery repellent, but its power cannot be denied. In Exodus the warrior God is on the side of the weak, and this imagery has continued to inspire and support liberation movements down to modern times.

Conclusion

In the end, very little can be said about the exodus as history. It is likely that some historical memory underlies the story, but the narrative as we have it is full of legendary details and lacks supporting evidence from archaeology or from nonbiblical sources. The story of the crossing of the sea seems to have arisen from attempts to fill out the allusions in the hymn preserved in Exodus 15. The references to drowning are poetic and cannot be pressed for historical information.

Regardless of its historical origin, however, the exodus story became the founding myth of Israel (especially in the northern kingdom) and of later Judaism. It is more important than any other biblical story for establishing Israelite and Jewish identity. It can fairly be regarded as one of the most influential stories in world literature.

Further Reading

Commentaries

Brueggemann, Walter. "The Book of Exodus." In *NIB* 1:677–981.

Childs, Brevard S. *The Book of Exodus*. OTL. Philadelphia: Westminster, 1974.

Fretheim, Terence. *Exodus*. Interpretation. Louisville: Westminster, 1991.

Meyers, Carol. *Exodus*. NCBC. Cambridge: Cambridge Univ. Press, 2005.

Propp, William H. C. *Exodus 1–18*. AB 2; New York: Doubleday, 1998.

Historical Issues

Frerichs, Ernest S., and Leonard H. Lesko, eds. *Exodus: The Egyptian Evidence*. Winona Lake, Ind.: Eisenbrauns, 1991.

Religious and Literary Themes

Batto, Bernard F. *Slaying the Dragon*, 102–52. Louisville: Westminster, 1992.

Cross, Frank Moore. *Canaanite Myth and Hebrew Epic*, 112–44. Cambridge: Harvard Univ. Press, 1973.

Dozeman, Thomas B. *God at War: Power in the Exodus Tradition*. New York: Oxford Univ. Press, 1996.

6

The Revelation at Sinai

KEY POINTS

- **Sinai and Exodus originally distinct.**
- The **covenant at Sinai** bears important similarities to **treaties** between unequal partners in the ancient Near East. In these treaties, the more powerful party is the **suzerain**, the less powerful party is the **vassal.**
- **Exclusive allegiance** to one and only one God is reminiscent of Near Eastern suzerainty treaties.
- There are two main types of laws:
  —**Apodictic laws:** direct commandments or prohibitions, e.g., "Do not steal."
  —**Casuistic laws:** in the form "if x, then y."
- The **Decalogue**, or **Ten Commandments**, in Exodus 20: usually attributed to E.
  —The first four commandments deal with the relationship with God.
  —The last six commandments deal with human society.
- The **Book of the Covenant: primarily casuistic laws** similar to ancient law codes from other Near Eastern societies.
- A second formulation of the laws given at Sinai is found in Exodus 34, especially in vv. 17-26. This passage is sometimes called the **J Decalogue**, or the **ritual Decalogue.**

The exodus from Egypt leads to Mount Sinai. It is likely that the traditions of Sinai and the exodus were originally distinct, but in the Bible as we have it, they are integrally related. Liberation, or salvation, has its fulfillment in the giving of the law, and the motivation for keeping the law is supplied by the memory of the exodus. This combination of history and law is essential to what we call the Sinai, or Mosaic, covenant.

> The Hittites lived in the area corresponding to modern Turkey in the second millennium B.C.E.

Treaty and Covenant

Much light has been shed on the structure of the Sinai covenant by analogies with ancient Near Eastern treaties. Two clusters of these treaties are especially important: a group of Hittite treaties from the period 1500 to 1200 B.C.E. and a group of Assyrian treaties from the eighth century. These treaties are called *vassal* or *suzerainty* treaties. They are not made between equal partners but involve the submission of one party (the vassal) to the other (the suzerain). The typical pattern in the Hittite treaties is as follows:

1. The *preamble,* in which the suzerain identifies himself.
2. The *historical prologue,* or history, that led up to the making of the treaty.
3. The *stipulations,* requirements, or terms of the treaty. These are often couched in highly personal terms. An Assyrian king, Esarhaddon, demands loyalty to his son Ashurbanipal by telling his subjects, "You will love as yourselves Ashurbanipal." It is essential to these treaties that the vassal "recognize no other lord."
4. There is provision for the *deposition or display of the text* of the treaty and sometimes for its periodic recitation.
5. There is a list of *witnesses,* consisting of the gods before whom the treaty oath is sworn.
6. Finally, there is a list of *curses and blessings* that indicate the consequences of observing or breaking the treaty.

The essential logic of the treaty is found in the second, third, and sixth elements. The heart of the treaty lies in the stipulations. These are supported by the recollection of the sequence of events that led up to the making of the treaty and by the prospect of blessings or curses to follow. The historical prologue is a distinctive feature of the Hittite treaties. The Assyrian treaties are distinguished by the prominence of the curses.

All the elements of this treaty form are paralleled in the Hebrew Bible, but they are scattered in various books. The most complete parallels are found in Deuteronomy. Exodus 20 ("I am the LORD your God, who brought you out of the land of Egypt") combines the introductory preamble with a very brief historical prologue. The stipulations are amply represented by the Ten Commandments and other laws. Exodus, however, does not address the deposition of the document, the witnesses, or the curses and blessings. It does not appear then that the Sinai revelation in Exodus follows the full form of the vassal treaties, although it resembles them in some respects.

The parallels with the Hittite treaties have been especially controversial, since they have potential implications for the date at which the covenant was conceived. The Hittites lived in Asia Minor, in what is now eastern Turkey. They were active in the area of Syria only in the Late Bronze Age (ca. 1500–1200 B.C.E.), precisely the time in which Israel is thought to have emerged. If it could be shown that the Israelite conception of the covenant was modeled specifically on the Hittite treaties, then it would follow that the covenant was indeed a very early element in the religion of Israel.

The argument for Hittite influence rests primarily on the role of history in both Hittite and Israelite texts. Nothing is more characteristic of the Hebrew Bible than the repeated summaries of "salvation history." The primary examples of these summaries, however, are found in Deuteronomy and Deuteronomistic texts (see, for example, Deut 6:21-25; 26:5-9; Josh 24:2-13) that are no earlier than the late seventh century B.C.E. Moreover, Deuteronomy has several clear parallels with Assyrian treaties of the eighth century B.C.E. It is possible that Israel developed its interest in the recitation of history independently of the Hittite treaties and that the similarity in this respect is coincidental.

The treaty analogies shed some light on the Sinai covenant in any case. The demand for exclusive allegiance in Exod 20:3, "You shall have no other gods before me," is directly comparable to the demands that Hittite and Assyrian sovereigns made on their subjects. Also, the covenant follows the same logic as the treaties. The Israelites are obligated to obey the law because of what God has done for them in bringing them out of Egypt. The treaty analogies serve to underline the political and social character of biblical religion. The parallels between Exodus and the Hittite treaties are not so close, however, as to guarantee that this understanding of the relation between history and law was present already in the time of Moses or in the beginnings of Israelite history.

The Sinai Theophany

The immediate prologue to the giving of the law in Exodus is not a recitation of history but a description of a theophany (manifestation of God) on Mount Sinai. Sinai was associated with theophany before it became the mountain of the law. The account in Exodus 19 exploits the old tradition of YHWH appearing in fire on the mountain and uses it as the backdrop for the giving of the law.

Exodus 19 is clearly composite. Verses 3-8 are generally agreed to be a Deuteronomistic insertion. Only here is the word "covenant" used to characterize what happens at Sinai in Exodus 19. (Verse 6, which speaks of a priestly kingdom and a holy nation, may derive from the P source.) It is also agreed that v. 2, which gives the stages of the journey to Sinai, is from P. Much of the narrative has a cultic character and has to do with setting limits for the people. They are not to touch the mountain or go near a woman. Moses assumes the role of mediator, but at the end he is invited to bring up his brother, Aaron the priest. The emphasis on the holiness of the mountain and the need for the people to observe limits is a typical concern of the P tradition. But an interest in holiness and cultic restrictions was not unique to P, and the attribution of sources remains uncertain. It is more important for our purpose to recognize the cultic character of this material. This is no eyewitness account of events at Sinai, but a narrative about how people should behave in the presence of the divine that is constructed on the basis of cultic experience.

The revelation on Sinai is framed by another cultic passage in Exodus 24. Here again there are manifold signs of different hands; witness how often Moses is said to ascend the mountain. Some of the ritual is Priestly, and the description of the glory of YHWH in vv. 15-18 is usually assigned to the P source. The reference to the "book of the covenant" in v. 7 is Deuteronomic. Verses 9-11, however, which say that seventy elders, as well as Moses, Aaron, Nadab, and Abihu, went up on the mountain and saw the God of Israel, are an old tradition. The text is remarkable for its blunt statement that "they saw the God of Israel" and yet lived. The usual biblical position is that humans cannot see God and live, but there are several notable exceptions in the prophetic literature (Isaiah 6; Ezekiel 1; the story of Micaiah ben Imlah in 1 Kings 22). It is not clear here whether the elders are thought to have a meal in the presence of the Lord. The phrase "and they ate and drank" may be a way of saying that they continued to live. The covenant is sealed with a sacrifice. The blood of the covenant, splashed on the people and on the altar, signifies that the people are joined to God in a solemn agreement. The idea of the blood of the covenant becomes important in the New Testament in the interpretation of the death of Jesus as a sacrifice.

The Laws of the Covenant

The laws given to Moses are of two kinds. The Decalogue (in Exodus 20) is *apodictic law*: it consists of absolute commandments or (more often) prohibitions, with no conditional qualifications. The Book of the Covenant (in Exodus 21–23) is *casuistic* law, of the type "if x, then y." There was a long-standing legal tradition in the ancient Near East, reaching back to the end of the third millennium B.C.E. Famous law codes were associated with the names of the Mesopotamian kings Ur-Nammu (twenty-first century B.C.E.), Lipit-Ishtar (twentieth century), and Hammurabi (eighteenth century). These great law codes are made up primarily of casuistic laws.

Fig. 6.1. Royal head, perhaps depicting Hammurabi (1792–1740 B.C.E.), from Susa. Louvre, Paris. Photo: © Erich Lessing / Art Resource, N.Y.

The Decalogue

The Ten Commandments as found in Exodus 20 are usually attributed to the E source of the Pentateuch. Another series of laws in Exod 34:11-26 is called "the Yahwist Decalogue," although it is clearly not a decalogue. The clos-

est parallel to Exodus 20 is Deut 5:6-21. Other lists of commandments that partially overlap the Decalogue are found in Lev 19:1-18 and Deut 27:15-26. The requirements of the covenant are said to be "ten words" in Exod 34:28; Deut 4:13; 10:4. In fact, there is some variation in the way that the commandments are counted. Jewish tradition distinguishes five positive commandments (down to honoring parents) and five negative. Christians generally distinguish between obligations to God and obligations to one's neighbor. In some Christian traditions (Catholic, Anglican, Lutheran), the obligations to God are counted as three. (The prohibition of idolatry is subsumed under the first commandment). A distinction is made between coveting one's neighbor's wife and coveting property. The Reformed tradition groups the commandments as four and six, distinguishing the prohibition of idolatry and regarding the prohibition of coveting as a single commandment. This division of the commandments seems to be most in line with the text of Exodus.

The first four commandments deal with Israel's obligations to YHWH. The first forbids the worship of any other gods. This is not yet monotheism: the existence of other gods is not denied. The prohibition is directly analogous to the requirement in the treaty texts that the vassals serve no other overlord. The only analogy for restricting worship in this way in the ancient world is found in the so-called Aten heresy in Egypt, when Pharaoh Ahkenaten suppressed the worship of all gods except Aten, the sun disk. The imagery of YHWH's manifestation on Mount Sinai is much closer to the tradition of the Canaanite god Baal than to that of the Egyptian deity. Egyptian influence on the idea of monotheism cannot be ruled out, but it does not explain very much of the Israelite conception of God.

Other deities besides YHWH were in fact worshiped in ancient Israel. The prophets and historical books repeatedly condemn the Israelites for worshiping the Canaanite Baal. Moreover, we now know that the Canaanite goddess Asherah was worshiped in Judah in connection with YHWH. Inscriptions from the eighth century B.C.E. found at Khirbet el-Qom, near Hebron, south of Jerusalem, and at Kuntillet Ajrud, a stopover for caravans in the Sinai desert, refer to YHWH and "his Asherah." Many scholars deny that Asherah in these inscriptions is the name of a goddess, since the possessive pronoun is not normally used with a proper name. They suggest that the reference is to a wooden image of some kind, a pole or tree, that is mentioned some forty times in the Hebrew Bible. But the wooden image was a symbol of the goddess Asherah, and so the inscriptions testify to the veneration of the goddess in any case. Moreover, more than two thousand figurines of a nude female figure, presumably a fertility goddess, have been found by archaeologists throughout the land of Israel.

In light of this evidence, there is some doubt as to whether the demand that Israel worship only YHWH really goes back to the beginning of Israel at the time of Moses. The

---

The Unwritten Law

The whole law was revealed to Moses on Mount Sinai, but the whole law is not contained in the Hebrew Bible. One problem was, how did the people who lived before Moses, such as the patriarchs, know what to do? The philosopher Philo, in the first century C.E., addressed the problem as follows: "The first generations, before any at all of the particular statutes was set in writing, followed the unwritten law with perfect ease . . . For they were not scholars or pupils of others, nor did they learn under teachers what was right to say or do; they listened to no voice or instruction but their own; they gladly accepted conformity with nature, holding that nature itself was, as indeed it is, the most venerable of statutes, and thus their whole life was one of happy obedience to law" (Philo, On Abraham, 5–6).

According to the book of Jubilees, God had the angel of the presence dictate to Moses another, fuller revelation. There may have been a basis for this in Exodus. Exod 24:12 speaks of God writing the tablets, whereas in Exod 34:27 it is Moses who writes. According to Jubilees, God revealed to Moses some things that are not explicit in the Pentateuch, such as the proper calendar (which for Jubilees was 364 days). The Temple Scroll, from Qumran, is another rewriting of the revelation at Sinai, which harmonizes the different biblical laws, among other things. According to rabbinic tradition, God had revealed to Moses the true interpretation of the Torah, which was then passed down through the centuries as the oral law.

prophets in the ninth and eighth centuries who demanded the worship of YHWH alone seem to have been a minority. It is possible that the restriction of worship to one god was the result of the preaching of these prophets.

The second commandment, which forbids the making of idols or images, complements the previous one. Worshipers in the ancient world did not think that the image was actually a god or goddess, although biblical writers often caricature them in this way (see Isa 44:9-20). Rather, the statue was where the god manifested his presence. In the cult in Jerusalem there were statues of cherubim, mythical creatures of Near Eastern art, part human, part animal, part bird, over which YHWH was thought to be enthroned. The golden calves set up by Jeroboam may also have been supposed to be thrones of YHWH, rather than the Deity himself. The existence of the golden calves and of the cherubim shows that neither Israelite nor Judahite religion completely renounced the making of images. At some point, the making of images of other deities was forbidden, and we have no evidence that YHWH was ever represented by images or statues. The prohibition in Exod 20:4 refers in the first instance to an image carved from wood or stone. Exodus 20:23 forbids the making of gods of silver and gold. It has been suggested that the origin of this opposition to images lay in an old tradition whereby the deity was represented by standing stones, which were not carved or sculpted.

The third commandment, which prohibits wrongful use of YHWH's name, refers to false or frivolous oaths.

The fourth commandment requires observance of the Sabbath day. The name is derived from a Hebrew verb meaning "to rest." The origin of the custom is unknown. In ancient Babylon, the Akkadian word *šappatu* designated the middle day of the month, the festival of the full moon. The Sabbath is associated with the festival of the new moon in Amos 8:5 and Isa 1:13. It may be that the Sabbath was originally linked to the waxing and waning of the moon. The rationale given for the observance of the Sabbath in Exodus 20 derives from the Priestly source and links it to the account of creation in Genesis 1.

The remaining commandments concern relations in human society. The command to honor father and mother is a staple element of Near Eastern wisdom literature, as we shall see in Proverbs and Ben Sira.

The sixth commandment is usually translated, "You shall not kill," but it is clear from the following chapters that a blanket prohibition on

Fig. 6.2. "Shrine of the Steles," Canaanite temple from Hazor. Basalt. Israel Museum (IDAM), Jerusalem. Photo: © Erich Lessing / Art Resource, N.Y.

all forms of killing is not intended. The effect of this law is not to prevent all killing, but to regulate the taking of life and to make it subject to community control.

The prohibition of adultery is concerned with violations of marriage; it does not encompass other kinds of fornication. Warnings against adultery figure prominently in the wisdom literature, especially in Proverbs 1–9.

The commandment against stealing does not offer any specification of what is stolen. Some scholars have argued that it was originally concerned with stealing persons (kidnapping), but the commandment as it stands is more general.

The importance of truth in witnessing is illustrated by those cases where someone is put to death on the basis of false witness (e.g., the story of Naboth's vineyard in 1 Kings 21).

Finally, the tenth commandment supplements the injunctions against adultery and stealing by forbidding even the coveting of another's goods. The most notable aspect of this commandment is surely the inclusion of the neighbor's wife along with his slaves and his ox and donkey. We need not conclude from this that adultery was considered only a property offense. It was also regarded as shameful and an offense against God. But it was also regarded as a property offense.

The Book of the Covenant

The Decalogue is followed by a collection of mainly casuistic laws, known as "the book of the covenant" (cf. Exod 24:7). These qualify the absolute character of the apodictic laws. For example, we are given several cases where killing is permissible, or even commanded. These laws were formulated in a settled agrarian community; they are not the laws of nomads wandering in the wilderness. We do not know exactly when they were formulated. They are clearly presupposed in Deuteronomy. Various

Fig. 6.3. A massebah, or standing stone, from Hazor. Photo: John J. Collins.

scholars have argued that these laws should be associated with the setting up of the northern kingdom by Jeroboam I in the late tenth century B.C.E., or with the reform of King Hezekiah of Judah in the late eighth.

The first issue raised may surprise the reader in the context of the exodus: "When you buy a Hebrew slave. . . ." If Israel had its origin in liberation from slavery, how could buying a Hebrew slave be condoned? But slavery is taken for granted right through the biblical corpus, including the New Testament (see the letter to Philemon). The most common cause of enslavement in the ancient world was debt: people who could not pay their debts were forced to sell their children, or themselves, into slavery. Prisoners taken in battle were also often sold into slavery. From early times, people in the ancient Near East saw the need to set some limits to debt slavery. The Edict of Ammisaduqa, a king of Babylon in the seventeenth century B.C.E. (*ANET*, 526–28) includes a provision for the release of slaves who had sold themselves or their families into slavery. It goes on to state that this does not apply to people who were born in servitude. The law in Exodus is more systematic insofar as it provides that the service of Hebrew slaves be always limited to six years. No such limit is imposed in the case of foreign slaves. Moreover, if the master gives the slave a wife, she and her children remain the master's property, and the slave may decline his liberty because of his family ties. The biblical law, then, is only a modest advance over the Near Eastern precedent. Moreover, women who have been sold into slavery are not granted the same right of liberation after six years. They are granted rights, however, and are entitled to their freedom if these rights are denied. These laws on slavery are revised and liberalized somewhat in Deuteronomy 15 (the distinction between men and women is erased), but the institution of slavery is not questioned.

The rights of slaves are again at issue in Exod 21:20. An owner who beats a slave to death is liable to punishment, but only if the slave dies immediately. Here, as in the laws just discussed, there seems to be an attempt to balance the rights of the slave with the interests of the slave owners. The casuistic form of the laws suggests that they resulted from a process of negotiation.

In general, the laws of Exodus stand in the legal tradition of the ancient Near East. The classic example is the case of the ox that gores (Exod 21:28). Laws on this subject are found in the codes of Eshnunna (§§53–54) and Hammurabi (§§250–51) in the early second millennium B.C.E. The Mesopotamian codes place greater emphasis on monetary compensation. The biblical law requires that an ox that kills a person be stoned and its flesh not eaten. If an ox kills another ox, the price of the live ox and the meat of the dead ox must be divided (Exod 21:35). This prescription corresponds exactly to the Code of Eshnunna §53.

Several laws in this collection deal with the consequences of violence. The most famous is undoubtedly that found in Exod 21:22-25. The first part of this law relates to the case where people who are fighting injure a pregnant woman so that she suffers a miscarriage. This law was later interpreted as prohibiting abortion, a subject that is not otherwise addressed in the biblical laws. The discussion in Exodus goes on to enunciate a general principle: "If any harm follows, then you shall give life for life, eye for eye, tooth for tooth, hand for hand, foot for foot, burn for burn, wound for wound, stripe for stripe." This law has often been derided for inculcating a spirit of vengefulness. In the Sermon on the Mount in the Gospel of Matthew, Jesus cites this law as an example of the old order that he is superseding: "But I say to you, Do not resist any evildoer, but if anyone strikes you on the right cheek, turn the other also" (Matt 5:38–39). But Jesus was enunciating a moral ideal; he was not legislating for a community. Taken in context, "an eye for an eye" is not vengefulness, but moderation. The point is that you may not kill someone who knocks out your eye.

The modern reader cannot fail to be struck by the frequency with which the death penalty is prescribed in these laws. It is unlikely that the death penalty was enforced in all these cases, but modern reformers who reject the death penalty find no support here. This is only one of many examples of the gulf that divides ancient and modern sensibilities on ethical issues.

Exodus 22:16 stipulates that, if a man seduces a virgin, he must pay the bride-price for her and make her his wife. The woman is not consulted as to her feelings. The issue is primarily an economic one. A woman who had been defiled would not be able to find another husband (compare the story of the rape of Dinah in Genesis 34).

I have already commented on 22:29, "The firstborn of your sons you shall give to me," in connection with the sacrifice of Isaac in Genesis 22. In Exod 34:20 this commandment is qualified; the firstborn son must be redeemed by offering something else in his place. This qualification is not found in Exodus 22. It is difficult to believe that any society would systematically require the sacrifice of the firstborn sons, but it may have been proposed as an ideal in early Israel.

The need to give thanks by giving back to God underlies the cultic regulations in Exodus 23. The Sabbath law is spelled out in 23:12. The motivation that is given is practical: that people and livestock may be refreshed. Similarly the land is to be allowed to rest every seventh year. It is possible that the law in Exodus could be interpreted in terms of rotation of fields—not all the land need lie fallow at the same time.

Later, however, this law is clearly taken to refer to a general practice in fixed years.

The cultic calendar in 23:14-17 specifies three major feasts. These were occasions when the males were to "appear before the Lord" by going to a sanctuary. The first is the Festival of Unleavened Bread, which marked the beginning of the barley harvest. The new bread was eaten without leaven. This festival was not yet linked with the Passover. Passover was not a pilgrimage festival but was celebrated in the home. The second festival is here called the harvest festival and is related to the wheat harvest. It is later known as the Feast of Weeks. Finally, the third festival was that of Tabernacles or Sukkoth at the end of the year (in ancient Israel, the year began and ended in the fall). This was the most important and joyful of the three festivals. In Leviticus it is called simply "the feast of YHWH." In Exodus 23 it is called the festival of ingathering. This was the celebration when all the produce of the fields had been gathered in, including the grapes that were used to make wine.

One final law must be noted because of its far-reaching effect on later Jewish life: "You shall not boil a kid in its mother's milk" (23:19). It is because of this law that Jews do not combine meat and dairy products in the same meal. No reason is given for the prohibition. The most plausible explanation is that to cook a kid in its mother's milk is unnatural and violates the life-giving character of mother's milk.

The Golden Calf and the Second Giving of the Law

Another formulation of the laws given at Sinai is found in Exodus 34, especially in vv. 17-26. This passage is sometimes called the J Decalogue, or the ritual decalogue, because of the prominence of laws concerning cult and sacrifice. It duplicates the laws of Exodus 20–23 at some points.

The occasion for the second giving of the law is provided by the story of the golden calf in Exodus 32. The division of sources in this chapter is problematic. Verses 7-14 are a Deuteronomic addition. The remainder of the narrative is variously attributed to J or E. On the one hand, it is extraordinary that Aaron, brother of Moses and high priest, is said to take the lead in making an idol for the people. Aaron was the ancestor of the priestly line that officiated in the Jerusalem temple. The story implicating him in idolatry can only have been composed as a polemic against the Jerusalem priesthood. This points to a northern origin for this part of the story and would make good sense as part of the E narrative. On the other hand, the golden calf recalls the foundation of the northern kingdom by Jeroboam (1 Kgs 12:28-29). The king "made two calves of gold" and said to the people: "Here are your gods, O Israel, who brought you up out of the land of Egypt." This is exactly how the people acclaim the golden calf in Exod 32:4. Since the golden calf is regarded as an idol in Exodus 32 as well, this story throws a negative light on the cult established by Jeroboam. Polemic against the northern cult points to an origin in the southern kingdom of Judah. Most probably, the story has been edited more than once.

Even though the celebration is said to be "a festival to the Lord" (Exod 32:5), Moses is enraged by the reveling as well as by the golden calf. The Levites rally to his support and put out the celebration by killing "brother, friend, and neighbor" (32:27). The Levites were the country clergy, who served the rural shrines especially in northern Israel. They were later displaced when the country shrines were suppressed and worship was centralized in Jeru-

salem, and they were made subordinate to the Aaronide priesthood. Exodus 32 can be read in part as the revenge of the Levites on the line of Aaron.

Exodus 32 presents YHWH as a jealous and wrathful God. But there is also another side that is emphasized in Exod 34:6-7, where Moses addresses him as "The LORD, the LORD, a God merciful and gracious, slow to anger, and abounding in steadfast love and faithfulness, keeping steadfast love for the thousandth generation, forgiving iniquity and transgression and sin." This formula is often repeated in the Hebrew Bible (e.g., Num 14:18; Ps 86:15; Neh 9:17). It does not negate the "jealous" character of God, but it qualifies it. This biblical portrayal of God is not unique in the ancient world. A Babylonian prayer to Marduk addresses him as "warrior Marduk, whose anger is the deluge, whose relenting is that of a merciful father" (B. R. Foster, *From Distant Days* [Bethesda, Md.: CDL, 1995], 247).

Further Reading

Commentaries

See chapter 5.

Other Studies

Dozeman, Thomas B. *God on the Mountain.* SBLMS 37. Atlanta: Scholars Press, 1989.

Levenson, Jon D. *Sinai and Zion: An Entry into the Jewish Bible*, 15–86. Minneapolis: Winston, 1985.

Propp, William C. Exodus 19–40. AB2A. New York: Doubleday, 2006.

Roth, M. T. *Law Collections from Mesopotamia and Asia Minor.* SBLWAW 6. Atlanta: SBL, 1997.

7

The Priestly Theology:
Exodus 25–40, Leviticus, and Numbers

KEY POINTS

- The **core of the Priestly source** is found in Exodus 25–40, Leviticus, and Numbers 1–10.
- P legislates the building of a tent shrine (**the tabernacle**) for God, similar to tent shrines known from elsewhere in the Near East; it provides a way of imagining a central sanctuary even while Israel was wandering in the wilderness.
- Leviticus 1–7: **the sacrificial system**.
- Leviticus 16: the rituals for the **Day of Atonement**, which include the ritual of the scapegoat.

- **Aaron's sons** form the priesthood according to Leviticus; they are distinguished from the subordinate class of **Levites**, who also perform ritual duties.
- Leviticus 11–15: laws of **ritual purity**, including dietary laws.
- Leviticus 17–26: the **Holiness Code** (or H).
- Leviticus 23: **calendar of cultic festivals**.
- The narratives in the book of Numbers underscore the authority of Moses.
- **The story of Balaam** traditionally ascribed to the J source.

The core of the Priestly source is found in Exodus 25 through Leviticus up to Numbers 10. Moses is given instructions about the sanctuary, the sacrificial system, the consecration of priests, the distinction between pure and impure, and the Day of Atonement. Leviticus 17–26 stands out as a distinct section known as the Holiness Code. The early chapters of Numbers provide instructions for the arrangement of the camp in the wilderness. Taken together, these laws constitute a symbolic system that embodies a distinct theology.

The Tabernacle
(Exodus 25–31; 35–40)

Tent-shrines for deities are attested in the Semitic world. In the Ugaritic myths the god El had a tent. The ancient Phoenicians had tent-shrines that they carried into battle. Such tent-shrines have survived down to modern times. Most scholars, however, have felt that the tabernacle described in Exodus 26–40 is too elaborate to have been transported in the wilderness. It may reflect a later, settled shrine, possibly at Shiloh, where the tabernacle is set up in Josh 18:1 (Shiloh is the site of "the house of the Lord" in the time of Samuel, before the building of Solomon's temple). Alternatively, it may be an ideal construction, imagined by later Priestly writers. It does not correspond to what we know of the Jerusalem temple, although it incorporates some of its features, notably the statues of winged cherubim guarding the mercy seat (Exod 25:21).

The significance of the tabernacle in P is that it provides a way of imagining a central sanctuary even while Israel was wandering in the wilderness. The presence of God is associated with the ark of the covenant, which is housed within the tabernacle. God is manifested over the mercy seat, between the cherubim that are on the ark (Exod 25:22). The centralization of worship was a major innovation in the reform of King Josiah in 621 B.C.E. The Priestly source, as reflected in Exodus 26–40, seems to presuppose this centralization. While there may well have been a tent-shrine in ancient Israel, it is unlikely that it ever served as the focus for the cult of all Israel in the way that the tabernacle does in P.

Leviticus

The Sacrificial System (Leviticus 1–7)

A sacrifice is something that is made sacred by being offered to a god. In the case of animals, and sometimes of human beings, the offering requires that they be killed, and so made to pass over into the world of spirit. There is also provision for offerings of inanimate objects, such as cereal.

Various kinds of sacrifices are distinguished in Leviticus 1–7. The burnt offering (ʿōlāh) literally means "that which ascends." The equivalent Greek term is "holocaust," which means "wholly burned." In such a sacrifice, the victim is given completely to God. In contrast, the sacrifice of well-being (šǝlāmim) was a communion sacrifice, where the victim was

Fig. 7.1. Israelites carrying the ark of the covenant from the gates of paradise by Ghiberti, Lorenzo (1370–1455). Baptistery, Florence, Italy. Photo: © Timothy McCarthy / Art Resource, N.Y.

eaten by the worshipers. Since the slaughter of animals was permitted only in the context of sacrifice in early Israel, these sacrifices were the occasions on which people could eat meat. The cereal or grain offerings (Leviticus 2) were less expensive than the meat sacrifices and could be offered more frequently.

In ancient times people thought of sacrifices as a way of feeding the gods. This idea is reflected in the Atrahasis myth, in which the gods are distressed when they are deprived of their offerings. It is also parodied in the story of Bel and the Dragon, which is one of the additions to the book of Daniel in the Greek Bible. In Leviticus, however, there is no suggestion that God needs the offerings in any way. Rather, the sacrificial system provides a symbolic means for people to express their gratitude and indebtedness to God, or to make amends for their sins.

Leviticus prescribes special sacrifices for sin, even inadvertent sin, and purification (chaps. 4–7). Sin is regarded as an objective fact—it must be atoned for even if it was not committed intentionally.

The Day of Atonement

The most vivid example of ritual atonement in Leviticus is found in chapter 16. This ritual requires the sacrifice of a young bull and the offering of two goats. The high priest (Aaron) designates one goat for the Lord. The other goat is designated "for Azazel" and is driven away into the wilderness. Azazel is not attested elsewhere but is evidently a demon. In the ancient Near East, all sorts of problems were explained as being due to angry demons that had to be appeased by offerings or other means. There are scarcely any references to demons in the biblical writings. (They do appear, however, in Jewish writings of the Hellenistic period, such as Tobit and *1 Enoch*.)

Leviticus 16 provides a good illustration of the way ritual works. The priest "shall lay both his hands on the head of the live goat, and confess over it all the iniquities of the people of Israel, and all their transgressions, all their sins, putting them on the head of the goat. . . . The goat shall bear on itself all their iniquities" (16:21-22). Iniquities (sins) are not material objects that can be packaged and put on an animal's head. They are deeds that people have done (murder, for example), and in many cases they cannot be undone. The action of the priest, then, is symbolic, and the effectiveness of his action depends on the belief of everyone involved. When the ritual is performed correctly, the sins of the people are deemed to be carried away into the wilderness. Just as a judge in a court has the power to declare someone guilty or innocent, the priest has the power to declare sin forgiven.

We can imagine that people who approached the Day of Atonement burdened by a sense of sin would feel a great sense of relief as they watched the goat bearing their sins disappear into the wilderness. Such people might well resolve to avoid sinful conduct in the future, although this is not necessarily the case. We can also understand that an individual who made an offering for sin would be pardoned not only by God but also by the society that acknowledged the validity of the ritual. The efficacy of the ritual, however, depends on its acceptance. A person who did not believe that the goat carried the sin of the people into the wilderness could hardly feel any relief when it went out of sight.

The Priestly laws in Leviticus may give the impression that the sacrifices work automatically, but elsewhere in the Bible we often find an awareness that rituals are only effective when they give expression to genuine human intentions. The prophets are often very critical of the sacrificial cult when it was not accompanied by the practice of justice (see especially Amos 5). The psalmists also were aware of the limits of ritual. "For you have no delight in sacrifice," says Ps 51:16-17; "if I were to give a burnt offering you, would not be pleased. The sacrifice acceptable to God is a broken spirit; a broken and contrite heart, O God, you will not despise." Leviticus, however, assumes that God is pleased by burnt offerings and that the ritual is effective when it is performed properly.

The Consecration of Priests

The instructions for the building of the tabernacle included directions for the consecration of the sons of Aaron as priests in Exodus 29. The actual consecration is described in Leviticus 8–10. Leviticus takes pains to emphasize that the consecration of the priests is stamped with divine approval. Any improper use of the priesthood is presented as highly dangerous. When Aaron's sons Nadab and Abihu "offered unholy fire" before the Lord (10:1-2), they were consumed by fire. We are not told what made their fire unholy. The point is that any neglect of proper ritual may prove fatal.

The Levites were another class of priests, depicted as subordinate to the descendants of Aaron in Numbers 8. They serve in the tent of meeting in attendance on Aaron and his sons. (The relationship is spelled out further in Numbers 18.) The account in Numbers 8 suggests that this was a harmonious arrangement, but there are indications that it was not always so. In Numbers 16 we are told that a descendant of Levi named Korah, supported by Dathan and Abiram, rebelled against Moses and Aaron, saying, "You have gone too far! All the congregation are holy, every one of them, and the Lord is among them. So why then do you exalt yourselves against the assembly of

the Lord?" (v. 3.). The dispute is resolved when the earth opens and swallows Korah and his followers. The Priestly writers claim absolute, divine authority for the cultic order, and specifically they claim that the Aaronide priesthood is divinely ordained to a higher rank than the Levites.

The stories of Nadab and Abihu and of Korah and his followers bring to mind one other story of instantaneous divine judgment in the book of Numbers. This is found in chapter 12 and concerns a challenge to the authority of Moses by Aaron and Miriam "because of the Cushite woman whom he had married." In the postexilic period, marriage to foreign women was a controversial issue in Judah. Some people found the marriage of Moses to a foreign woman to be an embarrassment. The story in Numbers makes the point that no one should question the authority of Moses, regardless of what he may have done. The point is made all the more forcefully by the fact that the people who are rebuked are Aaron and Miriam, sister of Moses (only Miriam is actually punished for her grumbling). There is no suggestion, however, that Moses' marriage to a foreign woman sets a precedent for anyone else.

Each of these stories serves to assert not only the authority of God but also that of God's human surrogates, Moses and Aaron. Religious leaders throughout history have often claimed such divine endorsement, as indeed have political leaders. We shall find in the prophetic literature that there were also good reasons to question such claims, as they served all too neatly the interests of the people who made them.

The Impurity Laws

Leviticus 11–15 deals with various matters that can cause impurity. Impurity, or uncleanness, is not in itself a sinful state, but it renders a person unfit to approach the altar. Some defilement is unavoidable, but it can be removed by ritual action. There was a tendency in Second Temple Judaism for some groups (Pharisees, Dead Sea Scrolls) to insist on stricter standards of purity in everyday life.

Dietary laws have always been important in Judaism. We have already encountered the prohibition against cooking a kid in its mother's milk in the Book of the Covenant (Exod 23:19). In the same context, the Israelites are forbidden to eat any meat that is mangled in the field, because "you shall be a people consecrated to me" (23:31). Such concerns are found in the oldest stratum of Israelite laws. More elaborate laws are found in Leviticus 11. Animals that do not have divided hooves and chew the cud, and sea creatures that lack fins and scales are prohibited, as are a list of twenty wild birds. All winged insects are "detestable."

The traditional, orthodox view is that these laws reflect the inscrutable will of God, so that no explanation should be sought. Already in the Middle Ages Jewish interpreters such as Maimonides argued that the forbidden animals were carriers of disease—the pig, for example, carries trichinosis. But this cannot be shown to apply to all the forbidden creatures. Others have tried to find symbolic explanations for the prohibitions (e.g., birds of prey were symbols of injustice). Others have sought an ethical explanation, arguing that the restriction of what humans may eat arises from reverence for life. Only cattle, sheep, and goats, which are bred for the purpose, may be eaten. The pig is excluded because it is disgusting. This kind of explanation makes some sense in the case of the kid in its mother's milk, or in the prohibition of eating meat with the blood. It is difficult to see, however, how reverence for life could lead to classifying animals as abominations, or

warrant a distinction between fish that have fins and scales and those that do not. In fact, ethical considerations (concern for the effect of actions on other human beings or on animals) are singularly absent from the Priestly code. The purpose of the Holiness Code in Leviticus 17–26 was largely to remedy this lack in the older laws.

The only rationale given in Leviticus is that the Israelites should not defile themselves but be holy because the Lord is holy (Lev 11:44-45). Holiness is primarily the attribute of God. Human beings are holy insofar as they come close to God. The opposite state is "profane." While the positive character of holiness is difficult to grasp, negatively it implies a contrast with the normal human condition. Holy people and places are set apart and consecrated. Observance of a distinct set of laws makes the Israelites holy insofar as it sets them apart from the rest of humanity. But the concept of holiness in itself does not explain why sheep may be eaten but not pigs.

One popular interpretation is offered by anthropologist Mary Douglas. Animals that may be eaten are judged to be normal, the others as abnormal. The decision as to what is normal is based on observation but draws a line that is arbitrary to a degree. It is characteristic of the Priestly authors that they like clear and distinct dividing lines. By categorizing things in this manner, they impose a sense of order on experience, and this in turn gives people a sense of security, which is especially attractive in times of crisis and uncertainty. Such a system can have unfortunate consequences for people who are themselves deemed to deviate from what is considered normal in their society. One of the ways in which a person was seen to be abnormal was by bodily defects. A priest who was blind or lame or had a mutilated face or other deformity was disqualified from service at the altar (Lev 21:16). Animals that were blemished were not acceptable for sacrifice (chap. 22). Anyone who was leprous or had a discharge or was impure from contact with a corpse was to be excluded from the camp (Num 5:1-5).

Some scholars have also sought to give an ethical character to impurity laws by arguing that the sources of impurity symbolize the forces of death. Three sources of impurity are discussed in Leviticus 11–15: dead bodies, bodily emissions, and scale diseases. In the case of dead bodies, the association with death is obvious. But the attempt to relate impurity to death breaks down in Leviticus 12, which discusses impurity caused by childbirth. A woman who bears a male child is ceremonially unclean for seven days, and her time of blood purification is thirty-three days. She is impure for double that length of time if she gives birth to a female. The uncleanness here is caused by bodily emissions, which are messy and do not fit in neatly distinct categories. Compare the discussion of bodily discharges, male and female, in Leviticus 15. Neither the birth of a child nor a discharge of semen can be said to symbolize death. Impurity laws preserve vestiges of old taboos, based on the fear of the unknown. They have more to do with primal fears about life and death and loss of human control over the body than with ethical principles in the modern sense.

The Holiness Code

Leviticus 17–26, the Holiness Code (H), has a distinctive style and vocabulary. Although the various units are still introduced by the formula "The LORD spoke to Moses saying," they have the character of a direct address by God to Israel. These chapters attempt to integrate eth-ical commandments of the type found in the Decalogue and emphasized in Deuteronomy and the prophets, with the more specific cultic and ritual laws of the Priestly tradition.

Slaughter and Sacrifice

Leviticus 17 opens with a remarkable command: "If any [Israelite] slaughters an [animal] . . . and does not bring it to the entrance of the tent of meeting . . . as an offering to the LORD . . . , he shall be held guilty of bloodshed" (vv. 3-4). One of the great turning points in the history of the religion of Israel was the Deuteronomic reform of King Josiah in 621 B.C.E., which forbade sacrifice outside the one place that the Lord had chosen (Jerusalem). Since many Israelites lived at some distance from Jerusalem, Deuteronomy allowed that animals could be slaughtered for meat without being sacrificed; that is, it permitted profane slaughter. Since there is only one tent of meeting, H is insisting on the centralization of sacrificial worship, but unlike Deuteronomy, it refuses to allow profane slaughter. Such a law would have been difficult to implement. I shall return to the centralization of the cult in discussing the relationship between the Priestly tradition and Deuteronomy.

Improper Relations

The next issue raised in the Holiness Code is the distinction of Israel from the nations: "You shall not do as they do in the land of Egypt, where you lived, and you shall not do as they do in the land of Canaan to which I am bringing you" (Lev 18:3). Most of the issues involve improper sexual relations. In modern times, only one of these laws is controversial, namely, 18:22: "You shall not lie with a male as with a woman." Leviticus 20:13 specifies that both men would have committed an abomination and must be put to death.

CLOBBER PASSAGE

The biblical prohibition of male homosexual intercourse is unique in the ancient world. Leviticus does not give an argument for the prohibition. It simply declares such intercourse to be an abomination. These are the only passages in the Hebrew Bible where homosexual intercourse is explicitly prohibited. The narratives in Genesis 19 (Sodom) and Judges 19, where hosts offer women to protect their male guests, involve other issues besides homosexuality (rape and the violation of hospitality). In the New Testament, Paul draws a contrast between the "shameless acts" of men with each other and natural intercourse with women (Rom 1:27). Homosexuality is also denounced in several lists of vices in the New Testament (1 Cor 6:9; Gal 5:19; 1 Tim 1:10).

All the issues in Leviticus 18 are sexual, except one (child sacrifice). Procreation is the common theme. Waste of reproductive seed is an issue here. This concern was not peculiar to P or H—compare the story of Onan in Genesis 38 (and see Prov 5:15-16). There is no prohibition of sex between women (lesbianism) in Leviticus. This omission cannot be explained by the male-centered focus of these laws. The following verse carefully indicates that the prohibition of sex with animals applies to women as well as to men (Lev 18:23; cf. 20:16). Presumably, sex between women did not concern the Priestly legislators because there was no loss of semen involved. In contrast, Rom 1:26-27 condemns "unnatural intercourse" on the part of both males and females.

Procreation, however, is not the only issue here. There is also an intolerable degree of defilement. Not only is the passive male partner condemned to death in Lev 20:13, but also animals with which humans have sexual relations must be killed, although there can be no question of responsibility on the part of the animals. The juxtaposition of the prohibition of male homosexuality with that of bestiality and the fact that the death penalty is prescribed for all parties in both cases shows that the issue is not exploitation of the weak by the strong.

One other passage in the Holiness Code may throw some light on the prohibition of male homosexuality: "You shall not let our animals breed with a different kind; you shall not sow your field with two kinds of seed; nor shall you put on a garment made of two different materials" (Lev 19:19; cf. Deut 22:9-11). Certain combinations are deemed improper. In Lev 19:19 the concern is with combinations of pairs of different materials; in the prohibition of homosexuality, the issue is combining two of the same kind. In all these cases, however, there is a preoccupation with order, with clear definitions of what combinations are permitted or not. The prohibition of male homosexuality must be understood in this context.

Finally, some comment must be made on the relevance of these laws for the modern world. They seem to be quite unequivocal in their condemnation of male homosexuality. Whether one considers any of these laws still binding is another matter. Few people in the modern world worry as to whether their garments are made of different materials. Many other factors besides the teaching of Leviticus would have to be considered in a discussion of the morality of homosexuality in the modern world.

Ethics and Holiness

The strategy of the Holiness Code in revising the Priestly tradition is most clearly evident in Leviticus 19. The chapter begins with the programmatic assertion: "You shall be holy, for I the LORD your God am holy" (v. 2). In the

Priestly source, holiness was defined primarily by ritual requirements, although reverence for life was certainly implied. In Leviticus 19, however, we find ritual regulations interspersed with ethical commandments (note the echoes of the Decalogue in 19:2-3, 11-13). Leviticus 19:10 echoes Deuteronomy when it says that the edges and gleanings of the harvest must be left for the poor. Also characteristically Deuteronomic is the reason why one should not oppress the alien: "for you were aliens in the land of Egypt" (19:36). The code does not lessen the importance of ritual and purity regulations, but it puts them in perspective by alternating them with ethical commandments. Holiness is not only a matter of being separated from the nations. It also requires ethical behavior toward one's fellow human beings.

The Cultic Calendar (Leviticus 23)

The cultic calendar in Exodus had only three celebrations—Unleavened Bread, Weeks, and Tabernacles. Leviticus lists these three, but it also includes the Passover as a "holy convocation." Two new festivals are mentioned in the seventh month: Rosh Hashanah (the fall New Year's festival) on the first day of the month, and Yom Kippur (the Day of Atonement) on the tenth day. The Priestly calendar gives precise dates for each of the festivals, using the Babylonian calendar, which began in the spring. The fixed dates for the festivals indicate that they are less closely connected to the rhythm of the agricultural year than was the case in the older calendars.

This is a more developed calendar than we find even in Deuteronomy. It cannot have reached its present form until a relatively late date, long after the exile. The book of Nehemiah, which cannot have been written before the late fifth century B.C.E., has an account of the festivals in the seventh month in chapter 8. There is one on the first of the month, but this is followed by the Festival of Tabernacles or Sukkoth. There is no mention of a Day of Atonement on the tenth day. In Nehemiah 9, however, we find that on the twenty-fourth day of the seventh month the people wore sackcloth and assembled to fast. It may be that the Day of Atonement was celebrated after Sukkoth, but, in any case, this account of the festivals does not conform to what we find in Leviticus.

Another distinctive observance is added in Leviticus 25: the Jubilee Year, in the fiftieth year (after seven weeks of years). There would be general emancipation, and the land would lie fallow. This would require that the land lie fallow for two consecutive years, as the forty-ninth year was a sabbatical year. There is no evidence that the Jubilee Year was ever actually observed. The original practice of the sabbatical year was probably a way to avoid overuse of the land and allow it to recover. The laws in Leviticus, however, have a strictly religious rationale: they are a reminder that the land belongs not to the people but to YHWH.

Blessings and Curses

The blessings in Leviticus 26 are given briefly. They promise a utopian condition of prosperity and peace. Distinctively Priestly is the promise that God will place his dwelling in the midst of the people. The curses are given in more detail and entail war, famine, and pestilence. People will be reduced to eating the flesh of sons and daughters. Again, there is a distinctively Priestly nuance in the prediction that "the land shall enjoy its sabbath years as long as it lies desolate" (v. 34). The passage concludes, however, with the assurance that if the people confess their sin and make amends, "when they are in the land of their enemies," then God will remember his covenant (v. 44). The reference here to "the land of their enemies" clearly presupposes the Babylonian exile.

The Book of Numbers

The book of Numbers begins with "a census of the whole congregation of Israelites, in their clans, by ancestral houses" (1:2). List making and genealogies are among the favorite activities of P. These lists impose order on reality, and the genealogies establish relationships and places in society. The genealogies became especially important after the Babylonian exile, when Israelite society had been disrupted.

Numbers 11–12 picks up the theme of rebellion in the wilderness, which was found already in Exodus 16–17 (J). The stories of miraculous food in the wilderness (quails and manna) and the water from the rock (Exodus 17) illustrate Israel's ingratitude for deliverance from Egypt and its complete dependence on divine providence. The stories in Numbers reinforce the authority of Moses.

Balaam

The story of Balaam is mainly derived from the Yahwist. Balaam is now also known from an inscription discovered in 1967 at Tell Deir 'Alla in the East Jordan valley that dates from the eighth century B.C.E., which describes him as "a seer of the gods." The content of this prophecy has no relation to the Balaam texts in Numbers but bears a general similarity to the prophecies of "the day of the LORD" (e.g., Amos 5:18).

The stories in Numbers 22–24 tell how Balaam is summoned by the king of Moab to curse Israel but is prevented from performing the task. First, God speaks to him in the night and forbids him to do so (this part of the story is usually attributed to E). Then the angel of the Lord blocks his path. Balaam's donkey sees the angel before Balaam does. This episode is vintage J storytelling (cf. the talking snake in the Garden of Eden). The blessing of Israel seems all the more sure because it is put on the lips of a pagan prophet. Balaam is acknowledged as a man of God—indeed, he acknowledges YHWH as his God, although he is not an Israelite. The Hebrew Bible seldom appeals to the testimony of Gentiles in this way. (Another example is found in 2 Kings 5, in the story of Naaman the Syrian.)

One of the oracles attributed to Balaam was especially important in later times: "A star shall come out of Jacob, and a scepter shall rise out of Israel . . ." (Num 24:17). In the Hellenistic and Roman periods, this oracle was taken as a messianic prediction. The leader of the last Jewish revolt against Rome, in 132–135 C.E., Simon Bar Kosiba, was hailed by Rabbi Akiba as the messiah foretold in this oracle. Because of this, he is known in Jewish tradition as Bar Kokhba (literally, "son of the star").

Phinehas and the Ideal of Zealotry

The incident at Shittim in Numbers 25 bears the distinct stamp of the Priestly writers. The Israelites engage in sexual relations with foreign (Moabite) women. When Phinehas, son of Eleazar, son of Aaron sees an Israelite man take a Midianite woman into his tent, he follows them and pierces the two of them with his spear. He did this "because he was zealous for the LORD," and his action is reported as making atonement and stopping a plague among the Israelites. For this God gives him a covenant of peace and an eternal priesthood.

The woman is Midianite, although in the context we should expect a Moabite. The significance of a Midianite woman is clear: Moses had married one. The Priestly author wants to make clear that the precedent of Moses does not apply to anyone else. The zeal of Phinehas represents a particular kind of religious ideal that had a long and fateful history in Israel. Much later, in the second century B.C.E., the Maccabees would invoke the model of Phinehas as inspiration for their militant resistance to persecution by the Syrian king Antiochus Epiphanes. The rebels against Rome in the first century C.E. take their name, Zealots, from the same source.

Finally, P adds an interesting notice in Num 31:8, 16. The Moabite women, we are told, acted on the advice of none other than Balaam, and the Israelites accordingly killed Balaam with the sword. The Priestly writers were evidently uncomfortable with the idea of a "good" pagan prophet and undermine the older JE account of Balaam by this notice. It is also axiomatic for the Priestly writer that the women who tempted the Israelites must not be allowed to live.

The Phinehas story underlines some of the fundamental tensions in the Priestly tradition. On the one hand, that tradition was characterized by respect for life, human and animal, as is shown by the prohibition against eating meat with the blood, and the account of creation in Genesis 1. On the other hand, the violence of Phinehas, like the summary executions of dissidents like Korah, shows an attitude of intolerance, where the demands of purity and holiness take precedence over human life. The intolerance shown in this story has its root in the certitude of Phinehas and those he represents that their way is God's way.

Further Reading

Commentaries

Dozeman, Thomas B. "The Book of Numbers." In *NIB* 2:1–268.

Gerstenberger, Erhard. *Leviticus*. Trans. D. W. Scott. OTL. Louisville: Westminster John Knox, 1996.

Levine, Baruch A. *Leviticus*. JPSTC. Philadelphia: Jewish Publication Society, 1989.

———. *Numbers 1–20*. AB 4. New York: Doubleday, 1993.

———. *Numbers 21–36*. AB 4A, New York: Doubleday, 2000.

Milgrom, Jacob. *Leviticus 1–16*. AB 3. New York: Doubleday, 1991.

———. *Leviticus 17–22*. AB 3A. New York: Doubleday, 2000.

———. *Leviticus 23–27*. AB 3B. New York: Doubleday, 2001.

Studies

Douglas, Mary. *Purity and Danger*, 41–57. London: Routledge and Kegan Paul, 1966.

Knohl, Israel. *The Sanctuary of Silence*. Minneapolis: Fortress Press, 1995.

8

Deuteronomy

KEY POINTS

- Deuteronomy's structure:
  1. **Motivational speeches** (1–11)
  2. **The laws** (12–26)
  3. **Curses and blessings** (27–28)
  4. **Concluding materials** (29–34).
- Composed with **Near Eastern suzerainty treaties** in mind.
- The analogies with Assyrian suzerainty treaties and the associations with the reforms of King Josiah point to the **7th century** B.C.E.
- As in E, mountain of God is called **Horeb**, not Sinai.

- Limits sacrifice to **one location** only; allows slaughter of animals for food in a nonsacrificial manner.
- Deuteronomy is typified by a **concern for the poor** and marginalized.
- **Passover celebrated in Jerusalem**, as pilgrimage feast, as in the account of Passover during King Josiah's reign in 2 Kings 23.
- Primary authors: **Jerusalem scribes**, initially in the service of Josiah. The editing went on long after Josiah's reign.
- Similarities to **wisdom literature**.

The book of Deuteronomy takes its name from the Greek translation of the phrase "a copy of the law" in Deut 17:18: *deuteros nomos,* "a second law." It is presented as the farewell address of Moses in which he recalls the giving of the law. There are two introductions, which probably reflect two stages in the composition of the book: 1:1, "These are the words that Moses spoke to all Israel," and 4:44-49, "This is the law that Moses set before the Israelites." The word for "law," *tôrāh,* can also mean "instruction," but the translation "law" is justified in the case of Deuteronomy. The two introductions nicely capture the composite character of the book.

It is a collection of laws (primarily in chaps. 12–26), but it also has a strongly homiletical character, especially in chapters 1–11.

The structure of Deuteronomy as a whole may be summarized as follows:

1. Motivational speeches, including some recollection of Israel's history (1–11)
2. The laws (12–26)
3. Curses and blessings (27–28)
4. Concluding materials, some of which have the character of appendices (29–34)

Apart from the closing chapters, the book has a consistent and distinctive style.

The Treaty Model

In chapter 6, I noted the debate about the relevance of Hittite treaties from the second millennium to the biblical idea of covenant. In the case of Deuteronomy, much closer parallels are found in the Vassal Treaties of Esarhaddon (VTE), an Assyrian king who ruled in the seventh century B.C.E. (681–669).

The basic structure of Deuteronomy, which draws on history as a motivational tool and reinforces the commandments with curses and blessings, corresponds to that of the ancient vassal treaties. The recollection of history is not as prominent in the Assyrian treaties as in the older Hittite examples, but it is not entirely absent. The most distinctive element of these treaties is the curses. The Assyrian treaties were essentially loyalty oaths imposed by the king of Assyria to ensure submission to his successor. In Deuteronomy, Moses is handing on authority to Joshua, but the loyalty of the people is pledged to their God, YHWH. Other elements in Deuteronomy that recall the treaty form include the invocation of heaven and earth as witnesses (4:26; 30:19; 31:28; cf. VTE §3 [line 25], *ANET*, 534), the deposition of the document (Deut 10:1-5; 31:24-26) and provision for periodic reading (31:9-13), and the making of copies (17:18-19).

The most striking correspondences between Deuteronomy and the treaties concern vocabulary and idiom. In both documents, the word "love" means loyalty, and subjects are commanded to love their lord with all their heart and soul (cf. VTE §24 [line 266]: "If you do not love the crown prince designate Ashurbanipal . . . as you do your own lives . . ."). Other standard terms for loyalty, both in Deuteronomy and in the treaties, are "to go after," "to fear," and "to listen to the voice of. . . ."

Fig. 8.1. Esarhaddon, Assyrian king (7th century B.C.E.). Photo: John J. Collins.

VTE §10 (108) warns of seditious talk by "a prophet, an ecstatic, a dream interpreter," among other people. Deuteronomy 13 warns against "prophets or those who divine by dreams" who try to induce people "to go after" other gods. The series of curses in Deut 28:23-35 is paralleled in VTE §§39–42 [419–30]. Even the order of the curses of leprosy and blindness is the same in both.

Deuteronomy is not structured as a treaty text. Rather, it is an address that is informed by the treaty analogy. It appeals to history as a motivating factor more often than is the case in the Assyrian treaties (see especially Deuteronomy 26).

Deuteronomy provides an alternative to the Assyrian loyalty oaths: the people of Judah are to pledge their loyalty and "love" to YHWH. Hence the key formulation in Deut 6:4-5: "Hear, O Israel: The LORD is our God, the LORD alone. You shall love the LORD your God with all your heart and with all your soul, and with all your might." This is not a theoretical assertion of monotheism. It is an assertion of allegiance. Other gods may exist, but the loyalty of the Israelite is pledged to YHWH alone.

The Date of Deuteronomy

The parallels with the Assyrian vassal treaties constitute a powerful argument that the book of Deuteronomy was not formulated in the time of Moses but in the seventh century B.C.E. The date of Deuteronomy had become apparent long before the vassal treaties were discovered, because of the correspondence between Deuteronomy and the "book of the law" that was allegedly found in the temple in 621 B.C.E. (2 Kings 22–23). Josiah assembled the people and "read in their hearing all the words of the book of the covenant that had been found in the house of the LORD" (23:2). All the people subscribed to

this covenant. Then he proceeded to purge the temple of the vessels made for Baal and Asherah, and to tear down the "high places" or rural shrines all over the country. Then the king celebrated the Passover "as prescribed in this book of the covenant. No such passover had been kept since the days of the judges who judged Israel" (vv. 21-22). The novelty of this Passover is that it was not a family observance in the home, but a pilgrimage festival celebrated in Jerusalem.

Not only did Josiah prohibit the worship of deities other than YHWH, but he banned sacrificial worship outside Jerusalem by tearing down the "high places." According to 2 Kgs 18:4, a similar reform had been tried unsuccessfully by King Hezekiah about a hundred years earlier.

According to Deuteronomy 12:2-3, "You must demolish completely all the places where the nations whom you are about to dispossess served their gods, on the mountain heights, on the hills, and under every leafy tree. Break down their altars, smash their pillars, burn their sacred poles with fire, and hew down the idols of their gods." This was the program of Josiah's reform. Moreover, the Israelites are told, "When you cross over the Jordan . . . then you shall bring everything that I command you to the place that the LORD your God will choose as a dwelling for his name" (vv. 10-11). It is apparent that the restriction of sacrificial worship to a single location was an innovation in the time of Josiah (except for the alleged but unsuccessful attempt of Hezekiah).

These analogies suggest that Deuteronomy is related to Josiah's reform. It is possible, of course, that Deuteronomy also includes some older laws, but if so, they were reformulated in Deuteronomic idiom. It should also be noted that Deut 29:28 ("the LORD uprooted them from their land in anger, fury, and great wrath") presupposes the exile of the northern tribes to Assyria in 722 B.C.E.

The Laws of Deuteronomy

The Recollection of Horeb

The laws in Deuteronomy are presented as divine revelation, originally received by Moses on the mountain. In this case the mountain is called Horeb, which means simply "the wilderness." It would seem that the identification of the mountain of the law with Sinai was not yet universally accepted when Deuteronomy was written.

Moses reminds the Israelites "how you once stood before the LORD your God at Horeb" (4:10). The direct address in Deuteronomy is an attempt to re-create the experience. Moses emphasizes the verbal character of the revelation: "You heard the sound of words but saw no form; there was only a voice" (4:12). The content is summarized as "his covenant," "the ten words," and "statutes and ordinances" that Moses should give them to observe when they enter the land. The Ten Commandments in Deuteronomy correspond closely to Exodus 20. One significant variation concerns the motivation for keeping the Sabbath day. Where Exod 20:11 grounded this commandment by recalling how God rested on the seventh day of creation, Deuteronomy puts the emphasis on compassion. Not only should the Israelites rest, but so also their slaves and their livestock, for "remember that you were a slave in the land of Egypt." The recollection of the experience of slavery as a reason to be compassionate is typical of the rhetoric of Deuteronomy.

The Statutes and Ordinances

The concerns of Deuteronomy are much broader than the centralization of the cult. Some of the distinctive emphases can be appreciated by comparison with the Book of the Covenant (Exodus 21–23).

Deuteronomy 15:1-11 picks up the laws of sabbatical release. Every seventh year is an occasion for remission of debts. The remission did not apply to foreigners, who might otherwise take advantage of it. It is primarily a way of reinforcing the cohesion of the people of Israel, but Deuteronomy urges an open and generous attitude.

A more direct comparison with the Book of the Covenant is provided by the law for the release of slaves in Deut 15:12-18. Exodus 21 prescribed that male Hebrew slaves must be set free after six years. Deuteronomy applies this law to all slaves, whether male or female. It retains the provision that a slave may elect to stay with his master, but the slave is no longer faced with the choice between his own freedom and remaining with his wife and children, as was the case in Exodus. Deuteronomy also goes beyond the older code in its exhortation to "provide liberally" for the liberated slave, because "you were a slave in the land of Egypt."

Similar concern for the poor and the marginal appears in several other laws. The corpse of an executed criminal must not be left all night on a gibbet (21:22-23). People have responsibility for a neighbor's livestock (22:1-4). One must not take a mother bird with its young (22:6). Slaves who have escaped from their owners should not be given back (23:6). Deuteronomy 24 contains provisions protecting the rights of poor wage earners, aliens, and orphans. Some of these concerns are already found in the Book of the Covenant in Exodus, but they are more developed in Deuteronomy.

Chapter 20 sets humanitarian restraints on war. People besieging a town should not cut down its trees. And yet the laws for treating conquered people sound barbarically harsh to modern ears. Within the land, the Israelites must not let anything that breathes remain alive. In other cities, people who submit peacefully are to be enslaved. Yet again, in 21:10-14 we find a more humane discussion of the treatment of captive women. Ancient warfare was savage, and little mercy was shown to captives. Nonetheless, the Deuteronomic insistence that the Canaanites be annihilated is in jarring conflict with the generally humane attitudes of the book.

The Effects of Centralization

The prohibition of sacrificial worship outside Jerusalem radically changed the nature of Israelite religion. Up to this time there was widespread worship of Baal and Asherah. This picture is now confirmed by archaeology, which has brought to light inscriptions mentioning YHWH's Asherah and over two thousand terra-cotta figurines depicting a nude female figure (presumably a fertility goddess). Some of the practices suppressed by Josiah had venerable histories. The patriarchs in Genesis had consecrated places of worship that were now torn down (e.g., Bethel) and had set up pillars and planted trees by them. Objects consecrated to the sun had allegedly been set up by "the kings of Judah" (2 Kgs 23:11). Even human sacrifice could be justified by appeal to Exod 22:29 ("the firstborn of your sons you shall give to me") and had also been practiced by Judean kings.

The worship of YHWH was also transformed. People who lived at a distance from Jerusalem could now offer sacrifices only on the rare occasions when they made a pilgrimage to the temple. Prior to this time, meat was eaten only when it had been sacrificed (except in the case of some wild animals). Deuteronomy allowed that "whenever you desire you may slaughter and eat meat within any of your towns" (12:15). Some sacral activities were

now treated as profane, and cultic rituals would henceforth play a much smaller role in the lives of most of the people.

In the Book of the Covenant, Passover was not a pilgrimage feast. Deuteronomy 16:2, however, requires it be celebrated "at the place that the Lord will choose," and it is clearly combined with the Festival of Unleavened Bread. In 2 Kgs 23:21-23 we are told that King Josiah commanded the people to observe the Passover in accordance with the book of the covenant (that is, Deuteronomic law, not the Book of the Covenant in Exodus) and that they did so in Jerusalem, although no such Passover had been kept since the days of the judges.

The Levites at the country shrines were practically put out of business by the centralization of the cult. Their situation is addressed in Deut 18:6-8, which says that any Levite who chose to go up to Jerusalem could minister at the temple there and share in the priestly offerings. This provision inevitably made for tensions between the Jerusalem priesthood and the newly arrived Levites. According to 2 Kgs 23:9, "the priests of the high places did not come up to the altar of the LORD in Jerusalem." Nonetheless, we shall find in Ezekiel 44 that relations between priests and Levites in Jerusalem remained controversial after the Babylonian exile.

Centralization and Control

Deuteronomy also tends toward a more centrally controlled society in other respects. Chapter 13 contains a warning against prophets and other diviners who might offer rival claims about the will of God. A prophet who speaks in the name of gods other than YHWH is false, but Deuteronomy also recognizes that a prophet may speak falsely in the name of the Lord. Deuteronomy 18 offers one simple criterion: a prophecy that is not fulfilled is thereby shown to be false. But prophets did much more than make predictions. The more far-reaching implication of Deuteronomy 18 is that a true prophet is "a prophet like Moses." The book of Deuteronomy was an attempt to express revelation in written, definitive form, so that it would be the standard against which all other forms of revelation would be measured.

A number of laws in Deuteronomy curtail the power of the father over the affairs of his family (21:15-21). The most remarkable assertion of control, however, concerns the king, in 17:14-20. The king may not be a foreigner. He must not "acquire many horses," which would be necessary for building up an army, nor acquire many wives (as Solomon would do), nor acquire much gold and silver. Instead, he should have a copy of this book of the law and read it all the days of his life. The king must be subject to the law. Even though Josiah was very young when he began to reign and was presumably subject to his advisers for a time, it is difficult to believe that he would have promulgated such a restrictive law of the kingship. Most probably, this passage was added later to the book, after the kingship had definitively failed in the Babylonian crisis.

Purity Concerns in Deuteronomy

Purity concerns are not prominent in Deuteronomy. But they are not entirely absent either. Deuteronomy 14 gives a list of forbidden foods that is very similar to what we find in Leviticus 11. In chapter 22 there are prohibitions against cross-dressing (22:5), against plowing with an ox and an ass, and against combining wool and linen in a garment (22:10-11).

Purity is also a consideration in laws concerning marriage and sexual relations. Adultery (sex with the wife of another man) is punishable by death for both partners. The law recognizes that a woman is not at fault in case of rape, but if she is unmarried, the penalty for the man is that he has to marry her and cannot divorce her. In this case, the motivation is the woman's well-being, since she would find it difficult to find a husband if she had been defiled. The discussion of divorce in Deuteronomy 24, however, seems to be concerned more with purity. If a man divorces his wife and she becomes the wife of another but is divorced a second time, then the first husband may not marry her again. There is no legislation concerning divorce in the Hebrew Bible. The practice is simply assumed. Deuteronomy 24:1-4 became the focal text for discussions of divorce in later tradition. Verse 1 envisions the case of a man who divorces a woman "because he finds something objectionable about her"— most probably impurity or sexual misconduct. There was a famous debate about the meaning of the phrase between the schools of Shammai and Hillel in the first century B.C.E. The Shammaites attempted to restrict the man's power of divorce to cases of adultery, but the school of Hillel ruled that divorce was permitted "even if she spoiled a dish for him" (Mishnah *Gittin* 9–10). Rabbi Akiba went further: "Even if he found another fairer than she."

The Authors of Deuteronomy

The language of the book, which is influenced by the Assyrian treaties, does not permit a date much earlier than the time of Josiah. Moreover, the policy of centralization, which is central to the book, was Josiah's policy, and the book seems to have been either composed or edited to support it. The elements that deal with centralization, either of the cult or of authority, were surely the work of Josiah's scribes. Other elements in the book, however, such as the discussion of divorce, are not obviously related to centralization. They suggest that the scribes drew on a legal tradition, which included, but was not limited to, the Book of the Covenant that is now found in Exodus 21–23. The description of a covenant ceremony at Shechem in Deuteronomy 27–28 is also independent of Josiah's policies and can hardly have been composed by people who wanted to centralize worship in Jerusalem. Some of these traditions had their origin in northern Israel (e.g., the covenant at Shechem). Despite the fact that the place that the Lord has chosen to centralize the cult is certainly Jerusalem, there are no allusions in Deuteronomy to Mount Zion or to traditions that can be associated with Jerusalem. There are many affinities between Deuteronomy and the northern eighth-century prophet Hosea (exodus, love of God, rejection of other gods). In contrast, there are few points of contact between Deuteronomy and the Jerusalem prophet Isaiah. There was a huge influx of northerners into Jerusalem after the fall of the northern kingdom. (We know from archaeological evidence that the size of the city more than doubled at that time.) It is not unreasonable, then, to suppose that some of the traditions found in Deuteronomy had originated in the north. Besides prophetic circles, of which Hosea might be representative, Levitical priests may have been the carriers of these traditions. The Levites figure prominently in the covenant ceremony in chapters 27–28 and are mentioned frequently throughout the book.

There can be little doubt, however, that the primary authors of Deuteronomy were Jerusalem scribes, initially in the service of Josiah. The editing of the book presumably went on for some time after Josiah's reign. The historical books of Joshua through Kings were also edited from a Deuteronomic perspective,

and so we should imagine a Deuteronomistic school whose activity continued even after the Babylonian exile. Josiah's scribes would presumably have been familiar with the Assyrian treaties that provide a model for the book in some respects.

Deuteronomy and Wisdom

Deuteronomy also has extensive affinity with wisdom literature. The "statutes and ordinances" are presented as a kind of wisdom: "You must observe them diligently, for this will show your wisdom and discernment to the peoples" (Deut 4:6). The Torah is to be Israel's counterpart to the wisdom teachings of other peoples. Similarly, the judges appointed by Moses in Deut 1:13 are described as "wise, discerning, and reputable."

Several ordinances found in Deuteronomy (against removing boundaries or falsifying weights and measures) are paralleled in wisdom writings. Deuteronomy 23:21-23 warns that a person who makes a vow should not postpone fulfilling it, and adds, "But if you refrain from vowing you will not incur guilt." This attitude contrasts with the positive attitude to vows in Leviticus 27. The wisdom book of Qoheleth (Ecclesiastes) similarly warns against postponing the fulfillment of a vow and says that "it is better that you should not vow than that you should vow and not fulfill it" (Qoh 5:5). Deuteronomy 23:15, which prohibits sending a runaway slave back to his master, corresponds to Prov 30:10 ("Do not slander a slave to his master"). In contrast, the laws of Hammurabi declared that sheltering a runaway slave was punishable by death (Code of Hammurabi §15; *ANET*, 166-7).

Despite these wisdom influences, Deuteronomy is unmistakably a law code and is presented as revealed law rather than as the fruit of human experience. Nonetheless, the wisdom it presents has a human, earthly character (Deut 30:12: "It is not in heaven"). While the law itself is revealed, no further revelation is necessary in order to understand it. Deuteronomy leaves little space for prophecy or other forms of revelation.

The Effects of the Deuteronomic Reform

The long-term effects of the reform were more profound than anyone could have anticipated in 621 B.C.E. Less than a generation later, Jerusalem and its temple were destroyed and the leading citizens were taken into exile in Babylon. The exiles in Babylon had to live without their temple, but they had "the book of the law," which acquired new importance in this setting. Henceforth, Judaism would be to a great degree a religion of the book. Study of the law would take the place of sacrifice. The synagogue would gradually emerge as the place of worship, first for Jews outside the land of Israel, later even within Israel itself. These changes took place gradually, over centuries, but they had their origin in the Deuteronomic reform, which put a book at the center of religious observance for the first time.

The increasing emphasis on the written law brought the class of scribes to the fore as important religious personnel. They were the people who could copy the book of the law and edit it. They were also the people who could read and interpret it. The role of the scribes would increase gradually over the centuries.

We do not know when Deuteronomy was combined with the material found in Genesis through Leviticus. It was originally joined to the historical books, Joshua through Kings. Some time after the Babylonian exile, the book of the law was detached and linked with the other accounts of revelation of the laws. Some Deuteronomic phrases found their way into the earlier books, but the evidence for Deuteronomic redaction of these books is much less obvious than the evidence for Priestly editorial work. It seems that the books of Genesis through Leviticus were edited by Priestly writers. Deuteronomy was added to this corpus, but there was relatively little Deuteronomic editing in the first four books.

Together with the Priestly edition of the Torah, Deuteronomy was a major influence on Jewish theology in the Second Temple period. Those who kept the law would prosper and live long in the land. This theology, however, did not go unquestioned. We find a major critique of it in the book of Job. But Deuteronomic theology should not be construed too narrowly as a legalistic religion. Its core teachings were love of God and of one's neighbor. The saying attributed to Jesus in the Gospels (Matt 22:34-40; Mark 12:28-31; Luke 10:25-28) on the twofold greatest commandment, sums up at least one strand of Deuteronomic theology.

Appendix: The Relationship between Deuteronomy (D) and the Priestly Code (P)

Up to the mid-nineteenth century, scholars usually assumed that P was the oldest stratum of the Pentateuch. The classic work of Karl Heinrich Graf and Julius Wellhausen in the second half of the nineteenth century reversed the order and argued that P presupposes Deuteronomy and is the latest stage. This order was accepted as standard through most of the twentieth century. In Wellhausen's view, the

Priestly theology reflected the decline of Israelite religion, from the spiritual heights of the prophets to the legalism of "late Judaism." The value judgment is a separate issue from the dating. One could as well argue that the later material represents a higher stage of development. Regardless of his prejudices, Wellhausen offered serious arguments for the late date of P:

1. The centralization of the cult was an innovation in the time of Josiah. It is taken for granted in P.
2. Profane slaughter is introduced in D and taken for granted in P.
3. Deuteronomy does not distinguish clearly between priests and Levites, and often refers to "Levitical priests." In the Priestly source, the Levites are clearly subordinated to the priests.
4. The cultic calendar in Leviticus is more developed than that of Deuteronomy.

On the other side, various arguments have been offered for the antiquity of P. Laws dealing with ritual and purity, sin and sanction, were an integral part of Near Eastern religion in the second millennium B.C.E. Interest in such matters can no longer be regarded as late. The language of P is different from that of postexilic Judaism. Several key terms in P either fall out of use (*ʿēdāh* for community) or acquire a different meaning (*ʿăbōdāh*, "work," comes to mean "worship"). This shows that the language of P was not invented in the exilic or postexilic period. But liturgical language is often archaic. (Compare the use of Latin in the Roman Catholic Mass up until the 1960s.) So the retention of archaic language in P does not necessarily prove that the composition is ancient.

Some scholars have argued that there are several cases of Priestly influence on D. For example, Deuteronomy sometimes tells the Israelites to do "as I have commanded them" when the relevant commands are found in Leviticus (e.g., Deut 24:8, with reference to scale disease, which is the subject of Leviticus 13–14). Also, the dietary laws in Deuteronomy 14 are said to be adapted from Leviticus 11 (such laws are typical of Leviticus but exceptional in Deuteronomy). But it is possible that these laws were known in Israel apart from the book of Leviticus, even before the Priestly laws were written down. Also, it has often been suggested that these elements were introduced into Deuteronomy by editors who were influenced by P.

This latter point highlights an ambiguity in the entire discussion. It is generally granted that Deuteronomy was not complete in its present form at the time of Josiah's reform but was edited and expanded by scribes for many decades thereafter. It is also likely that the Priestly code evolved over a period of time. Even if we can show that one depends on the other at a specific point, this does not necessarily mean that the entire book or tradition is later.

The central issue has always been whether P presupposes the centralization of the cult. Neither P nor H ever explicitly demands that sacrificial worship be confined to one place, but P speaks of the tabernacle and the tent of meeting as one central place of worship. The question is, did the Priestly authors imply that Israel should also have one central place of worship when they came into the land? An interesting test case is provided by the Passover in Exodus 12: the lamb should be sacrificed by "the whole assembly of the congregation of Israel." The language here is most easily taken to mean that the lamb is sacrificed in a cultic assembly. But Passover was a family celebration down to the time of Josiah's reform. It seems, then, that P presupposes the Deuteronomic transformation of Passover into a pilgrimage festival. Nonetheless, the text is not so explicit as to settle the issue beyond doubt. If indeed P was compiled after Josiah's reform, then the attempt of H to forbid profane slaughter must be seen as a reactionary move, rejecting one of the major innovations of Deuteronomy.

The changing relations between priests and Levites are also more easily explained if the Priestly legislation is later than Josiah's reforms.

Finally, Wellhausen was indisputably right that the Priestly calendar in Leviticus 23 is the most developed such calendar in the Hebrew Bible. Not only does it include the Passover among the pilgrimage feasts, but it includes two important festivals that are not found even in Deuteronomy, Rosh Hashanah, and Yom Kippur. Even Nehemiah 8–9, written long after the Babylonian exile, does not yet reflect the Priestly calendar for these festivals.

It would be too simple to say without qualification that P is later than Deuteronomy. Both of these sources contain ancient traditions, and both went through extensive editing over a lengthy period of time. Some of the traditions contained in P may be quite old. It seems, however, that the Priestly strand of the Pentateuch was edited after Josiah's reform and was influenced by the centralization of the sacrificial cult.

The P material was integrated with JE to a much greater extent than was Deuteronomy, which was originally linked with the historical books that follow it. We do not know when Deuteronomy was detached from the history and integrated into the Torah as the fifth book of Moses. Nonetheless, the climactic position eventually accorded to Deuteronomy ensured that for many people it would provide the lens through which the Pentateuch would be interpreted.

Further Reading

Commentaries

Clements, Ronald E. "The Book of Deuteronomy." In *NIB* 2:268–538.

Miller, Patrick D. *Deuteronomy*. Interpretation. Louisville: Westminster John Knox, 1990.

Nelson, Richard D. *Deuteronomy*. OTL. Louisville: Westminster John Knox, 2002.

Rad, Gerhard von. *Deuteronomy*. Trans. D. Barton. OTL. Philadelphia: Westminster, 1966.

Weinfeld, Moshe. *Deuteronomy 1–11*. AB 5. New York: Doubleday, 1991.

Studies

Levinson, Bernard M. *Deuteronomy and the Hermeneutics of Legal Innovation*. New York: Oxford Univ. Press, 1997.

Lohfink, Norbert. *Theology of the Pentateuch: Themes of the Priestly Narrative and Deuteronomy*. Trans. L. M. Maloney. Minneapolis: Fortress Press, 1994.

Weinfeld, Moshe. *Deuteronomy and the Deuteronomic School*. Oxford: Clarendon, 1972 (reprint, Winona Lake, Ind.: Eisenbrauns, 1992).

9

Joshua

KEY POINTS

- The books of Joshua, Judges, Samuel, and Kings (known traditionally as the Former Prophets) form, together with Deuteronomy, **the Deuteronomistic History (Martin Noth)**.
- The book of Joshua: occupation of the land of Canaan.
- Models to understand the occupation:
  —The **immigration model**: Israelites came from outside, first settling the central highlands, and only later the coastal plains.
  —The **conquest model**: violent conquering of indigenous cities and peoples; this model is largely refuted by archaeological evidence.
  —The **revolt model**: the incoming Israelites allied with disaffected Canaanites against oppressive urban centers.

- —The **gradual emergence model**: differs from the revolt model mainly in that it does not ascribe Israel's emergence to ideology and an egalitarian drive.
- The stories of conquest in Joshua are **most likely fictions**, underpinned by the Deuteronomic claim that the land had been granted to Israel by God.
- The second half of Joshua is concerned with the **territorial allotments** to the various tribes.
- The book concludes with a **covenant ceremony** at Shechem (chap. 24), which is highly deuteronomistic in character.

The books of Joshua, Judges, Samuel, and Kings (traditionally known as the Former Prophets) are known in modern scholarship as the Deuteronomistic History.

The view that the book of Deuteronomy once constituted a literary unit with the historical books was argued by Martin Noth in 1943 and has been generally accepted since then, although some scholars have questioned it in recent years. These books contain diverse kinds of material and evidently drew on older sources and traditions. Other scholars before Noth had noticed the influence of Deuteronomy. The

books of Kings frequently condemn northern Israel for continuing "the sin of Jeroboam," its first king, who erected places of worship at Bethel and Dan. This criticism clearly presupposes Josiah's prohibition of sacrificial worship outside of Jerusalem. Noth, however, argued that similar language and ideology runs through all these books. The editor is called Deuteronomistic because history is judged in the light of Deuteronomic theology.

Key points in this history are marked by speeches. A speech by Joshua in Joshua 1 marks the beginning of the conquest, and another in Joshua 23 marks its conclusion. Samuel's speech in 1 Samuel 12 marks the transition to the time of the monarchy. Solomon's prayer in 1 Kings 8 at the consecration of the temple also marks an important point in the history. Other Deuteronomistic passages take the form of narrative summaries: Joshua 12; Judg 2:11-22; 2 Kgs 17:7-18, 20-23. The promise to David in 2 Samuel 7 also has structural importance and is often recalled in 1–2 Kings.

Noth argued that the entire Deuteronomistic History was composed by one editor during the Babylonian exile. The purpose of the work would then be to explain the disaster that befell Israel and Judah as divine punishment for their failure (and especially the failure of the kings) to keep the covenant. But this is not the only theme in the history. There is also a positive view of the kingship that is reflected in the promise to David in 2 Samuel 7 and in the account of Josiah's reform. Various alternatives to Noth's single editor have been proposed. The most influential of these is the view of F. M. Cross that there were two editions of the history, the first in the reign of Josiah, with a positive view of the monarchy, and the second in the Babylonian exile, after the release of King Jehoiachin from prison in 562 B.C.E., the last event reported in 2 Kings. The second edition was colored by the destruction of Jerusalem and placed greater emphasis on the failure of the monarchy. Other scholars have proposed more complex theories. A theory of three editions, one with a historical focus, one prophetic, and one nomistic (emphasizing law), has enjoyed wide support in German scholarship. Some scholars argue that there was a pre-Josianic edition of the history that culminated in the reign of Hezekiah.

Three considerations should be borne in mind in reading these books. First, this history was put together and edited no earlier than the late seventh century B.C.E., several hundred years after the supposed time of the conquest and the judges. The final edition is no earlier than the Babylonian exile, possibly later.

Second, these books have a clear ideological character. They are heavily influenced by Deuteronomic theology, seeing a pattern of reward and punishment in history. They are written from a Judean perspective, with a strong belief in the divine election of Jerusalem and the Davidic line, and are unsympathetic to the kings of northern Israel.

Third, the history contains some diversity of editorial perspective. Some passages have a negative view of the monarchy; others are more positive. This diversity is most easily explained by supposing that there were different editions of the book. Moreover, each of the books has its own character, which is shaped by the underlying traditions on which it draws.

The Book of Joshua

The book of Joshua describes how the Israelite tribes took possession of the land of Canaan west of the Jordan. In the opening verses, the Lord tells Joshua that he is giving him the land "from the wilderness and the Lebanon as far as the great river, the river Euphrates," essentially the land promised to Abraham in Genesis 15. Later summary statements suggest that Joshua did indeed overrun the entire country (e.g., Josh 10:40).

Closer reading suggests a more limited conquest. Most of the action in chapters 2–10 takes place in a small area around Jericho, Shechem, and Jerusalem. The summary in 10:40-43 claims the comprehensive conquest of the southern part of the country. Chapter 11 describes a campaign against Hazor in the far north. The actual narratives of conquest appear quite spotty as compared with the sweeping claims in the summaries. Moreover, Judges 1 gives a long list of places from which the Canaanites were not driven out, including major sites such as Taanach and Megiddo. There are also troubling inconsistencies. Judges 1:8 says that "the people of Judah fought against Jerusalem and took it," but according to 1:21, "the Benjaminites did not drive out the Jebusites who lived in Jerusalem." Later we will find that Jerusalem was captured only in the time of David. Hazor, allegedly captured by Joshua in Joshua 11, is still in Canaanite control in Judges 4 and 5. The biblical evidence for a sweeping conquest, then, is not as straightforward as it might initially appear.

Four models of the origin of Israel have been influential in scholarship in the twentieth century: the immigration model, favored especially by German scholars in the mid-twentieth century; the conquest model, defended especially in North America; the revolt hypothesis, which tries to explain the origin of Israel as social upheaval; and the model of gradual evolution, which suggests that the Israelites originated as Canaanites and only gradually attained a distinctive identity.

The Origin of Israel in Canaan

The Immigration Model

The immigration model is associated especially with the names of Albrecht Alt and Martin Noth. Alt observed that the main cities were in the plains, whereas the central highlands were sparsely inhabited in the second millennium. He proposed that the Israelites first occupied the highlands and only gradually extended their control to the plains. This view of the Israelite settlement could claim support from the account in Judges 1, which admits that the

Canaanites were not initially driven out from many of the lowland cities. Some patriarchal stories from Genesis could also be understood as part of this process of settlement. Alt and Noth accepted the biblical account insofar as they assumed that the Israelites came from outside the land.

The Conquest Model

American scholarship in the early and mid-twentieth century was dominated by the rise of archaeology. The Near East is dotted with *tells,* flat-topped mounds that were the sites of ancient cities. These mounds grew because of the frequency with which cities were destroyed. After the destruction, the ruins were leveled off and the city rebuilt on top of them. Typically, a "destruction layer" of debris was trapped under the new floors. If the cities of Canaan had been violently destroyed, there should be evidence that could be found by the archaeologists. The leader in this endeavor was William Foxwell Albright. The Albrightean account of the history of Israel was given classic expression in John Bright's *History of Israel.* The attempt to corroborate the biblical account by archaeological research, however, backfired: the archaeological evidence does not match the biblical account of the conquest.

According to the biblical accounts, the first phase of the conquest took place in Transjordan. The account in Numbers 21 claims that there was a settled population in this region and specifically mentions the cities of Heshbon and Dibon. Both of these sites have been excavated and shown to have been unoccupied in the Late Bronze period.

Similar results were obtained at Jericho and Ai, the two showpieces of the conquest in Joshua. Neither was a walled city in the Late Bronze period. Of nearly twenty iden-

Israelite Settlement

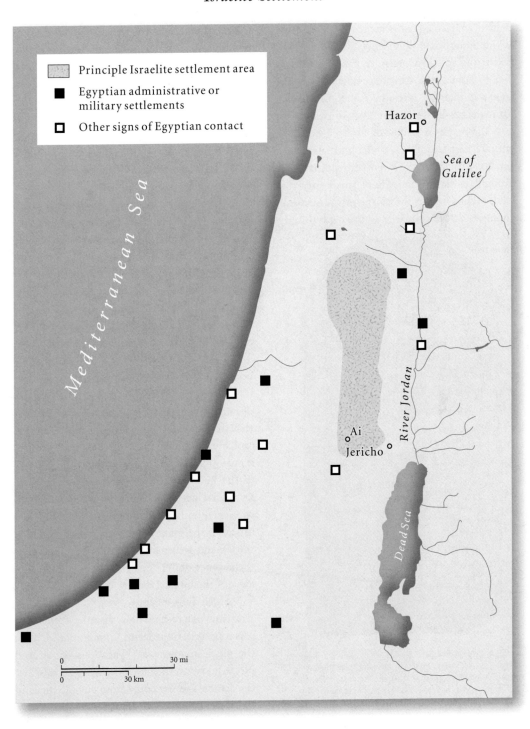

tifiable sites that were captured in the biblical account, only two, Hazor and Bethel, have yielded archaeological evidence of destruction at the appropriate period. Ironically, Hazor is said to be still in Canaanite hands in Judges 4–5. In light of the available evidence, we must conclude that the account of the conquest in Joshua is largely if not entirely fictitious.

The results of archaeology have not been entirely negative. Excavations and surveys in the last quarter of the twentieth century have brought to light hundreds of small sites that were established in the thirteenth to eleventh centuries B.C.E., primarily in the central highlands. The identification of these settlements as Israelite is suggested by the fact that this region is the stronghold of early Israel according to the biblical account, and it was clearly Israelite in later times. A commemorative stele of the Egyptian pharaoh Merneptah, erected about 1220 B.C.E., boasts of his victories in Canaan and that "Israel is laid waste, his seed is not" (*ANET*, 378). It is not clear here whether Israel is a people or a place but in either case an entity called Israel existed in Canaan in the late thirteenth century B.C.E.

The most remarkable thing about these settlements in light of the biblical account is that their material culture is essentially Canaanite. Archaeologists of an earlier generation thought they had found some distinctively Israelite features in the central highlands. The typical style of house there is usually referred to as "the four-roomed courtyard house" (consisting of a cluster of rooms around a courtyard). This has often been called "the Israelite-style house," and it was indeed the typical kind of house in ancient Israel, but a growing number of such houses have now been found at sites that were obviously not Israelite. Similarly, the "collar-rimmed jar" is typical of these settlements but not unique to them. The pottery in the new villages is usually of poorer quality than what is found in Canaanite cities such as Gezer, but of the same general type. (One aspect of the material remains of the highland settlements that may be distinctive, however, is the absence of pig bones, which is of interest in view of the biblical dietary laws.)

Since these villages were not fortified, they lend support to the view that the settlement was a process of peaceful immigration. Unlike the older immigration hypothesis of Alt and Noth, however, the new evidence suggests that the settlers did not come from outside the land but were of Canaanite origin.

Fig. 9.1. Grey granite double-sided stele called the "Israel Stele" or "the Victory Stele of Merneptah" inscribed with a list of defeated peoples including the first mention of Israel, erected by Merneptah 1213–1204 B.C.E. Photo: © The Art Archive / Egyptian Museum Cairo / Dagli Orti.

The Revolt Model

The hypothesis that Israel had its origins in a social revolution within Canaan was first proposed by George Mendenhall in 1962. The basic idea was derived from the Amarna letters, which had been found in Egypt in 1888. These letters were written in Akkadian on clay tablets by people in Canaan, and addressed to the pharaohs Amenophis III and Amenophis IV or Akhenaten in the fourteenth century B.C.E. The latter pharaoh had launched a religious revolution in Egypt by promoting the cult of the sun-god Aten to the exclusion of other deities (the Aten heresy). The letters from Canaan frequently complain about groups who were causing turmoil and challenging Egyptian authority. These troublemakers are often called Habiru/Hapiru or 'Apiru. This is not an ethnic term but refers to people who were on the margins of society, as mercenaries, slaves, or outlaws. Especially interesting are the references to one Labayu, who allegedly "gave Shechem to the Habiru." Shechem figures prominently in Deuteronomy and Joshua as an early Israelite center, but there is no account of its capture in the book of Joshua.

The Amarna letters date from a time more than a century before the usual date for the exodus, so they cannot be taken as referring to upheavals caused by the emergence of Israel. But conditions in Canaan probably did not change very much over a century or so. Mendenhall suggested that the Israelites who had escaped from Egypt made common cause with disaffected Canaanites. Israel was

---

Say [t]o the king, my lord: Message of 'Abdi-Heba, your servant. I fall at the feet of my lord, the king, 7 times and 7 times. What have I done to the king, my lord? They denounce me: . . . (I am slandered) before the king, my lord, "'Abdi-Heba has rebelled against the king, his lord." Seeing that, as far as I am concerned, neither my father nor my mother put me in this place, but the strong arm of the king brought me into my father's house, why should I of all people commit a crime against the king, my lord? As truly as the king, my lord, lives, I say to the commissioner of the king, [my] lord, "Why do you love the 'Apiru but hate the mayors?" Accordingly, I am slandered before the king, my lord. May the king, my lord, know that (though) the king, my lord, stationed a garrison (here), Enhamu has taken i[t al]l away. . . . [Now], O king, my lord, [there is n]o garrison, [and so] may the king provide for his land. May the king [pro]vide for his land! All the [la]nds of the king, my lord, have deserted. Ili-Milku has caused the loss of all the land of the king, and so may the king, my lord, provide for his land. For my part, I say, "I would go in to the king, my lord, and visit the king, my lord," but the war against me is severe, and so I am not able to go in to the king, my lord. And may it seem good in the sight of the king, [and] may he send a garrison so I may go in and visit the king, my lord. In truth, the king, my lord, lives: whenever the commissioners have come out, I would say (to them), "Lost are the lands of the king," but they did not listen to me. Lost are all the mayors; there is not a mayor remaining to the king, my lord. May the king turn his attention to the archers so that archers of the king, my lord, come forth. The king has no lands. (That) 'Apiru has plundered all the lands of the king. If there are archers this year, the lands of the king, my lord, will remain. But if there are no archers, lost are the lands of the king, my lord. [T]o the scribe of the king, my lord: Message of 'Abdi-Heba, your [ser]vant. Present eloquent words to the king, my lord. Lost are all the lands of the king, my lord.

—Letter #286, The Amarna Letters, trans. Moran, 326–27.

not originally an ethnic group but the union of people fleeing oppression who joined together in the worship of the liberator god YHWH. This revolt hypothesis was developed further by Norman Gottwald.

The revolt hypothesis is in fact compatible with the archaeological evidence, but it has little support in the biblical text. There is no suggestion that Joshua was engaged in the liberation of Canaan. The revolt model is widely viewed as anachronistic, a myth of ancient Israel that conforms to one set of modern ideals.

The Gradual Emergence Model

In fairness to the revolt model, no account of early Israel can reconcile the biblical account and the archaeological evidence. The consensus on the subject at the beginning of the twenty-first century favors the view that the Israelites were basically Canaanites who gradually developed a separate identity. Their emergence as a distinct entity is reflected in the settlement of the central highlands. The people who founded these settlements had apparently migrated from the lowlands. We do not know why. They may have been disaffected with an oppressive society in the Canaanite city-states, as the revolt model suggests. Alternatively, they may have fled because of the instability of life in the lowlands due to the invasion of the Sea Peoples who became the Philistines, and who emerge into history about the same time as the Israelites, or for other reasons. The main difference over against the revolt model is that this model does not assume that the Israelites were motivated by egalitarian ideals. It is true that early Israel, according to the Bible, did not have a king, but this may have been due to the relative lack of political organization rather than to ideological reasons.

The Account of the Conquest

Gilgal and Jericho

Some of the early stories in Joshua have a ritualistic character. Before the crossing of the Jordan, Joshua tells the Israelites to sanctify themselves as they had before the revelation at Sinai. The waters part before the Israelites when the priests enter the river, and the people cross on dry ground. This directly recalls the crossing of the Red Sea and may reflect a ritual reenactment of the exodus at Gilgal.

According to Joshua 5, Joshua had all the Israelites circumcised before proceeding to attack Jericho. Such an action is wildly implausible at the beginning of a military campaign (cf. Genesis 34, where the sons of Jacob sack Shechem while the Shechemites are still sore after circumcision). Here again the editor of the story seems to be more concerned with ritual propriety than with historical plausibility.

Before the attack on Jericho, Joshua has a vision of a figure who identifies himself as "commander of the army of the Lord" (5:14). The point is made that Israel does not rely only on its own human resources. Rather, it is engaged in a "holy war," aided by angelic hosts. (A similar view of "holy war" is found much later in the "Scroll of the War of the Sons of Light against the Sons of Darkness" from Qumran.)

And Chemosh said to me, "Go take Nebo from Israel!" So I went by night and fought against it from the break of dawn until noon, taking it and slaying all, seven thousand men, boys, women, girls and maid-servants, for I had devoted them to destruction for (the god) Ashtar-Chemosh.

—The Moabite Stone, trans. W. F. Albright, ANET, 320.

The textbook example of the theological, or ritual, theory of warfare is the siege of Jericho in Joshua 6. The Israelites march around the city for six days. On the seventh they shout, and the walls fall down. The victory is given miraculously by the Lord. If, as the archaeologists have concluded, Jericho was not even occupied in the late thirteenth century, then the biblical writer was free to compose an ideal account of theologically correct conquest, unhindered by any historical traditions.

The Moral Problem of the Conquest

Historicity is not the only problem posed by Joshua. A more fundamental one is posed by the morality of the story. Joshua instructs the Israelites that "the city and all that is in it shall be devoted to the Lord for destruction" (6:17), with the exception of the prostitute Rahab, who helped the Israelite spies. When the Israelites enter the city, "they devoted to destruction by the edge of the sword all in the city, both men and women, young and old, oxen, sheep, and donkeys" (6:21). This dedication and destruction is known as ḥērem, or the ban. The custom was known outside Israel. King Mesha of Moab, in the ninth century B.C.E., boasted that he took Nebo from Israel, "slaying all, seven thousand men, boys, women, girls and maidservants, for I had devoted them to destruction for (the god) Ashtar-Chemosh" (ANET, 320). The story of the capture of Jericho is almost certainly fictitious, but this only makes the problem more acute. We are not dealing in Joshua with a factual report of the ways of ancient warfare. Rather, the slaughter of the Canaanites, here and elsewhere, is presented as a theologically correct ideal.

The savagery of the destruction here is bound up with its sacral character: the victims are dedicated to the Lord. The ḥērem was essentially a religious act, like sacrifice. It not only condoned indiscriminate slaughter; it sanctified it. Compare the story of the zeal of Phinehas in Numbers 25, where the summary killing of an Israelite with a Moabite woman is rewarded with a covenant of peace and an eternal priesthood.

The brutality of warfare in antiquity was no greater than it is in modern times, and arguably less. We should not be surprised that the Israelites, like other peoples, gloried in the destruction of their adversaries. What is troubling in the biblical text is the claim that such action is justified by divine command and therefore praiseworthy. Such violence is generally disavowed by later Jewish and Christian tradition. But the examples of Joshua and Phinehas are still enshrined in Scripture and are therefore likely to lend legitimacy to such actions. This is a case where biblical authority can be dangerous and misleading.

Josiah's reform was, among other things, an assertion of national identity, and this entails differentiation from others, especially from those who are close but different. The ferocity of Deuteronomic rhetoric toward the Canaanites may be due in part to the fact that Israelites were Canaanites to begin with. It may also be due in part to the fact that Israelites traditionally had followed Canaanite cultic practices.

Underlying the whole Deuteronomic theology, and indeed most of the Hebrew Bible, is the claim that the Israelites had a right to invade Canaan because it was given to them by God. This claim is found already in the promise to Abraham in Genesis and is repeated constantly. It would not be problematic if the land were empty, but it was not. The God of Israel, it would seem, did not care much for the Canaanites. The biblical story has often served as a paradigm for colonial conquest (North America, South Africa, modern Israel). We should be wary of any attempt to invoke the example of the conquest as legitimation for anything in the modern world.

The final redaction of the Deuteronomistic History, including Joshua, was most probably done in the Babylonian exile. In that situation, the Judeans were not invincible conquerors but the hapless victims. It is one of the ironies of the biblical story that the people of Israel and Judah suffered the kind of violent conquest that they supposedly had inflicted on the Canaanites.

The Story of Ai

The story of the attack on Ai is most probably also a fiction designed to give a clear illustration of the Deuteronomist's theology. When the initial attack fails, it is assumed that the reason is the displeasure of the Lord. Sure enough, the Lord informs Joshua that Israel has broken the covenant by disobeying a commandment. Achan had violated the ban by taking things for himself. After the perpetrator has been executed, the Israelites are able to capture Ai and destroy it. Perhaps the most remarkable aspect of the story is the sense of corporate responsibility. The Israelite army is defeated and some thirty-six people are killed because of the sin of one man. Moreover, not only is Achan executed, but also his sons and daughters and livestock, and even the goods that he had taken are stoned, burned, and buried under a heap of stones. There is a strong sense here that the family is a unit, but there is also a sense of defilement that has spread even to material objects.

The execution of Achan's family is all the more remarkable because Deut 24:16 says explicitly that "parents shall not be put to death for their children, nor shall children be put to death for their parents; only for their own crimes may persons be put to death." The story is presumably older than Deuteronomic law. According to Exod 20:5, the Lord punishes children for the iniquity of their parents even to the third and fourth generation, and this was the traditional idea in Israel, roughly down to the time of the Deuteronomic reform or the Babylonian exile. The doctrine of individual responsibility is an innovation in Deuteronomy 24. It is most strongly articulated in Ezekiel 18.

The Tribes

The second half of the book of Joshua is dominated by the allotment of territory to the tribes. Biblical tradition is unanimous that the twelve tribes of Israel were descended from twelve sons of Jacob, who was also called Israel. Such a simple genealogical model, whereby each tribe is descended from one individual, is clearly a fiction, but the tradition that early Israel consisted of associated tribes can hardly be denied. The tribes are listed in several places in the Pentateuch, with some variations (Genesis 29–30, Genesis 49, Numbers 26). It is evident that some historical changes are reflected in these lists. Linguistic evidence suggests that the list in Genesis 49 is older than that in Numbers 26. But attempts to reconstruct the history of the tribes are of necessity hypothetical. It has been suggested that the tribal lists in Numbers and Joshua reflect administrative districts under the monarchy, but here again clear confirming evidence is lacking. What is clear is that each tribe, with the exception of the priestly tribe of Levi, was identified with specific territory. Presumably the identity of the tribes and their territories evolved over time. The story of the allotment of territory in Joshua 13–19 projects into the early history of Israel the kind of centralized control

12 Tribes of Israel

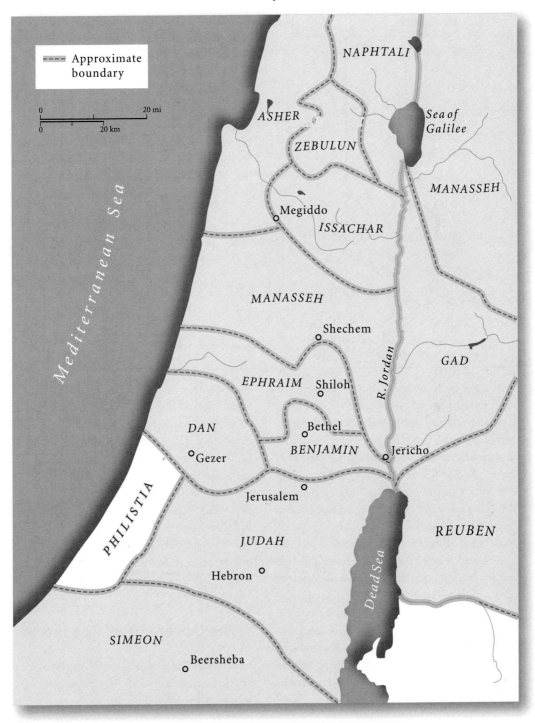

Tribal Lists in the Biblical Texts		
Genesis 49	**Numbers 26**	**Joshua**
Leah's offspring:	Reuben	Judah
Reuben	Simeon	Manasseh
Simeon	Gad	Ephraim
Levi	Judah	Reuben
Judah	Issachar	Gad
Zebulun	Zebulun	Benjamin
Issachar	Manasseh	Simeon
	Ephraim	Zebulun
Bilhah and Zilpah's	Benjamin	Issachar
offspring:	Dan	Asher
Dan	Asher	Naphtali
Gad	Naphtali (12)	Dan (12)
Asher		
Naphtali		
Rachel's offspring:		
Joseph		
Benjamin (12)		

that came only with the monarchy and was aggressively pursued by Josiah.

The Israelite tribes were evidently associated in some way. The Song of Deborah in Judges 5 commemorates a battle between Israelite tribes and Canaanite kings, "at Taanach, by the waters of Megiddo." Ephraim, Benjamin, Machir (= Manasseh), Zebulun, Issachar, and Naphtali all reported for duty. The Transjordanian tribes of Reuben and Gilead (= Gad) and the coastal tribes of Dan and Asher did not. Judah, Simeon, and Levi are not mentioned. The song singles out the otherwise unknown Meroz to be cursed, because its inhabitants did not come to the aid of the Lord. The song suggests that there was an alliance of tribes who worshiped YHWH. There was some obligation of mutual defense, but there are no sanctions against the tribes that did not show up, with

the exception of Meroz (which may not have been a tribe at all). The alliance did not extend to all twelve tribes. The omission of Judah is significant. The bond between Judah and the northern tribes was weak, and this eventually led to the separation of the two kingdoms after the death of Solomon.

Judah is included in the Blessing of Moses in Deuteronomy 33, but there Simeon is missing. It would seem that the number twelve was not as stable in the premonarchic period as is often supposed.

The Covenant at Shechem

Joshua concludes with a covenant ceremony at Shechem (chap. 24). The passage is now recognized as Deuteronomistic because of its

The Walls of Jericho

The walls of Jericho have played a symbolic role in the modern study of the Bible. If the walls came tumbling down, archaeologists should be able to find them. For a time, they thought they had. British archaeologist John Garstang identified the ruins in 1932 and dated them about 1400 B.C.E., a date compatible with the biblical record. Another British archaeologist, Kathleen Kenyon, returned to the site in the 1950s and concluded that the ruins identified by Garstang were actually several hundred years older. Jericho was not a walled city in the second half of the second millennium B.C.E., at any time when Joshua might have conquered it.

Biblical archaeology had its origin in the nineteenth century in the desire to identify biblical sites. In the late nineteenth century, biblical criticism was dominated by the literary theories of Julius Wellhausen, who had a skeptical view of the historical value of the early parts of the Bible. But then Heinrich Schliemann showed that the places mentioned in Homer's epics, such as Troy and Mycenae, actually existed, and that their material remains could be found. Biblical archaeology arose as an attempt to counter Wellhausenian scholarship, by finding material evidence relevant to the patriarchs and the conquest. "The theory of Wellhausen will not bear the test of archaeological examination," wrote William Foxwell Albright. Archaeologists such as Albright and his student G. E. Wright were by no means fundamentalists. They were submitting the biblical record to tests to verify it and often had to modify it as a result. (When the destruction of Ai by Joshua could not be verified, Albright suggested that it had been confused with nearby Bethel.) But they worked with a strong presumption of the basic historical reliability of the biblical record.

There were too many cases like Jericho, however, where the archaeological findings did not support the biblical record. Eventually, a reaction set in. More scholars came to realize that the assumption of historical reliability often led to hasty and unwarranted interpretations of archaeological sites. The entire concept of "biblical archaeology" became discredited. Instead, archaeologists came to view the archaeology of Israel/Palestine as part of the wider enterprise of Near Eastern archaeology, and to be more critical of the use of the Bible as supporting evidence.

Nonetheless, archaeological findings continue to be of enormous interest to biblical scholars. Some conservative scholars continue to defend the historicity of the biblical narratives. So, for example, one scholar claims that the relevant evidence at Jericho was lost "by erosion." But responsible scholars can only interpret the evidence they actually find. At present, the balance of that evidence inclines to a skeptical view of the historicity of the early biblical books (Genesis through Joshua).

idiom. It is not an old source incorporated by the historian. It has many of the elements of the treaty form. The historical prologue is developed at great length. The people are called to witness against themselves (in place of the pagan gods of the Near Eastern treaties). The words of the covenant are recorded in a book, and a stone is set up to commemorate the covenant. The statutes of the covenant are not recited, but they are implied. Possession of the land is contingent on serving the Lord. The main elements of the covenant that are missing are the blessings and curses. In contrast, blessings and curses are amply represented in the covenant at Shechem in Deuteronomy 27–28. The prominence of Shechem in these Deuteronomic writings strongly suggests that there was a tradition of covenant renewal at that site. It does not necessarily follow that all twelve tribes were ever involved in such a ceremony. Moreover, we find in Judg 8:33 that Israelites at one point worshiped Baal-berith (Baal of the covenant), and we know that there was a temple of Baal-berith at Shechem. Indeed, Shechem appears to have been a Canaanite city through much of the period of the judges. The tradition of a covenant ceremony at Shechem may have been older than the cult of YHWH.

The need for fidelity to "all that is written in the law of Moses" is also emphasized in Joshua 23, the farewell speech of Joshua. Joshua concedes that the Canaanites have not been wiped out and warns against intermarriage with them (23:12-13). The prohibition of intermarriage is found already in Deuteronomy 7 with reference to the seven peoples of the land. It did not necessarily apply to all peoples. Some distinctions between Gentiles were possible. Deuteronomy 23 distinguishes between the Ammonites and Moabites, who may not be admitted to the assembly of the

Lord "even to the tenth generation," and the Edomites and Egyptians, who may be admitted after the third. The thrust of Deuteronomy, however, is to maintain a distinct identity, and this could be threatened by intermarriage with any Gentiles. After the Babylonian exile, moreover, a significant part of the Jewish people lived outside the land of Israel, and the need for boundaries over against the Gentiles became more urgent. In this context, distinctions between Ammonites and Edomites lost its significance and all intermarriage was discouraged.

Further Reading

Joshua

Boling, Robert G. "Joshua, Book of." In *ABD* 3:1002–15.

Coote, Robert B. "Joshua." In *NIB* 2:555–716.

Nelson, Richard D. *Joshua*. OTL. Louisville: Westminster John Knox, 1997.

Deuteronomistic History

Campbell, Antony F., and Mark A. O'Brien. *Unfolding the Deuteronomistic History*. Minneapolis: Fortress Press, 2000.

McKenzie, Steven L. "Deuteronomistic History." In *ABD* 2:160–68.

Noth, Martin. *The Deuteronomistic History*. JSOTSup 15. Sheffield: JSOT Press, 1991.

Pury, Albert de, Thomas Römer, and Jean-Daniel Macchi, eds. *Israel Constructs Its History: Deuteronomistic Historiography in Recent Research*. JSOTSup 306. Sheffield: Sheffield Academic Press, 2000.

Schearing, Linda S., and Steven L. McKenzie, eds. *Those Elusive Deuteronomists: The Phenomenon of Pan-Deuteronomism*. JSOTSup

268. Sheffield: Sheffield Academic Press, 1999.

Early History of Israel

Dever, William G. *Who Were the Early Israelites and Where Did They Come From?* Grand Rapids: Eerdmans, 2003.

Finkelstein, Israel, and Neil Asher Silberman. *The Bible Unearthed: Archaeology's New Vision of Ancient Israel and the Origin of Its Sacred Texts*, 72–122, 329–39. New York: Free Press, 2001.

Gottwald, Norman. *The Tribes of Yahweh.* Maryknoll, N.Y.: Orbis, 1979.

Moran, William L., ed. and trans. *The Amarna Letters.* Baltimore: Johns Hopkins Univ. Press, 1992.

Particular Themes

Collins, John J. *Does the Bible Justify Violence?* Minneapolis: Fortress Press, 2004.

Rowlett, Lori L. *Joshua and the Rhetoric of Violence: A 'New Historicist' Analysis.* JSOT-Sup 226. Sheffield: Sheffield Academic Press, 1996.

Whitelam, Keith W. *The Invention of Ancient Israel and the Silencing of Palestinian History.* London: Routledge, 1996.

10

Judges

KEY POINTS

- **Judges** consists of **folkloristic stories** about local heroes who distinguished themselves in battle with Canaanites, Midianites, or Philistines, at a time when "there was no king in Israel."
- The portrait of the Israelite "conquest" in Judges 1 differs from that in Joshua and is more historically plausible in many respects.
- The "judges" described were primarily **charismatic** military leaders against neighboring groups such as the Midianites and Philistines.

- The story of **Jephthah's vow**, like the story of Abraham's near sacrifice of Isaac, serves not to disparage the practice of child sacrifice, but tacitly attests it as an accepted practice.
- The last four stories in the book are framed in such a way as to suggest that the lack of a king led society to become unstable and to disintegrate.

Judges is different in character from Joshua. It consists of folkloristic stories about local heroes who distinguished themselves in battle with Canaanites, Midianites, or Philistines when "there was no king in Israel." They preserve local color and provide some vivid glimpses of life in early Israel, but they contain little that can be verified by extrabiblical evidence. The individual stories deal with conflicts in different regions. Ehud fights the Moabites in Transjordan. Deborah and Barak campaign against the kings of Canaan near Mount Tabor in northern Israel. Gideon fights the Midianites in the south. Abimelech is involved in civil war in Shechem. Jephthah battles the Ammonites in Transjordan. Samson is involved with the Philistines. These stories were edited into a sequential (but episodic) narrative by the Deu-

teronomist. There is a programmatic introduction in 2:11—3:6 that provides an overview of the period from the point of view of the editors.

Judges and History

Since the book of Judges appears to describe a period of Israel's early history, some comment on its historical value is required. The summary of the "conquest" in Judges 1, which lists extensive areas where the Canaanites were not driven out, is widely regarded as more accurate than the picture of sweeping conquest in Joshua. But the account in Judges is not without its problems. It includes contradictory notices about Jerusalem (1:8, 21). Gaza,

Ashkelon, and Ekron are all said to be conquered by Judah in 1:18, but they are subsequently known to be Philistine strongholds. Taanach, which, according to Judg 1:27, was not conquered, was apparently destroyed in the thirteenth century and replaced by a village like those in the central highlands. Hazor, which was allegedly destroyed in Joshua 11 and was in fact destroyed at some time during the thirteenth century, still appears in Canaanite hands in Judges 4–5. The prominence of the Philistines in the book of Judges is appropriate to the period. Also, the book depicts the land of Canaan in a state of transition from the city-states of the Bronze Age to the emerging national entities of Israel, Philistia, Aram, and so forth. This transition is appropriately located in the period around 1200–1000 B.C.E. Many of the stories in Judges, however, deal with local events, which would be difficult to verify.

The Deuteronomistic Introduction

After the summary of the situation in Judges 1, the narrative continues with the death of Joshua in chapter 2. Before Joshua dies, the angel of the Lord appears to assure the people and warn them not to make a covenant with the peoples of the land. Rather, they are to "tear down their altars" (cf. Deuteronomy 12). The angel is the mouthpiece of the Deuteronomistic editor. The editor speaks in his own voice in 2:11—3:6. Israel "did what was evil in the sight of the Lord" by worshiping Baal, Astarte, and other deities. Then the anger of the Lord was kindled against them, and he gave them into the hand of their enemies. Then he was moved to pity and raised up a judge to deliver them. Whenever the judge died, however, the Israelites relapsed into their old ways and the anger of the Lord was kindled against them again.

Judges in Israel		
Judge	**Opponent**	**Reference**
Othniel	Cushan-rishathaim of Aram	3:7-11
Ehud	King Eglon of Moab	3:12-30
Shamgar	Philistines	3:31
Deborah/Barak	Jabin, king of Canaan, and his general Sisera	4–5, which include the "Song of Deborah"
Gideon	Midianites	6–8
Abimelech	Kills his seventy brothers, becomes king of Shechem	9
Tola		10:1-2
Jair		10:3-5
Jephthah	Ammonites	10:6—12:7
Ibzan		12:8-10
Elon		12:11-12
Abdon		12:13-15
Samson	Philistines	13–16

In the long-term view of the Deuteronomistic History, this pattern explained the great destructions of Israel and Judah at the hands of the Assyrians and Babylonians. In the shorter perspective of the book of Judges, it led to the institution of the monarchy as a way of providing permanent leadership. The monarchy, however, would have its own problems.

The English word "judges" is somewhat misleading. These are primarily military leaders. They are charismatic figures, in the sense that they are not officeholders but are chosen to deal with a crisis. They are not necessarily chosen for their virtue. Jephthah was the son of a prostitute and had been driven out by his legitimate brothers, so he supported himself by banditry. Samson's major qualification was brute strength. After the crisis had passed, the judge continued to rule Israel for the rest of his life. In normal times, the judge might well be called upon to judge cases. Deborah sat under a palm tree, and all Israel came to her for judgment. Samuel, the last of the judges, also acted as a judge in the usual sense of the word. Neither Deborah nor Samuel, however, was a warrior, and so they deviate from the typical pattern.

The Deuteronomist imposes a schematic design on Judges that does some violence to the stories that make up most of the book. The judges are typically local heroes, and they lead what is at most a temporary alliance of tribes. Worship of deities other than YHWH does not appear to be an issue, except in the story of Gideon. Neither are the judges guided by the laws of the covenant nor by the recollection of the exodus. (There are recollections of the exodus in the story of Gideon in Judges 6 and again in the Jephthah story, but the relevant passages are clearly Deuteronomistic additions.) The covenantal context is not an integral part of the stories but is imposed by an editor. The tales themselves give us a glimpse of a pre-Deuteronomic view of Israel, whether it accurately portrays the period before the monarchy or not.

The Early Judges (Chapters 3–5)

Some judges are passed over quickly. Othniel, is dispatched in three verses (3:9-11). Ehud is credited with one of the more colorful exploits in the book. His daring assassination of King Eglon of Moab is accomplished by deception. Moab is clearly the oppressor, and Ehud is a freedom fighter or rebel leader.

Deception is also a factor in the killing of Sisera, the Canaanite general, in Judges 4. Judges 4 is the prose counterpart of the Song of Deborah in Judges 5. It may be that the prose account was extrapolated from the poetry (cf. the relationship between Exodus 14 and 15). According to Judges 4, the Lord delivered Israel into the hand of King Jabin of Hazor. One might assume, then, that Jabin was the oppressor. The song in chapter 5, however, gives a different impression, as it boasts that the Israelites were successfully plundering the caravan routes. The battle that ensued was not a war of liberation but simply a clash between two groups that had competing economic interests.

Deborah forewarns Barak that the campaign will not end in his glory, "for the Lord will give Sisera into the hand of a woman" (Judg 4:9). The woman, however, is not Deborah but Jael, the wife of a Kenite. Jael is a marginal figure on two accounts—she is a woman and not an Israelite. Yet she becomes the heroine of the battle by luring Sisera into her tent and killing him with a tent peg while he was asleep. For this she is pronounced "most blessed of women" in

5:24. The morality of her action is problematic. Her clan was at peace with the Canaanites. She simply seems to have decided to back the winners in the battle. Moreover, the violation of a guest was regarded as a particularly heinous crime in the ancient world. Since Jael's opportunism works to the benefit of Israel, however, no questions are raised about its morality.

Gideon and Abimelech (Chapters 6–10)

Gideon receives more attention than any other judge in the book except Samson. The occasion is a conflict in the southern part of the country, caused by marauding Midianites. Gideon is chosen by the angel of the Lord because of his weakness rather than his strength. Like other judges, he goes to battle under the influence of the spirit of the Lord.

The story of Gideon is marked by tensions between old traditions and clear interventions by the Deuteronomistic editors. Like the patriarchs, Gideon builds an altar to mark the site of the apparition of the angel of the Lord (6:24; despite the Deuteronomic prohibition of multiple altars). We are told in 7:1 that he was also known as Jerubbaal (meaning "Baal will contend"). This would seem to indicate that he was at one time a Baal worshiper. His sons are still known in chapter 9 as the sons of Jerubbaal, and the people of Shechem are said to revert to the worship of Baal-berit, Baal of the covenant, after Gideon's death. After the defeat of the Midianites, Gideon collects precious metals from his soldiers and constructs an idol. None of this suggests that Gideon was a devout Yahwist. He shows himself a ruthless fighter in taking vengeance on the Midianites and also on Israelites who refused to help him. His ferocity as a fighter, rather than piety, is what qualifies him as a savior of his people.

In contrast, a few passages cast Gideon in a more orthodox Deuteronomic mold: he recalls the exodus (6:13) and tears down his father's altar of Baal (6:25-32)—an action that seems quite inconsistent with his subsequent idol worship.

Gideon's success against the Midianites provides the occasion for the first proposal of kingship in Israel. The people invite him to "rule over us, you and your son and your grandson also" (8:22). The people in question are ostensibly the whole of Israel, but only the tribes of Manasseh and Ephraim have been involved in the story. Gideon declines the offer. Kingship is also at issue in the story of Abimelech ("my father is king") in Judges 9. Abimelech has no reservations about claiming the kingship, and he clears his path by murdering his seventy brothers, except for the youngest, Jotham, who escapes. Like Jephthah in Judges 11, Abimelech is of dishonorable birth; he is the son of a slave woman. Unlike Jephthah or some other underprivileged figures in the Hebrew Bible, he is not asked to assume leadership but pursues it murderously. Abimelech is king of Shechem, not of Israel, and Shechem appears here to be a Canaanite city, with a temple to Baal-berit.

The people of Shechem soon tire of Abimelech, and civil war breaks out. According to Judges 9, Abimelech razed the city and burned its tower. The archaeological evidence indicates that Shechem was destroyed in the mid- to late twelfth century. (Whether this destruction is reflected in the story of Abimelech, we do not know). It is of interest that the biblical story provides an instance of the destruction of a Canaanite city that has nothing to do with invaders. Internal warfare between Canaanites was also a cause of destruction in Canaan in the Early Iron Age.

Abimelech encounters poetic justice in the end. He is mortally injured when a woman throws an upper millstone on his head—no small feat for a woman!

Jephthah (10:6—12:7)

The story of Jephthah is as gripping as any story in the Hebrew Bible. Jephthah operates in Gilead in Transjordan, and the adversaries are Ammonites. Like Abimelech, he is of dishonorable birth and is expelled by the legitimate children. He rises to prominence as an outlaw, however, and is recalled by the elders because of his prowess as a fighter. He agrees to help on condition that he will become ruler if he succeeds. (Compare the bargain made by the Babylonian god Marduk in *Enuma Elish*.)

The spirit of the Lord comes upon Jephthah (11:29), and he makes a vow to the Lord that "whoever comes out of the doors of my house to meet me, when I return victorious from the Ammonites, shall be the LORD's, to be offered up by me as a burnt offering" (11:31). He did not anticipate that the person in question would be his only daughter. Unlike Abraham, he is given no reprieve. Jephthah is often criticized for making a rash vow, but this criticism is not made in the text, where he appears to act under the influence of the spirit of the Lord. In the New Testament he is celebrated as a hero of faith (Hebrews 11). His daughter is more heroic than he. She urges him to keep his vow and asks only for time to bewail her virginity. The text is unambiguous that he "did with her according to the vow that he had made" (Judg 11:39). While the story in Judges certainly appreciates the tragedy of the outcome, there is no hint that Jephthah did wrong either by making the vow (for which he was rewarded with victory) or in fulfilling it.

Samson (Chapters 13–16)

Samson, the most colorful character in the book of Judges, is marked as a hero by his birth to a barren mother, announced by an angel of the Lord. Similar stories are told of Samuel and of John the Baptist in the New Testament (Luke 1; the virgin birth of Jesus is related to this pattern but has a heightened miraculous character). He is set aside as a nazirite, who must abstain from wine and strong drink and never cut his hair (cf. Num 6:1-6).

The people with whom Samson interacts are the Philistines, who were emerging as a power at the same time as Israel. It is unlikely that they had dominion over all the Israelite tribes, but they controlled the coastal plain and came into conflict with the neighboring tribe of Judah. The story of Samson implies that there was considerable coming and going between Judah and Philistia, and a major feature of Samson's career is his involvement with Philistine women. Samson is described as a man of legendary strength, who can tear apart a lion with his bare hands. He is vulnerable, however, to the "weaker sex." The only religious note in all this is that "the spirit of the LORD" comes upon him and enables him to kill thirty men of Ashkelon. The spirit of the Lord manifests itself in an outburst of physical force. In these stories, the spirit has nothing to do with wisdom or virtue.

Samson's downfall, inevitably, comes from his inability to resist the charms of a Philistine woman, Delilah. He has one last mighty deed when he pulls down the temple of Dagon on himself and his Philistine tormentors. The Deuteronomist portrays this as an answer to prayer. Judges 16:22 hints at a different explanation: his hair had grown back.

The story of Samson is a popular folktale about a legendary strong man, not unlike the

Greek tales about the labors of Heracles. At no point is Samson motivated by concern for Israel. He does not seem to be constrained by any moral code except honor and vengeance. His story is preserved in the Bible as part of the lore of Israel, and it is a gripping and entertaining story. The Deuteronomist gives it only a light sprinkling of piety and never suggests that Samson is a moral exemplar. Rather, he is a tragic hero, a person of extraordinary (if brutish) talent who has a fatal weakness in his attraction to Philistine women. The story could easily serve to discourage marriage with foreign women, a favorite Deuteronomic theme, but the readers are left to draw their own inferences in this regard.

The final irony of the Samson story is found in the Epistle to the Hebrews (11:32), which includes Samson among those "who through faith conquered kingdoms, administered justice, obtained promises," among other things. Samson was often considered to

Samson

Samson is marked out as special even before his birth. His mother is told that he will be a nazirite. She must drink no wine or strong drink, and the boy must not cut his hair. The law pertaining to nazirites is set out in Numbers 6:2-5: "When either men or women make a special vow, the vow of a nazirite, to separate themselves to the LORD, they shall separate themselves from wine and strong drink; they shall drink no wine vinegar or other vinegar, and shall not drink any grape juice or eat grapes, fresh or dried. All their days as nazirites they shall eat nothing that is produced by the grapevine, not even the seeds or the skins. All the days of their nazirite vow no razor shall come upon the head; until the time is completed for which they separate themselves to the LORD, they shall be holy; they shall let the locks of the head grow long." The nazirites were also forbidden to go near a corpse.

It should be noted, however, that the Priestly legislation in Numbers does not fit Samson perfectly. Numbers envisions the nazirite state as temporary and voluntary. The long hair has no special connection with strength. Samson is a nazirite for life, and he is not free to choose. Samson is never said to drink wine or strong drink, but drink is not an issue in the story. It may well be that Samson's long hair was a folkloric motif related to his strength, and that he was called a nazirite to bring him within the categories of biblical law. Or it may be that the significance of the nazirite vow evolved over time. Originally, it may have pertained to the status of special warriors, related to their exceptional strength. Later it became a way of expressing a particular type of piety. Samson does not seem to be concerned with holiness, but he does seem to channel divine power, which is somehow associated with his hair.

prefigure Christ in later Christian interpretation because of his suffering and the manner in which he meets his death with outstretched arms.

"In Those Days There Was No King"

The last four chapters of the book of Judges are framed by statements that "in those days there was no king in Israel; all the people did what was right in their own eyes" (17:6; 21:25). The stories suggest that when there was no king the society tended to disintegrate. There are two main episodes in these chapters. The first concerns the relocation of the tribe of Dan. The second describes a conflict between Benjamin and the other tribes.

The Danites lost their original territory to the Philistines and then settled on Laish in the extreme north of Israel as their new home. Even though their mission is portrayed in terms that recall the initial conquest by Joshua (especially in the matter of spying out the land), we are told twice that the people of Laish were "quiet and unsuspecting." The naked aggression of the Danites is not disguised. Moreover, the cult of YHWH that is established at Dan is of questionable origin. It involves idols that were stolen from the house of Micah in Ephraim and a Levite who is portrayed as a rather mercenary character. Later, during the monarchy, Dan was the site of one of the temples set up by King Jeroboam I of the northern kingdom of Israel, in opposition to Jerusalem. This was considered an abomination by the Deuteronomists. The account of the founding of Dan in Judges 17–18 is not flattering. Nonetheless, the story is told without much editorial comment. Readers are free to see for themselves how things were in Israel when there was no king.

The conflict between Benjamin and the other tribes involves one of the "tales of terror" of the Hebrew Bible. Benjamin was the only tribe that remained with Judah after the division of the kingdom. It was also the home tribe of Saul, the first king. In this case the conflict is entirely within Israel.

The story begins with a Levite from Ephraim, who took a concubine from Bethlehem who subsequently left him. When he was bringing her back, they found themselves near Jerusalem at nightfall. Since Jerusalem was then a Jebusite city, they pressed on to Gibeah in Benjamin. The assumption that it is safer to lodge among Israelites than among Gentiles proves to be tragically mistaken. The story that unfolds is very similar to the story of Sodom in Genesis 19. The men of Gibeah want to abuse the stranger. The man who has taken him in is horrified and offers them his virgin daughter and the Levite's concubine instead. In Genesis Lot's offer of his virgin daughters is rendered unnecessary by divine intervention. There is no such intervention here. The Levite's concubine is sacrificed to the cause, raped all night, and found dead in the morning. The story is chilling, not only because of the wickedness of the men of Gibeah, but also because of the Levite's willingness to sacrifice his concubine and the host's offer of his virgin daughter. The story reaches a grisly climax when he dismembers her corpse and sends a piece to each of the tribes. The outrage of the Israelites against Gibeah is well merited. The conduct of the Levite is scarcely less outrageous but receives no comment in the biblical text.

The fate of Gibeah is not as severe as that of Sodom. The Israelites defeat the Benjaminites, but only after initial setbacks. Eventually all but six hundred Benjaminite men are slaughtered. When the Israelites swear that they will not give their daughters to the men of Benjamin, the future of the tribe seems in doubt. Eventually they are given the virgin daughters of Jabesh-gilead, and, in a scene reminiscent of the Roman tale of the Sabine women, the Benjaminites are allowed to snatch the young women who came out to dance at the festival of the Lord at Shiloh. The book ends on a positive note, insofar as the tribe of Benjamin is restored—but at the expense of the women, who are repeatedly treated as disposable commodities. Like many of the stories in Judges, this one is not edifying. It can contribute to moral education by showing the horror of some kinds of behavior. Later tradition would labor to portray the judges in a positive light (as in Hebrews 11). The biblical text, however, seems designed to show the depravity of human, and specifically Israelite, nature and its need for divine mercy.

Further Reading

Commentaries

Niditch, Susan. "Judges." In *The Oxford Bible Commentary*, ed. J. Barton and J. Muddiman, 176–91. Oxford: Oxford Univ. Press, 2001.

Soggin, J. Alberto. *Judges*. Trans. J. Bowden. OTL. Philadelphia: Westminster, 1981.

Historical Issues

Halpern, Baruch. *The First Historians*. San Francisco: Harper & Row, 1988.

Literary and Feminist Studies

Ackerman, Susan. *Warrior, Dancer, Seductress, Queen*. New York: Doubleday, 1998.

Bal, Mieke. *Death and Dissymetry: The Politics of Coherence in the Book of Judges*. Chicago: Univ. of Chicago Press, 1988.

Trible, Phyllis. *Texts of Terror: Literary-Feminist Readings of Biblical Narratives*. OBT. Philadelphia: Fortress Press, 1984.

11

First Samuel

KEY POINTS

- 1 and 2 Samuel incorporate **extensive source documents** that have been only lightly edited by the Deuteronomist.
- 1 Samuel is replete with **duplicate accounts** and **various tensions**.
- Samuel : **last judge and first prophet**.
- **Capture and recovery of the ark** (1 Sam 4:1b-7:1).
- **Two accounts of election of Saul**
- The story of **David's rise**: a historical novel, composed to defend David against various charges of wrongdoing.
- **Picture of David not uniform**: loyal servant, an outlaw, a mercenary, etc.

The two books of Samuel were originally one book in Hebrew. They were divided in Greek and Latin manuscripts because of the length of the book. In the Greek, the Septuagint (LXX), they are grouped with the books of Kings as 1–4 Reigns. The Greek text of Samuel is longer than the traditional Hebrew text (MT). Some scholars had thought that the translators had added passages, but the Dead Sea Scrolls preserve fragments of a Hebrew version that corresponds to the Greek. It is now clear that the Greek preserves an old form of the text and that some passages had fallen out of the Hebrew through scribal mistakes.

There are various tensions and duplications in 1 Samuel that are obvious even on a casual reading of the text. Samuel disappears from the scene in chapters 4–6 and then reemerges in chapter 7. In chapter 8 the choice of a human king is taken to imply a rejection of the kingship of YHWH. Yet the first king is anointed at YHWH's command. There are different accounts of the way in which Saul becomes king (10:17-27; chap. 11) and different accounts of his rejection (chaps. 13 and 15). There are two accounts of how David came into the service of Saul (chaps. 16 and 17). David becomes Saul's son-in-law twice in chapter 18, and he defects to the Philistine king of Gath twice in chapters 21 and 27. He twice refuses to take Saul's life when he has the opportunity (chaps. 24 and 27).

The Deuteronomistic editor does not seem to have imposed a pattern on the books of Samuel such as we find in Judges or Kings.

Deuteronomistic passages have been recognized in the oracle against the house of Eli in 1 Sam 2:27-36 and 3:11-14, in Samuel's reply to the request for a king in 8:8, and especially in Samuel's farewell speech in chapter 12. The most important sign of editorial activity is the presence of two quite different attitudes to the monarchy. First Samuel 9:1—10:16; 11; 13–14, had a generally favorable view of the monarchy. Chapters 7–8; 10:17-27; 12; and 15 view the kingship with grave suspicion. The easiest explanation is that the first Deuteronomistic edition in the time of Josiah was positive toward the monarchy, and that the more negative material was incorporated in a later edition during the exile, after the monarchy had collapsed. Both editions may have drawn on older traditions. The net result, however, is a complex narrative that shows the range of attitudes toward the monarchy. The historical accuracy of these stories is moot, since we have no way of checking them. They have the character of a historical novel, which clearly has some relationship to history but is concerned with theme and character rather than with accuracy in reporting.

The Birth and Call of Samuel (1:1—4:1a)

The story of Samuel's birth is similar to that of Samson's but more elaborate. His mother Hannah is barren, but eventually the Lord answers her prayer and Samuel is conceived. In thanksgiving, Hannah dedicates her son as a nazirite to the Lord. Unlike Samson, who was also a nazirite, Samuel is dedicated to service at the house of the Lord at Shiloh. Psalm 78:60 describes the shrine at Shiloh as a *miškan,* or tent-shrine, and Josh 18:1 and 19:51 refer to the tent of meeting there. Some scholars have argued that the tabernacle described in the Priestly source was located at Shiloh.

The Song of Hannah in 1 Samuel 2 is a hymn of praise, which refers to God's ways of dealing with humanity rather than to a specific act of deliverance. It was probably chosen for this context because of v. 5: "The barren has borne seven, but she who has many children is forlorn." The theme of the song is that God exalts the lowly and brings down the mighty. Hannah's song is the model for the Magnificat, the thanksgiving song of the virgin Mary in the New Testament (Luke 1:46-55).

The manner of Samuel's birth links him with the judges. His call anticipates that of the later prophets. The call of the prophets takes either of two forms: it can be a vision (Isaiah 6; Ezekiel 1), or it can be an auditory experience (Moses, Jeremiah). Samuel's call is of the auditory type. Unlike Moses or Jeremiah, however, Samuel is not given a mission. Rather, he is given a prophecy of the destruction of the house of Eli. The revelation establishes his credentials as a prophet. We shall find that he functions as a prophet in other ways. He is a seer, who can find things that are missing (chap. 9). In 1 Sam 19:20, he appears as conductor of a band of ecstatic prophets. More important, he anoints kings and can also declare that they have been rejected by God. Samuel's interaction with Saul prefigures the interaction between kings and prophets later in the Deuteronomistic History.

The Ark Narrative (4:1b—7:1)

The story of Samuel is interrupted in 4:1b—7:1 by the story of the ark, in which he plays no part. The ark is variously called the ark of God, the ark of YHWH, the ark of the covenant, or the ark of testimony. In Deut 10:1-5 Moses is told to make an ark of wood as a receptacle for the stone tablets of the covenant. The story in 1 Samuel 4–6, however, makes clear that it is no mere box. It is the symbol of the presence of the Lord. It is carried into battle to offset the superior force of the Philistines, in the belief that YHWH is thereby brought into the battle. But YHWH's enemies are not scattered before him. The capture of a people's god or gods, represented by statues, was not unusual in the ancient Near East. Nonetheless, the capture of the ark in battle was a great shock to the Israelite and led directly to the death of Eli.

The story of the ark, however, has a positive ending for the Israelites. YHWH mysteriously destroys the statue of the Philistine god Dagon and afflicts the people with a plague. As a result, the Philistines send back the ark. Nonetheless, it is significant that shortly after this episode the Israelites begin to ask for a king. The old charismatic religion of the judges, which relied heavily on the spirit of the Lord, was not adequate for dealing with the Philistines.

The Move to Monarchy (1 Samuel 7–12)

Samuel reappears on the scene in 1 Sam 7:3 and is said to judge Israel after Eli's demise. Unlike the older judges, however, he is not a warrior. He secures the success of the Israelites in battle by offering sacrifice.

Like Eli, Samuel has sons who do not follow in his footsteps, and so the people finally ask for a king. The exchange between Samuel and the people in 1 Samuel 8 represents the negative view of the kingship. The people are said to have rejected YHWH as king. Moreover, the prediction of "the ways of the king" reflects disillusionment born of centuries of experience and is quite in line with the cri-

tiques of monarchy by the prophets, beginning with Elijah in 1 Kings 21.

There are two accounts of the election of Saul as the first king. The first is a quaint story in which he goes to consult the seer Samuel about lost donkeys. This story speaks volumes about early Israelite society. Lost donkeys were a matter of concern for prophets and for future kings. This is the first case in which a king is anointed in ancient Israel. The king was "the Lord's anointed" par excellence. It is from this expression that we get the word "messiah," from the Hebrew *māšîaḥ*, "anointed."

According to the second account of the election of Saul, he was chosen by lot (1 Sam 10:20), the formal method for discerning the divine will favored by the Deuteronomists. Also distinctively Deuteronomistic is the notice that Samuel wrote the rights and duties of the kingship in a book and gave it to Saul (compare the law of the king in Deut 17:14-20). Initially, Saul acts like a judge, summoning the tribes by sending around pieces of oxen and being inspired by the spirit of the Lord. After the victory over the Ammonites, the people assemble at Gilgal to make him king. There are several steps, then, in the process by which Saul becomes king: divine election, designation by a prophet (Samuel), and finally acclamation by the people.

The accession of Saul is completed by the apparent retirement of Samuel in chapter 12. Samuel's protestation of innocence provides a concise summary of the conduct expected from a good ruler. He should not abuse the people by taking their belongings, or defraud them, and he should not take bribes to pervert justice. Samuel seems reluctant, however, to yield the reins of power. He chides the people for asking for a king. In the end he grants that things will be all right if they do not turn aside from following the Lord. What is important is keeping the law, regardless of whether there is a king.

The Trials of Saul (1 Samuel 13–15)

Samuel does not stay retired. He clashes with Saul in two incidents, in chapters 13 and 15. The first concerns the preparation for a battle against the Philistines. Samuel is late, and Saul is concerned about the morale of his soldiers, so he presumes to offer the sacrifice himself. No sooner does he do so than Samuel appears and judges him harshly. If he had kept the commandment, his kingdom would have been confirmed, but now it will not continue.

This is clearly a theological reading of the failure of Saul's kingship. According to the Deuteronomists, success comes from keeping commandments, and failure comes from disobedience. As a prophet, Samuel speaks for God and is not to be questioned. Also implicit in the story is the assumption that success in battle depends on ritual rather than on strategy or force of arms. The ritual is not automatically efficacious but depends on the obedience of the performer.

There is a blatant conflict of interest between the two men, as to which of them is ultimately in control. This is plausible psychologically, although we have no way to verify whether it has any historical basis. There is also, however, a conflict between two theologies. Samuel represents an ethic of unconditional obedience, while Saul represents a moderate pragmatism. From the viewpoint of the Deuteronomists, the trouble with kings was that they took things into their own hands instead of deferring to the word of God as revealed by the prophets. But the word of God is always mediated by human agents who have their own interests in the proceedings. The claims of figures like Samuel to speak for God must be viewed with some suspicion in view of their own interests.

The conflict between Saul and Samuel is resumed in chapter 15. This time Samuel orders Saul to attack Amalek and slaughter every man, woman, and child—and even the animals. Saul partially complies but spares the king and the best of the animals to offer them as sacrifices. Because of this, he is again repudiated as king. Once again, the issue is authority and control. It is not apparent that Samuel's command, either here or in chapter 13, is for the greater good of the people, unless one assumes that it is always better to obey the prophet who claims to speak for God.

Samuel's rebuke to Saul has a prophetic ring to it: "Has the LORD as great delight in burnt offerings and in sacrifices as in obeying the voice of the LORD? Surely, to obey is better than sacrifice, and to heed than the fat of rams" (1 Sam 15:22). There is a close parallel to this in the prophet Hosea: "For I desire steadfast love and not sacrifice, the knowledge of God rather than burnt offerings" (Hos 6:6). Hosea and Samuel agree that sacrifice is no substitute for right conduct, but they have rather different ideas about what constitutes right conduct. For Hosea, it is steadfast love and the knowledge of God. For Samuel everything comes down to obedience, even if what is commanded is the slaughter of other human beings.

The two stories of conflict between Samuel and Saul, in 1 Samuel 13 and 15, frame another engrossing story that illustrates a similar conflict in values. In the battle against the Philistines after the incident at Gilgal, Saul laid an oath on the troops, cursing any man who tasted food before the enemy was defeated. His son Jonathan, the hero of the battle up to this point, was unaware of the oath and ate some honey. When he is told of the oath, Jonathan shrugs it off: the men would fight better if they had food. Here again we see a clash between a moderate pragmatism on the one hand and an ethic that attaches great importance to oaths and vows on the other. In this case Saul is cast as the defender of the ethic of obedience. He declares that if Jonathan is guilty he must die. This story, however, ends very differently from either that of Abraham and Isaac or that of Jephthah and his daughter. Jonathan is not executed, and the reprieve does not come from divine intervention. Instead, the troops intervene to rescue Jonathan from his father's oath. In this case pragmatism wins out.

The stories in 1 Samuel 13–15 capture brilliantly the sense of a society in transition, where deference to custom and to religious authorities collides with a growing sense of pragmatism.

The Rise of David

The second half of 1 Samuel and the opening chapters of 2 Samuel tell the story of David's rise to power. It is widely agreed that the Deuteronomist drew on an older source document here. The "History of David's Rise" is usually identified as 1 Sam 16:14—2 Samuel 5; 1 Sam 16:1-13 is sometimes included. A major turning point in this story is the death of Saul.

The story of David reads like a historical novel rather than the kind of chronicle we find in Kings. It cannot be verified from nonbiblical sources. Some scholars have gone so far as to question whether David ever existed, but most would regard this as undue skepticism. The ruling family in Judah for some four hundred years was known as the "house of David." This title has now been found in an inscription from Tel Dan. It is reasonable to assume that David was a historical person, like Omri, who gave his name to a dynasty in northern Israel. That said, we have simply no way of checking whether the historical David bore any resemblance to the figure described in the biblical narratives.

Related to this issue is the genre of the story. One influential hypothesis is that it was composed as an apology for King David—that is, a propaganda document, intended to refute charges that might be brought against him. It shows that David was not an outlaw, a deserter, or a Philistine mercenary, that he was not implicated in Saul's death or in the deaths of some of Saul's family and followers. Nonetheless, for the modern reader, at least, the story conveys the impression that David at various times *was* an outlaw, a deserter, and a Philistine mercenary, and he was at best conspicuous by his absence when Saul was killed. If this is apologetic literature, it is exceptionally subtle and only partially successful. The appeal of this story lies precisely in the ambiguity of its hero. He is chosen by God, but he is by no means flawless or innocent.

The Election of David

As in the case of Saul, there is more than one account of how David became king. First, he is anointed by Samuel (1 Sam 16:1-13). This story follows a familiar biblical pattern in the exaltation of the lowly: David is the youngest of the sons of Jesse and initially thought to be of no account.

First Samuel 16:14-23 gives a different account of the discovery of David. He is picked out because of his skill as a musician. Saul has now lost the spirit of the Lord and instead is afflicted by "an evil spirit from the LORD" (16:14). Saul is unaware that David has been anointed as his replacement.

Yet another account of the discovery of David follows in the story of his combat with Goliath in 1 Samuel 17. There are actually two stories here. The first is found in 17:1-11, 32-40, 42-48a, 49, 51-54. The second is in 17:12-31,

41, 48b, 50, 55-58; 18:1-5, 10-11, 17-19, 29b-30. The verses that make up the second story are missing from the Old Greek translation. It is generally agreed that in this case the Greek preserves the older text.

Few stories in the Hebrew Bible have such popular appeal as that of David and Goliath. It has become the proverbial story of the under-dog. David triumphs by wit and agility over the huge but rather immobile Philistine. The Deuteronomist sees another dimension in the conflict. Goliath comes with sword and spear, but David comes in the name of the Lord of hosts (17:45). Despite its legendary character, the story of Goliath fits the most plausible scenario of David's rise. He was successful in battle and outshone Saul. Hence the popular acclaim: Saul has killed his thousands, but David his tens of thousands.

The relationship between Saul and David is complicated by David's friendship with Saul's family. Jonathan, Saul's son, loved David as himself (18:1). Much has been made of the relationship between David and Jonathan as a possible homosexual relationship. Homosexual attraction is certainly a factor in male bonding, especially in all-male institutions like the army (up to modern times). But if there is a sexual dimension in this relationship, it is never acknowledged explicitly.

David also has relationships with Saul's daughters. In 1 Samuel 18 the initiative for marriage comes from Michal, who loves David, with Saul's approval. David, then, cannot be accused of marrying for expediency. When David is estranged from Saul, Michal becomes the wife of another man, but David recalls her after Saul's death, when he is trying to secure the kingship over all Israel. After the kingship has been consolidated, however, she is cursed with childlessness, ostensibly for disapproving of David dancing before the ark. The story may be intended to defend David from allegations that he used Michal and dumped her when he no longer needed her, but it is difficult not to read between the lines and suspect that he was motivated by political expediency.

The stories of interaction between David and Saul in 1 Samuel 19–24 provide the closest analogies to the genre of apology. Saul repeatedly tries to kill David for no reason other than jealousy. Members of Saul's own family, Jonathan and Michal, side with David. Saul commits an outrage by slaughtering the priests of Nob (a shrine north of Jerusalem, near Gibeah), for befriending David. Nonetheless, when David has Saul at his mercy, he refrains, declaring, "I will not raise my hand against the Lord's anointed" (24:10). Even Saul admits, "You are more righteous than I" (24:17). Finally, Saul acknowledges that David will succeed to the kingship and asks only that David not "wipe out my name from my father's house."

David as Outlaw and Mercenary

The later chapters of 1 Samuel paint a more complex picture of David as bandit leader and mercenary. When he is not in the service of a king, he must support his troops by whatever means available. In 1 Samuel 25 he does this by demanding a protection payment from a sheep farmer in Carmel. The farmer is named Nabal, which means "fool." His folly lies in his failure to recognize the threat posed by the bandit's demand. In contrast, his wife, Abigail, is clever and beautiful, and she intervenes to buy David off. When Nabal hears what happened, he dies suddenly, and David takes Abigail as a wife. Frequent invocation of the name of the Lord cannot hide the fact that David is engaged in extortion.

Finally, David is called on to join the Philistines in battle against Israel. He declares his willingness, and the king of Gath does not doubt his loyalty. Other Philistine commanders, however, are distrustful, and so David is sent back. Thus he is saved from the dilemma of either fighting against his own people or being disloyal to his current master. Here again the story serves as an apology, to defend David of complicity in the death of Saul.

The death of Saul has a certain aura of heroism. He falls on his sword rather than be captured by the Philistines. Suicide has generally been condemned in Jewish and Christian tradition, but some cases have always been admired—most notably the mass suicide of the Zealots at Masada at the end of the Jewish revolt against Rome in the first century C.E. There is no hint of disapproval of the suicide of Saul. For all his faults, he is recognized as a champion of Israel in its struggle with the Philistines and other neighboring peoples.

Further Reading

Commentaries

Birch, Bruce C. "1 and 2 Samuel." In *NIB* 2:949–1383.

Hertzberg, Hans Wilhelm. *I and II Samuel*. OTL. Philadelphia: Westminster, 1964.

Klein, Ralph W. *1 Samuel*. WBC 10. Waco, Tex.: Word, 1983.

McCarter, P. Kyle, Jr. *1 Samuel*. AB 8. New York, Doubleday, 1980.

Literary-Historical Analyses

Halpern, Baruch. *David's Secret Demons: Messiah, Murderer, Traitor, King*. Grand Rapids: Eerdmans, 2001.

McKenzie, Steven L. *King David: A Biography*. New York: Oxford Univ. Press, 2000.

Fig. 11.1. Beth-Shean tell and lower city. Photo: John J. Collins.

12

Second Samuel

Like 1 Samuel, 2 Samuel incorporates extensive source documents that have been only lightly edited by the Deuteronomist. The key Deuteronomistic passage is the account of the promise to David in 2 Samuel 7, although here too the editor is adapting an older source. The history of David's rise, which dominated the second half of 1 Samuel, is continued in 2 Samuel 1–5. The section from 2 Samuel 9 to 2 Kings 2 is often identified as the "Court History of David" or the "Succession Narrative." The account of the rebellion of Absalom in 2 Samuel 13–20 is a tightly structured narrative, which may be a distinct unit. First Kings 1–2 is an apology for the accession of Solomon to the kingship.

The Conclusion of David's Rise (1:1—5:10)

After the death of Saul, David goes to Hebron, where he is anointed king by his own tribe, Judah. Hebron was associated with Abraham in Genesis.

David's claim to monarchy was not undisputed. Ishbaal, son of Saul, became king over the rest of Israel. (Ishbaal means "man of Baal." The fact that a son of Saul, the king of Israel, had a name honoring Baal indicates that other deities besides YHWH were worshiped in Israel at this time.) Eventually Ishbaal is murdered. David not only disavows responsibility but executes the murderers. Eventually, the only living heir to the house of Saul is the crippled son of Jonathan, who is no threat to David. His name, Mephibosheth, is probably a euphemism, concealing the name of Baal (*bosheth* means "shame"). The name is given as Meribaal in 1 Chron 8:34 and 9:40. This entire strand of the narrative fits perfectly with the view that the Rise of David is an apologetic or propaganda document. But again it is not difficult to read the story against the grain and arrive at a rather unfavorable picture of David.

The rise of David reaches its climax in 2 Samuel 5. He is again acclaimed as king at Hebron, this time by all Israel. Then he captures Jerusalem, the Canaanite, Jebusite, city. Jerusalem was an ideal capital for David because it was easy to defend and it had not hitherto been associated with any Israelite tribe, although it was in the territory of David's own tribe, Judah. The acclamation of David is complete when he is acknowledged by the king of Tyre.

By bringing the ark to Jerusalem, David made the old Jebusite city the center of worship for the tribes of YHWH.

The Promise to David

Second Samuel 7 is one of the key passages in the Hebrew Bible. The promise to David is the foundation charter of the Davidic dynasty, and eventually became the basis for messianic hope, that is, the hope that the Davidic kingship would be restored and last forever.

Palace and temple were often associated in the ancient Near East. The same Hebrew word, *hēkāl*, is used for both. Accordingly, David worries that his "house of cedar" is grander than the tent-shrine of the Lord. At this point, the prophet Nathan appears on the scene. Nathan is in David's service. His initial reaction is precisely what we should expect a retainer to tell his employer: "Go, do all that you have in mind; for the LORD is with you" (v. 3). Nathan, however, has second thoughts, and he receives a second oracle for David. YHWH insists that he has never wanted a house. He likes the mobility of a tent. Rather, he will build David a house, in the sense of a dynasty. His son will reign after him. While his descendants will be punished for their iniquities, YHWH will not take the kingdom away from them as he took it from the house of Saul: "Your house and your kingdom shall be made sure forever before me; your throne shall be established forever" (v. 16).

Central to this oracle is the play on the double sense of "house." David may not build a house (temple) for YHWH, but the deity will build a house (dynasty) for David. It was not unusual in the ancient Near East for the founder of a dynasty to build a temple for his

Fig. 12.1. Head of King David. ca. 1150. The Metropolitan Museum of Art, New York. Photo: © The Metropolitan Museum of Art / Art Resource, N.Y.

patron god. The oddity of this passage is the rejection of the offer to build a temple. Some suggest that this oracle was meant to explain why it was Solomon rather than David who built the temple. But 7:13a, "He shall build a house for my name," is widely recognized as a secondary addition. That the house will be built "for my name" is a trademark of Deuteronomistic theology. Presumably, then, the reference to Solomon was added by a Deuteronomistic editor, and the basic oracle was older.

The role of the Deuteronomists in the composition of 2 Samuel 7 is controversial. The promise to David is certainly important in the Deuteronomistic view of Israel's history. There are several examples of Deuteronomistic language in the passage: the notion of "rest," the reference to the exodus, etc. But it is unlikely that the Deuteronomists would have invented an unconditional promise that the kingdom would last forever. In Deuteronomistic theology, covenants are conditional. The fortunes of the king depend on his observance of the law. The idea that God had promised David an everlasting dynasty by the oracle of Nathan was probably an established tradition in Jerusalem. The present formulation of the promise has been edited by the Deuteronomists, to emphasize that the king was still subject to punishment.

Punishment for transgression is certainly in line with Deuteronomic theology. But we also find such provisions in Near Eastern treaties. A thirteenth-century Hittite grant to one Ulmi-Teshshup, for example, promises: "After you, your son and grandson will possess it, nobody will take it away from them. If one of your descendants sins . . . the king will prosecute him at his court. . . . But nobody will take away from the descendant of Ulmi-Teshshup either his house or his land." Even if a king were executed, his son might be allowed to succeed him.

Scholars often refer to "the Davidic covenant," but the word "covenant" is not used in this passage (though it is used with reference to God's promise to David in Ps 89:3). The oracle has the character of an unconditional grant rather than of the vassal treaties discussed in connection with the Mosaic covenant. The nearest biblical analogy is provided by the covenant with Abraham in Genesis 15, which also was an unconditional grant. In Nathan's oracle, the essential point is that the Davidic dynasty will last forever. In fact, it lasted some four hundred years, which might be regarded as a reasonable approximation of "forever." When the Davidic kingdom was finally brought to an end by the Babylonians, the promise was thought to stand. If there was no king in the present, then God's promise must be fulfilled in the future by the restoration of the Davidic line. This is the origin of the hope for a messiah.

> Moreover the Lord declares to you that the Lord will make you a house. When your days are fulfilled and you lie down with your ancestors, I will raise up your offspring after you, who shall come forth from your body, and I will establish his kingdom. He shall build a house for my name, and I will establish the throne of his kingdom forever. I will be a father to him, and he shall be a son to me. When he commits iniquity, I will punish him with a rod such as mortals use, with blows inflicted by human beings. But I will not take my steadfast love from him, as I took it from Saul, whom I put away from before you. Your house and your kingdom shall be made sure forever before me; your throne shall be established forever.
> —2 Samuel 7:11b-16

The relationship between YHWH and the king is defined as that of father and son (2 Sam

7:14). There is no suggestion here that the king does not have a human father; the relationship is like adoption. Egyptian royal theology made a stronger claim that the king was divine, the incarnation of the god Horus. Kings of Damascus in the ninth century B.C.E. took the name or title of "Son of Hadad" (Hadad was another name for Baal). The claim that the Davidic king was son of YHWH is also found in the Psalms, most explicitly in Ps 2:7. In 2 Samuel 7 the idea that the king is God's son is linked directly to the idea that he should be chastised. (The idea that sons should be chastised is a favorite theme of the book of Proverbs.)

Excursus:
The Royal Ideology of Judah

The main window we have on pre-Deuteronomic kingship is provided by several psalms that deal with the kingship, and at least some of these are likely to date from the preexilic period. These include Psalms 2, 45, 72, and 110. Two other psalms, 89 and 132, speak of the promise to David in terms reminiscent of 2 Samuel 7. (I discuss the Psalms in detail in chapter 23.)

Some of these psalms depict the kingship in mythological terms. Psalm 2 implies that the king in Jerusalem is the rightful ruler over all the kings of the earth. If the Gentile nations resist, the Lord derides them. The psalmist reports the decree of the Lord, "You are my son, this day I have begotten you." Many scholars hold that this formula was recited by a prophet when a new king ascended the throne. What is striking in Psalm 2 is the kind of authority the king is supposed to enjoy: the nations are his inheritance and the ends of the earth are his possession. No king in Jerusalem ever actually reigned over such an empire.

> I will tell of the decree of the LORD:
> He said to me, "You are my son;
> today I have begotten you.
> Ask of me, and I will make the nations your
> heritage,
> and the ends of the earth your possession.
> You shall break them with a rod of iron,
> and dash them in pieces like a potter's
> vessel."
> —Psalm 2:7-9

The theme of divine sonship reappears in Psalm 110. In this case the king is addressed as *Adonai*, "my lord"—the phrase that came to be substituted for the divine name in later Judaism. YHWH bids him sit at his right hand. (This is probably a reference to the king's throne in the temple.) The Deity continues, "From the womb, from dawn, like dew I have begotten you" (Ps. 110:3; the Hebrew is corrupt and must be reconstructed with the help of the Greek). In this case the psalmist adds an intriguing detail: "You are a priest forever according to the order of Melchizedek." Melchizedek was the priest-king of Salem (Jerusalem) in Genesis 14. He was a Jebusite, which is to say, a Canaanite. He was priest of El Elyon, a Canaanite deity who was identified with YHWH in the Bible. If the Davidic kings claimed to be "according to the order of Melchizedek," this meant that they affirmed continuity with the old Canaanite religion that had been practiced in the city for centuries before David captured it.

An even more startling view of the kingship appears in Psalm 45. This seems to be a song for a royal wedding. It begins with unabashed praise (flattery?) of the king: "You are the most handsome of men!" The praise reaches its climax in v. 6: "Your throne, O God, endures forever and ever. Your royal scepter is a scepter of equity. You love righteousness and hate wickedness, therefore God, your God, has anointed you with the oil of gladness above your fellows." Here the king is addressed as *'elōhîm*, "god." This does not mean that he is put on the same level as the Most High. He is carefully distinguished from "God, your God," who has anointed him and on whom he depends. But the king is clearly regarded as a divine being, in some sense.

Psalm 45 also emphasizes the obligation of the king to uphold truth and righteousness. This obligation is also clear in Psalm 72. That psalm stops short of addressing the king as a god, but it prays that he may live as long as the sun and moon, and have dominion from sea to sea.

Seen against the background of these psalms, Nathan's oracle paints a much more modest picture of the king. True, he is like a son to God, but nothing is said of him being begotten by God, even metaphorically. As "son of God," he is subject to chastisement, a point not noted in these psalms. Second Samuel 7 represents a toned-down, even demythologized, form of the royal ideology. A later passage in the Deuteronomistic history goes further. Solomon's prayer in 1 Kgs 8:25 says that the promise is conditional: "if only your children look to their way, to walk before me." The covenant with David is also regarded as conditional in Ps 132:12.

The royal ideology is extremely important for the development of messianism in postexilic Judaism and its adaptation in early Christianity. It provided the basis for the view that the messiah is Son of God. Psalm 110 ("The LORD says to my lord, 'Sit at my right hand'") was taken as proof in early Christianity that the Messiah must ascend to heaven (Acts 2:34-36).

The Bathsheba Affair

Like many people in positions of power, David also had other conquests in mind. The story of his encounter with Bathsheba has several stock motifs. The woman bathes where she can be seen. Her husband, Uriah, carries the instructions for his own murder. Uriah is undone by his own piety and respect for tradition: he refuses to sleep with his wife while his companions are on a military campaign. David has his general, Joab, set Uriah up to be killed in battle and, after an appropriate interval, takes Bathsheba and marries her.

At this point the prophet Nathan enters the scene. He would hardly have needed a special revelation to figure out what had happened. What is remarkable is the courage of the prophet in confronting his king. He might, after all, have been given the next message to convey to Joab. Equally remarkable is the way that he confronts the king. Later prophets, such as Elijah or Amos, confront kings for wrongdoing by denouncing them harshly. Nathan takes a softer approach. He tells a parable. Like many of the parables of Jesus, this one induces the hearer to pass judgment on himself. Nathan does not refer to any specific law or remind the king about the exodus. The story assumes a common sense of justice, grounded in natural law, or at least in the common traditions of the ancient Near East. Kings were supposed to uphold justice and especially to defend the more vulnerable members of society (cf. Pss 45:7; 72:2). But anyone should know that it is wrong for a rich man to take from a poor man, and the story adds pathos by the fact that it involves the killing of a little ewe lamb. The approach of the prophet presupposes that the king is ultimately a person of goodwill, that he has the decency to deplore injustice. Nathan's technique would not work for an Elijah or an

Amos who had adversarial relations with the kings of their day. But where the parable can work, it is more likely to lead the listener to repentance than fiery denunciations.

The child born to Bathsheba dies. If this is punishment for David's sin, we must feel that the punishment is misplaced. It is characteristic of David that he escapes the consequences of his actions by well-timed repentance. Moreover, Bathsheba becomes the mother of David's eventual heir, Solomon. Once again, providence works in unexpected ways.

David

The historicity of David and Solomon has been controversial in recent scholarship. Despite the alleged splendor of Solomon's kingdom, it is not attested in the admittedly meager nonbiblical sources pertaining to the time. The temple, which was the showpiece of his reign, is supposedly hidden under the Temple Mount in Jerusalem and strictly off limits to archaeologists. In recent years, however, two pieces of evidence pertaining to David have come to light.

The first of these is an Aramaic inscription, found at Tell Dan in northern Israel in 1993, which mentions "the house of David." The inscription tells of an attack by Hazael, king of Damascus, on northern Israel about 835 B.C.E.: "[I killed Jeho]ram son of [Ahab] king of Israel, and [I] killed [Ahaz]iahu son of [Jehoram kin]g of the house of David. And I set [their towns into ruins and turned] their land into [desolation]." (Words in brackets are restored.)

This inscription shows that there was indeed a Davidic dynasty in the ninth century. (The royal line in northern Israel was called "the house of Omri" in Assyrian inscriptions). The inscription does not give us any information about David himself.

The second piece of new evidence is a large stone structure in Jerusalem, in the northern part of the ancient City of David, south of the Temple Mount. The excavator, Eilat Mazar, dates it to the middle of the tenth century B.C.E. and suggests that it was David's palace. She argues that it is unlikely to have been built by the Jebusites who occupied Jerusalem before David conquered it, as it would have had to be built in the very last days of their regime. Whether this interpretation of the site will win scholarly acceptance remains to be seen. It is based entirely on the supposed date of the structure. There is no inscription or anything that would provide an explicit interpretation. But in any case, the discovery will add fuel to the ongoing controversy about the historicity of the Bible's account of David's reign.

David and Absalom

David, however, does not get off scot-free. Second Samuel 13–20 tells a tragic family saga. It begins with the incestuous rape of David's daughter, Tamar, by her brother Amnon. Another brother, Absalom, bides his time but eventually kills Amnon in revenge. Absalom then has to flee. He is eventually brought back to Jerusalem, but then he rebels against his father. David has to flee from Jerusalem in mourning. Absalom enters Jerusalem and symbolizes his usurpation of David's throne by going in to his concubines. He meets his downfall, however, by following the advice of David's counselor and going into battle in person. His demise is comical—he gets caught in a tree by the long hair that was his pride. David, typically, takes no pleasure in his death but laments the loss of his son.

The story shows David in a very favorable light. He does not wish the death of any of his sons, neither Amnon nor Absalom, regardless of what they have done. David is also portrayed as compassionate and forgiving toward his enemies. Yet when a man named Sheba of the tribe of Benjamin (Saul's tribe) attempts to secede from Judah (chap. 20), David acts decisively to put down the revolt. As in several previous incidents, however, Joab and his brother are the ones who shed the blood. If there is guilt because of the violence, it can be imputed to them rather than to David.

The Psalms of David

The closing chapters of 2 Samuel contain two poetic compositions ascribed to David. According to 1 Sam 16:18, David was a skillful musician. In later tradition he would become the author of psalms par excellence. A composition found in the Dead Sea Scrolls credits him with 3,600 psalms and 450 songs (11Q5 col. 27)—a total rivaling the productivity of Solomon in 1 Kgs 5:12 (1 Kgs 4:32 in English versions). The psalm attributed to him in 2 Samuel 22 is also found in the Psalter as Psalm 18. It is a thanksgiving psalm that praises God for delivering the psalmist from the waves of death. It is notable for a description of a theophany of YHWH as a storm-god in 2 Sam 22:8-16.

The shorter poem, called "the last words of David," is notable in several respects. It mentions the "everlasting covenant" that was described at some length in 2 Samuel 7. But it also claims that "the spirit of the LORD speaks through me" (23:2). David, in effect, was a prophet, and he was widely regarded as such in antiquity. The composition from the Dead Sea Scrolls that lists the works of David says that David composed all his psalms and songs in the spirit of prophecy.

Even if we suspect that much of the portrayal of David in the books of Samuel originated as political propaganda, the character of David as depicted is exceptionally appealing. No other character in the Hebrew Bible is so well rounded. Here we have a fully human figure who is no saint. He is a hot-blooded individual who is guilty of murder, adultery, and sundry forms of extortion and exploitation. But he is also an emotional figure, whose grief for his friend Jonathan and for his son Absalom is moving. Even if the biblical authors tried to excuse and justify his actions, they nonetheless portrayed him as a man who was very fallible and even sinful. Later tradition enhanced the legend of David by crediting him with prophecy and the composition of psalms. In the process, it often depicts him as more pious than he appears in the books of Samuel. (We shall see this tendency in the books of Chronicles.) The charm of the biblical character, however, is precisely his human fallibility. It is this appreciation of the imperfection of human nature that marks the story of David as one of the finest pieces of literature to come down to us from antiquity.

Further Reading

Most of the literature cited in the previous chapter deals with both books of Samuel. In addition, note the following:

Commentary

McCarter, P. Kyle. *II Samuel*. AB 9B. New York: Doubleday, 1984.

Davidic Covenant and Royal Ideology

Day, John, ed. *King and Messiah in Israel and the Ancient Near East*. JSOTSup 270. Sheffield: Sheffield Academic Press, 1998.

Mettinger, T. N. D. *King and Messiah: The Civil and Sacred Legitimation of the Israelite Kings*. ConBOT 8. Lund: Gleerup, 1976.

Mowinckel, Sigmund. *He That Cometh*. Trans. G. W. Anderson. Nashville: Abingdon, 1955.

Schniedewind, William M. *Society and the Promise to David*. New York: Oxford Univ. Press, 1999.

Historicity

Finkelstein, Israel, and Neil Asher Silberman. *David and Solomon: In Search of the Bible's Sacred Kings and the Roots of the Western Tradition*. New York: Free Press, 2006.

13

First Kings 1–16:
Solomon and the Divided Monarchy

KEY POINTS

- Succession of Solomon: Realpolitik.
- Reign of Solomon:
  Historical questions about its grandeur.
  Solomon and wisdom.

The temple.
Temple piety in the Psalms.
- The division of the kingdom.
  The Omri dynasty in the north.

The first eleven chapters of 1 Kings deal with the accession and reign of Solomon. Thereafter 1 and 2 Kings chronicle the parallel histories of the northern and southern kingdoms (Israel and Judah).

A number of sources are explicitly identified in the books of Kings: "the book of the acts of Solomon" (1 Kgs 11:41), "the book of the annals of the kings of Judah" (14:29; 15:7, 23; et al.), and the corresponding annals of the kings of Israel (14:19; 15:31; 16:5, 14; et al.). None of these source books has survived. Chronicles were maintained at the royal courts of Egypt and Mesopotamia (for examples see *ANET*, 265–317). The "Babylonian Chronicle" may be roughly contemporary with the Deuteronomistic History. Historical information was also recorded in

royal inscriptions. The Near Eastern accounts are generally presented as lists of events, with little narrative elaboration. The books of Kings have much more developed narrative, but they are generally less expansive than the stories in Samuel.

The hand of the Deuteronomistic editors is more obvious in Kings than in Samuel. A typical introduction to a king of Israel reads: "In the x year of PN [proper name], king of Judah, PN the son of PN began to reign over all Israel in Samaria, and reigned for x years. He did what was evil in the eyes of YHWH." The introductions to the kings of Judah commonly add to this information the king's age at accession and the name of his mother. (The differences between the formulae for the two kingdoms supports the existence of source documents.) The end of a king's reign is likewise formulaic: "Now the rest of the deeds of PN, and all that he did, are they not written in the book of the annals of the kings of Israel? And PN slept with his fathers, and his son reigned in his stead." The Deuteronomist allows that some kings of Judah (Hezekiah, Josiah) did what was good in the eyes of YHWH, but they are exceptional. The main criterion is whether a given king allowed sacrificial worship outside the Jerusalem temple. The first king of Israel, Jeroboam, established temples at Bethel and Dan as rivals to Jerusalem. All subsequent northern kings "walk in the sin of Jeroboam." Other important Deuteronomistic themes in the books of Kings are the theology of the temple and the continuity of the Davidic dynasty in the southern kingdom.

The Succession to David (1 Kings 1–2)

The opening chapters of 1 Kings are an apology for the succession of Solomon to the kingship. Since he is the younger brother, his succession is brought about by palace intrigue. Solomon has the support of his mother, Bathsheba, and the prophet Nathan. David's support is decisive. Solomon is accepted by the people as the legitimate king.

Kingdoms of David & Solomon

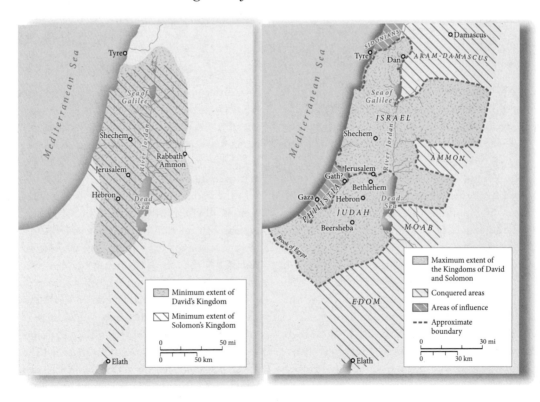

David tells Solomon to "act with the wisdom that is in you." Solomon becomes legendary for wisdom. In this case, however, his wisdom is a kind of street-smartness that leads him to kill his enemies before they kill him. In light of this unscrupulous Realpolitik, the beginning of David's farewell address in 1 Kings 2 is ironic: "Keep the charge of the Lord your God, walking in his ways and keeping his statutes, his commandments, his ordinances, and his testimonies, as it is written in the law of Moses" (1 Kgs 2:3). This is the Deuteronomic ideal for a king. It is evident, however, that Solomon was not greatly concerned about the law of Moses. He had more pressing concerns in the need to eliminate anyone who might present a threat to his kingship.

The Reign of Solomon (1 Kings 3–11)

The reign of Solomon is described in 1 Kings as a golden age. He is said to have entered into marriage alliances with all the surrounding peoples, and even to have received a daughter of the pharaoh in marriage. He built a palace, a house for Pharaoh's daughter, and, most famously, the temple. He is also credited with building up Hazor, Megiddo, and Gezer. He engaged in international trade and imported gold from Ophir (possibly in southern Arabia) and Tarshish (Spain?). The Queen of Sheba (modern Yemen?) came to visit.

Modern historians are skeptical about this account of Solomon's grandeur. Archaeology has shown that Jerusalem was a very small place until the end of the eighth century B.C.E. Prior to that time, it is argued, Jerusalem could have been no more than a local chiefdom, not unlike the traditional Canaanite city-states. The claim that all the territory from the border of Egypt to the Euphrates gave tribute to Solomon corresponds to the promise made to Abraham in Genesis 15 (cf. 1 Kgs 9:20). The claims made for Solomon may have been inferred from the promise. The great wealth that Solomon supposedly enjoyed (1 Kgs 10:14) has left no trace

Fig. 13.1. The "Solomonic" gate at Megiddo. Photo: John J. Collins.

in the material remains. Solomon's fabulous empire is now regarded by many scholars as a dream of glory from a later time.

The issue, however, is controversial and is likely to remain so. The most likely place for Solomon's palace and temple is on the site where Herod's temple later stood. This Temple Mount is one of the holiest sites of both Judaism and Islam. It is now impossible to excavate under it, and so it is impossible to verify the claims of Solomon's building projects in Jerusalem. Aside from Jerusalem, Hazor, Megiddo, and Gezer have been excavated extensively. At each of these sites, archaeologists identified a stratum as Solomonic. Characteristic of this stratum were huge gateways with six chambers. Some structures were also identified as stables. Some recent scholars have called the dating of these structures into question, arguing that they could come from the ninth century rather than the tenth. This issue is still contested. In part it depends on whether archaeologists are willing to use the biblical account as a key for interpreting their findings.

Those who defend the historicity of Solomon's splendor argue that the critics are arguing from silence. Such arguments are hazardous, especially when an important site like the Temple Mount is off limits to the archaeologists. In 1993 and 1994, fragments of an Aramaic inscription were found at Tel Dan in northern Galilee, which mentions "Beth David," the house of David. In 2005 archaeologists found a structure in Jerusalem outside the Temple Mount, which they claimed to be the palace of David, although there is no inscriptional evidence to prove the identification. Archaeology is an ongoing enterprise, and its results are never final.

Moreover, some of Solomon's practices were in flagrant violation of Deuteronomic law. It is unlikely that the Deuteronomist would have invented such an account out of whole cloth. Rather, the main features of Solomon's

Fig. 13.2. Tel Dan altar and high place. Photo: John J. Collins.

reign must have been established by an older tradition, probably a product of the royal court in Jerusalem.

Three aspects of the account of Solomon require further comment—his wisdom, the building of the temple, and his worship of foreign deities.

The Wisdom of Solomon

The wisdom of Solomon is proverbial. Wisdom literature was associated especially with scribes at the royal court. It may be that Solomon established a scribal school in Jerusalem. Other kingdoms, especially pharaonic Egypt, were well equipped with scribes. Yet nothing is said about such a school in the biblical text. Some scholars think that Jerusalem was too small a place in the tenth century to need a scribal school, and that the need for scribes would only have arisen in the time of Hezekiah, two centuries later.

First Kings addresses the wisdom of Solomon in chapter 3 and again in 4:29-34 (MT 5:9-14). First Kgs 3:3-14 reports a dream in which the Lord invites Solomon to "ask what I should give you." Solomon asks for an understanding mind to govern the people. The Lord grants his wish, but also grants the things for which he did not ask, riches and honor all his life. These things were supposed to be the gifts of wisdom (Prov 3:16). The account of Solomon's dream is clearly a Deuteronomistic composition. It concludes with a conditional promise: "If you will walk in my ways, keeping my statutes and my commandments, as your father David walked, then I will lengthen your life" (1 Kgs 3:14).

Solomon's wisdom is illustrated by his judgment on the two women who claimed the same child (chap. 3). A different kind of wisdom is highlighted in chapter 5. Here

wisdom consists of mastery of proverbs and songs, but also of an exhaustive knowledge of nature. There is nothing distinctively Israelite about this wisdom. The biblical book of Proverbs was influenced by Egyptian wisdom at some points. Wisdom was an international phenomenon, fostered especially at the royal courts.

The Temple

Arguably the most important achievement attributed to Solomon was the building of the temple. The materials for the temple were obtained in Lebanon, and at least some of the work was done by Phoenician craftsmen. The temple resembled other temples in Syria-Palestine. The basic plan was a rectangle, 100 cubits long and 50 cubits wide (approximately 165 x 84.5 feet). There were three main sections: the 'ûlām or vestibule, the hēkāl or main room (the same word is used for the temple as a whole), and the dᵉbîr or inner sanctuary (the Holy of Holies). Two bronze pillars, called Jachin and Boaz, stood in front of the temple. There was also a molten sea, a circular object, supported by twelve statues of oxen. The symbolism of these objects is not explained, but the sea recalls the prominence of Yamm (Sea) in the Ugaritic myths. In the inner sanctuary there were two enormous cherubim made of olivewood. These hovered over the ark, which represented the presence of God, who was often said to be enthroned above the cherubim.

In the ancient world, a temple was thought to be the place where the deity lived. While the god or goddess was present in the temple, no harm could befall the city. The Lament for the Destruction of Ur in the early second millennium B.C.E. complains that the various deities abandoned their temples (*ANET*, 455–63). Later Ezekiel has a vision of the glory of the

Lord leaving Jerusalem before it was destroyed by the Babylonians.

The theology associated with Solomon's temple can be seen in the Psalms. The psalmists sometimes speak unabashedly about the temple as the dwelling place of YHWH. "How lovely is your dwelling place, O LORD of hosts!" (Ps 84:1-2). According to Psalm 46, Jerusalem is "the city of God, the holy habitation of the Most High. God is in the midst of the city; it shall not be moved." Again, Mount Zion is said to be God's holy mountain "in the far north" (Mount Zion was not in fact in the north, but traditionally the holy mountain of Baal, Mount Zaphon, was associated with the north). The importance of the temple for the people of Judah is amply evident: "for a day in your courts is better than a thousand elsewhere" (84:10).

The Deuteronomistic theology of the temple is found in Solomon's prayer in 1 Kings 8. Solomon recalls the promise to David but understands it as conditional: "There shall never fail you a successor before me to sit on the throne of Israel, if only your children look to their way, to walk before me" (v. 25). He then goes on to reflect, "But will God indeed dwell on the earth? Even heaven and the highest heaven cannot contain you, much less this house that I have built!" (v. 27). This dilemma is resolved by the Deuteronomic compromise: God makes his *name* dwell there. The name still represents the presence of God, but it stops short of saying that God actually dwells in the temple. Solomon goes on to explain the temple as a place where people can have access to God, to bring their requests and atone for their sins. The temple has become a house of prayer, closer to the later synagogue than to God's dwelling.

Solomon's prayer at the consecration of the temple may have been written in the Bab-

ylonian exile or later, when the myth that Zion could not be captured had been shattered. The temple, however, remained the central focal point of Jewish worship throughout the biblical period. While Deuteronomy demythologized the temple by saying that God's *name* lived there, rather than the Deity himself, it increased the centrality of the temple by declaring it to be the only valid place for sacrificial worship.

Solomon as Idolater

Not only did Solomon offer sacrifice at high places (1 Kgs 3:3), but he "loved many foreign women" from the nations with whom the Lord had forbidden intermarriage. Moreover, he also succumbed to the worship of their gods and goddesses (11:5-8). Solomon's behavior makes good sense if indeed he was actively engaged in international affairs. One of the ways in which kings in the ancient world cemented alliances was by giving and taking each other's daughters in marriage. The claim that Solomon had seven hundred princesses among his wives, then, is a tribute not to his sexual energy but to his diplomacy. There is a parallel to Solomon's career in this regard in the reign of Herod the Great, almost a thousand years later. We can be confident that the tradition of Solomon's promotion of pagan deities was not invented by the Deuteronomist. Whether it is an accurate reflection of the reign of Solomon or not, it shows that, before Josiah's reform, there was a tradition of tolerance in Jerusalem toward the gods and goddesses of neighboring peoples.

For the Deuteronomists, Solomon's idolatry is the reason why the united monarchy did not persist. Ten tribes were allowed to secede under Jeroboam the son of Nebat because Solomon worshiped foreign deities (11:33). Nonetheless, the kingdom is not taken away entirely. The promise to David remains, despite Solomon's failure to keep the laws. It is somewhat ironic that the only tribe left under the kingdom of Judah is Benjamin, the tribe of Saul.

The Division of the Kingdom

The issue that sparked the revolt was the oppressive practice of forced labor, or corvée, introduced by Solomon. The old men in his retinue advised Rehoboam to lighten the burden on the people, while the young men told him to intensify it. He chose the latter course, and schism resulted. Jeroboam had been in charge of all the forced labor of the northern tribes. When he rebelled, with the encouragement of the prophet Ahijah, he fled to Egypt. There is a clear parallel here between the forced labor of Solomon and the oppression of the Israelites in Egypt in the exodus story. The same Hebrew word is used to refer to the corvée in both stories. After Solomon's death, Jeroboam came up from Egypt. When he became king, he made the recollection of the exodus central to the cult in Bethel and Dan (12:28). Jeroboam may have drawn a parallel with an older tradition about the exodus to lend legitimacy to his revolt, but it is also possible that the celebration of the exodus became central to the cult of YHWH only at this time.

Henceforth, the northern tribes would constitute the kingdom of Israel proper. It may be significant that the rebellion was launched at the old center of Shechem rather than at Hebron, where David had been crowned. Kingship in the north would remain much closer to the kind of charismatic leadership we saw in Judges than would the dynasty in the south.

Jeroboam built up Shechem as the first capital of the northern kingdom. He also built two shrines, one at Bethel, not far from Jerusalem, and one at Dan in the far north. Bethel was associated with Jacob, who had allegedly given it its name, "house of God."

The account of Jeroboam's actions is unsympathetic and bears the clear imprint of the Deuteronomist. He is accused of idolatry in setting up the two golden calves (cf. the story of the golden calf in Exodus 32). It is unlikely, however, that Jeroboam was guilty of idolatry. The deity may have been thought to stand on the calves, just as he was thought to sit above the cherubim in Jerusalem. Jeroboam's crime in the eyes of the Deuteronomists was that he promoted sacrificial worship outside Jerusalem. This is what is called the sin of Jeroboam. In fact, Jeroboam was more closely attuned to the traditions of the tribes than was Rehoboam, whose capital had been a Jebusite stronghold little more than a generation earlier.

The Deuteronomists provide an explicit judgment on Jeroboam in 1 Kings 13, where a man of God is said to prophesy that a Davidic king named Josiah would one day tear down the altar at Bethel. The explicit mention of Josiah here leaves no doubt but that this king's reform is the climax of the history. An even more explicit judgment is pronounced in chapter 14 by Ahijah the Shilonite. Jeroboam is to have no male descendant. Anyone who has read the books of Samuel must appreciate the irony when Jeroboam is told that he has not been like "my servant David, who kept my commandments and followed me with all his heart, doing only that which was right in my sight" (14:8).

Omri (16:16-17; ca. 885 B.C.E.) is the first king of Israel or Judah to leave an imprint in nonbiblical sources. The Moabite Stone, which was discovered in 1868, tells of the conflict between Mesha, king of Moab, and Omri, who humbled Moab for many years but was

Israel and Judah

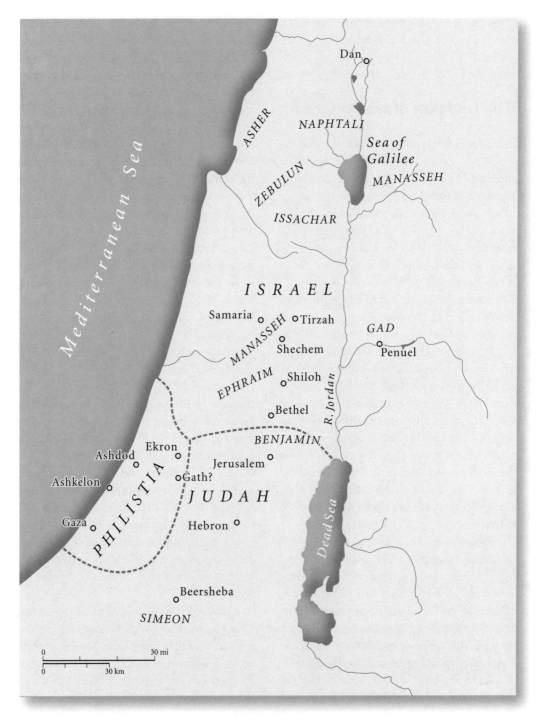

eventually defeated (*ANET*, 321). The inscription is remarkable for the similarity it shows between the religion of Moab and that of Israel. Mesha acts at the behest of his god, Chemosh, just as the Israelites act at the behest of YHWH. Most remarkable is that Mesha boasts of having slaughtered every man, woman, and child in Nebo, "for I had devoted them to destruction for (the god) Ashtar-Chemosh." Omri's son, Ahab, is mentioned in the Monolith Inscription of the Assyrian king Shalmaneser as having contributed two thousand chariots and ten thousand foot soldiers to an Aramean coalition that halted an Assyrian advance (*ANET*, 279). Assyrian records continued to refer to Israel as "the house of Omri" long after Omri's descendants had ceased to rule. Omri and Ahab were kings to be reckoned with. There is much more evidence outside the Bible for their power and influence than was the case with Solomon.

It is Omri who bought and fortified the hill of Samaria, which remained the capital of Israel from that time forward. Archaeology has shown that it was a splendid city. The royal acropolis covered an area of four acres, the size of a typical town of the time. One of the buildings on the acropolis contained a hoard of carved ivories, the most important collection of artwork from ancient Israel. The Omride dynasty also either built or expanded Hazor and Megiddo, and fortified them with massive walls.

The southern, Deuteronomistic, editor dismisses Omri summarily: "Omri did what was evil in the sight of the LORD; he did more evil than all who were before him" (16:25). His son Ahab proves to be a much more colorful character: "And as if it had been a light thing for him to walk in the sins of Jeroboam son of Nebat, he took as his wife Jezebel, daughter of King Ethbaal of the Sidonians, and went and served Baal, and worshiped him" (16:31). The advent of Ahab and Jezebel sets the stage for a major confrontation between the devotees of YHWH and the cult of Baal, and the first sustained discussion of prophecy in the Hebrew Bible.

Further Reading

Commentaries

Cogan, Mordechai. *1 Kings*. AB 10. New York: Doubleday, 2000.

Long, Burke O. *1 Kings, with an Introduction to Historical Literature*. FOTL 9. Grand Rapids: Eerdmans, 1984.

Seow, C. L. "The First and Second Books of Kings." In *NIB* 3:1–296.

Historical Background

Finkelstein, Israel, and Neil Asher Silberman. *David and Solomon: In Search of the Bible's Sacred Kings and the Roots of the Western Tradition*. New York: Free Press, 2006.

Miller, J. Maxwell, and John H. Hayes. *A History of Ancient Israel and Judah*, 189–286. Philadelphia: Westminster, 1986.

Na'aman, Nadav. "Cow Town or Royal Capital? Evidence for Iron Age Jerusalem." *BAR* 23/4 (1997): 43–47.

Studies

Knoppers, Gary N. *Two Nations under God: The Deuteronomistic History of Solomon and the Dual Monarchies*. Vol. 1: *The Reign of Solomon and the Rise of Jeroboam*, HSM 52. Atlanta: Scholars Press, 1993.

Levenson, Jon D. *Sinai and Zion*, 89–184. Minneapolis: Winston, 1985.

Kings of Judah and Israel

Judah		Israel	
Judah		**Israel**	
Rehoboam	922–915	Jeroboam	922–901
Abijah (Abijam)	915–913		
Asa	913–873	Nadab	901–900
		Baasha	900–877
		Elah	877–876
		Zimri	876
		Omride Era	
		Omri	876–869
Jehoshaphat	873–849	Ahab	869–850
		Ahaziah	850–849
Jehoram	849–843	Jehoram	849–843
Ahaziah	843–842		
		Jehu Dynasty	
		Jehu	843–815
Athaliah	842–837		
Joash	837–800		
		Jehoahaz	815–802
Amaziah	800–783	Jehoash	802–786
Uzziah (Azariah)	783–742	Jeroboam II	786–746
		Assyrian Intervention	
Jotham	742–735	Zechariah	746–745
		Shallum	745
		Menahem	745–737
		Pekahiah	737–736
Ahaz	735–727 or 715	Pekah	736–732
		Hoshea	732–722
Hezekiah	727 or 715–687		
		Fall of Samaria	**722**
Manasseh	687–642		
Amon	642–640		
Josiah	640–609		
Jehoahaz	609		
Jehoiachim	609–598		
Jehoiachin	598–597		
First capture of Jerusalem by Babylonians	597		
Zedekiah	597–586		

Destruction of Jerusalem   586

14

First Kings 17–Second Kings 25: Tales of Prophets and the End of the Kingdoms of Israel and Judah

---

KEY POINTS

- Stories about prophets in the books of Kings
  - —**Micaiah ben Imlah** and the normal situation of prophecy.
  - —**Elijah** and the prophets of Baal.
  - —Elijah and social justice: **Naboth's vineyard**.
- **Jehu's coup**: religion and violence.

- The **Assyrian destruction of Israel**.
- **Hezekiah and Sennacherib**: miraculous deliverance or abject surrender?
- The **Babylonian conquest** of Judah.

The narratives in 1 Kings 17–22 and 2 Kings 1–9 are unlike the annalistic reports on the reigns of kings. They are legendary stories about prophets. These stories most probably circulated independently before they were incorporated into the Deuteronomistic History. They shed light on the place of prophecy in Israelite society under the monarchies.

Micaiah ben Imlah

An impression of the normal context of prophecy may be gleaned from the story of Micaiah ben Imlah in 1 Kings 22. The kings of Israel and Judah agree to launch a campaign against the disputed city of Ramoth-gilead. The king

of Judah proposes that they "inquire first for the word of the Lord." There is no mention of Baal here, as we might expect from the other narratives about the reign of Ahab.

The king of Israel assembles four hundred prophets. Most prophets were not isolated individuals but were members of a guild. One of the functions of prophets seems to have been to whip up enthusiasm at the beginning of a campaign. Here the prophets hold a virtual pep rally for the king. Not only do they promise that God will give him victory, but they symbolically act out the battle on the threshing floor in the gate of Samaria. The threshing floor was an open space like a town square, where public assemblies were held. Later, in the prophetic books, we often find "oracles against the nations" proclaiming woes upon the enemies of Israel. First Kings 22 illustrates the *Sitz im Leben*, the setting in life, of such oracles.

The messenger who goes to fetch Micaiah is exceptionally candid: "The words of the prophets with one accord are favorable to the king; let your word be like the word of one of them and speak favorably." This is tantamount to an admission that the prophets as a group tell the king what he wants to hear. Micaiah, inevitably, does not. He claims to have had a vision of all Israel scattered like sheep without a shepherd. The implication is that the king will be killed in battle.

We might have expected Micaiah to accuse the prophets of conspiring, as they surely had. To do so, however, might undercut belief in prophecy altogether. Instead, Micaiah reports an extraordinary vision of his own. He saw the Lord sitting on his throne. According to one strand of Israelite tradition, a human being could not see God and live (cf. Exod 33:20). Micaiah, however, represents a tradition in which prophets claim to have had visions of God (cf. Isaiah 6 and Ezekiel 1). We cannot fail to notice the similarity between the Lord on his throne, surrounded by his host, and the kings of Israel and Judah. The prophet hears the deliberations of the heavenly council. The Lord asks his heavenly courtiers: "Who will entice Ahab, so that he may go up and fall at Ramoth-gilead?" The Lord is setting the king up for disaster, just as he had set up the pharaoh in the exodus story by hardening his heart. The solution is provided by a "spirit" that volunteers to be a lying spirit in the mouths of the prophets. Micaiah does not deny that his fellow prophets are inspired. The problem is that the spirit of inspiration may be deceitful.

If inspiration can be deceitful, whom should the king believe? Both he and Micaiah adopt an attitude of "wait and see." The king

does not have Micaiah killed on the spot but has him imprisoned, pending the outcome of the battle. Micaiah agrees that if the king returns from the battle, "the LORD has not spoken through me." In the event, Micaiah is vindicated, but it is too late by then for the king to do anything about it.

The story of Micaiah ben Imlah illustrates both the way prophecy worked in Israelite society and the problems that were inherent in it. The prophets claimed to speak the word of the Lord, and this is what made their utterances powerful. But sometimes they disagreed and contradicted each other. How then could one decide which one was right? Ultimately, the only satisfactory way to know whether a prophecy was right was to wait and see, and that might well be too late. The king would have been better advised to decide whether to go to war on the merits of the case: was this a necessary war, that he should risk his life to pursue it?

Elijah

The stories about Elijah are closely related to those about Elisha. Each prophet performs a miracle on behalf of a widow by causing her store of oil to increase (1 Kgs 17:8-16; 2 Kgs 4:1-7). Each raises a child from the dead (1 Kgs 17:17-24; 2 Kgs 4:18-37). The stories about Elijah, however, reflect a greater theological interest. Elijah is engaged in polemic against the worship of Baal, and he emerges as a champion of social justice, whereas Elisha is more simply a wonder-worker. Accordingly, some scholars regard the Elisha stories as older than those about Elijah. There is some doubt about the historicity of Elijah. His name means "YHWH is my God," and the stories about him have obvious symbolic significance.

Elijah's Narratives

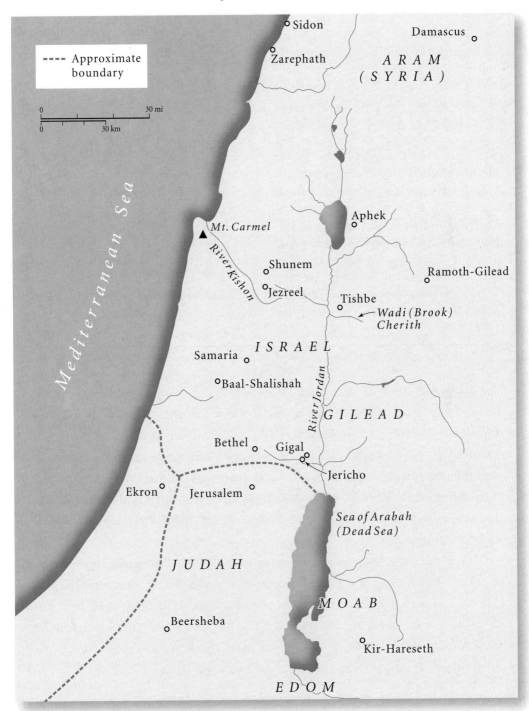

The extent to which these stories were edited by Deuteronomists is disputed. The charge against Ahab in chapters 17–19 is that he "followed the Baals," not that he walked in the sin of Jeroboam. Elijah offers a burnt offering on Mount Carmel, despite the Deuteronomic restriction of sacrifice to Jerusalem. Some have suggested that the Elijah cycle was incorporated into 1 Kings later than the Deuteronomistic edition of the work. But the stories surely originated in northern Israel before Josiah's reform. Ostraca found at Samaria show that "Baal" was a common element in proper names, and this supports the view that his worship was widespread. It is clear from the prophet Hosea that Baal worship continued to flourish in the eighth century, down to the end of the northern kingdom. The strongest case for a Deuteronomistic insertion can be made in chapter 19, where Elijah goes to "Horeb the mountain of God" and takes on the character of "a prophet like Moses" (cf. Deut 18:15).

The conflict between the cult of YHWH and that of Baal comes to a head in 1 Kings 17 because of a drought, which Elijah interprets as a punishment on Ahab because of the worship of Baal. Baal was a storm-god, the "rider of the clouds," and was supposed to provide rain, which made fertility and life possible. In the words of the prophet Hosea, the dispute in Israel concerned which god provided "the grain, the wine, and the oil," YHWH or Baal (cf. Hos 2:8). This is also the issue in the Elijah stories.

The challenge posed by Elijah is that "the god who answers with fire is indeed God." The prophets of Baal use various techniques to whip themselves into ecstasy. Elijah mocks them and suggests that their god is asleep. The story is polemical and is not concerned with

---

Elijah

The prophet Elijah has a special place in Jewish legend. Because he did not die but was taken up to heaven, the legend arose that he would come again. This legend first appears at the end of the book of Malachi: "Lo, I will send you the prophet Elijah before the great and terrible day of the LORD comes. He will turn the hearts of the parents to their children and the hearts of children to their parents, so that I will not come and strike the land with a curse." In the New Testament (Mark 9:11-13), the disciples ask Jesus "Why do the scribes say that Elijah must come first?" and he responds that he has already come (presumably in the person of John the Baptist).

In rabbinic times, Elijah was imagined as an angelic figure who could traverse the world with four strokes of his wings and could help people in various ways. He was also thought to be a priest and a teacher of Torah. Since he had raised the dead during his earthly life, it was expected that he would be God's agent in the resurrection. A place is still reserved for him at the Passover meal. Finally, he is supposed to slay the satanic figure Samael at God's command and banish evil forever.

fair representation of the opponents. The manner in which Elijah produces fire, by pouring water on the offering and in a trench, makes one suspect that some trickery (involving a flammable liquid) is involved. But we do not know whether there is any historical basis for this story. The narrator wished to give the impression that a decisive test was carried out, which proved beyond doubt that YHWH was God. Elijah seizes his advantage by having all the prophets of Baal slaughtered.

Elijah is impelled by the hand of the Lord, which imbues him with strength and enables him to outrun the king's chariots. He manifests a kind of charismatic religion, such as we saw in Judges. The massacre of the prophets is in the spirit of the total slaughter that was commanded on some occasions in Joshua and 1 Samuel, and of which the Moabite king Mesha boasted. (In later tradition Elijah was remembered as a figure of zeal and was even identified with Phinehas, the paradigmatic zealot of Numbers 25). This readiness to slaughter one's opponents in the name of God is hardly a religious ideal that we should wish to emulate in the modern world.

One other aspect of Elijah's contest is troubling. He and the prophets of Baal agree that "the god who answers with fire is indeed God." Is this an adequate criterion for identifying God? YHWH was originally worshiped as a god who manifested himself in fire on a mountain, not unlike the Canaanite storm-god Baal. In the Bible, however, YHWH differs from Baal above all by his ethical character. This difference is not apparent in the story of Elijah on Mount Carmel in 1 Kings 18.

This story, however, is followed immediately by another one, in chapter 19, that serves as a corrective, and that is at least in part the work of a Deuteronomistic editor. Elijah has to flee from the wrath of Jezebel, and he betakes

himself southward, to the wilderness. He is fed miraculously in the desert, as Israel was during the exodus. Then he proceeds for forty days and forty nights to "Horeb the mountain of God." The forty days and nights correspond to the forty years spent by the Israelites in the wilderness. The motif is picked up in the New Testament story of the temptation of Jesus.

At the mountain, Elijah has an experience similar to that of Moses in Exod 33:21-23. Moses was not allowed to see God's face but only his back. Elijah does not see God in human form, but he does experience his presence. The Deity, we are told, was not in the wind, the earthquake, or the fire that were the typical trappings of a theophany, even in the account of the revelation on Mount Sinai in Exodus 19. Instead, God was in "a sound of sheer silence" (1 Kgs 19:12). God must not be confused with the forces of nature. The word translated "sound" also means "voice." In Deuteronomic theology, Israel at Horeb "heard the sound of words but saw no form; there was only a voice" (Deut 4:11-12). The theophany to Elijah in 1 Kings 19 corrects the impression that might have been given by chapter 18, that God is manifested primarily in fire or in the power of nature. Instead, God is manifested primarily by the voice and the words of commandment.

But while the Deuteronomist corrects the theology of the traditional story, there is no correction of the ethics of Elijah. The virtue of his (murderous) zeal is affirmed, and he is given a new mission, to anoint a new king in Syria and to anoint Jehu as king of Israel. In fact, it is Elisha who anoints Jehu, but Elisha derives his authority from Elijah. As we learn in 2 Kings, Jehu acts with the same kind of zeal as Elijah in slaughtering the enemies of YHWH. Elijah is also told to anoint Elisha as his successor. He is not actually said to anoint the younger prophet, but he casts his mantle over him, which has the same effect. The act of anointing does not have to be taken literally. He confers authority on Elisha and appoints him to the task of prophecy.

A different kind of story is told about Elijah in 1 Kings 21. Here the issue is not Baal worship but social injustice. Ahab wants the vineyard of Naboth the Jezreelite. When Naboth refuses to sell it, Jezebel has him murdered. The situation is reminiscent of David and Bathsheba. There also the king was confronted by a prophet. There is a striking contrast, however, between the approach of Nathan and that of Elijah. Nathan induced David to condemn himself by appealing to values that the king shared. Such an appeal may not have been possible in the case of Ahab. Elijah makes no attempt to win the king over but pronounces a judgment, in effect a curse, on both Ahab and Jezebel. In fact, the coup that terminated Ahab's line came not in his lifetime but in that of his son. The Deuteronomist explains this by saying that Ahab humbled himself and was given a reprieve.

The end of Elijah's earthly career is described in 2 Kings 2. His affinity with Moses is underlined when he parts the waters of the Jordan. Then he is taken up to heaven in a fiery chariot. Because Elijah had not died, it was believed that he would come back to earth "before the great and terrible Day of the Lord" (Mal 4:5). According to the New Testament (Matt 17:10; Mark 9:11), Elijah is supposed to come before the Messiah. In Jewish tradition, a place is set for Elijah at the Passover in anticipation of his return.

Elisha

Some of Elisha's miraculous deeds are very similar to those of Elijah. Nonetheless, the careers of the two prophets are quite different. Elisha is not engaged in conflict with the cult of Baal, and he never fights for social justice, as Elijah did in the case of Naboth's vineyard. Some of his miracles are, at best, amoral. He curses small boys who jeer at him, so that they are mauled by she-bears (2 Kgs 2:23-25). He makes an iron axe float on the water (6:1-7). He prophesies that the Lord will enable the kings of Israel and Judah to ravage Moab, although there is no evident moral issue at stake. He also discloses the secret plans of the king of Aram and performs various miracles to aid the Israelites in battle against him. These stories are concerned with manifestations of supernatural power with little concern for moral issues.

Jehu's Coup

The career of Elisha reaches its climax in 2 Kings 9 in the story of Jehu's coup. King Ahaziah of Judah is killed as well as Joram of Israel. Jezebel's fate is gruesome. In the end, Jehu kills all who were left of the house of Ahab and everyone who was associated with the royal house. He also slaughters the kin of Ahaziah of Judah, whom he meets on the way. Finally, he kills every worshiper of Baal in Samaria. This whole bloodbath is justified by "the word of the LORD that he spoke to Elijah" (10:17). In view of the way that Jehu's actions are justified by appeal to prophecy, it seems quite plausible that the prophetic stories were edited at the court of one of his descendants. (Four of his descendants reigned in Samaria, and the dynasty lasted a hundred years.) The Deuteronomistic editor added only a characteristic note of disapproval: even though Jehu allegedly stamped out the worship of Baal, he still walked in the sin of Jeroboam (2 Kgs 10:29). The "sin of Jeroboam" was not an issue at all in the stories in 1 Kings 17—2 Kings 9.

Even in northern Israel, the attempt to justify Jehu's bloody coup was not entirely successful. About a hundred years afterward, toward the end of Jehu's dynasty, the prophet Hosea announced that God would punish the house of Jehu for the bloodshed of Jezreel. This judgment did not bespeak any sympathy for the house of Omri but acknowledged that the way in which Jehu carried out his coup was blameworthy.

The End of the Kingdom of Israel

There was rapid turnover of rulers in the last years of Israel. Six kings ruled in the space of just over twenty years. Four of these were assassinated. Menahem (745–737) had to deal with a new factor in Israelite history, the encroachment of the Assyrian Empire. Menahem paid a heavy tribute to the Assyrian king, Tiglath-pileser, and in return was confirmed on his throne (2 Kgs 15:19). Menahem's son, Pekahiah, was assassinated by one Pekah, son of Remaliah, who is mentioned in Isaiah 7. During his reign, Tiglath-pileser of Assyria captured territory in the north of Israel, in Gilead, Galilee, and Naphtali, and took the people captive to Assyria. Shortly thereafter Pekah was assassinated by Hoshea, the last king of Israel. He ruled for nine years, paying tribute to Assyria, but in the end he made the disastrous mistake of conspiring with Egypt and withholding tribute. In 722 Samaria was destroyed by the Assyrians, and the area was placed under direct Assyrian rule.

The account in 2 Kgs 17:5-6, 24 is essentially in agreement with this, but it is aston-ishingly brief from a historical point of view. The Deuteronomists were primarily interested in a theological explanation: "This occurred because the people of Israel had sinned against the LORD their God" (17:7), by worshiping other gods and by having high places, complete with pillars and poles. Most of all, "Jeroboam drove Israel from following the LORD" (17:21) by promoting sacrificial worship outside Jerusalem. The disaster had been foretold by the prophets. In reality, many other factors were involved, primarily Assyrian expansionism and military power.

> The numerous Assyrian inscriptions from this period often mention Israel. Sargon II states: "I besieged and conquered Samaria, led away as booty 27,290 inhabitants of it. . . . The town I rebuilt better than it was before and settled therein people from countries which I myself had conquered. I placed an officer of mine as governor over them and imposed upon them tribute as is customary for Assyrian citizens."
> —ANET, 284–85.

The biblical account and the Assyrian records agree that people from other places were settled in Samaria. According to 17:33, "they worshiped the Lord but they also served their own gods." The editors insist: "They do not worship the Lord and they do not follow the statutes or the ordinances or the law or the commandment that the Lord commanded the children of Jacob" (17:34). In the view of the Deuteronomistic editors, the new inhabitants of Samaria were not legitimate descendants of ancient Israel. This judgment on the people of Samaria would be a source of conflict after the Babylonian exile, in the time of Ezra and Nehemiah, and would complicate relations between Jews and Samaritans in the Second Temple period.

Judah in the Assyrian Crisis

In Judah, Hezekiah conducted a reform that was similar to the one later carried out by Josiah. He removed the high places, broke down the pillars, and cut down the sacred poles. He even destroyed the bronze serpent, Nehushtan, that had been made by Moses in the wilderness (Num 21:6-9). It is difficult to judge the scope of Hezekiah's reform, or even the point at which it took place. According to 2 Kgs 18:1, Hezekiah began to reign in the third year of Hoshea, and Samaria fell in the

sixth year of his reign. This would require a date around 727 B.C.E. for his ascent to the throne. But Sennacherib's invasion, which is known to have taken place in 701, is said to have been in the fourteenth year of Hezekiah (18:13). This would place his accession in 715. Moreover, he is said to have been 25 when he began to reign (18:2) although his father, Ahaz, is said to have died at age 36, and so would only have been eleven when Hezekiah was born! Some of these figures are evidently mistaken.

We know from archaeology that the size of Jerusalem was greatly expanded during Hezekiah's reign. There was presumably an influx of refugees from the north. The suppression of the high places can be understood as

Assyrian Empire

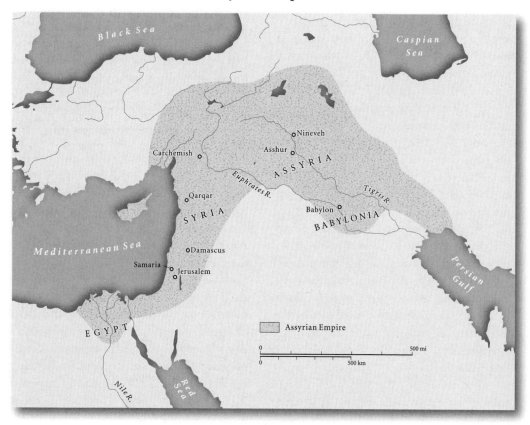

Plate A. Akhenaton and Nefertiti offering to the sun god Aton. Painted limestone stele. From el-Amarna. 18th dynasty, c.1353–1336 B.C.E. Egyptian Museum, Cairo. Photo: © Scala / Art Resource, N.Y.

Plate B.
The "Baal of Lightning" found in a sanctuary at (Ugarit) Ras Shamra, Syria. 17th–13th B.C.E. (limestone, 142 x 50 cm). Louvre, Paris. Photo: © Scala / Art Resource, N.Y.

Plate C. Smiting God, probably Reshef or Baal, from Megiddo. Bronze figurine, Canaanite. Israel Museum (IDAM), Jerusalem. Photo: © Erich Lessing / Art Resource, N.Y.

Plate D. High Place (altar) of the Canaanites. Tel Megiddo, the legendary Armageddon of Revelation, was a fortified city during King Solomon's time. Megiddo, Israel. Photo: © Erich Lessing / Art Resource, N.Y.

Plate E. Horned altar, from Megiddo. Limestone (around 900 B.C.E.). Israel Museum (IDAM), Jerusalem. Photo: © Erich Lessing / Art Resource, N.Y. ART43606

Plate F. The walls and a city gate of Megiddo. The settlement dates back some 6,000 years. During Solomon's kingdom, it was a fortified chariot city (1 Kings 9:15). Photo: © Erich Lessing / Art Resource, N.Y.

Plate G. High Place, Shechem, Israel. According to the Bible, Abraham built an altar at Shechem, Jacob bought a piece of land, Joseph's body was brought here from Egypt for burial, and Joshua renewed the covenant with God there. The ruins of Shechem are near the town of Nablus. Photo: © Erich Lessing / Art Resource, N.Y.

Plate H. Remains of the City of David. At one time, this area, now outside the city walls of Jerusalem, was inside, under the rule of King David. Israel. © Richard T. Nowitz/CORBIS.

Plate I. Jehu, King of Israel, prostrating himself before King Shalmaneser III of Assyria. Basalt bas-relief on the black stele of Shalmaneser III. Assyrian, 9th century B.C.E. British Museum, London. Photo: © Erich Lessing / Art Resource, N.Y.

Plate J. Assyrian warriors with their spoil from the conquest of the Israelite town of Lachish (battle 701 B.C.E.). Relief from the palace of Sennacherib at Nineveh, Mesopotamia (Iraq). British Museum, London. Photo: © Erich Lessing / Art Resource, N.Y.

Plate K. Pillar figurine from a tomb in Bethlehem, Israel, ca. 7th century B.C.E. Such figurines may be related to a fertility cult associated with the goddess Astarte, an ancient Canaanite fertility goddess.British Museum, London. Photo: © HIP / Art Resource, N.Y.

Plate L. The tunnel of Siloam brings water from the spring of Gihon to the Pool of Siloam inside the city of Jerusalem. The tunnel was constructed under King Hezekiah, 700 B.C.E., to insure the water supply of the city during a siege. Photo: © Erich Lessing / Art Resource, N.Y.

Plate M. The Assyrian Grand King Ashurbanipal (668–627 B.C.E.) leads the vanquished by a nose-ring. The kneeling figure on the left is Ushanakhuru, son of Pharaoh Taharq; on the right, the Baal of Tyrus. Granite stele from Babylon, Mesopotamia (Iraq). Neo-Assyrian relief, 7th century B.C.E. Vorderasiatisches Museum, Staatliche Museen zu Berlin. Photo: © Erich Lessing / Art Resource, N.Y.

Plate N. The Ishtar Gate, main gate of Babylon built during the reign of Nebuchadnezzar II (605–562 B.C.E.). Enamelled tiles, mythical animals, lions, and gods embellish the gate, which was dedicated to the goddess Ishtar of Babylon. Vorderasiatisches Museum, Staatliche Museen zu Berlin. Photo ©: Erich Lessing/Art Resource, N.Y.

Plate O. Lion. Detail of procession road to the Ishtar Gate. Enamelled tile frieze. 105 x 227 cm. Neo-Babylonian, 7th B.C.E. Louvre, Paris. Photo: © Erich Lessing/Art Resource, N.Y.

Plate P. Cyrus Cylinder, Babylonian, from Babylon, southern Iraq, ca. 539–530 B.C.E. This clay cylinder represents a declaration of good kingship. It is inscribed in Babylonian cuneiform with an account by Cyrus, king of Persia (559–530 B.C.E.), of his conquest of Babylon in 539 B.C.E. and capture of Nabonidus, the last Babylonian king. British Museum, London. Photo: © HIP / Art Resource, N.Y.

Plate Q. Mausoleum of Cyrus the Great. Achaemenid period. Pasargadae, Iran. Photo: © SEF / Art Resource, N.Y.

Plate R. Darius I the Great (550–486 B.C.E.) giving audience. Detail of a relief in the Treasury of the Palace at Persepolis, 491–486 B.C.E. Persia, Achaemenid period. Persepolis, Iran. Photo: © SEF / Art Resource, N.Y.

Plate S. Tetradrachm of Antiochus IV Epiphanes (175–163 B.C.E.), Seleucidan king of Syria who, by his imposition of Greek law and customs in Judea, provoked the Maccabean Revolt (167 B.C.E.). Israel Museum (IDAM), Jerusalem. Photo: © Erich Lessing / Art Resource, N.Y.

Plate T. Ink pot. Found at the Qumran excavations. Israel, 3rd century B.C.E.–1st century C.E. Shrine of the Book, Jerusalem. Photo: © Erich Lessing / Art Resource, N.Y.

Plate U. A few lines (in Hebrew square writing) from one of the two scrolls of Isaiah found in the cave of the scrolls of Qumram, north-west of the Dead Sea. Herodian period. Israel Museum (IDAM), Jerusalem. Photo: © Erich Lessing / Art Resource, N.Y.

Plate V. Bronze coin with a tripod and Greek inscription, from the period of Herod the Great, King of Judea (37–44 C.E.). Diameter 24.5 cm. Reifenberg Collection. Israel Museum (IDAM), Jerusalem. Photo: © Erich Lessing / Art Resource, N.Y.

Plate W. Scale model of Jerusalem and the Second Temple at the time of King Herod the Great (ca. 20 B.C.E.). The picture shows the Temple compound. Holy Land Hotel, Jerusalem. Photo: © Erich Lessing / Art Resource, N.Y.

part of a strategy of centralization and tightening control in light of the Assyrian threat. But if Hezekiah attempted to suppress the high places, he had little success. All these cults were flourishing a century later when Josiah undertook his reform.

Sennacherib's Invasion

It is uncertain whether Hezekiah was already on the throne at the time of the destruction of Samaria. Jerusalem escaped destruction at that time, presumably by paying tribute. Sargon II, who resettled Samaria, claimed in an inscription to be "the subduer of the country of Judah which is far away" (*ANET*, 287). The main narrative in 2 Kings is concerned with events after the death of Sargon in 705 B.C.E. Hezekiah had made preparations for rebellion. This included the construction of the Siloam tunnel, to bring the water from the Gihon spring to a more secure location (the construction of the tunnel is the subject of a famous inscription, *ANET*, 321). He also formed an alliance with other kings in the area. Inevitably, the rebels relied on Egyptian support. The new Assyrian king, Sennacherib, had to attend to rebellions in various areas, including Babylon, but in 701 he turned his attention to Syria-Palestine. The campaign is described in his inscriptions (*ANET*, 287–88) and in 2 Kings

18–19. The account in Kings is repeated in Isaiah 36–37, although the first paragraph, 2 Kgs 18:13-16, is not found in Isaiah.

Sennacherib describes his dealings with Hezekiah as follows:

As to Hezekiah, the Jew, he did not submit to my yoke, I laid siege to 46 of his strong cities, walled forts and to the countless small villages in their vicinity and conquered (them) by means of well-stamped (earth)ramps, and battering-rams brought (thus) near (to the walls) (combined with) the attack by foot soldiers, (using) mines, breeches as well as sapper work. I drove out (of them) 200,150 people, young and old, male and female, horses, mules, donkeys, camels, big and small cattle beyond counting, and considered (them) booty.

Fig. 14.1. The Siloam tunnel, cut through the rock at Jerusalem, by order of King Hezekiah. Photo: © Erich Lessing / Art Resource, N.Y.

Himself I made a prisoner in Jerusalem, his royal residence, like a bird in a cage. . . . Thus I reduced his country, but I still increased the tribute. (*ANET*, 288)

The tribute included thirty talents of gold, eight hundred talents of silver, and Hezekiah's own daughters, concubines, and male and female musicians. The biblical account says that Hezekiah paid thirty talents of gold and three hundred talents of silver (2 Kgs 18:14). Hezekiah gave the Assyrians all the silver that was in the house of the Lord and in his own palace, and he stripped the gold from the doors and doorposts in the temple. There is, then, reasonable correspondence between the Assyrian account and 2 Kgs 18:14-16. The Assyrian records also confirm that Hezekiah was neither killed nor deposed and that Jerusalem was not destroyed.

The biblical account continues, however, with a colorful and problematic narrative. Assyrian emissaries come up to Jerusalem from Lachish and taunt the king. The gods of other peoples had not been able to rescue them from the god of Assyria. Faced with humiliation and disaster, Hezekiah consults the prophet Isaiah. This is a rare mention of a canonical prophet in the historical books. (Jonah is mentioned briefly in 2 Kgs 14:25.) Since this material is repeated in the book of Isaiah, I shall discuss Isaiah's response in that context, in light of Isaiah's whole career.

The manner of the deliverance is miraculous. The angel of the Lord struck down 185,000 in the camp of the Assyrians. Sennacherib had no choice but to return home. What are we to make of this as a historical report?

It is certainly surprising that Sennacherib did not destroy Jerusalem. Various explanations are possible. An epidemic in the Assyr-

ian army might have given rise to the tradition that the angel of the Lord had intervened. Another possibility is suggested by the words of Isaiah in 2 Kgs 19:7: "I will put a spirit in him so that he shall hear a rumor and return to his own land." No doubt, Sennacherib could have conquered Jerusalem, but it would have taken time. He may have had pressing affairs back home. Timely submission by Hezekiah may have saved the city and his own life.

There is no doubt that Judah was brought to its knees by the Assyrians, but the more remarkable thing was that the city was not destroyed. This unexpected deliverance is celebrated in the story of the angel of the Lord. It contributed to the myth of the inviolability of Zion. According to Ps 46:5, "God is in the midst of the city; it shall not be moved; God will help it when the morning dawns." Psalm 48 tells how kings who came up against Jerusalem were seized with panic and fled. It is possible that these psalms were inspired by the fact that Sennacherib did not destroy Jerusalem. More probably, the belief that the city was protected by YHWH was older, but it was powerfully reinforced by this deliverance. A century later, the confidence inspired by this myth would prove to be false—when the city was destroyed by the Babylonians.

The End of the Kingdom of Judah

The "good" King Hezekiah is followed in 2 Kings 21 by Manasseh, who reigns for 55 years and does everything of which the Deuteronomists disapprove, restoring the high places that Hezekiah had torn down, erecting altars for Baal, and even making his son "pass through fire" as a burnt offering. The Deuteronomists paint Manasseh in lurid colors, in part to explain why there were so many abuses when Josiah came to the throne, and in part to explain the fate that ultimately befell Judah, despite the reforms of Hezekiah and Josiah. According to 21:10-15, it is because of the sins of Manasseh that the Lord resolves to destroy Jerusalem.

I have already discussed the reforms of Josiah in connection with the book of Deuteronomy. The account indirectly gives a vivid picture of religion in Judah before the reform, with widespread worship of Baal and Asherah. The reforms represent the climax of the Deuteronomistic History. We might expect that the reform would earn Judah a reprieve in the eyes of the Lord, but this is not what happens. Josiah is killed by the pharaoh at Megiddo. The parallel account in 2 Chron 35:20-24 makes clear that Josiah went to fight the pharaoh. The account in Kings is ambiguous. The pharaoh may have had him executed. The premature death of the reforming king confounds the expectations of Deuteronomic theology. The editors, however, provide an explanation. Josiah is to be spared the destruction of Jerusalem by the Babylonians. The problem with this explanation is that death at the hands of the pharaoh was hardly a peaceful demise.

Year 7, month of Kislimu: The king of Akkad moved his army into Haddi land, laid siege to the city of Judah, and the king took the city on the second day of the month Addaru. He appointed in it a (new) king to his liking, took heavy booty from it and brought it into Babylon.
—Babylonian Chronicle, trans. A. Leo Oppenheim; ANET, 564.

The actual account of the destruction of Jerusalem is quite terse. (An even terser account is found in the Babylonian Chronicles). Babylon now replaced Assyria as the invading power, under the leadership of Nebuchadnezzar II. Josiah's son Jehoiakim submitted for a while, but then revolted. He died before he could be punished. His son Jehoiachin promptly surrendered and was taken prisoner to Babylon in 597 b.c.e., together with thousands of the upper echelon of Judean society. Jehoiachin's uncle, Zedekiah, was made king in his place. He served Babylon for a time but eventually succumbed to the temptation to rebel. His punishment was brutal. His sons were killed before his eyes, and his eyes were then put out. Jerusalem was destroyed and the temple burned down. The Babylonians allegedly carried into exile "all the rest of the population," except for some of the poorest people, who were left to be vinedressers and tillers of the soil (25:12).

The Deuteronomistic explanation of these disastrous events is simple, even simplistic: "Surely this came upon Judah at the command of the LORD, to remove them out of his sight, for the sins of Manasseh" (24:3). Babylonian policy and Near Eastern politics are of little account. It was a merit of this explanation that it encouraged the Jewish people to look to themselves for the cause of their misfortunes rather than to pity themselves as the victims of history. But, ultimately, this explanation of history would not prove satisfactory. It placed too much blame on the victims.

The Deuteronomistic History, however, ends on a positive note. After thirty-seven years of exile, King Jehoiachin was released from prison and treated with respect by the king of Babylon. Life would go on. Jewish exiles would return to Jerusalem. The destruction of the states of Israel and Judah would set the stage for the emergence of Judaism as a worldwide religion.

Further Reading

Commentaries

Cogan, Mordechai, and Hayim Tadmor. *II Kings*. AB 11. New York: Doubleday, 1988.

Long, Burke O. *2 Kings*. FOTL 10. Grand Rapids: Eerdmans, 1991.

Seow, C. L. "The First and Second Books of Kings." In *NIB* 3:1–296.

Historical Issues

Finkelstein, Israel, and Neil Asher Silberman. *The Bible Unearthed: Archaeology's New Vision of Ancient Israel and the Origin of Its Sacred Texts*. New York: Free Press, 2001, 206–25, 229–95.

Miller, J. Maxwell, and John H. Hayes. *A History of Ancient Israel and Judah*, 314–415. Philadelphia: Westminster, 1986.

Literary and Redactional Studies

Knoppers, Gary N. *Two Nations under God: The Deuteronomistic History of Solomon and the Dual Monarchies*. Vol. 2: *The Reign of Jeroboam, the Fall of Israel, and the Reign of Josiah*. HSM 53. Atlanta: Scholars Press, 1994.

McKenzie, Steven L. *The Trouble with Kings: The Composition of the Book of Kings in the Deuteronomistic History*. VTSup 42. Leiden: Brill, 1991.

Rofé, Alexander. *The Prophetical Stories*. Jerusalem: Magnes, 1988.

Sweeney, Marvin A. *King Josiah of Judah: The Lost Messiah of Israel*. New York: Oxford Univ. Press, 2001.

15

Amos and Hosea

KEY POINTS

- **Prophecy** in the ancient Near East.
  Mari
  Assyria
- **Amos**: "I am no prophet."
- **Structure of the book:**
  Oracles against various nations, concluding with Israel
  (1:3 –2:16).
  Short oracles (chaps. 3–6).
  Vision reports (chaps. 7–9).
- **Israel and the nations**: no special privilege.
- The **Day of the Lord** as a day of judgment.
- **Social justice** is more important than the sacrificial cult.

- An **end** is coming to Israel.
- "Are you not like the **Ethiopians** to me?"
- The **Judean edition** of Amos.
- **Hosea**: 2 main sections:
  Chaps 1-3: the marriage metaphor for a covenantal
  relationship.
  Chaps 4-14: religion and politics in the last years of Israel.
- **Critique of the cult.**
- **Critique of royal politics.**
- **When Israel was a child**: human analogies for God.
- The **Judean redaction** of Hosea.

Introduction

The word "prophecy" comes from the Greek *prophētēs*, "proclaimer," and refers to one who speaks on behalf of a god or goddess. Prophets typically receive their revelations in a state of ecstasy, either by seeing visions or by direct inspiration. In the Hebrew Bible, the most frequent term for such intermediaries is *nābî'*, which probably means "one who is called." "Seers" (*rō'eh*, *ḥōzeh*) and "men of God" are also used. Prophecy is distinguished from divination, which attempts to discern the will of the deity by technical means.

Prophecy in the Ancient Near East

Prophecy was widespread in the ancient Near East. One major source of information is found in the royal archives of Mari on the Euphrates, from the eighteenth century B.C.E. The oracles typically assure the king of success or warn of dangers. They sometimes warn that cultic acts have been neglected. While these prophecies were taken seriously, they seem to have been regarded as inferior to technical divination and were subject to confirmation by court diviners.

Another major source is found in Assyrian archives from the seventh century B.C.E. Here again, the texts come from royal archives and typically provide assurance of divine support in time of crisis, often telling the king to "fear not." Not all Assyrian oracles were favorable to the kings or accepted as authentic. One of the treaty texts of Esarhaddon requires the vassal to inform the king of any negative utterance by a prophet.

Apart from these Mesopotamian archives, there is other scattered evidence. The tale of the Egyptian Wen-Amon, from the eleventh century B.C.E., reports a case of ecstatic prophecy in the Canaanite or Phoenician coastal city of Byblos (*ANET*, 26). A plaster inscription from Tell Deir 'Alla in Jordan, from about 700 B.C.E., refers to Balaam, son of Beor, a "seer of the gods" (cf. Numbers 22–24). An inscription from Syria from about 800 B.C.E. reports how King Zakkur of Hamath prayed to Baal-shamayn during a siege, and Baal answered him by means of visionaries and told him to "fear not."

Prophecy in Israel

It is of the essence of prophecy that the prophets addressed specific situations in highly concrete terms. Nonetheless, like many of the Assyrian prophecies, the biblical oracles come to us embedded in collections that were made for later generations. Moreover, the biblical prophetic books are often edited with later situations in mind. There is inevitable tension between the words of the prophets in their original context and the "canonical shape" given to their oracles by later editors. Much of the history of scholarship over the last two hundred years has been concerned primarily with the original words of the prophets. In recent years

the pendulum has swung toward a focus on the final form of the prophetic books in their canonical context. Both interests are clearly legitimate, and even necessary, but it is important to recognize the tension between them. The historical prophets whose oracles are preserved in these books were often highly critical of the political and religious establishments of their day. The scribes who edited their books were part of the establishment of later generations. Consequently, they often try to place the older oracles in the context of an authoritative tradition. The editorial process often takes the edge off powerful prophetic oracles and dulls their effect. The preference of an interpreter for the original prophets or for the canonical editors often reflects his or her trust or distrust of political and religious institutions in general.

Amos

The preface to the book of Amos identifies him as a shepherd from Tekoa and dates his prophecy to the time of King Jeroboam son of Joash (785–745 B.C.E.). Tekoa is in Judah, some ten miles south of Jerusalem. Yet Amos seems to have prophesied at Bethel, which was one of the royal sanctuaries of the northern kingdom but was only ten to eleven miles north of Jerusalem. Did Amos regard the boundary between Israel and Judah as insignificant because all were one people of YHWH? Or was he a Davidic loyalist, who was especially critical of the cult at Bethel because of the separation of the northern kingdom from Jerusalem? There is no doubt that the book in its canonical form presents a Judean perspective. In 1:2 "The LORD roars from Zion," and the concluding promise is that the Lord will raise up "the booth of David that is fallen" (9:11-15). It is not at all clear, however, that the eighth-century prophet Amos was promoting Davidic rule. He was also critical of "those who are at ease in Zion" (6:1). It might have been more difficult to preach in Jerusalem, on the doorstep of the king, than in Bethel, where he was at some distance from the royal court.

Amos prophesied the destruction of the northern kingdom. His prophecy was fulfilled by the Assyrian destruction of Samaria in 722 B.C.E. But the Assyrian threat was not in evidence during the reign of Jeroboam and developed only in the reign of Tiglath-pileser III, whose reign began about the time of Jeroboam's death. Amos never mentions Assyria in his oracles, but a few passages refer to the punishment of exile, which was typical Assyrian policy (5:5, 27). These oracles are more easily explained if they are dated somewhat later, when Assyria was a threat to Israel.

Apart from the introductory preface, the only biographical notice is in 7:10-14, which relates an encounter between Amos and the priest of Bethel. Amos was preaching that divine punishment was about to befall the kingdom of Israel. The priest, Amaziah, was understandably nervous about this. Therefore he tells Amos to go back to Judah, for Bethel is a royal sanctuary and loyal to Jeroboam. The response of Amos has given rise to much commentary: "I am no prophet, nor the son of a prophet." The Hebrew literally reads: "No prophet I" (the term for "prophet" is *nābî'*). Some scholars translate, "I was no prophet," since Amos goes on to say that he was a herdsman and a dresser of sycamores until the Lord called him. But Amos does not say that he became a *nābî'*, and Amaziah calls him not a *nābî'* but a *ḥōzeh* (seer). The point is that Amos is not a member of a prophetic guild, of the "sons of the prophets" who ate at the king's table (cf. 1 Kings 22). He is a freelancer and not beholden to the king.

The style of Amos's prophecy is confrontational, in the tradition of Elijah rather than that of Nathan. The prophecy that Amaziah's wife would become a prostitute could only enrage the priest. It may also have functioned as a curse that was intended to bring about what was predicted. We do not know what happened to Amaziah. Jeroboam certainly did not die by the sword. That this prophecy was not fulfilled argues strongly for its authenticity. Why would a later editor have ascribed to Amos a prophecy that was manifestly incorrect? The editors may have felt that Amos's prophecies were substantially fulfilled by the Assyrian conquest and may have added the references to the exile of Israel to clarify the point.

The Oracles of Amos

The book of Amos can be divided into three parts: (1) a series of oracles against various nations, concluding with Israel (1:3—2:16); (2) a collection of short oracles (chaps. 3–6); and (3) a series of vision reports, with the account of the confrontation with Amaziah (chaps. 7–9).

The Oracles against the Nations

We have seen the kind of situation in which oracles against foreign nations might be uttered in 1 Kings 22, where the prophets conduct a pep rally before the start of a military campaign. There are long sections of such oracles in other prophetic books (e.g., Isaiah 13–19; Jeremiah 46–51). The nations mentioned here are Israel's immediate neighbors. The list has been expanded in the course of transmission. The focus on "the law of the LORD" in the oracle against Judah is Deuteronomic and contrasts with the highly specific charges in the other oracles. But the structure of this section is clear enough. Israelite prophets were expected to denounce foreign nations. The shock comes when Amos denounces Israel just like all the others.

The grounds for the denunciations are generally humanistic. Damascus threshed Gilead (in Transjordan) with sledges of iron. Gaza sold entire communities as slaves to Edom. The Ammonites ripped open pregnant women in Gilead. Each of these cases could be read as instances of aggression against Israel, but Amos's concerns are not nationalistic. So he condemns Moab "because he burned to lime the bones of the king of Edom" (2:1). This is a crime of one Gentile against another and can only be viewed as a crime against humanity. Amos operates with a concept of universal justice, such as we often find in the wisdom literature.

The accusations against Israel are likewise humanistic in nature. To be sure, they also evoke the laws of the Pentateuch (e.g., Exod 22:25 and Deut 24:17, garments taken in pledge). The condemnation of father and son who sleep with the same girl (2:7) is at least in the spirit of Leviticus 20. The entire condemnation of Israel has been read as an example of a "covenant lawsuit" or *rib* (the Hebrew word for disputation). YHWH reminds the Israelites of the favors he has shown them and threatens them with punishment because of their disobedience. The structure of the argument, which appeals both to the recollection of history and to the consequences of obedience or disobedience, is similar to the "covenant form" derived from ancient Near Eastern treaties, especially in Deuteronomy. Some scholars suspect, however, that the similarity to Deuteronomy is due to Deuteronomistic editors. The concern for prophets and nazirites in vv. 11-12 seems out of context in Amos. The oracle against Israel is similar to those against the other nations except for vv. 9-12, precisely the verses that give the passage a Deuteronomic, covenantal flavor.

The point at issue here is important for understanding the ethics of a prophet such as Amos and his place in the history of Israelite religion. One view of the subject regards the covenant as foundational and assumes that such a covenant was known already in the beginnings of Israel, before the rise of the monarchy. On this view, prophets such as Amos were traditionalists, calling Israel back to the observance of its original norms. The other view sees the covenant as found in Deuteronomy as a late development, influenced by the preaching of the prophets. On this view, the prophets were highly original figures who changed the nature of Israelite religion and influenced its ultimate formulation in the Bible. The second view does not deny that the exodus was celebrated in the Israelite cult before the rise of the prophets or that there was a concept of election of Israel from early times. The issue is whether that concept of election entailed moral obligation or was tied to a corpus of laws in the earlier period.

The Central Oracles

The understanding of the exodus and of the election of Israel is brought to the fore in Amos 3:2, "You alone have I known of all the families of the earth; therefore I will punish you for all your iniquities." If YHWH has known Israel alone, this should be good news. As in the series of oracles against the nations, Amos subverts the expectations of his hearers. Amos does not dispute that YHWH brought Israel out of Egypt, but he questions the significance attached to it. Election only means greater responsibility.

Two themes predominate in the central oracles of Amos. One is social injustice. Colorful examples are found in 4:1-3, which caricatures the women of Samaria as "cows of Bashan" (Bashan was a fertile area in Transjordan), and 6:4-7, which derides those who lie on beds of ivory and drink wine from bowls. The luxury of Samaria is confirmed by archaeology. One of the most spectacular finds was a collection of ivories, which came from furniture and inlaid walls in the royal palaces. Amos even condemns music as part of the excessive luxury. Those who were at ease, whether in Zion or Samaria, enjoyed their leisure at the expense of the poor, who were forced into slavery when they could not pay their debts.

Fig. 15.1. Kneeling falcon-headed god with small seated Maat. Samaria. Israel Museum (IDAM), Jerusalem. Photo: © Erich Lessing / Art Resource, N.Y.

The other recurring theme is condemnation of the cult, especially at Bethel. "Come to Bethel and transgress; to Gilgal and multiply transgressions" (4:4). It is possible to read this pronouncement from a Deuteronomistic perspective: the cult at Bethel was inherently sinful because it was not in Jerusalem. No doubt this is how the passage was read by many after Josiah's reform.

The original concerns of Amos, however, emerge most clearly in 5:18-27. This famous passage pronounces woe on those "who desire the day of the LORD" (5:18). There has been much debate as to what is meant by "the day of the LORD." In later times it came to mean the day of judgment. In this context, however, it clearly refers to a cultic celebration, perhaps the Festival of Tabernacles or Sukkoth, which was known as "the feast of YHWH" in later times. Tabernacles was celebrated at the end of the grape harvest. It was a joyful festival, marked by drinking wine. It was a day of light, in the sense of being a joyful occasion. For Amos, however, the day of the Lord was darkness and not light, gloom with no brightness. He is sweeping in his rejection of the sacrificial cult, in all its aspects. Instead, he asks that "justice roll down like waters."

> Alas for you who desire the day of the LORD!
>   Why do you want the day of the LORD?
> It is darkness, not light;
>   as if someone fled from a lion,
>   and was met by a bear;
> or went into the house and rested a hand
>   against the wall,
>   and was bitten by a snake.
> Is not the day of the LORD darkness, not light,
>   and gloom, with no brightness in it?
> I hate, I despise your festivals,
>   and I take no delight in your solemn
>   assemblies.
> Even though you offer me your burnt offerings
>   and grain offerings,
>   I will not accept them;
> and the offerings of well-being of your fatted
>   animals
>   I will not look upon.
> Take away from me the noise of your songs;
>   I will not listen to the melody of your harps.
> But let justice roll down like waters,
>   and righteousness like an everflowing
>   stream.
> —Amos 5:18-24

Criticism of the sacrificial cult is a prominent theme in the eighth-century prophets, and it was directed against the cult in Jerusalem as well as that in Bethel (cf. Isa 1:12-17; Mic 6:6-8; Hos 6:6). It is difficult to imagine that anyone in antiquity could have envisioned the worship of a deity without any organized cult or without offerings of some sort. But the prophets are not addressing the problem in the abstract. They are reacting to the cult as they knew it. In the case of Amos, the rejection is unequivocal. He does not say that sacrifice would be acceptable if the people practiced justice. The rhetorical question, "Did you bring to me sacrifices and offerings the forty years in the wilderness?" (5:25) clearly implies the answer no. Amos presumably did not know the priestly laws of Leviticus. The question implies that people could serve God satisfactorily without sacrifices and offerings.

The critique of the cult puts in sharp focus the question of what is important in religion. For Amos to serve God is to practice justice. The slaughter of animals and the feasting and celebration that accompanied sacrifice did not contribute to that goal. On the contrary, it gave the people a false sense of security, since they felt they were fulfilling their obligations to their God when in fact they were not. For this reason, sacrifices, even if offered at great expense, were not only irrelevant to the service of God, but actually an impediment to it. The service of God is about justice. It is not about offerings at all.

The Visions

Chapters 7–9 report a series of five visions, each of which warns of a coming judgment. The message of Amos is summed up concisely in 8:1-2. The vision involves a wordplay in Hebrew. He sees "a basket of summer fruit" (Hebrew *qāyṣ*) and is told that "the end"

(Hebrew *qēṣ*) is coming on Israel. The expectation of "the end" later comes to be associated especially with apocalyptic literature, such as the book of Daniel. (The word "eschatology," the doctrine of the last things, is derived from the Greek word for "end," *eschaton*.) Eventually it comes to mean the end of the world. In Amos it means simply the end of Israel. In fact, a few decades after Amos spoke, the kingdom of northern Israel was brought to an end by the Assyrians and was never reconstituted.

The final vision concerns the destruction of the temple at Bethel. The most striking passage in this chapter is found in 9:7-8: "Are you not like the Ethiopians to me, O people of Israel?" The cult at Bethel celebrated the exodus as the defining experience of Israel. The people who celebrated it either did not think it entailed covenantal obligations or paid no heed to them. The significance of the exodus was that it marked Israel as the special people of YHWH. Amos does not deny that God brought Israel out of Egypt, but he radically questions its significance. It was the same God who brought the Philistines from Caphtor (Crete) and the Arameans from Kir (location unknown, but cf. Amos 1:5; 2 Kgs 16:9). For Amos, YHWH is the God of all peoples and responsible for everything that happens, good and bad. The movements of the Arameans and Philistines were just as providential as those of the Israelites. In the eyes of God, Israel is no different than the Ethiopians.

The final word of Amos is found in 9:8a-b: "The eyes of the Lord GOD are upon the sinful kingdom, and I will destroy it from the face of the earth." It is unthinkable that the prophet from Tekoa would have added "except that I will not utterly destroy the house of Jacob." To do so would have taken the sting out of the oracle of judgment. For a later editor, however, the addition was necessary. After all, Judah was also part of the house of Jacob.

The Judean Edition of Amos

Naturally enough, Amos found little acceptance from the political and priestly leadership of the northern kingdom. His oracles were preserved in Judah. No doubt, people were impressed that the destruction he had predicted happened a mere generation later. The final edition of the book was probably after the Babylonian exile. A few passages stand out as editorial markers. These include the superscription in 1:1, explaining who Amos was, and the verse asserting the priority of Jerusalem as the abode of God in 1:2. The oracle against Judah, "because they have rejected the law of the LORD" (2:4), betrays the influence of the Deuteronomic reform. The book is punctuated by doxologies, short passages giving praise and glory to God (4:13; 5:8-9; 9:5-6). The most notable editorial addition, however, is found in 9:11-15, which promises that "on that day" the Lord will raise up the booth of David that is fallen. The phrase "on that day" often indicates an editorial insertion in the prophetic books. Such passages give the whole book an eschatological cast, insofar as they purport to speak about a time in the indefinite future when the conditions of history will be radically altered. The "fallen" booth of David indicates that this passage dates after the Babylonian exile. It looks for a restoration of the kingship in Jerusalem under the Davidic line. The editors ended on a note of hope. Judah, after all, survived its destruction, and the hope remained that YHWH would yet fulfill his promise to David.

Hosea

Hosea was a younger contemporary of Amos. He prophesied in the reign of Jeroboam of Israel, but also in the reigns of Uzziah, Jotham, Ahaz, and Hezekiah of Judah. Since even Uzziah's reign extended after the death of Jeroboam, it is clear that the editor had a Judean perspective, even though Hosea was a northern prophet.

The book falls into two main sections. Chapters 1–3 are dominated by the metaphor of marriage to a promiscuous woman, which serves as a metaphor for the relationship of YHWH and Israel. Chapters 4–14 comment on the political and religious affairs of the northern kingdom in the last decades of its existence.

The Marriage Metaphor

Hosea is commanded by the Lord to "take for yourself a wife of whoredom and have children of whoredom." One of the ways in which prophets communicated with their audience was by symbolic action. (Cf. Isaiah 20, where the prophet goes naked and barefoot for three years.) Hosea's marriage must be seen in that context. Some scholars have suggested that Hosea discovered his wife's promiscuous disposition only after he married her, but the symbolism of the action requires that she was known to be promiscuous from the start. Some have thought that she must have been a prostitute, perhaps even a sacred prostitute who played a ritual part in the cult of the Canaanite god Baal. Recent scholarship, however, has cast severe doubt on whether prostitution played any part in the cult of Baal. Hosea's wife may have been a prostitute, or she may have been a woman with a reputation for promiscuous behavior.

> When the LORD first spoke through Hosea, the LORD said to Hosea, "Go, take for yourself a wife of whoredom and have children of whoredom, for the land commits great whoredom by forsaking the LORD."
> —Hosea 1:2

The children of Hosea and his wife, Gomer, are made to bear the prophet's message by symbolic names. The first was named Jezreel, the summer palace of the kings of Israel. It was at Jezreel that Jehu had slaughtered Jezebel and the royal family (2 Kings 9). According to 2 Kings, Jehu acted with the sanction of the prophet Elisha, but his bloodshed nonetheless warranted punishment in the eyes of Hosea. The second child is named *lō' ruḥāmāh*, which may be translated "not pitied" or "not loved" (the name is related to the Hebrew word for womb, *reḥem*). The point is that Israel will no longer be pitied. The third child receives an even harsher name, *lō' 'ammî*, "not my people." The phrase echoes the common formula for divorce ("she is not my wife") and reverses the common formula for marriage. The optimistic conclusion to the chapter is surely supplied by an editor.

The use of Hosea's marriage as metaphor implies a covenantal relationship. It is clear that Hosea, like Amos, saw this relationship as conditional. It entailed certain ethical and cultic requirements. If Israel failed to comply, the relationship could be broken off. All of this corresponds to the understanding of the Mosaic covenant in Exodus and Deuteronomy. It is also clear that the people addressed by the prophets did not share that understanding. Instead of the analogy of international treaties, Hosea uses marriage as his guiding metaphor.

The marriage metaphor is developed at length in chapter 2. This long poetic oracle is presented as a legal indictment (Hebrew *rîb*). It is sometimes called a "covenant lawsuit," but the metaphor is one of divorce proceedings rather than of treaty violation. The grounds for divorce are the wife's adultery. In ancient Israel, only the husband could initiate divorce, and the view of adultery was usually one-sided, a point noted later by Hosea (4:14). The punishment for adultery here, "I will strip her naked," is not attested elsewhere in the Hebrew Bible, except in Ezek 16:37-39, which may be influenced by Hosea (cf. also the story of Susanna 1:32). In biblical law the punishment for adultery is death by stoning (Deut 22:23-24; both Ezekiel and Susanna also envision an ultimate death penalty). In Genesis 38 Judah condemns Tamar to be burned. The punishment of stripping allows the prophet in Hosea 2 to speak metaphorically of the stripping of the land, to make it like a wilderness.

The adultery of Israel consisted of worshiping Baal, the Canaanite god, who was widely revered in the northern kingdom of Israel. Baal was attractive because he was a fertility deity, the "rider of the clouds" and bringer of rain. People believed that he provided "the grain, the wine, and the oil." Hosea insists to the contrary that YHWH is the deity who provides these goods. (Compare the story of Elijah and the prophets of Baal.)

Hosea differs from Amos in two crucial respects. First, the primary sin of which Israel is accused is Baal worship. Hosea is also concerned about social justice, but it plays a secondary role. Second, he vacillates between judgment and oracles of salvation. The wilderness was, on the one hand, a place of death and punishment. But it was also the place where Israel had encountered YHWH in the exodus tradition. Hosea recalls the wilderness period of the exodus as the courtship of YHWH and Israel. If Israel is again reduced to wilderness, this is also an opportunity for a new beginning. Israel would no longer address its god as "baal," which meant "lord, husband" (but was also the name of the god), but as *'îšî*, "my man/husband," with a connotation of partnership rather than subordination. In effect, YHWH and Israel would renew their marriage.

The marriage metaphor for the relationship between God and Israel is not without its problems. The prophet takes the common assumptions about the roles of husband and wife as his point of departure. The adulterous wife could be humiliated and even put to death. It is not the purpose of Hosea 1–3 to say how husbands should treat their wives but to explain how YHWH reacts to Israel's behavior. The use of human analogy is one of the most distinctive and appealing aspects of Hosea's prophecy, but it runs the danger of making God conform to the cultural norms of the time. Should God behave like a jealous or outraged husband? Hosea was not unaware of the problem of using human analogies for God (cf. chap. 11), but he does not reflect on it in his use of the marriage metaphor. Moreover, there is always the danger that people may take the conduct ascribed to God as exemplary. If God can strip and expose Israel, may not a human husband punish an unfaithful wife in like manner? The very negative use of female imagery in the prophets has contributed to negative stereotypes of women and even, on occasion, to physical abuse.

Chapters 4–14

The main corpus of oracles in Hosea begins with another indictment: There is no faithfulness or loyalty and no knowledge of God in the land. Instead, there is "swearing, lying, murder, stealing, and adultery." All these sins are mentioned in the Decalogue. Accordingly, many scholars see here another "covenant lawsuit." Hosea links law and covenant explicitly in 8:1: "They have broken my covenant and transgressed my law." There is a close relationship between Hosea and Deuteronomy. Both condemn the worship at the high places in similar language. Both use the exodus as a major point of reference. Both speak of the danger of "forgetting" God (Hos 2:13; 8:14; 13:6; Deut 6:12; 8:14, 19). Both emphasize the love of God. They differ insofar as "love" in Deuteronomy refers to the loyalty of a vassal, whereas Hosea conceives it on the analogy of the love between husband and wife or father and son (chap. 11). Hosea stands in the same tradition as Deuteronomy and shares much, though not all, of its understanding of the covenantal relationship. Like Deuteronomy, Hosea makes clear that while the covenant requires the observance of laws, it more fundamentally requires an underlying attitude of faithfulness, loyalty, and "knowledge of God" (cf. the emphasis on the love of God in Deut 6:5).

Priesthood and Cult

Hosea is scarcely less vehement than Amos in his criticism of the priests and their cult. His charges against the priests are outlined in 4:4-14. He appears to reject sacrifice in chapter 6: "I desire steadfast love and not sacrifice." Hosea is not interested in reforming the sacrificial cult any more than Amos was. Sacrifices are not what the Lord wants, and those who offer them are misled into thinking they have fulfilled their obligations when they have not.

The Critique of Royal Politics

Unlike Amos, Hosea does not dwell on the theme of social injustice. He comments repeatedly, however, on the political intrigue that racked the kingdom of Israel in the final decades of its existence. Hosea finds little to approve in this tragic history. His basic critique is that Israel repeatedly looked for political solutions instead of turning to the service of YHWH. The reliance on Egypt is especially ironic in view of Israel's origin. Israel only ensured its own destruction by its attempts to resist Assyria and to form coalitions against it. Furthermore, attempts to solve its problems by changing kings were futile.

The Understanding of God

No book of the Hebrew Bible is so rich in metaphorical expressions as Hosea. Often the metaphors are applied to Israel, either to express YHWH's affection for her ("like grapes in the wilderness," 9:10), or her wayward behavior ("a luxuriant vine," 10:1). Even more striking is Hosea's use of metaphor to portray God. I have already explored one such metaphor, the jealous husband. In chapter 11 Hosea develops another: the loving father. Here God remembers Israel as a child, whom he taught to walk and lifted to his cheek. So now, despite their disobedience, he cannot bring himself to destroy them. "I will not execute my fierce anger; I will not again destroy Ephraim; for I am God and no mortal, the Holy One in your midst, and I will not come in wrath" (11:9). On the one hand, God is portrayed in very human terms as someone who can be overcome by emotion. On the other hand, he is "God and no mortal." What then is the difference between God and a human being? God can overcome the more destructive emotions and be guided by the better, whereas human beings often succumb to the worst. We have no better way to imagine God than in the likeness of human beings, but we should attribute to God what is best in human nature, not human weakness or malevolence.

Unfortunately, the generous promise, "I will not again destroy Ephraim," made perhaps when Samaria survived the invasion of Tiglath-pileser, was not fulfilled. It is contradicted outright in 13:9: "I will destroy you, O Israel; who can help you?" God will not ransom them from the power of Sheol: "O Death, where are your plagues? O Sheol, where is your destruction? Compassion is hidden from my eyes" (13:14; this verse is cited in 1 Cor 15:55 in a very different sense). In the end God's burning anger seems to prevail. The contradictions in Hosea's prophecy arose from the changing fortunes of Israel in its final years. They also illustrate one of the fundamental problems of all human speech about God. On the one hand, there is the conviction, eloquently expressed by Hosea, that God is good and must be imagined in accordance with the highest ideals of humanity. On the other hand, there is belief that God is revealed in history, and specifically in the history of Israel. The first conviction leads to the assertion that God is merciful and compassionate, but this conviction is often hard to reconcile with the death and destruction to which human beings are subject and which were all too often the fate of Israel.

The Judean Edition of Hosea

Like Amos, Hosea was preserved and edited in the south, after the fall of Samaria. Hosea himself had commented on Judah as well as Israel on occasion. So, for example, he comments on the sickness of both Israel and Judah in the context of the Syro-Ephraimite war (5:13). A number of passages, however, contrast Judah with Israel, and these are likely to come from the Judean editors. Hosea 1:7 assures the reader that God will have pity on the house of Judah. Hosea 3:5 inserts a reference to "David, their king" that is inconsistent with Hosea's attitude toward kings of any sort. Hosea 4:15 warns Judah not to become guilty by worshiping at Gilgal or Bethel, probably reflecting the Deuteronomic condemnation of worship outside Jerusalem. Perhaps the most obvious editorial contribution to the book, however, is the positive ending, which promises restoration if only the people will return to the Lord. The final saying ("Those who are wise understand these things") is typical of the wisdom literature and shows the hand of the scribes who were finally responsible for the edition of the book. From the viewpoint of these scribes, the oracles provided a moral lesson on the consequences of following "the ways of the LORD." This lesson could be applied to individuals as well as to kingdoms.

Further Reading

Prophecy in General

Blenkinsopp, Joseph. *A History of Prophecy in Israel*. 2nd ed. Louisville: Westminster John Knox, 1996.

Huffmon, Herbert B. "Prophecy, Ancient Near Eastern." In *ABD* 5:477–82.

Nissinen, Martti, ed. *Prophecy in Its Ancient Near Eastern Context: Mesopotamian, Biblical and Arabian Perspectives*. SBLSymS 13. Atlanta: SBL, 2000.

Petersen, David L. *The Prophetic Literature: An Introduction*. Louisville: Westminster John Knox, 2002.

Sweeney, Marvin A. *The Prophetic Literature*. Nashville: Abingdon, 2005.

———. *The Twelve Prophets*. BerO. Collegeville, Minn.: Liturgical, 2000.

Wilson, Robert R. *Prophecy and Society in Ancient Israel*. Philadelphia: Fortress Press, 1977.

Amos

Jeremias, Jörg. *The Book of Amos*. Trans. D. W. Scott. OTL. Louisville: Westminster John Knox, 1998.

King, Philip J. *Amos, Hosea, Micah: An Archaeological Commentary*. Philadelphia: Westminster John Knox, 1988.

Mays, James Luther. *Amos: A Commentary*. OTL. Philadelphia: Westminster, 1969.

Paul, Shalom M. *Amos*. Hermeneia. Minneapolis: Fortress Press, 1991.

Wolff, Hans Walter. *Amos the Prophet*. Trans. F. R. McCurley. Philadelphia: Fortress Press, 1973.

———. *Joel and Amos*. Hermeneia. Philadelphia: Fortress Press, 1977.

Hosea

Davies, G. I. *Hosea*. Grand Rapids: Eerdmans, 1992.

Sherwood, Y. *The Prostitute and the Prophet: Hosea's Marriage in Literary-Theoretical Perspective*. JSOTSup 212. Sheffield: Sheffield Academic Press, 1996.

Weems, Renita N. "Gomer: Victim of Violence or Victim of Metaphor?" *Semeia* 47 (1989): 87–104.

Wolff, Hans Walter. *Hosea*. Trans. G. Stansell. Hermeneia. Philadelphia: Fortress Press, 1974.

Yee, Gale A. "The Book of Hosea." In *NIB* 7:197–297.

16

Isaiah

```
                                    KEY POINTS

Isaiah: complex book. Compiled over several hundred years.    Chaps 36–39 = 2 Kgs 18:17—20:19.
   Chaps. 1–39: First Isaiah.                               • The Isaianic Memoir: chaps. 6–8.
   Chaps. 40–55: Second Isaiah.                               Call vision in chap. 6.
   Chaps. 56–66: Third Isaiah.                                Prophecy of Immanuel in chap. 7.
   Only part of First Isaiah is likely to derive from the  • Prophecies of an ideal king.
      8th-century prophet.                                    Isa 9:1–7: an enthronement oracle?
   Chaps. 24–27 = the so-called "Apocalypse of Isaiah"       Isa 11:1–9: a messianic king. Probably postexilic.
      (postexilic)                                            Isaiah and social justice: Isaiah 5.
   Chaps. 34–35 are like Second Isaiah.                       Isaiah and Sennacherib.
```

The Book

I saiah is arguably the most complex book in the Hebrew Bible. It is introduced as "the vision of Isaiah son of Amoz, which he saw concerning Judah and Jerusalem in the days of Uzziah, Jotham, Ahaz, and Hezekiah, kings of Judah." The death of Uzziah is dated variously from 742 to 734 B.C.E. A major episode in the book concerns the invasion of Sennacherib in 701 B.C.E. Isaiah, then, was active thirty to forty years.

Only a small part of the book, however, can be associated with the prophet of the eighth century. Chapters 40–66 clearly relate to the Babylonian exile and its aftermath. Cyrus of Persia, who lived in the sixth century B.C.E.,

is mentioned by name in Isa 44:28 and 45:1. These oracles were composed by an anonymous sixth-century prophet dubbed "Second Isaiah" or "Deutero-Isaiah," although there is no evidence that he spoke in the name of Isaiah. Chapters 56–66 are usually distinguished as "Third Isaiah" or "Trito-Isaiah." For the last century or so, it has been customary to refer to chapters 1–39 as "First Isaiah."

Not everything in chapters 1–39 can be attributed to the eighth-century prophet. The oracles against Babylon in chapters 13–14 are most naturally dated to a time after Babylon had replaced Assyria as the dominant power. The provenance of some of the other oracles against foreign nations is uncertain. Isaiah 24–27, often called "the Isaiah apocalypse," is usually dated to a time after the exile, by analogy with other late prophetic writings. Chapters 34 and 35 are similar to Second Isaiah in tone and theme. Several shorter passages in chapters 1–39 appear to date from a time after the Deuteronomic reform (2:1-4) or after the end of the monarchy (11:1-9). Passages introduced by the phrase "on that day" (e.g., 7:18-25; 11:10-11) are usually thought to be editorial additions.

Scholars have labored to find signs of intelligent editorial intentions in the way the book was put together. The final edition was certainly later than the Babylonian exile, and it was guided by thematic rather than historical interests. Even though the vision in chapter 6 is usually thought to describe the call of the prophet, it does not stand at the beginning of the book (contrast Jeremiah and Ezekiel). It may be that it originally introduced a separate booklet, consisting of 6:1—8:22. The final editors, however, were less concerned with the career of Isaiah than with the theme of judgment. This theme is revisited at the end of the book, in chapter 66. Chapters 40–66 were probably attached to chapters 1–39 because of their common concern for the fate of Jerusalem. But, by modern standards, the book as a whole is not tightly structured. Some chapters are grouped together because of either common subject matter (chaps. 7–8) or a common theme (the oracles against the nations in chaps. 13–19). Chronology is sometimes a factor. (Material relating to the Syro-Ephraimite war comes early in the book; the crisis with Sennacherib at the end of "First Isaiah.") In other cases the reason for the placement of oracles is difficult to discern. While we can identify some principles in the editing of the book, the degree of intentionality should not be exaggerated.

In this chapter my concern is with the prophet of the eighth century. I shall reflect on the final shape of the book in chapter 19, "The Additions to the Book of Isaiah."

Isaiah's Vision

Two main sections in the book offer biographical information: chapters 6–8 and chapters 36–39.

Near the end of chapters 6–8 the prophet gives a command to "bind up the testimony, seal the teaching among my disciples" (8:16). Similarly, in 30:8 he says, "Go now, write it before them on a tablet, and inscribe it in a book." Apparently the prophet had a group of disciples who were entrusted with preserving his "testimony." It is plausible to suppose that the testimony in 8:16 contained some form of the prophet's oracles to Ahaz. It is equally plausible that additions were later made to this testimony (e.g., in the passages beginning "on that day"). Chapter 7 is written in the third person and does not pretend to be the prophet's own account. But, whatever the origin of these chapters, they do much to establish the persona of the prophet.

The vision in chapter 6 is similar to the vision of Micaiah ben Imlah in 1 Kings 22. Like Micaiah, Isaiah claims to have seen the Lord seated on his throne. This claim stands in defiance of another biblical tradition, that mortals cannot see God and live (cf. Exod 33:20). In contrast, other prophets (e.g., Jeremiah) experience an auditory call, by hearing only, as Moses did at the burning bush. The report of a vision such as this was a powerful claim for the legitimacy of the prophet.

Unlike the vision of Micaiah, that of Isaiah is set in the Jerusalem temple, where YHWH was believed to be enthroned above the cherubim (cf. Isa 37:16). Micaiah had seen the host of heaven. Isaiah sees "YHWH of hosts," one of his favorite designations for God. The seraphim are "burning ones," representatives of the host in attendance on YHWH. They proclaim the holiness of God, in a form that influenced the liturgical traditions of both Judaism (the q'dûšāh) and Christianity (the *trisagion* or *sanctus*). God is often called "the Holy One of Israel" in all sections of Isaiah.

Isaiah confesses that he is a man of unclean lips, living among an unclean people, and so he is unworthy to see the Lord. It is not apparent that Isaiah is guilty of any specific violation. Any human being is impure in relation to God. Isaiah is purified by having his lips touched with a burning coal. The implication is that the human condition can only be purified by the painful and radical remedy of burning. This will have implications for the fate of the people of Judah.

The discussion in the divine council is rather similar to what was reported by Micaiah ben Imlah. The Lord asks for a volunteer to do his bidding. The prophet volunteers. He is given a strange command:

> Make the mind of this people dull,
>   and stop their ears,
>   and shut their eyes,
> so that they may not look with their eyes,
>   and listen with their ears,
> and comprehend with their minds,
>   and turn and be healed. (6:10)

Isaiah's mission to Ahaz failed, in the sense that Ahaz did not accept his advice. But according to chapter 6, the mission was supposed to fail. There is an obvious analogy here with the hardening of Pharaoh's heart in the book of Exodus. Judah is being set up for punishment. The mission of the prophet only increases the guilt, as now there is no excuse.

The prophet asks how long he must carry out this frustrating mission. The answer implies that he must continue until Judah is utterly destroyed and "the LORD sends everyone far away"—a reference to the Assyrian policy of deportation. Even if a remnant survives, it will be burned again. We shall meet the motif of the remnant again in Isaiah. The final statement,

that "the holy seed is its stump," is an obvious gloss. From the perspective of the postexilic editor, the destruction was not absolute. The image of the stump left room for a new beginning. We shall find a similar image in chapter 11.

The Encounter with Ahaz

Isaiah's encounter with Ahaz is set in the context of the Syro-Ephraimite war (734 B.C.E.), when the kings of Israel and Syria tried to coerce Judah into joining a coalition against Assyria. The prophet meets the king "near the conduit of the upper pool," where he was checking the water supply in anticipation of a siege. Isaiah is accompanied by his son, Shear-yashub (meaning "a remnant shall return"). Isaiah's children, like Hosea's, are walking billboards, bearing their father's message. In chapter 8 we meet Maher-shalal-hash-baz ("hasten for spoil, hurry for plunder"). The implication of the name Shear-yashub is that *only* a remnant shall return. At a time when no Judeans had been taken into exile, this seems like a disastrous prospect. Later the survival of a remnant would be the seed of hope.

Isaiah's prophecy to Ahaz begins like the typical Assyrian prophecies of the day, "Do not fear." The campaign of the Arameans and northern Israelites would fail. Ahaz must have faith and trust that the crisis will pass: "If you are not firm in faith, you will not be made firm" (7:9). The underpinning of this advice is to be found in the Zion theology in the Psalms, which we have already considered in connection with Solomon's temple. Psalm 46 declares that "God is our refuge and strength. . . . Therefore *we will not fear*, though the earth should change, though the mountains shake in the heart of the sea" (emphasis added). It goes on to say that "God is in the midst of the city," and that "the LORD of hosts is with us." But in fact, "when the house of David heard that Aram had allied itself with Ephraim, the heart of Ahaz and the heart of his people shook as the trees of the forest shake before the wind" (7:2). Isaiah challenged Ahaz to believe the proclamation of the psalm, which was easy to recite in times of peace but difficult to accept when there was an enemy at the gates.

Isaiah offers Ahaz a sign. The king demurs, saying that he will not put the Lord to the test, but the answer is hypocritical. The sign would make it more difficult for him to reject the prophet's advice. The actual sign is one of the most controversial passages in the Old Testament: "The young woman is with child and shall bear a son, and shall name him Immanuel." The Hebrew word for "young woman" is 'almāh, which can, but does not necessarily, refer to a virgin (the unambiguous Hebrew word for virgin is bᵉtûlāh). The Greek translation of Isaiah, however, uses the word parthenos, "virgin." This Greek reading was cited in the New Testament as a proof text for the virgin birth of Jesus (Matt 1:23). Consequently, the text was a battleground for Jewish and Christian interpreters for centuries. The medieval Jewish interpreters (Ibn Ezra, Rashi) rightly argued that in order for the sign to be meaningful for Ahaz it had to be fulfilled in his time, not seven hundred years later.

> Again the Lord spoke to Ahaz, saying, Ask a sign of the Lord your God; let it be as deep as Sheol or high as heaven. But Ahaz said, I will not ask, and I will not put the Lord to the test. Then Isaiah said: "Hear then, O house of David! Is it too little for you to weary mortals, that you weary my God also? Therefore the Lord himself will give you a sign. Look, the young woman is with child and shall bear a son, and shall name him Immanuel. He shall eat curds and honey by the time he knows how to refuse the evil and choose the good. For before the child knows how to refuse the evil and choose the good, the land before whose two kings you are in dread will be deserted.
>
> —Isaiah 7:10-16

Various suggestions have been offered for the identity of the young woman. One candidate is the wife of the prophet. In Isa 8:3 Isaiah goes in to "the prophetess" and she conceives Maher-shalal-hash-baz, but then she can hardly have been the mother of Immanuel at about the same time. The more likely candidate is the wife of the king. The name Immanuel, "God is with us," is an allusion to the royal ideology; compare Psalm 46:7, "The Lord of hosts is with us" (cf. also 2 Sam 7:9; 1 Kgs 1:37; 11:38; Ps 89:21, 24). The birth of a royal child would have greater import for Ahaz. There has been much debate as to whether the child in question was Hezekiah, but the chronology of the period is confused. It may be significant that 2 Kgs 18:7 says of Hezekiah that "the Lord was with him."

There is no reason to think that Isaiah was predicting a miraculous birth. The birth of a child in the time of crisis was an assurance of hope for the future of the dynasty. Isaiah predicts that the child "shall eat curds and honey by the time he knows how to refuse the evil and choose the good. For before the child knows how to refuse the evil and choose the good, the land before whose two kings you are in dread will be deserted." The crisis will pass within a few years. Milk and honey were the original trademarks of the Promised Land (Exod 3:8, 17; 33:3). Isaiah is assuring Ahaz that the Davidic line will survive and prosper. Such a rosy prediction, however, would be difficult to reconcile with the ominous names of the prophet's children, and there is another side to it. This is brought out in a series of additions to the passage, each introduced by the formula "on that day." Isaiah 7:21-25 explains that "on that day" everyone will eat curds and honey because the population will be decimated. The vineyards will be ravaged and there will be little agriculture. Ahaz might not appreciate a diet of milk and honey, but it would nonetheless be good, even wonderful. Isaiah was not prophesying easy deliverance, but he was affirming that the promises to David would be honored.

The negative side of the prediction is developed in chapter 8. The name of the prophet's second child is a prediction of the destruction of Samaria and Damascus. But there is also judgment against Judah, exacerbated by the refusal of Ahaz to heed the prophet's advice. The people have rejected the waters of Shiloah by failing to put their faith in the promises to David and Zion (cf. the reference in Ps 46:4 to the streams that gladden the city of God). Ahaz showed his lack of faith by appealing to Assyria for help. Therefore the Lord will bring upon them the floodwaters of Assyria, which will be destructive, though not fatal. Like Hosea, Isaiah rejects the attempts of the king and his counselors to solve their problems by political means. Isaiah's advice would have been difficult for any ruler to follow. It required that he simply put his faith in the Lord, not try to defend himself by making alliances, and certainly not by appealing to Assyria. In Isaiah's estimation, YHWH was more to be feared than either the Syrian-Israelite coalition or Assyria.

The Ideal King

There is, however, a very positive oracle appended to chapters 7–8 in 9:1-7 (MT 8:23—9:6), announcing, "Unto us a child is born." The "child" is given hyperbolic names: Wonderful Counselor, Mighty God, Everlasting Father, Prince of Peace. In Christian tradition, this passage is read as a messianic prophecy and used in the Christmas liturgy with reference to the birth of Christ. Some scholars argue that it was originally composed as a messianic prophecy, but there is no indication that a restoration of the kingship is involved. Many scholars

hold that the oracle was originally part of an enthronement liturgy. Compare Psalm 2, where the king is told, "You are my son, this day I have begotten you." The names given to the child can then be taken as the throne names of the king. We have seen in Psalm 45 that the king can be addressed as 'elōhim, "god." The possibility cannot be excluded, however, that the poem celebrates the birth of child in the royal household. A famous analogy for such a birth poem is found in Virgil's Fourth Eclogue.

The oracle refers explicitly to the throne of David and his kingdom in 9:7. Such an oracle would make most sense after the fall of Samaria. We know from archaeological evidence that Jerusalem was greatly expanded at that time, presumably by refugees from the north (cf. 9:3, "You have multiplied the nation"). When there was no longer a king in Samaria, it was possible to rekindle dreams of Davidic rule over all of Israel. If Hezekiah came to the throne in 715 B.C.E., as is suggested by Isa 36:1 (= 2 Kgs 18:13), his enthronement would provide a plausible setting for this poem. The chronology of Hezekiah's reign is problematic, however, and so the matter must remain in doubt.

The king in Isaiah 9 is not a messiah in the later sense of the term—a future king who would restore the Davidic line. He was rather a successor to the throne who was still at the beginning of his reign, when one might hope for great things. This concept of an ideal king is at the root of later messianic expectation.

This theme comes to the fore again in 11:1-9, which is one of the most widely cited messianic texts in the Dead Sea Scrolls and other Jewish literature from around the turn of the era. In this case there is an indication that the Davidic line has been interrupted and must be restored. The metaphor of the shoot sprouting from the stump implies that the tree has been cut down (cf. Job 14:7). The king in question, then, is properly called a messiah. It is possible that Isaiah could have uttered such an oracle after the devastation of Judah by Sennacherib, but it is easier to suppose that it comes from a time after the exile, possibly from the period of the restoration, when some people hoped for a restoration of the Davidic line. The new king would be characterized by wisdom, but above all by the fear of the Lord. Even if this oracle is late, however, it taps into the traditional royal ideology, which also informed the preaching of Isaiah. The hope for a righteous king is found in another oracle of uncertain provenance in 32:1.

The motif of the holy mountain (11:9) also appears in 2:1-5. This motif is especially prominent in Third Isaiah (Isaiah 56–66). While the motif of the holy mountain is old, the idea that *tōrāh*, whether "law" or "instruction," radiates from Jerusalem is typical of the Second Temple period, and probably later than the Deuteronomic reform. The explanation of this oracle is complicated by the fact that it is also found in Mic 4:1-5. This suggests that it was a traditional oracle of uncertain attribution. Here again we have a relatively late oracle that revives old ideas of a mythical kingdom of universal peace.

Themes in the Preaching of Isaiah

Isaiah's encounter with Ahaz during the Syro-Ephraimite war is balanced in chapters 36–38 with an exchange with Hezekiah during the invasion of Sennacherib in 701 B.C.E. In between, the chronological setting of the oracles is only occasionally apparent. It is difficult in many cases to tell whether an oracle came from Isaiah or was added to the collection because it was judged to be thematically appropriate.

Some of the oracles in the early part of the book recall the preaching of Amos. Isaiah also appears to reject the cult absolutely: "trample my courts no more . . . your new moons and your appointed festivals my soul hates" (vv. 12-14). To be sure, he hates them because of the wrongdoing of the people, but he does not entertain the possibility of sacrifices offered by righteous people. The sacrificial cult is a distraction from the real service of the Lord, which is to defend the orphan and plead for the widow. The demand that people "wash yourselves, make yourselves clean" is not intended to substitute one ritual for another. The washing is metaphorical. (This verse was, however, invoked later as a warrant for ritual washings, which proliferated in Judaism around the turn of the era, and for early Christian baptism.) The critique of the cult is repeated in 29:13, which says that the people honor God with their lips, while their hearts are far from him. This passage is quoted in the New Testament in Matt 15:8-9 and Mark 7:6-7.

Isaiah comes close to Amos's concern for social justice in the Song of the Vineyard in chapter 5. The choice of the vineyard may be determined by the kind of offenses that Isaiah was condemning: those who joined house to house and field to field. The story of Naboth's vineyard (1 Kings 20) comes to mind. Small landowners were forced to mortgage their property to pay their debts, and so the land came to be concentrated in fewer and fewer hands. The vineyard was a symbol of luxury. It produced the wine that fueled the drunkenness of the wealthy. Consequently, if "every place where there used to be a thousand vines, worth a thousand shekels of silver, will become thorns and briars" (Isa 7:23), from the prophet's perspective this was not altogether bad. The stripping of the land has much the same function in Isaiah that it had in Hosea. It is the painful but necessary condition for a new beginning.

One of the most characteristic themes of Isaiah's preaching is the condemnation of human pride and the demand for humility before the majesty of God. Isaiah articulates his vision of "the day of the LORD," which has lost its reference to a festival day and is simply the day of judgment: "For the LORD of hosts has a day against all that is proud and lofty, against all that is lifted up and high" (2:12). He is especially derisive of the women of Jerusalem who walk daintily and adorn themselves with jewelry (3:16-24). He is also dismissive of the rulers and counselors, who trust in their own competence (3:1-5). The destruction wrought by the Assyrians, then, served to remind people of the abject condition of humanity and the majesty of God.

In 10:5-19 he describes Assyria as the rod of YHWH's anger. It executes YHWH's punishment on Israel and Judah. But this was not how the Assyrians saw their role, or what they proclaimed in their propaganda. Their pride also required punishment. It was as if an instrument should think itself more important than its maker.

The theme of bringing down the proud is

Isaiah

Isaiah seems to have enjoyed a good relationship with King Hezekiah, who is remembered in the biblical tradition as a good king. But Hezekiah was succeeded by Manasseh, who has a very bad reputation, and so people wondered how Isaiah might have fared in his reign. The story is told in a book called The Ascension of Isaiah, which was transmitted by Christians but may contain some Jewish traditions. It is known to have existed in the early third century C.E. and was composed some time before that.

According to the legend, Isaiah prophesied to Hezekiah that he would become a martyr under Manasseh. Sure enough, after the good king died, Manasseh turned to evil ways and became a servant of Beliar. Isaiah withdrew, first to Bethlehem and then to the mountains. He and his followers spent two years mourning and fasting because of the sins of Manasseh. Then the false prophet Belchira discovered his retreat. (The name seems to be a combination of Belial or Beliar, a name for Satan, and Melchira, "king of evil"). Isaiah was then accused before Manasseh on three grounds: that he had claimed to see God, that he had prophesied the destruction of Jerusalem, and that he had referred to Jerusalem and its people as Sodom and Gomorrah. Manasseh had Isaiah sawn asunder with a wooden saw. Belchira and the false prophets stood by and taunted him.

When Bernhard Duhm, arguably the greatest modern interpreter of Isaiah, proposed that the book of Isaiah should be divided into three parts (First, Second, and Third Isaiah), a conservative reviewer entitled his review "Sawn Asunder."

perhaps the most consistent theme that unites the various oracles in Isaiah 1–39. A classic example is found in 14:12-20, a passage of uncertain provenance. It evokes the myth of the Day Star, son of Dawn, who tried to set his throne above the stars of El and was cast down to the Pit. The higher they rise, the lower they fall. It is essentially the same pattern that we found in the story of Adam and Eve, who tried to be like gods knowing good and evil, only to find that they were naked.

Distaste for human arrogance also underlies the prophet's critique of Jerusalemite politics in chapters 29–31. Isaiah had an especially strong distaste for the class of "wise men" who functioned as political advisers. So he predicts that "the wisdom of the wise shall perish" (29:14; cf. 1 Cor 1:19). The counselors do not consult the Lord, which is to say that they do not pay attention to the prophet.

The recurring element in the plan of the "wise" is to seek help from Egypt (30:1-5; 31:1-3) and trust in horses and chariots. Isaiah formulates the problem concisely: "The Egyptians are human, and not divine; their horses are flesh, and not spirit" (31:3). The contrast between flesh and spirit goes to the heart of Isaiah's theology. That which is merely flesh, which is to say mortal, human, is of no avail. The human role is to trust (30:15). But this goes

against the grain of a basic human instinct to take control of one's destiny.

Fig. 16.1. Colossal statue of a winged human-headed bull from the North-West Palace of Ashurnasirpal II (Room S), intended to protect the palace against demonic forces. Nimrud (ancient Kalhu), northern Iraq. Neo-Assyrian, ca. 883–859 B.C.E. Height 309 cm. Inv. 118872. British Museum, London. Photo: © British Museum / Art Resource, N.Y.

The Invasion of Sennacherib

The narrative about Sennacherib's invasion in chapters 36–38 and the visit of the Babylonian envoys in chapter 39 is found also in 2 Kings 18–20. The most notable difference between the two accounts is that 2 Kings also includes a short notice in vv. 13-16 that says that Hezekiah submitted to the Assyrian king and paid him tribute, as is also claimed in the Assyrian annals. I have already discussed this narrative in the context of 2 Kings. Here my concern is with the portrayal of the prophet Isaiah.

There are two interventions by the prophet. First, in Isa 37:2-4 Hezekiah sends delegates to Isaiah to ask him to intercede. Isaiah's response is in accord with his oracle to Ahaz in Isaiah 7 and with the typical Assyrian prophecies of the era, insofar as it tells the king not to fear. The Assyrian king will return home because of rumors in his own land.

The second intervention is at Isaiah's own initiative, in 37:21-35. It has three parts. First there is a poetic taunt song, professing the contempt of Zion and her God for the invader (cf. Psalm 2). We should expect an oracle addressed to Hezekiah here rather than a lengthy poem. This taunt song is an unequivocal affirmation of the traditional Zion theology, whereby YHWH defends his city against his enemies. It has a triumphalist tone that is difficult to reconcile with the other prophecies of Isaiah and is likely to be a later composition.

The following oracle in vv. 30-32 is considerably more nuanced. Here Isaiah gives the king a sign, as he did with Ahaz. For two years people will have to eat what grows of itself, because it will not be possible to grow crops (compare the curds and honey in Isaiah 7). Only in the third year will it be possible again to plant and reap. This prediction is similar to Isaiah's use of the remnant theme in connection with the Syro-Ephraimite crisis. A remnant will survive, but it will not enjoy the kind of easy deliverance suggested by the taunt song.

Finally, in vv. 33-35 Isaiah predicts that Sennacherib would not enter or conquer Jerusalem. It is quite possible that Isaiah made such a prediction. The narrative presents Hezekiah as a righteous king who prays in time of crisis, in contrast to Ahaz, who lacked faith. Isaiah affirmed the traditional belief that God would be with the Davidic dynasty and its city, but he did not imply that the people would be unscathed or would not suffer. Another oracle that may relate to the crisis under Sennacherib is in 29:1-7. In that case the prophet predicts that the city would be besieged, as it once was by David, but that its enemies would suddenly be dispersed. In fact, Jerusalem was not destroyed, and its escape was remembered as a miracle.

While the narrative may have preserved some memory of Isaiah's oracles, however, the portrayal of the prophet here is very different from what we find in the rest of the book. Here he provides only reassurance. Even other oracles that probably relate to this crisis, however, such as 1:2-9 and 29:1-8, speak of punishment (for rebellion, in chap. 1) and of suffering. The judgmental side of the prophet's persona has been eliminated in the narrative of chapters 36–39.

The account of the envoys from Babylon provides a transition to the second half of the book, which is focused on the Babylonian exile.

Further Reading

Blenkinsopp, Joseph. *Isaiah 1–39*. AB 19. New York: Doubleday, 2000.

Childs, Brevard S. *Isaiah*. OTL. Louisville: Westminster John Knox, 2001.

Clements, R. E. *Isaiah 1–39*. NCB. Grand Rapids: Eerdmans, 1980.

Seitz, Christopher R. "Isaiah, Book of (First Isaiah)." In *ABD* 3:472–88.

———. *Isaiah 1–39*. Interpretation. Louisville: Westminster John Knox, 1993.

Sweeney, Marvin A. *Isaiah 1–39, with an Introduction to Prophetic Literature*. FOTL 16. Grand Rapids: Eerdmans, 1996.

Wildberger, Hans. *Isaiah 1–12*. Trans. T. H. Trapp. CC. Minneapolis: Fortress, 1991.

———. *Isaiah 13–27*. Trans. T. H. Trapp. CC. Minneapolis: Fortress, 1997.

———. *Isaiah 28–39*. Trans. T. H. Trapp. CC. Minneapolis: Fortress, 2002.

Williamson, H. G. M. *The Book Called Isaiah: Deutero-Isaiah's Role in Composition and Redaction*. Oxford: Clarendon, 1994.

17

The Babylonian Era:
Jeremiah and Lamentations

KEY POINTS

Jeremiah
- The **Greek text** is shorter. Shorter Hebrew text in Dead Sea Scrolls.
  Four kinds of material:
  1. poetic
  2. prose narratives about Jeremiah
  3. sermonic prose (Deuteronomistic)
  4. oracles against nations
- **Call of Jeremiah**. More like Moses than Isaiah. Early preaching, like Hosea (Jeremiah 2–3).
- **Criticism of scribes**: (chap. 8).

- **Critique of kingship**: no descendant of Jehoiachin would rule again in Jerusalem.
- **Messianic oracles** in chaps. 23 and 33. At least chap. 33 is a later addition.
- **Critique of prophets** and criteria for true prophecy (chap. 28).
- **Submission to Babylonians** as God's instruments.
- **Later prophecies of hope** (chaps. 31–33). The **confessions** of Jeremiah: no reward, but fire in the bones.
  Lamentations: between guilt and horror.

The prophetic books of the Hebrew Bible cluster around the great catastrophes that befell the kingdoms of Israel and Judah. Nahum and Zephaniah are somewhat exceptional in this regard. Nahum prophesied on the occasion of the fall of Assyria. Zephaniah was a little earlier in the reign of Josiah. This was a transition era in the ancient Near East, between the decline of Assyria and the rise of Babylon. Neither Nahum nor Zephaniah addressed the problems presented by the rising power. These prophets, however, were contemporaries of the young Jeremiah, whose later career would be dominated by the shadow of Babylon. Another "minor" prophet,

Habakkuk, is also set against the backdrop of the coming of Babylon. Here I will focus on the major prophets of the era, Jeremiah and, in the following chapter, Ezekiel.

Jeremiah

According to Jer 1:1, Jeremiah was "son of Hilkiah, of the priests who were in Anathoth," and began to prophesy in the thirteenth year of Josiah (627 B.C.E.). Anathoth was located no more than three miles northeast of Jerusalem. Jeremiah continued to prophesy until the fall of Jerusalem to the Babylonians.

The Composition of the Book

The book of Jeremiah rivals that of Isaiah in complexity, although the period of its formation does not cover as wide a time span. There are obvious differences between the Hebrew (Masoretic) text and the Greek (Septuagint, LXX) translation. The Greek text is about one-eighth shorter than the Hebrew. Most of the differences concern single verses, but some longer passages are also absent from the Greek (33:14-26; 39:4-13; 51:44b-49a; 52:27b-30). Also the oracles against foreign nations, which appear at the end of the book in Hebrew (chaps. 46–51), are found in the Greek after 25:13. The historical appendix in chapter 52 is borrowed from 2 Kgs 24:18—25:21. One of the fragmentary Hebrew copies of the book found at Qumran (4Q Jer[b]) corresponds to the Greek, and so it now appears that the Greek preserves the older form of the book.

There are three kinds of material in the book: poetic oracles, conventionally designated (A); narratives about Jeremiah, especially in the second half of the book (B); and sermonic prose passages that bear a strong resemblance to Deuteronomic style (C). The oracles against the nations are yet a fourth kind of material.

The narratives about Jeremiah are often attributed to his assistant, Baruch. The C

Babylon and Judah

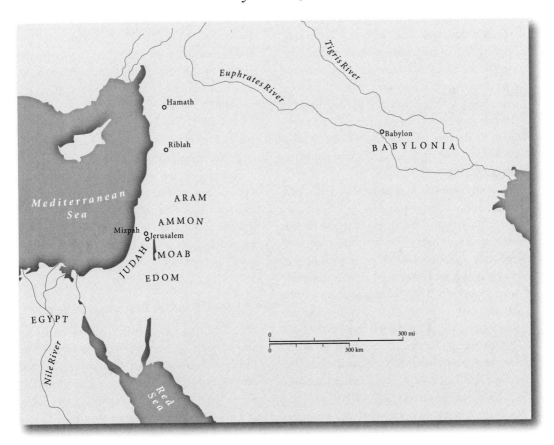

maerial is the work of Deuteronomistic editors but may nonetheless contain paraphrases or recollections of actual oracles of the prophet. Some scholars regard the whole book as a reliable witness to the words and life of Jeremiah. Others regard it as largely a product of anonymous scribes in the postexilic period. The view that distinguishes A, B, and C material remains the most reasonable.

Some light may be shed on the formation of the book by an incident reported in chapter 36. In the fourth year of Jehoiakim, 605 B.C.E., Jeremiah received a divine command to take a scroll and write all the words spoken to him. So Jeremiah called Baruch, son of Neriah, who was evidently a scribe, who wrote down the words at Jeremiah's dictation. Baruch read the scroll in the temple on a fast day, since Jeremiah was barred. The officials who heard it became concerned and felt it must be reported to the king. They told Baruch and Jeremiah to go and hide themselves while they took the scroll and read it to the king. As the king heard it read, he cut off columns of the scroll and burned them in the fire. Jeremiah, however, dictated the words again to Baruch, who wrote them on another scroll, "and many similar words were added to them" (36:32).

Many scholars have argued that the substance of this scroll is found in Jer 1:1—25:13a (25:13a refers to "everything written in this book"). These chapters do not, however, contain the unedited oracles of Jeremiah, and they contain some material that is explicitly later than 605 (21:1-10 relates to the reign of Zedekiah, after 597). It may be that the oracles transcribed by Baruch formed the basis of these chapters, which were then edited by Deuteronomistic scribes, to illustrate how the people had failed to listen to "his servants the prophets." In the second half of the book, apart from the oracles against the nations, prose predominates. Whoever may have been the author of these narratives, they constitute a presentation of the prophet that attempts to enlist his authority in support of a particular interpretation of the Babylonian conquest. They cannot be taken as an objective account of the historical events.

There is a rough chronological order in the book, but it is not consistent. The episode in the reign of Zedekiah in chapter 21 appears out of sequence, and there are two prose accounts of Jeremiah's temple sermon (chaps. 7 and 26). Jeremiah, like other prophetic books, is primarily a collection of oracles and of narratives about the prophet. Attempts to find systematic logic in the order are anachronistic and misunderstand the nature of this kind of literature.

The Call of Jeremiah

The call of Jeremiah in chapter 1 follows the pattern of the call of Moses in Exodus rather than that of Isaiah. There is no vision. Jeremiah protests his unsuitability, as Moses does in Exod 4:10-17. The Lord encourages the chosen one and confirms him in his mission. Jeremiah is presented as "a prophet like Moses" (cf. Deuteronomy 18). The designation of Jeremiah as a prophet to the nations is somewhat puzzling. Most of his oracles are addressed to Judah and Jerusalem. The oracles against foreign nations are generic pieces that could have been composed by any prophet.

Jeremiah and the Deuteronomic Reform

Some of the early oracles of Jeremiah are like Hosea's. He recalls the origin of Israel as YHWH's bride in the wilderness (Jer 2:1) and uses the metaphor of divorce (3:1). The complaint here is twofold: worship of the Baals and other gods, and seeking political alliances with Egypt and Assyria. At this point Jeremiah addresses northern as well as southern Israel (3:12) and holds out the prospect of repentance. The polemic against the worship of other gods would presumably have been congenial to the Deuteronomic reform, as would the prediction that God would reunite northern Israel with Jerusalem if it repented (3:14). The only passages that refer to the reform explicitly, however, are in sermonic prose, and are part of the Deuteronomistic edition of the book. Jeremiah preached "in the days of King Josiah"

that Judah was repeating the cultic adultery that had led to the destruction of the northern kingdom (3:6–11). Jeremiah 11:1-8 appeals to "the words of this covenant," which can only mean the Deuteronomic law. There are also clear overtones of Deuteronomy in the prose account of Jeremiah's temple sermon in 7:1—8:3, which takes the people to task for trusting in "these deceptive words: 'This is the temple of the LORD, the temple of the LORD, the temple of the LORD.'" Josiah had torn down the places of worship outside Jerusalem, but this

---

Baruch

Baruch is mentioned in Jeremiah 36 as a scribe who recorded some prophecies of Jeremiah. In later tradition, several hundred years after his death, he became quite prolific. His name is associated with no fewer than four books:

Baruch: An apocryphal book that is added to the book of Jeremiah in the Greek and Latin manuscripts. It was probably composed in Hebrew, but no fragment of the Hebrew has survived. It contains a historical introduction, claiming that it was written by Baruch in Babylon, but it is thought to have been written no earlier than the second century B.C.E. It includes a lengthy confession of sin and a poem in praise of wisdom.

2 Baruch: a lengthy apocalypse written after the destruction of Jerusalem by the Romans, at the end of the first century C.E. It is preserved in Syriac. It contains lengthy prophecies of the course of history.

3 Baruch: another apocalypse from the end of the first century C.E, which survives in Greek and Slavonic. It is thought to have been composed in Egypt. It describes the ascent of Baruch through five heavens, where he sees the places of reward and punishment after death.

4 Baruch also comes from the aftermath of the destruction of Jerusalem. In Greek, it is known as the Paraleipomena Ieremiou, "Things omitted from Jeremiah." It is also preserved in Ethiopic, where it is called "The Rest of the Words of Baruch." Jeremiah is instructed to hide the temple vessels before the destruction by the Babylonians. Jeremiah is then told to accompany the exiles to Babylon (in contrast to the biblical account) and to leave Baruch in Jerusalem.

only added to the importance of the Jerusalem temple as the one center of legitimate worship, and so indirectly strengthened the Zion theology. Jeremiah's sermon in 7:1—8:3 can be read as an indictment of the people for not truly following the requirements of Deuteronomy, by practicing justice and avoiding the worship of other gods. As a result, YHWH would do to Jerusalem what he had done to Shiloh. This episode is also recounted in chapter 26, where it is dated to the first year of King Jehoiakim, son of Josiah. It is very plausible that Jeremiah delivered oracles condemning the facile temple theology and predicting that Jerusalem would be made like Shiloh. The language of the sermon, however, reflects an interpretation of his oracles by Deuteronomistic editors.

Jeremiah certainly shared basic values of the Deuteronomic reform—opposition to the worship of deities other than YHWH and to social injustice. But he was reluctant to identify the law of the Lord with the contents of a book promulgated by scribes. The clearest evidence of this point is found in Jer 8:4-12. Jeremiah complains that the people are blinded by false security. They say, "We are wise, and the law of the Lord is with us" (8:8). The law of the Lord, here, is surely the law promulgated by Josiah. But, according to Jeremiah, this law has been corrupted: "The lying pen of the scribes has made it into a lie." There is animosity between the prophet and the scribes. Both claimed to speak for God. If the law was contained in a book, then the rest was interpretation, and for that role the scribe was better equipped than the prophet. The charge that the scribes had falsified the Torah and made it into a lie can be understood in various ways. Jeremiah may have been aware that the scribes added to the original scroll that was allegedly found in the temple. It is more likely, however, that in his view they falsified it by absolutizing it and

leading those who had it to trust too easily in their own wisdom.

Ultimately, Jeremiah's oracles were preserved and edited by Deuteronomists. The editors undoubtedly viewed the prophet through the lens of their own theology and made him sound more Deuteronomistic than he had actually been. Nonetheless, it is remarkable that they preserved his biting criticism of the scribes, and this fact inspires some confidence that they did not deliberately distort his message.

A Sense of Impending Doom

One of the most distinctive features of Jeremiah's prophecy is the acute sense of impending disaster that informs much of his poetic oracles. He evokes the sheer terror of military conquest from the victim's point of view: "My anguish, my anguish! I writhe in pain! Oh, the walls of my heart! My heart is beating wildly; I cannot keep silent; for I hear the sound of the trumpet, the alarm of war" (4:19). He sees the coming devastation in cosmic terms: "I looked on the earth, and lo, it was waste and void" (4:23)—creation undone. The prophet also upbraids the people for various offenses, and he sometimes calls for repentance, but most of his oracles give the impression that doom is inevitable. He is especially scathing to those who proclaim peace when there is no peace (8:11).

The Critique of the Kingship

While the coming disaster might be inevitable, Jeremiah does not hesitate to lay blame on various leaders and to hold them responsible: "from the least to the greatest, everyone is greedy for unjust gain; from prophet to priest everyone deals falsely" (8:10-11). He devotes only passing remarks to the priests and the cult, but he says enough to show that he shared the basic attitudes of earlier prophets: "Your burnt offerings are not acceptable, nor are your sacrifices pleasing to me" (6:20).

The most biting social criticism in the book is found in 22:13-17, in an oracle addressed to King Jehoiakim, son of Josiah, who was installed as a puppet king by the Egyptians, after his brother, Jehoahaz (Shallum) had been deposed: "Woe to him who builds his house by unrighteousness and his upper rooms by injustice; who makes his neighbors work for nothing and does not give them their wages." Jehoiakim is concerned with the trappings of royal rank, such as the splendor of his palace. Jeremiah predicts a shameful end for him: "With the burial of an ass he will be buried." In fact, Jehoiakim died before Jerusalem fell to the Babylonians and so escaped humiliation. The oracle, however, is reminiscent of the invective of Elijah or Amos. It was not calculated to win over the king but to denounce him, and possibly to curse him.

The sharp critique of Jehoiakim raises the question of Jeremiah's attitude to the Davidic line. The oracle on Jehoiakim is followed by another on his son Jehoiachin (Coniah), who was only eighteen when he began to reign and had to surrender to the Babylonians three months later. Even if he were the signet ring on the hand of the Lord, as kings claimed to be, he would be shown no mercy. The oracle in 22:28-30 can be read as sympathetic to the young king, doomed to a life of exile, but the last verse is chilling in its finality: "Record this man as childless, a man who shall not succeed in his days; for none of his offspring shall succeed in sitting on the throne of David and ruling again in Judah." So much, it would seem, for the promise to David. Jeremiah was not opposed to kingship in principle (cf. the comments on righteous kingship in 22:1-5). The comment on Jehoiachin is simply a realistic assessment of his prospects. In fact, none of his offspring ever sat on the throne of David. The last king of Judah, appointed by the Babylonians when Jehoiachin was taken into exile, was his uncle, Zedekiah.

Nonetheless, a few passages in Jeremiah entertain a brighter future for the Davidic line. In 23:5-6 the Lord promises, "I will raise up for David a righteous Branch, and he shall reign as king and deal wisely . . . and this is the name by which he will be called: 'The Lord is our righteousness.'" There is a play here on the name Zedekiah ("righteousness of YHWH"). The phrase "the days are surely coming" seems to indicate a break in the continuity of the kingship. Either Jeremiah affirmed that the line would be restored after an interruption, or an editor supplied this hope, to balance the pessimistic oracle on Jehoiachin. There is a further elaboration of this oracle in 33:14-18, which affirms that the prophecy will be fulfilled "in those days and at that time," which is to say, in God's good time. The later passage adds that there will always be a Davidic king and a Levitical priest. The balancing of the kingship with the priesthood is typical of postexilic Judaism. The passage in chapter 33 is not found in the Greek translation, and it is certainly a late addition to the text. The designation of the future king as the "Branch" became an important way of referring to the Messiah in later times.

The Critique of the Prophets

Like Amos and others, Jeremiah is critical of the professional prophets (23:9-40). The problem is not that they prophesy by Baal, like the prophets of Samaria, but that they strengthen the hands of evildoers by prophesying peace. Unlike Micaiah ben Imlah, Jeremiah does not attribute false prophecy to a lying spirit from

YHWH. He denies that it is authentic prophecy at all: these prophets have not stood in the council of the Lord. He makes a distinction between the dream of a false prophet and the vision of a true one. This distinction would be difficult to maintain on a purely phenomenological basis. A prophetic vision, especially one received at night, is difficult to distinguish from a dream. The difference between true and false prophecy is a matter of evaluation of the contents, not a difference in the means of revelation.

The issues between Jeremiah and his contemporary prophets are clarified in the prose narratives in chapters 27 and 28. The incident is set in the reign of Zedekiah, when envoys had come to Jerusalem from several neighboring states, presumably to foment rebellion. Jeremiah makes himself a yoke to symbolize that Judah must submit to the yoke of Babylon. The sight of the prophet parading as a symbol of submission must have been galling to any Judean who entertained hopes of independence. Moreover, he declared that the Lord had given over the earth to "Nebuchadnezzar of Babylon, my servant" (27:6). This statement was extremely provocative.

Jeremiah's message of submission brought him into conflict with other prophets, who were predicting that the Lord would bring back the exiles and the temple vessels from Babylon. One Hananiah broke Jeremiah's yoke. Jeremiah replaced it with a yoke of iron. His response to Hananiah offers another criterion for distinguishing between true and false prophecy: "The prophets who preceded you and me from ancient times prophesied war, famine, and pestilence against many countries and great kingdoms. As for the prophet who prophesies peace, when the word of that prophet comes true, then it will be known that the Lord has truly sent that prophet" (28:8-9). At the least,

a prophet who predicted disaster could not be accused of currying favor with anyone or of acting in his own interest. Ultimately, only time would tell whether a particular prediction was right. By then, of course, it would be too late to be of much help. In this case, time would prove Jeremiah right. There can be little doubt, however, that the disagreements between prophets during the Babylonian crisis contributed to the eventual decline in prophecy in the postexilic period.

The Attitude to Babylonian Rule

According to the prose accounts, Jeremiah consistently advocated submission to Babylon and incurred the wrath of his contemporaries as a result. While these accounts have some basis in the recollection of Jeremiah, they also dovetail with the interests of the Jewish community in Babylon after the deportation.

Already in the time of Jehoiakim, before the initial capture of Jerusalem, Jeremiah prophesied that Judah would serve Babylon for seventy years (25:11; cf. 29:10). He also prophesied that Zion would be made like Shiloh (chap. 26), and for this some people wanted to put him to death. His friends at court prevailed by invoking the precedent of Micah of Moresheth, but another prophet, Uriah son of Shemaiah, was not so fortunate. Even though he fled to Egypt, he was brought back and executed. Prophesying bad tidings to the king was a dangerous business.

After the initial deportation in 597 B.C.E., Jeremiah allegedly sent a letter to the exiles (chap. 29), telling them to settle in Babylon and seek its welfare, "for in its welfare you will find your welfare" (29:8). In chapter 24 the Jewish community in Babylon is contrasted with those who remained in the land under Zedekiah. Jeremiah is shown two baskets of figs, one good and one bad. The good figs represent the exiles, while the bad represent Zedekiah and his officials. The exiles are destined for good: "I will plant them and not pluck them up" (cf. 1:10). These passages clearly reflect the viewpoint of the exilic editors of Jeremiah's oracles.

The issues become more acute during the final siege of Jerusalem. In Jeremiah 21 Zedekiah asks the prophet "to inquire of the LORD on our behalf" in the hope that the Lord would do a mighty deed as in the time of Sennacherib. Jeremiah provides no comfort. On this occasion, the divine warrior is on the side of the Babylonians. This response proceeds on the assumption that YHWH is the Lord of all history, and that whatever happens is his will. To discern the will of the Lord on this occasion, all Jeremiah or Zedekiah had to do was look over the city wall at the Babylonian army and draw their own conclusions.

But Jeremiah does not only predict disaster. He goes on to counsel treason and desertion: "See, I am setting before you the way of life and the way of death. Those who stay in this city shall die by the sword, by famine, and by pestilence; but those who go out and surrender to the Chaldeans . . . shall have their lives as a prize of war" (21:8-10). The reference to the way of life and way of death alludes to Deut 30:15. In that case the way of life was to keep the commandment of the Lord. By implication, the will of God was now to surrender to the Babylonians (cf. Jer 37:3-10). The message attributed to Jeremiah in these passages goes against the grain not only of national pride but of the human instinct for self-assertion. Nonetheless, it must be admitted that submission was the only way to self-preservation for Judah in face of the Babylonian army.

The officials in Jerusalem took exception to Jeremiah's prophecies of doom on the grounds that he was discouraging the soldiers. According to a narrative in chapter 38, they lowered him into an empty but muddy cistern to await a slow death, but he was rescued. The Babylonians are said to have treated the prophet with respect after the conquest and offered to take him to Babylon. He declined, but he also resisted those who advocated flight to Egypt after the governor Gedaliah was murdered (chaps. 42–43). Nonetheless, he was finally forced to flee. He continued to be critical of the community in Egypt because of alleged idolatry (chap. 44). The discussion of the worship of "the queen of heaven" in this context gives an interesting insight into Judean popular religion, even after the fall of Jerusalem.

Whether Jeremiah himself was actually so loyal to Babylon is open to question. There is at least one piece of discordant evidence. Chapters 50 and 51 consist of oracles against Babylon that are attributed to Jeremiah. At the end of these oracles a narrative account claims that Jeremiah "wrote in a scroll all the disasters that would come on Babylon" and gave them to Seraiah, brother of Baruch, when he accompanied Zedekiah to Babylon, and told him to submerge it in the Euphrates, saying, "thus shall Babylon sink, to rise no more." If this material includes any reminiscences of the words of Jeremiah, he cannot have been quite as docile toward the Babylonians as he is portrayed in the prose sections of the book.

Hope for the Future?

According to Jer 30:1, "The days are surely coming when I will restore the fortunes of my people, Israel and Judah." The following chapters contain words of consolation, which stand in sharp contrast to the predictions of "war, famine, and pestilence" that dominate the book. Some oracles in this section date from early in the prophet's career and envision the restoration of northern Israel. Others suggest restoration at the end of the exile and resemble Second Isaiah (Jer 30:10; 31:11-12). It is likely that some of these oracles were added after the time of Jeremiah to relate the prophecies to the restoration from Babylon.

One of the best-known prophecies in the book is Jer 31:31: "The days are surely coming, says the LORD, when I will make a new covenant with the house of Israel and the house of Judah." This passage is part of the C stratum of the book, the Deuteronomistic sermonic prose. The most striking aspect of the new covenant is that it will be written on the people's hearts. It will, in effect, be an unbreakable covenant. We find here a significant shift in expectations about the future. It was of the essence of the Sinai covenant that it demanded free choice, and therefore entailed the possibility of a negative response. But this covenant is judged to have failed. The new internalized covenant will be foolproof, but at a price. A situation where people are programmed, so to speak, to behave in a certain way would no longer correspond to human history as we know it. There is always some tension between utopian thinking, the dream of a perfect society, and free will, which inevitably leads to imperfection. This tension will grow stronger in the apocalyptic writings of the Second Temple period.

In chapter 32 Jeremiah buys a field in Anathoth, to keep it in the family. He did so, as a sign that "houses and fields and vineyards shall again be bought in this land" (32:15). It was in character for Jeremiah to preach doom when everyone else was clinging to hope but to entertain hope when everyone else was in a state of despair.

Jeremiah 33:10-13 contains one of the most beautiful visions of hope in the Hebrew Bible: "In the towns of Judah and the streets of Jerusalem that are desolate, without inhabit-

ants, human or animal, there shall once more be heard the voice of mirth and the voice of gladness, the voice of the bridegroom and the voice of the bride, the voices of those who sing, as they bring thank offerings to the house of the LORD."

The Confessions of Jeremiah

A series of passages in chapters 11–20 seem to have a more personal character than the other oracles and are often singled out as the "confessions" or "laments" of Jeremiah. These passages are 11:18-23; 12:1-6; 15:10-21; 17:14-18; 18:18-23; and 20:7-18. They resemble the individual laments found in the Psalms (e.g., Psalms 3, 5, 6, 7). Some commentators regard them as anonymous additions to the book, but we should hardly be surprised if the prophet expressed himself in traditional forms. We can never be certain that they were composed by Jeremiah, but they certainly contribute to the persona of the prophet as it is presented in the book.

In each of these passages the prophet calls on God, reports some of the speech of his enemies, declares his own innocence, and prays for vengeance. The complaint in 12:1-6 is of a general nature, reminiscent of Habakkuk: "Why does the way of the wicked prosper?" Other passages are more directly personal. According to 11:18-23, Jeremiah's enemies planned to have him killed. The prophet was at first unaware, "like a lamb led to slaughter," but is outraged by the discovery. Jeremiah is not the "turn the other cheek" kind of prophet. He reacts with passion: "Let me see your vengeance on them." He is even more explicit in his demand for vengeance in 18:19-23. There is no concept here of loving your enemies, but there is certainly a passion for justice.

The other poems relate more directly to the experience of prophecy. Jeremiah 15:10-21 begins on a bitter note: "Woe is me, my mother, that you bore me" (cf. 20:15). Nobody likes him; everybody curses him. A further indication of his isolation is found in chapter 16, where he is forbidden to take a wife or to have children, to symbolize the fact that children born in Jerusalem at that time were likely to perish. Other passages indicate ambivalence even about the prophetic calling. The word of the Lord has become a source of reproach and derision. Yet, "If I say, 'I will not mention him, or speak any more in his name,' then within me there is something like a burning fire shut up in my bones; I am weary with holding it in, and I cannot" (20:8-9). Jeremiah prophesies because he cannot help himself. Compare Amos 3:8: "The lion has roared; who will not fear? The Lord GOD has spoken; who can but prophesy?"

These passages raise the question of the motivation of a prophet. Not only does he not stand to gain anything, but he opens himself to abuse and possible death. The reassurance he receives from the Lord in 15:19-20 is modest: his enemies will not prevail over him. There is no promise here of any reward after death, or of much by way of public recognition. Jeremiah did not suffer a violent death, but he died in exile, against his will. Ultimately, the motivation of the prophet comes from the fire in his bones—the compulsion to speak what he believes to be true. We might speak here of an ethical imperative, an obligation to do the right thing whether it is in our personal interest or not.

Lamentations

The book of Lamentations has traditionally been ascribed to Jeremiah, beginning with the LXX, although it is placed among the Writings in the Hebrew Bible. The consensus of modern scholarship is that Jeremiah was not the author.

These laments are highly stylized poems that stand in a long tradition of laments for cities that dates back to the end of the third millennium (cf. the Lament for Ur, *ANET*, 455).

> How lonely sits the city
> that once was full of people!
> How like a widow she has become,
> she that was great among the nations!
> She that was a princess among the provinces
> has become a vassal.
> She weeps bitterly in the night,
> with tears on her cheeks;
> among all her lovers
> she has no one to comfort her,
> all her friends have dealt treacherously with her,
> they have become her enemies.
> —Lamentations 1:1-2

Lamentations contains confession of sin and acknowledgment that "the LORD is in the right" (1:18). This is outweighed, however, by the expression of suffering. The poet stops short of accusing the Lord of excess, but one might draw that inference from his question: "Look, O LORD, and consider! To whom have you done this? Should women eat their offspring, the children they have borne? Should priest and prophet be killed in the sanctuary of the Lord?" (2:20).

In the final poem, the confession of guilt recedes further. "Our ancestors have sinned; they are no more, and we bear their iniquities" (5:7). This sentiment comes close to the proverb, "The fathers have eaten sour grapes," which is vehemently rejected in Ezekiel 18, and is said not to apply to the future in Jeremiah 31. In this poem the emphasis is on innocent suffering: women raped, men abused, people starving. The poet concludes by asking God to restore the people, "unless you have utterly rejected us, and are angry with us beyond measure" (5:22). Here again there is a hint that this degree of suffering cannot be fully explained as just punishment from God.

The book of Lamentations is cherished mainly for its poetic expression of unspeakable horror. As such, it has lent itself readily to recurring situations in every century.

Further Reading

Jeremiah

Brueggemann, Walter. *A Commentary on Jeremiah: Exile and Homecoming*. Grand Rapids: Eerdmans, 1998.

Carroll, Robert P. *Jeremiah*. OTL. Philadelphia: Westminster, 1986.

Holladay, William L. *Jeremiah*. 2 vols. Hermeneia. Philadelphia: Fortress Press, 1986–1989.

King, Philip J. *Jeremiah: An Archaeological Companion*. Louisville: Westminster, 1993.

Miller, Patrick D. "The Book of Jeremiah." In *NIB* 7:555–1072.

Lamentations

Berlin, Adele. *Lamentations*. OTL. Louisville: Westminster John Knox, 2002.

Dobbs-Allsopp, F. W. *Lamentations*. Interpretation. Louisville: Westminster John Knox, 2000.

Linafelt, Tod. *Surviving Lamentations. Catastrophe, Lament and Protest in the Afterlife of a Biblical Book*. Chicago: Univ. of Chicago Press, 2000.

O'Connor, Kathleen M. "Lamentations." In *NIB* 6:1013–72.

Westermann, Claus. *Lamentations: Issues and Interpretation*. Trans. C. Muenchow. Minneapolis: Fortress Press, 1994.

18

Ezekiel

KEY POINTS

Ezekiel

Chaps. 1–24: mostly judgment, ending in destruction of Jerusalem.

Chaps. 1–11: framed by visions of the glory of the Lord.

Chaps 25–32: oracles against nations.

Chaps 33–48: consolation and restoration.

Chaps. 40–48: new Jerusalem.

• Frequent use of **date formulae**.

• **Call vision** and Jewish mysticism.

• **Symbolic actions**. How the prophet bears the sin of his people, to get their attention.

• **The vision of destruction**. Justifying the wrath of God.

• **Jerusalem as a promiscuous woman** (chap. 16).

• **Individual responsibility** (chap. 18).

• **The valley of dry bones**. Restoration as resurrection.

• The eschatological enemy: **Gog**.

• The new Jerusalem: main concerns for cult, hierarchy, and purity. The king or "prince" is subordinated to the priests.

zekiel was a younger contemporary of Jeremiah. He too was from a priestly family, most probably a Zadokite from Jerusalem. He was among the elite of the land who were deported to Babylon in the company of Jehoiachin in 597 B.C.E. (2 Kgs 24:15). He was already in Babylon when he had his inaugural vision (chap. 1), which is dated to "the thirtieth year," or the fifth year of the exile of King Jehoiachin. The thirtieth year presumably reflects his age. After his call as a prophet, he became a figure of some importance among the exiles.

The book of Ezekiel is more highly structured than other prophetic books. The most obvious division in the book comes at the end of chapter 24, which marks the destruction of Jerusalem. Up to this point, the great majority of the oracles pronounce judgment on Judah and Jerusalem. Chapters 1–11 are framed by the great visions of the glory of the Lord in chapters 1 and 8–11. The oracles of judgment in chapters 12–24 are marked by extended and colorful allegories. There follows a collection of oracles against foreign nations in chapters 25–32. The remainder of the book, chapters 33–48, prophesies consolation and restoration. The sequence then is judgment on Jerusalem, judgment on foreign nations, consolation for Jerusalem.

One of the distinctive features of the book is the frequency with which date formulae are used—fifteen times. They range from the fifth year of the exile (1:2) to the twenty-fifth

(40:1), mostly in chronological order. The latest date is the twenty-seventh year of the exile (571/570 B.C.E., in 29:17). This is one of the many features that relate the book of Ezekiel to the Priestly tradition.

The book begins with visions of the destruction of Jerusalem and ends with an elaborate vision of its restoration. There is no doubt that it exhibits a deliberate order. Whether that order was imposed by the prophet himself or by a disciple is a matter of controversy. The bulk of the prophecies must be dated to the early exilic period. There is no reference to the capture of Babylon by Cyrus. The main doubts about authenticity concern the prophecies of restoration at the end of the book, especially the long vision of the restoration of Jerusalem in chapters 40–48. In part, this vision reflects the struggle for control of the sanctuary after the return of the exiles (chap. 44), but it may be that a prophecy of Ezekiel was updated and expanded. There are scarcely any references of a biographical nature in the second half of the book.

Ezekiel differs from other prophets in the prominence of his priestly concerns. Like the Holiness Code in Leviticus, he does not distinguish between moral and ritual laws, and much of his prophecy deals with issues of holiness and purity. Ezekiel's reaction to the fall of Jerusalem is to recoil in horror at the impurity of the city, which he sees as the primary cause of its downfall. There is little sense that conversion is possible before the destruc-

Fig. 18.1. The Ishtar Gate from Babylon. Vorderasiatisches Museum, Berlin. Photo: © Erich Lessing / Art Resource, N.Y.

tion. The objective of the prophet's mission is that the people should recognize the hand of the Lord in the fate that befalls them (hence the recurring statement, "You shall know that I am the Lord"). The book is also noteworthy for the prominence of symbolic actions and for the vivid, even bizarre symbolism of many of the visions.

Chapters 1–11: Glory and Destruction

The Opening Vision

The opening vision of Ezekiel is the most complex of all prophetic visions, and it became a cornerstone of later Jewish mysticism. The vision combines two traditions. The first is a storm theophany, in the tradition of Mount Sinai (cf. Judg 5:4-5; Ps 68:7-9; Hab 3:3-15; et al.). The presence of the Lord is associated with fire. In accordance with the imag-

ery of the storm-god, YHWH rides a chariot (Hebrew *merkābāh*). Later Jewish mysticism is known as Merkavah mysticism because it is concerned with visions of the divine throne-chariot.

The second tradition that informs Ezekiel's vision is that of the Jerusalem temple, where YHWH was enthroned above the cherubim (cf. Isaiah 6). These were hybrid creatures, combining features of various animals and endowed with wings, of a type often depicted in ancient Near Eastern art. The beings seen by Ezekiel are inspired by this tradition but are exceptionally bizarre. In their midst was something like burning coals of fire. Burning coals also figured in the vision of Isaiah (Isa 6:6). The Deity is enthroned above the living creatures, separated from them by a dome. Unlike Isaiah or Micaiah ben Imlah, however, Ezekiel does not simply see the Lord. He sees "something like" a throne, on which there was "something that seemed like a human form" but that was fiery and dazzling in appearance.

Fig. 18.2. Lion detail from the Ishtar Gate. Lion. Louvre, Paris. Photo: © Erich Lessing / Art Resource, N.Y.

This, we are told, was "the appearance of the likeness of the glory of the Lᴏʀᴅ." The glory (*kābôd*) was the symbol of the presence of God in the Priestly tradition. Ezekiel is at pains to emphasize the transcendent, surpassing nature of this God, who cannot be perceived clearly by human eyes. Throughout the book, Ezekiel is addressed as "son of man," meaning "mortal human being." The emphasis on the prophet's humanity contrasts with the awesome majesty of God.

The vision of the prophet is not an end in itself. As in the case of Isaiah, it is the occasion of a commissioning. The nature of the prophet's task is spelled out clearly in Ezek 3:16-21, by analogy with the role of a watchman. The watchman is bound to give warning of an impending danger. Whether anyone heeds that warning is not his responsibility. This view of the prophet's mission is closely bound up with Ezekiel's emphasis on individual responsibility, which we shall find more fully expounded in chapter 18. Both the watchman analogy and the teaching on individual responsibility are repeated in chapter 33, at the beginning of the oracles of consolation.

The vision is formally concluded by the departure of the glory of the Lord. The mobility of the divine chariot-throne is significant. It means that God can appear in Babylon as well as in Jerusalem. Ezekiel is also mobile. He is transported, like Elijah, by the spirit of the Lord.

Symbolic Actions

More than any other prophet, Ezekiel exhibits phenomena that are associated with unusual psychological conditions and that seem to call for psychological analysis. His personal life and his psychological condition were deeply affected by his prophetic calling.

The first symbolic action, in chapter 4, calls for the prophet to build a model of a city under siege. Next he was to lie on his left side, and "bear the iniquity of the house of Israel" for 390 days. Then he was to lie on his right side for 40 days to "bear the iniquity" of the house of Judah. We do not know how the prophet carried out these commands. One tradition of interpretation, going back to Maimonides, the great Jewish philosopher in the Middle Ages, argued the action was only within the context of the vision—that the prophet did not carry it out physically. It is of the essence of the symbolic actions of the prophets, however, that they are public signs, performed so as to attract the attention of bystanders. They have aptly been compared to street theater as a way of engaging public interest. We must assume, then, that Ezekiel did the things described. To lie on one side for 390 days would require (or cause!) a pathological condition, but we do not know whether he was allowed to leave his position periodically or to move.

By lying in these positions, the prophet is said to "bear the iniquity" of Israel and Judah in turn. "Bear the iniquity" is a technical term in the Priestly laws of the Pentateuch. In Lev 16:21-22 the scapegoat is said to "bear the sins" of the house of the people of Israel and carry them away to the desert. In Lev 10:17 the priests are given the sin offering "to bear the iniquity of the congregation." The scapegoat bears iniquity in the sense of removing it. The priests also remove it, in the sense of atoning for it. It is doubtful, however, whether Ezekiel is thought to atone for the sin of Israel by his ordeal of lying on his side. Rather, he seems to bear the punishment of the people, in the sense that he illustrates and dramatizes it. There is no implication that people are relieved of their guilt simply by looking at Ezekiel. The prophet's action is meant to help them recognize their guilt and their impending punishment. The 390 days and 40 days represent the number of years allotted for the punishment of Israel and Judah. Neither figure was historically accurate. The kingdom of Israel was never restored, and the Babylonian exile lasted more than forty years.

Ezekiel is given further instructions about his diet while performing these actions. His food is rationed, and he is to prepare it over human dung. The point is to show that the food is unclean. Ezekiel's reaction is visceral: "Ah Lord God! I have never defiled myself; from my youth up to now . . ." (4:14). He is allowed to substitute animal dung, which has been used as fuel in the poorer countries of the Middle East down to modern times. For a Zadokite priest like Ezekiel, defilement was a fate worse than death.

Ezekiel is given one further symbolic action to perform at this point. He is told to shave his head and his beard with a sword and divide the hair, to symbolize the fate of the inhabitants of Jerusalem. One-third would die of pestilence or famine, one-third would fall by the sword, and one-third would be scattered. Compare Lev 26:23-33, where the Israelites are threatened with sword, pestilence, famine, and exile if they disobey the laws.

The Abominations in the Temple

In chapter 8 Ezekiel sees a figure like the one on the throne in chapter 1, presumably an angel or a member of the heavenly court other than YHWH. This figure lifts the prophet by a lock of his hair and transports him to Jerusalem. (This motif reappears in the story of Bel and the Dragon). The transportation is said to be "in visions of God." We should not suppose that the prophet actually went to Jerusalem.

The vision of abominations in the temple is not necessarily an accurate depiction of what was happening there. Rather, it represents a fantasy of Ezekiel, what he imagined was going on in the temple, so as to explain the catastrophe that befell it. The glory of the God of Israel is there, in the inner court. But there is also "the image of jealousy, which provokes to jealousy." This is presumably a statue of another deity, which offends the jealous God, YHWH. The visionary character of the experience is shown by the statement that Ezekiel dug through a wall, something he could hardly have done with impunity in the actual temple. He observes a number of idolatrous practices. There is no parallel for veneration of loathsome animals in Israel or Judah. "Women weeping for Tammuz" refers to a Mesopotamian ritual that can be traced back to ancient Sumer in the third millennium, where it marked the death and descent into the netherworld of the shepherd-god, Dumuzi. This ritual was observed in the Near East for thousands of years. Whether it was observed in Jerusalem we do not know. Worship of the sun was practiced in Judah in the seventh century. Josiah is said to have suppressed it (2 Kings 23). There is also a reference to "filling the land with violence" in 8:17, but Ezekiel is primarily disturbed by cultic offenses. Whether in fact any of these "abominations" was practiced in Jerusalem in this period, we do not know. What the vision primarily shows is the kind of offenses that Ezekiel thought would trigger the destruction of Jerusalem.

The Vision of Destruction

The same figure who had guided Ezekiel in his vision now summons "the executioners of the city." These are six angelic figures, accompanied by "a man dressed in linen." This figure is commanded to go through Jerusalem and mark the foreheads of those who oppose the "abominations" with a *taw*, the last letter of the alphabet, which had the shape of an X in the Old Hebrew alphabet. The marking recalls the smearing of blood on the lintels and doorposts of the Israelites in Egypt, so that the angel of destruction would pass them by (Exod 12:23). In this case, however, the distinction is not between Israelite and Egyptian, but between the people of Jerusalem. The implication is that the people who are killed are sinners. This is a dangerous concept, which is surely not defensible. (The underlying logic, with regard to suffering in general, is criticized in the book of Job.)

As Ezekiel sees it, the slaughter in Jerusalem is the work not of the Babylonians but of YHWH. Jerusalem is destroyed because the inhabitants deserve it. This explanation is essentially similar to what we find in the Deuteronomists, but there are some distinct nuances in Ezekiel. He is especially concerned with the defilement of the temple. Ezekiel's way of dealing with the catastrophe that befell Jerusalem seems to be to persuade himself that it was utterly defiled so that destruction was the only remedy.

The destruction is completed in chapter 10, when the angel spreads burning coals over the city. In Isaiah's vision burning coals were used to purify the prophet's lips. Here too the burning can be understood as purgation. Jerusalem will rise again, in the last section of the book. For the present, the destruction is severe and complete. In conjunction with the destruction, the glory of the Lord abandons Jerusalem. It rises up from the temple and comes to rest on the Mount of Olives (Ezek 11:23). The entire destruction and abandonment are described without reference to the Babylonians.

In Ezekiel's view the responsibility for the destruction of Jerusalem was borne primarily by the people who had remained in the city with Zedekiah after the first deportation. In contrast, the exiles in Babylon are regarded as the hope for the future.

Chapters 12–24: Oracles of Judgment

Chapters 12–24 contain some twenty-five oracles, mostly introduced by the formula "the word of the LORD came to me." There are no visions in this section, although some of the oracles use highly pictorial language.

The Useless Vine

In chapter 15 Jerusalem is compared to a vine. This is a time-honored metaphor. According to Psalm 89, Israel was a vine brought out of Egypt that took deep root and filled the land. According to Hosea, it was a luxuriant vine that yielded fruit. It was a symbol of prosperity and fertility. The Song of Songs (8:12) refers to the beloved as a vineyard. Even the Song of the Vineyard in Isaiah 5, which is an oracle of judgment against Israel and Judah, assumes that a vineyard should be a good thing.

It comes as something of a shock, then, when Ezekiel asks what the vine is good for. In all the cases cited, the reference was to the cultivated vine, which yields grapes for wine. The wild vine, however, is useless, and this is the analogy that the prophet has in mind. Not only does Jerusalem have no intrinsic value; it is a vine that has been burned, so that, in the brutal formulation of 15:5, it can never be used for anything. Ezekiel expresses a disdain for Jerusalem that goes far beyond anything that we found in Isaiah or Jeremiah.

The Promiscuous Woman

That disdain finds its most extreme expression in chapter 16 (cf. Hosea 2). Ezekiel 16:9, which says that YHWH pledged himself to Jerusalem and entered into a contract or covenant with her, implies the metaphor of marriage. The beauty of the young woman, however, becomes an occasion for prostitution.

The punishment of unfaithful Jerusalem in this oracle is more severe than the fate of Israel in Hosea. Not only will she be stripped naked in public, but "they shall bring a mob against you, and they shall stone you and cut you to pieces with their swords" (16:40). The violence of this picture is undoubtedly inspired by the actual fate of Jerusalem, but it also carries the implication, or even a presupposition, that this is what a promiscuous woman deserves. Death by stoning was the punishment for adultery in biblical law (Deut 22:23-24). Stripping is the punishment in Hosea 2 (and later in the story of Susanna). There is no precedent for cutting in pieces as a punishment. There may be an allusion here to the Levite's concubine in Judges 19, who was cut in pieces after she had been raped, but this was not a punishment. Feminist scholars have quite rightly expressed concern that such rhetoric may seem to sanction violence against women. Some go so far as to describe it as pornographic. Of course, this is not the point of the oracle. The passage is an allegory and deals with the punishment of Jerusalem, not of actual women. But the allegory accepts as its premise that an adulterous woman deserves to be stoned or hacked to pieces, and the vivid imagery may well have contributed to violence against women, promiscuous or not, over the centuries. It may not be fair to characterize Ezekiel as a misogynist. He is grief stricken at the death of his wife,

whom he describes as "the delight of my eyes" (24:15-18). It is unfortunate that his use of female imagery is predominantly negative and associates women primarily with promiscuity and impurity (see also chapter 23, below).

Individual Responsibility

The most important contribution of this section of Ezekiel (and arguably of all of Ezekiel) to the theological tradition is the teaching on individual responsibility in chapter 18. This teaching was already touched on in chapter 3, in connection with the commission of the prophet, and in 14:12-20.

The prophet sets out to refute the popular saying, "The parents have eaten sour grapes, and the children's teeth are set on edge" (cf. Jer 31:29-30). According to this proverb, the people of Jerusalem were not punished for their own sins, but for those of their fathers—notably those of Manasseh in the previous century. Ezekiel argues that everyone is punished or rewarded for his or her own sins.

> The word of the LORD came to me: What do you mean by repeating this proverb concerning the land of Israel, "The parents have eaten sour grapes, and the children's teeth are set on edge"? As I live, says the Lord GOD, this proverb shall no more be used by you in Israel. Know that all lives are mine; the life of the parent as well as the life of the child is mine: it is only the person who sins that shall die.
> —Ezekiel 18:1-4

In the process, Ezekiel states what constitutes righteousness or wickedness. A sinner is one who engages in idolatry or in worship at the high places, defiles his neighbor's wife, and does not observe purity laws, but also one who oppresses the poor, takes interest on loans, or performs unjustly in any way. Ezekiel's concern for purity and related issues is evident on every page of the book. His concern for social justice is not so often spelled out but receives due prominence here. In this regard, Ezekiel resembles the Holiness Code, where moral and ritual requirements are placed side by side (see Leviticus 19). The righteous do more than avoid these offenses. They also feed the hungry and cover the naked. The ideal of righteousness, then, is a well-rounded one, and not as narrowly focused on purity issues as we might have inferred from some passages in Ezekiel.

Ezekiel insists that "the person that sins shall die." We have seen that the vision of the destruction of Jerusalem in chapter 9 seemed to take this principle quite literally: only the righteous were spared. Nonetheless, it is clear that Ezekiel did not think sinners were struck down automatically. He allows for the possibility that a wicked person may repent, or that a righteous person may stray from virtue. Further, there is no suggestion of significant life after death, so even the righteous die eventually. "To live" here most probably means to be right with God, and "to die" means to be in disfavor. But in light of the vision in chapter 9, we must also reckon that those who lived unrighteously were liable to premature destruction.

Ezekiel's teaching on individual responsibility is a watershed text in the Hebrew Bible. The blessings and curses of the covenant applied to the people as a whole, without exceptions for individual behavior. The novelty of Ezekiel's teaching was that it called for such discrimination, by God if not by the Babylonians. The prophet was still greatly concerned for the welfare of Israel as a whole, but he showed a new concern for individual justice in the eyes of God.

To the modern reader, raised in an individualistic culture, this teaching of Ezekiel seems clearly right. It would not have been so obvious to the ancients. According to Exod 20:5, YHWH is a jealous God, punishing children for the iniquity of parents even to the third and fourth generation. It is an experiential fact that the behavior of parents has consequences for their children. Moreover, such a simple correlation of virtue and reward, vice and punishment, lends itself to self-righteousness on the part of the successful and to unfair blame of the less fortunate.

The philosophical and theological merit of Ezekiel's doctrine of individual responsibility is suspect, but it had unquestionable pastoral merit. The attitude reflected in the proverb, blaming misfortune on the sins of the fathers, did the exiles no good. It was better for all to take responsibility for their own fate and to use it as an incentive to live better and more righteously.

The Final Blow

The most moving incident in the book of Ezekiel is undoubtedly the passage that concludes the "book of judgment," 24:15-27. The prophet is told that God will take away "the delight of his eyes," but he must not mourn. That evening his wife died. It seems clear from the passage that he loved his wife and wanted to mourn but was prevented by what he perceived as a divine command. The death of his wife is treated as a sign of the destruction of Jerusalem, which he also loved deeply but could not mourn.

The inability to mourn is viewed as a pathological condition in modern psychiatry. It reflects not indifference but a depth of trauma that leaves the person numb. (It leaves Ezekiel temporarily dumb.) This incident throws a new light on Ezekiel's vehement condemnations of Jerusalem. The destruction of the temple was a great trauma, not only because of his attachment to it, but because his tradition taught him that YHWH loved Zion. If YHWH nonetheless destroyed it or allowed it to be destroyed, Jerusalem must have been vile to deserve such a fate. The vehement denunciations of Jerusalem bespeak Ezekiel's desperate desire to vindicate what he perceived as the action of his God.

Chapters 25–32:
The Oracles
against the Nations

The main cluster of oracles in this section of the book is directed against Tyre, the Phoenician coastal city to the north. Tyre was besieged by Nebuchadnezzar for thirteen years. It eventually submitted, but it was not destroyed or pillaged as Ezekiel had prophesied. The failure of the prophecy is acknowledged in 29:17-18. Ezekiel predicted that Nebuchadnezzar would carry off plunder from Egypt as compensation for his effort against Tyre, and that Egypt would be desolate for forty years (29:13). This too did not happen. Egypt remained independent until it was conquered by the Persians in 525 B.C.E. In fact, the only prediction that Ezekiel got fully right was the destruction of Jerusalem.

The oracles against Tyre are striking for their use of mythic patterns to describe the human condition. The basic pattern is one of hubris, or arrogant pride, leading to a fall. It is familiar from Greek tragedy (which developed about a century later), and is often represented in the Bible (e.g, the stories of Adam and Eve and the Tower of Babel, and the allusion to Lucifer, son of Dawn, in Isaiah 14). The finest expression of the pattern is in Ezek 28:2: "Because your heart is proud and you have said 'I am a god; I sit in the seat of the gods, in the heart of the seas,' yet you are but a mortal, and

no god, though you compare your mind with the mind of a god." Tyre was an island fortress; hence the confidence that it was as inaccessible as the home of the gods. Especially interesting is the allusion in v. 13 to "Eden, the garden of God." Ezekiel's form of the story, however, is quite different from what we have in Genesis. The figure in the garden is not naked but adorned with precious stones, and the garden is equated with "the mountain of God."

The oracles against Tyre dwell at length on the wealth of Tyre, derived from its trading. There is evident envy in these oracles. They arise out of the mutual grudges between neighboring cities. The desire for revenge and the gloating over the fall of another are not among the most edifying material in the Bible. Nonetheless, these oracles have had a profound impact on later tradition, not least because of their influence on the book of Revelation, especially on the vision of the destruction of Rome in Revelation 17–18.

Chapters 33–48:
Oracles of Restoration

The last section of the book of Ezekiel is dominated by prophecies of restoration. Ezekiel did not envision, or want, a simple return to the status quo before the destruction. In order to be restored, Israel must be purified. Therefore, "I will sprinkle clean water upon you" (36:25), for a ritual cleansing. Moreover, "A new heart I will give you, and a new spirit I will put within you; and I will remove from your body the heart of stone and give you a heart of flesh. I will put my spirit within you, and make you follow my statutes" (vv. 26-27). In Ezekiel's view the old creation had failed. He does not say how Israel, or humanity, had come to have a heart of stone. It is presumably akin to the evil inclination of humanity before the flood (Gen 6:5). The new creation would remove the hazards of free will by making people obey the laws. Here, as in Jeremiah's concept of a new covenant, we find the totalitarian tendency of utopian thinking. Human nature as we know it inclines to evil. Only by radically redesigning human nature can good behavior be guaranteed.

The Valley of Dry Bones

One of the most memorable of Ezekiel's visions is that of a valley full of dry bones in chapter 37. The imagery may have been suggested by the Zoroastrian custom of laying out the dead to be picked clean by vultures. If so, this vision must be later than the time of Ezekiel, although it is faithful to his style. There was no tradition in Israel of the resurrection of the dead. Such a belief was held by the Zoroastrians from an early date. Ezekiel uses the vision of resurrection only metaphorically. He does not suggest that the individual dead will come back to life, only that "the whole house of Israel" will be restored. In later times, this vision would be reinterpreted as referring to literal resurrection, as already in 4Q386, in the Dead Sea Scrolls.

This vision is followed by a symbolic action, in which the prophet writes on a stick: "For Judah and the Israelites associated with it." The restoration must include all Israel, north and south, under "my servant David." The restored dynasty would last forever, and YHWH would dwell in the midst of them. The word translated "dwelling" in the NRSV is *miškan*, the term for the tabernacle or tent-shrine in the Priestly strand of the Pentateuch.

Gog of the Land of Magog

In chapters 38–39 we encounter a new kind of prophecy. The novelty is not formal. It is a judgment oracle like other oracles against foreign nations. The novelty lies in the fact that the enemy addressed is not an actual entity in the contemporary world of the prophet, but a legendary figure who takes on mythic proportions. The name Gog is most probably derived from Gyges of Lydia in western Asia Minor, who lived about a century before the time of Ezekiel. He is known from Assyrian texts, where he is called *gûgu*, and from the Greek historian Herodotus (Book 1). Gyges had absolutely no contact with Israel, and it is unlikely that Ezekiel knew much about him. His country is called Magog (= the place of Gog; the name appears in the list of nations in Gen 10:2). The figure described in these oracles only takes his name from Gyges. He is a figure of myth and fantasy.

Gog is identified as the enemy "of whom I spoke in former days by my servants the prophets" (38:17). He is said to come "out of the remotest parts of the north" (38:15), which suggests that he is the "foe from the north" in the prophecy of Jeremiah. Gog becomes the principal actor in the mythical conflict between the nations and Zion (cf. Psalm 2). He will be killed "on the mountains of Israel." The expectation of victory over the nations by the power of YHWH had not materialized in the Babylonian invasion. The prophecy insists that it will be fulfilled, in a definitive way, in the future.

It is not enough that Gog be defeated. His entire host must be annihilated. Then there is a gruesome feast. The birds and wild animals are assembled to "eat the flesh of the mighty, and drink the blood of the princes of the earth" (39:18). This is a sacrificial feast, as if Gog were a sacrificial victim. The drinking of blood, however, is extraordinary, especially in a book concerned with ritual purity to the degree that Ezekiel is. It is quite literally a bloodthirsty vision, which sets no limits to the destruction that is wished upon the nations. Here again Ezekiel has left his mark on later tradition. In Rev 20:8 the followers of Satan in the final conflict are Gog and Magog, while "the great supper of God" consists of the flesh of kings and the mighty, but also of all both small and great (Rev 19:17-19).

The banquet brings ritual closure to the drama of the final battle. We shall meet the motif of a final banquet again in one of the additions to the book of Isaiah (Isa 25:6-10). This motif is sometimes called the messianic banquet, but neither Ezekiel 39 nor Isaiah 25 speaks of a messiah in this context. The banquet is, however, part of the pattern of the old combat myth in which the good god defeats his enemies. This myth provides a way of imagining a satisfactory future that is increasingly prominent in Second Temple Judaism.

The New Jerusalem

The final vision of the book of Ezekiel occupies nine chapters, almost one-fifth of the book. It is written in the style of Ezekiel, and a nucleus of it may come from the prophet himself. On some matters, such as the role of the prince, its position seems to be developed beyond that of the earlier chapters, and some passages would seem to fit better in the context of the restoration, some decades after the time of Ezekiel (e.g., chap. 44). It provides a fitting conclusion to the book, which began with the departure of the divine presence from Jerusalem.

Formally, the vision is similar to the temple vision in chapters 8–11. The prophet is taken on a guided tour by an angel. Jerusalem is not mentioned by name, but is referred to as "the city." It is located in a consecrated area that runs from the Jordan to the sea, separating the territories of Judah to the south and Benjamin to

the north. Within this area, strips of land are set aside for the priests, the Levites, the city, and the prince. The temple is located in the middle of the territory of the priests. The area of the city proper is declared profane, and it occupies only half as much territory as that of the priests. The city of Jerusalem is clearly subordinated in importance to the temple area. This sanctified city has an Edenic character. A river flows out from it that makes the waters of the Dead Sea fresh (47:1-12; compare the river that flows out from Eden in Gen 2:10).

In Ezekiel's view, failure to protect the sanctity of the temple was a major cause of the disaster that had befallen Jerusalem. In the future, "no foreigner, uncircumcised in heart and flesh," would enter the sanctuary (Ezek 44:9). Levites and ordinary Israelites were restricted to the outer court. A sharp distinction is made between Levites and Zadokite priests. At the time of Josiah's reform, the Levites from the country shrines were invited to go up to Jerusalem and minister at the temple there. Ezekiel is not so welcoming. The Levites, we are told, must bear their punishment for contributing to the apostasy of Israel in the past. They are allowed to perform menial services in the temple, but are not to serve as priests. Pride of place in the new order is reserved for the Zadokite priests, who are credited with preserving the sanctuary when the rest of the people sinned, and who alone would be allowed to enter the inner court. They are given special linen garments and are not to wear anything that causes sweat. But they are to remove these garments when they go into the outer court "so that they may not communicate holiness to the people with their vestments" (44:19).

The purpose of these rules is to make a clear separation between the sacred and the profane, and so to preserve the special character of the holy. They also create a hierarchical structure, in which some people hold more power than others. The Levites are to a great degree disenfranchised, while power is vested in the hands of the Zadokite priests.

There is still a role in this vision for the "prince," the title given in chapters 34 and 37 to the Davidic king. In the new order, the prince has a place of honor but very little power. His main role is to provide victims and offerings for the altar (46:11-15).

Ezekiel's vision was never realized in Jerusalem. It was the model for several utopian prescriptions for a new Jerusalem in Second Temple times. A long section of the Temple Scroll from Qumran is devoted to regulations for an ideal temple. There is also a fragmentary vision of a New Jerusalem in Aramaic among the Dead Sea Scrolls. The book of Revelation, which is often influenced by Ezekiel, does not offer the kind of detailed instructions found in Ezekiel 40–48, but it does offer a vision of "the holy city, the new Jerusalem, coming down out of heaven from God, prepared as a bride adorned for her husband" (Rev 21:2).

Further Reading

Block, Daniel I. *The Book of Ezekiel*. 2 vols. NICOT. Grand Rapids: Eerdmans, 1997–1998.

Darr, Katheryn Pfisterer. "The Book of Ezekiel." In *NIB* 6:1075–1607.

Greenberg, Moshe. *Ezekiel 1–20*. AB 22. New York: Doubleday, 1983.

———. *Ezekiel 21–37*. AB 22A. New York: Doubleday, 1997.

Kaminsky, Joel S. *Corporate Responsibility in the Hebrew Bible*. JSOTSup 196. Sheffield: Sheffield Academic Press, 1995.

Levenson, Jon D. *The Theology of the Program of Restoration of Ezekiel 40–48*. HSM 10. Missoula, Mont.: Scholars Press, 1976.

Zimmerli, Walther. *Ezekiel*. Trans. R. E. Clements. 2 vols. Hermeneia. Philadelphia: Fortress Press, 1979–1983.

19

The Additions to the Book of Isaiah

KEY POINTS

Second Isaiah

- Presupposes defeat of Babylon by **Cyrus** of Persia, who is called "my anointed one."
- Return to Judah seen as a **new Exodus.**
- Polemic against **idolatry**, deriding gods of Babylonians.
- True God has been **hidden** but is now revealed.
- **Servant poems**, in 42:1-4; 49:1-6; 50:4-9; and 52:13—53:12.
  —These poems must be seen in the broader context of Second Isaiah.
  —The Servant of the Lord is identified as Jacob/Israel in several passages.
  —Isa 49:1-6 is confusing because the servant seems to have a message for Israel and so must be either a remnant or the true/ideal Israel.
  —The servant is a **light to the nations**. Second Isaiah believed that the exile and restoration of Judah would get the attention of the nations and convince them that Yahweh is the true God.
  —Isa 50:4-9 does not mention the servant and probably refers to the prophet.
  —The most important servant poem is 52:13—53:12, which describes the suffering and death of the Servant. The nations confess that the Servant **bore the sins of others** and suffered their punishment.
  —The suffering of the Servant is supposed to have an effect on others by having them realize what they deserve and changing their lives.
  —The death and apparent resurrection of the Servant reflects the destruction and restoration of Israel/Judah in the exile.
  —Early Christians understood the **death of Jesus** in light of these poems.
  —These poems open up the possibility that suffering may not be just punishment for sin, but may have another purpose.
  —The Servant was not understood as the Messiah in ancient Judaism before the Christian period. The promise to David is transferred to the whole people in chap. 55.

Third Isaiah (Isaiah 56–66) reflects sharp division in the postexilic community. It questions the importance of the **temple** and hopes for a **new creation.**

- The so-called **Apocalypse of Isaiah** (Isaiah 24–27) describes cosmic collapse. It cannot now be related to any one specific historical crisis.
- Isa 24–27 resembles later apocalyptic literature (Daniel) in using highly mythological imagery to describe a radical cosmic transformation, including the **defeat of death.**
- The **book of Isaiah** as a whole moves attention away from the prophet to the message of judgment and hope for restoration.

For at least two hundred years, modern scholarship has been aware that some parts of the book of Isaiah cannot have originated with the eighth-century prophet. Chapters 40–66 come from a time during or after the Babylonian exile. Cyrus of Persia, the king who overthrew Babylon in 539 B.C.E., is twice mentioned by name (Isa 44:28; 45:1). Since the end of the nineteenth century, it has been conventional to distinguish between "First Isaiah" (chaps. 1–39), "Second (Deutero-) Isaiah" (chaps. 40–55), and "Third (Trito-) Isaiah" (chaps. 56–66). The line between Second and Third Isaiah is blurred by chapters 60–62, which are closely related to Second Isaiah in style and in spirit. Also, chapter 35 seems to belong with Second Isaiah. Chapters 24–27, often dubbed the "Apocalypse of Isaiah," are likely to be later than anything in chapters 40–66. Some scholars argue that First Isaiah was edited by Second Isaiah. There are some themes that run through the entire book, such as the interest in Zion/Jerusalem, the designation of God as "the Holy One" and "King" of Israel, and the symbolism of light (2:5; 42:6; 49:6; 60:1). The theme of the new exodus in Isa 11:15-16 is typical of Second Isaiah but atypical of First Isaiah.

Second Isaiah

The opening words of Second Isaiah are among the best-known lines in the Bible because they are used in Handel's *Messiah* (KJV: "Comfort ye, comfort ye my people"). They also mark a major point of transition in the history of Hebrew prophecy. Up to this point, the prophets had delivered primarily oracles of judgment. Most prophets who attempted to reassure the people were judged to be false. Now we find a prophet whose main theme is consolation, who is accepted as a genuine prophet of YHWH.

The difference is due to the change of historical circumstances. The prophecies of judgment had all been fulfilled. Moreover, Second Isaiah prophesied at one of the most hopeful moments in the history of Israel and Judah. Cyrus of Persia conquered Babylon in the fall of 539 b.c.e. He changed not only the power structure of the Near East, but also the policy toward subject peoples. We know something of his policy from an inscription known as "the Cyrus Cylinder" (*ANET*, 316). He claimed that it was Marduk who had called him and led

him to Babylon to restore his cult. Cyrus did not ravage Babylon, and he restored the Babylonian gods to their shrines. He found it more effective to win over the people rather than to subdue them.

Cyrus adopted a similar policy toward Judah. He authorized Judeans to return from Babylon to Jerusalem and to rebuild the temple there. It seemed self-evident to Second Isaiah that such a turn of events could only have been brought about by the God of Israel.

The euphoria of (at least some) Jews at the edict of Cyrus rings loud and clear in Second Isaiah. The setting is Babylon. There is no awareness in chapters 40–55 of the problems that would confront the exiles when they returned to Judea. These oracles were probably delivered within a year or so of the coming of Cyrus, and they consist of a series of short poems. There is a shift in tone beginning in chapter 49. Chapters 40–48 are filled with the expectation of a new era to be inaugurated by Cyrus. Chapters 49–55 are concerned rather with the Jewish community and its internal problems.

The New Exodus

The opening oracle in Isa 40:1-11 is set in the divine council, like Isaiah's call vision in chapter 6. The speaker is not identified but is apparently an angelic being.

The message of comfort in Isa 40:1-2 acknowledges the familiar idea that the exile was a punishment for sin, but it adds a novel twist: Jerusalem has been punished "double for all her sins." This is the first suggestion that the punishment of YHWH is excessive. This opens up the possibility that the suffering may have a purpose other than punishment.

Another voice cries out in v. 3: "In the wilderness prepare the way of the LORD." The return from Babylon will be a reenactment of the exodus. Israel is given the opportunity to begin anew (cf. Hosea 2). There is also a suggestion of a new creation, because of the way in which the order of nature will be reversed.

The theme of the exodus recurs. In 43:16 the prophet speaks in the name of the Lord, "who makes a way in the sea, a path in the mighty waters." Yet a few verses later he says: "Do not remember the former things or consider the things of old. I am about to do a new thing. . . . I will make a way in the wilderness and rivers in the desert " (43:18-20). The exodus is not to be regarded as "a thing of old" but as a pattern of divine intervention that is being reenacted in the present.

The most striking instance of this typological understanding of the exodus is found in Isa 51:9-11, which calls on "the arm of YHWH" to awake as in the days of old. The prophet first recalls creation: "Was it not you who cut Rahab in pieces, who pierced the dragon?" This is not the account of creation that we find in Genesis but one that we know from passing allusions in Hebrew poetry, such as Job 26:12 or Ps 74:13-14. It is closely related to the stories of Baal and Yamm in the Ugaritic myths, and less directly to the Babylonian myth of Marduk and Tiamat. Second Isaiah juxtaposes this myth with the exodus: "Was it not you who dried up the sea, the waters of the great deep; who made the depths of the sea a way for the redeemed to cross over?" (51:10). The implication is that the exodus and the battle with the dragon at creation are analogous events. The prophet is not interested in ancient history. Both creation and exodus provide a model for what is happening in the present. When "the ransomed of the LORD" return to Zion, the dragon is pierced and the waters of the deep are once again dried up.

Fig. 19.1. The tomb of Cyrus at Pasargadae in Iran. Photo: © SEF / Art Resource, N.Y.

The Polemic against Idolatry

For Yahwists in Babylon, one of the galling aspects of their situation was the apparent failure of their God and the superiority of the Babylonian deities. One aspect of Babylonian worship that attracts a lot of attention in Second Isaiah is divination—the prediction of the future by ritual means. With the fall of Babylon and the restoration of Jerusalem, however, the situation was reversed. Second Isaiah claims that this is what YHWH had predicted all along: "The former things I declared long ago . . . then suddenly I did them and they came to pass" (48:3). It is not clear whether he had specific prophecies in mind.

The claims that Second Isaiah makes for his God are stronger than any we have hitherto encountered in the Hebrew Bible. He categorically denies that any other gods have power and comes close to denying their existence: "Before me no god was formed, nor shall there be any after me. I, I am the LORD, and besides me there is no savior" (43:10-11; cf. 44:6; 46:9). Because of statements like these, Second Isaiah is arguably the first monotheist in the tradition, but even he seems to grant the pagan gods a limited form of existence: "Bel bows down, Nebo stoops . . . they themselves go into captivity" (46:2). But statements like this are mere mockery. The prophet denies that there is any reality to these gods beyond the idols made by their worshipers.

The critique of idols in Second Isaiah must be seen against the background of the role of statues in Babylonian worship. The cult image was the basic means of representing the presence of the deity. These statues were the focus of the sacrificial cult, and they were carried in processions. When the images were carried off by conquerors, the gods were thought to go with them. The statues were consecrated in ceremonies that supposedly opened their eyes and mouths and thereafter were treated as if they

were alive. Food was placed before them twice a day. The "leftovers" were sent to the king or consumed by the temple clergy. The care and proper clothing of these statues was a major activity of the temple personnel.

Second Isaiah inaugurates a long tradition of satire against idols. He focuses on the process by which they were made. "A man cuts down a tree, makes a fire with part of it to warm himself and heat his food, and makes the rest into a god and calls on it to save him" (44:9-20). Of course the prophet is not being fair to the Babylonians. The statue was not the god or goddess, but only the instrument by which the god's presence was mediated. There are several such idol parodies in the later books of the Old Testament. A particularly entertaining example is found in the story of Bel and the Dragon, in the Greek additions to the book of Daniel.

While the prophet's mockery is aimed at the Babylonian gods, he does not acknowledge any gods besides YHWH. Despite his enthusiasm for Cyrus of Persia, he never mentions Ahura Mazda, the god of the Zoroastrians. In fact, there is a subtle rejection of the Persian deity in 45:7. In Zoroastrian theology Ahura Mazda presided over warring forces of light and darkness. According to Second Isaiah, it is YHWH who forms light and creates darkness.

A Hidden God

If YHWH was the true God after all, and was now vindicated by the turn of events, how was his apparent failure in the period of Babylonian ascendancy to be explained? For the prophet, it must have been part of a deliberate plan. "Truly, you are a God who hides himself, O God of Israel, the Savior" (45:15). By withdrawing from history for a time, YHWH could make his revelation all the more spectacular. The reversal of fortunes brought about by the fall of Babylon would catch the attention of the nations.

Second Isaiah calls on all peoples to worship YHWH. The universalism of the Hebrew prophet, however, should not be confused with modern pluralism. What he envisions is the subordination of all peoples to Jerusalem and its God. The prophet gloats over the fall of Babylon in chapter 47, just as Ezekiel had over the fall of Tyre. His vision may still reasonably be called universalistic, since he wants to include the whole universe in the dominion of YHWH. But it is universalism on Yahwistic terms, centered on Mount Zion.

The Servant of the Lord

One of the best-known features of Second Isaiah concerns the figure of "the servant of the LORD." The word "servant" occurs numerous times in these oracles, but four passages are usually singled out as "Servant Songs": 42:1-4; 49:1-6; 50:4-9; and 52:13—53:12. These passages are an integral part of the prophecy of Second Isaiah, and some of them are integral parts of longer passages. The servant in question has been variously identified as a collective figure (Israel) or as an individual. Several individual identifications have been suggested. The most widely supported are Moses, who is often called the servant of the Lord in the Deuteronomic tradition, Cyrus, and the prophet himself.

The first point to note is that Israel, or Jacob, is explicitly called "my servant" in several oracles: 41:8; 44:1-2; 44:21; 45:4. This is also the case in 49:3, a Servant Song, unless one resorts to textual emendation. However, 44:26, "who confirms the word of his servant and fulfills the prediction of his messengers," suggests rather that the servant is the prophet. The evidence, then, indicates that the servant is usually Israel, but that an individual interpretation cannot be ruled out in all cases.

The third Servant Song, 50:4-9, stands apart from the others and does not use the word "servant" at all. The figure, who speaks in the first person, is a teacher or prophet who endures much resistance and abuse. Jeremiah would seem to be the model here (cf. Jer 15:15-21). In this case the reference is most probably to the prophet himself.

The first two Songs, 42:1-4 and 49:1-6 are each part of a longer passage. In both, the servant recalls Jeremiah. In 49:3 the servant is addressed as "Israel," but he also seems to have a mission to Israel. It may be that the servant is an ideal Israel, or an idealized remnant within Israel, that acts as a leader toward the rest of the people. The servant is also a light to the nations. The divine plan in the restoration of Israel is not concerned only with the welfare of one people, but with the conversion of the entire world. Isaiah 49:7 is addressed to "one deeply despised, abhorred by the nations," assuring him that kings and princes would be startled because of what the Lord would do. This points forward to the beginning of the fourth Servant Song in 52:13-15. The "covenant to the people" and the release of prisoners in 49:8-9 harks back to 42:6-7. These links suggest that at least three of the Servant Songs, those in chapters 42, 49, and 52–53, have the same figure in mind.

Surely he has borne our infirmities
    and carried our diseases;
yet we accounted him stricken,
    struck down by God, and afflicted.
But he was wounded for our transgressions,
    crushed for our iniquities;
upon him was the punishment that made us
        whole,
    and by his bruises we are healed.
All we like sheep have gone astray;
    we have all turned to our own way,
and the LORD has laid on him
    the iniquity of us all.
—Isaiah 53:4-6

The longest and most famous Servant Song begins at 52:13 and runs through chapter 53. The first few verses, 52:13-15, summarize the servant's story: he was deformed beyond recognition but will be restored and exalted to the astonishment of kings. The main body of the poem, 53:1-10, is spoken by a collective group. If the servant is thought to be an individual, this group could be the Jewish community. If the servant is Israel, the speakers are the kings, whose astonishment is noted at the end of chapter 52. Again, they comment on the abject state of the servant, but now they add an explanation: "Surely he has borne our infirmities and carried our diseases . . . he was wounded for our transgressions, crushed for our iniquities, upon him was the punishment that made us whole." Moreover, we are told that the servant was "cut off from the land of the living, stricken for the transgression of my people" (53:8). His life is made an offering for sin. The final verses, 11-12, are spoken by YHWH, confirming that the servant will indeed atone for others, and that because of this "I will allot him a portion with the great."

Since the servant is said to be killed, he can hardly be the prophet himself. He could conceivably be a prophet, and the poem could be composed by his disciples, but this is an entirely hypothetical scenario. It is equally hypothetical to identify the servant with a royal figure (the heir to the throne?) and suppose that he had died "for the sin of my people." The explanation that requires least hypothetical speculation is that the servant is Israel, described metaphorically as an individual. In the exile, Israel was deformed beyond recognition and might even be said to have died (cf. Ezekiel's vision of a valley full of dry bones). The people whose iniquities he bore are the other nations. On this explanation, the exile was not punishment for the sin of Israel but vicarious suffering for the sins of other peoples. One of the problems of the poem is the statement in 53:10 that "he shall see his offspring and prolong his days," even though he was earlier said to be cut off from the land of the living. This is less of a problem if the servant is Israel than if he is an individual. There is no hint of individual resurrection anywhere else in Second Isaiah. Admittedly, no interpretation of this song is without problems, and it is easy to understand why many commentators insist that the servant must be an individual. Any individual interpretation, however, requires that we imagine a history for that individual for which we have no other information.

Regardless of whether the servant is individual or collective, the interest of the passage lies primarily in the idea of vicarious suffering, the idea that the sufferings of one person or people can atone for the sin of another. One analogy that comes to mind here is that of the scapegoat in Leviticus 16, which was said to bear the sins of the people and carry them into the wilderness. A closer analogy is provided by Ezekiel, who was said to bear the sin of the people by lying on his side in a symbolic action (Ezekiel 4). As we saw in the case of Ezekiel, the efficacy of such action depends on the reaction of the people for whom it is performed. In the context of Second Isaiah, the onlookers are astonished by the exaltation of the servant, after he had seemed beyond hope. It is this astonishment that leads to their conversion; compare Isa 45:20-25, where the ends of the earth are expected to turn to YHWH because of the astonishing salvation of Israel. The purpose of the exile, then, was to get the attention of the nations, so that they would become aware of YHWH and be astonished by the sudden revelation of his power. Israel was like a sacrificial victim, a lamb led to the slaughter (53:7; cf. Jer 11:19). By obediently going along with the divine plan, Israel makes righteous the many people who observe what happened. No one is automatically saved by the suffering of the servant, but it creates an opportunity for people to recognize their true situation and convert accordingly.

The importance of this passage is that it introduces the possibility of a positive understanding of suffering. This idea would prove extremely fruitful in later tradition and would be crucial to the understanding of the death of Jesus in early Christianity.

The Davidic Covenant

Second Isaiah's vision of restoration has no place for a renewed monarchy. The restoration, after all, was by permission of the Persians, and they were not about to grant Judah its independence. The prophet does refer once to the promise to David, in 55:3-5. The everlasting covenant will be renewed, but with the people as a whole rather than with a royal dynasty. The covenant with David, then, is not void, but it finds its fulfillment in the restoration of a community in

---

The Suffering Servant

Many Christians find it difficult to read Isaiah 53 as anything but a prophecy of the sufferings of Jesus. Yet in ancient Judaism it was not even read as a messianic prophecy until after the time of Christ. It is read as messianic in the Targum, an Aramaic paraphrase from the early centuries of the common era. But the Targum does not attribute the suffering to the Messiah. It begins with Isa 52:13: "Behold my servant, the messiah, shall prosper. . . . As the house of Israel hoped for him many days, for their appearance was wretched among the nations and their countenance beyond that of the sons of men." Isa 53:4 is read: "He shall pray on behalf of our transgressions and our iniquities shall be pardoned for his sake, though we were accounted smitten, stricken from before the Lord, and afflicted." Isa 53:7: "The mighty ones of the peoples he will deliver up like a lamb to the slaughter." 53:10: "It was the Lord's good pleasure to refine and to purify the remnant of his people, in order to cleanse their soul from sin: they shall look upon the kingdom of their messiah, they shall multiply sons and daughters. . . ."

In this way, suffering is attributed either to the Israelites or to the nations, but the Messiah is preserved as a strong and glorious figure.

The idea of a messiah who dies is attested in later Judaism. In the apocalypse of 4 Ezra, written at the end of the first century C.E., he dies at the end of a reign of 400 years. Later Judaism has a tradition about the messiah son of Joseph, who is killed. That tradition may have been suggested by the fate of Bar Kokhba, the man who led the revolt against Rome in 132–35 C.E. and was believed by some to be the Messiah. He was killed by the Romans.

Jerusalem. The prophet insists that no word of the Lord goes unfulfilled, although the ways of God are often mysterious to human beings.

Third Isaiah

Some of the oracles in Isaiah 56–66 are close to those of Second Isaiah in spirit and tone, especially those of chapters 60–62. Chapter 60 is a joyful prediction of the restoration of Jerusalem, familiar from Handel's *Messiah*: "Arise, shine, for thy light has come." The prophet envisions an open city. As in Second Isaiah, this is a universalistic vision, but a Zion-centered one. There is a place for all the nations in the restored order, but it is a subordinate place. Nonetheless, the contrast with the vision of the future in the last chapters of Ezekiel is striking. The Ezekiel tradition was concerned to create a holy city, where Jews would be separated from Gentiles. The Isaianic tradition also envisions a holy city, but one where Gentiles enhance the glory of Jerusalem by serving it.

The euphoric tone continues in Isaiah 61, where the prophet claims to be endowed with the spirit of the Lord. The mission of the prophet here is closely related to that of the servant in Second Isaiah—to bring good news to the oppressed and liberty to captives (cf. 42:7; 49:9). The "year of the LORD's favor" is an allusion to the Jubilee Year of Leviticus 25, but here it seems to have the character of a final, definitive jubilee. It is also the day of God's vengeance. Isaiah 61:1-2 figures prominently in the New Testament as the text for Jesus' inaugural sermon (Luke 4:18-19).

A Divided Community

Many of the other oracles in this section of the book of Isaiah have a very different tone, one of bitter recrimination that reflects disputes within the community. These oracles presuppose a situation after the return to Judah and are thereby distinguished from Second Isaiah. The rhetoric is especially bitter in chapter 65, but the specific references are obscure.

There is some evidence of tension between Third Isaiah and the Jerusalem priesthood. In 66:1-2 the prophet asks, in the name of the Lord: "Heaven is my throne and the earth is my footstool; what is the house that you would build for me?" This passage clearly dates from the period after the exile, when the temple was being rebuilt. The opening question echoes Solomon's prayer at the consecration of the temple in 1 Kgs 8:27: "But will God indeed dwell on the earth?" Solomon goes on to explain the value of the temple as a place where people could make their offerings. There is no such explanation in Isaiah 66. The implication of the question would seem to be that the temple is unnecessary, or at least not very important. The passage continues with some of the most startling verses in the Hebrew Bible. The Hebrew text juxtaposes a series of participles, literally: "slaughtering an ox, killing a man; sacrificing a lamb, breaking a dog's neck; presenting a grain offering, offering swine's blood." The NRSV translates: "Whoever slaughters an ox is like one who kills a human being," etc. On this interpretation, some of the hallowed practices of the Jewish cult were morally equivalent to murder or profanity. But the Hebrew can also be construed in another way: "The one who slaughters an ox also kills a man," etc.). On this interpretation, the problem is not that the cult itself is perverse, but that there is a gulf between the apparent piety of the worshipers and their conduct on other occasions. This would be more in line with the critique of sacrifice in the preexilic prophets. There is no consensus as to the identity of the people who are being condemned.

One other passage in Isaiah 56–66 is relevant to the issue of inner-community polemics. Isaiah 56:1-7 reassures eunuchs and foreigners who had joined themselves to the Lord that they are welcome on the holy mountain to minister to the Lord. (This passage shows, incidentally, that Third Isaiah did not reject the temple cult in principle.) This hospitable attitude is in conflict with Deut 23:1-8, which excludes from the assembly of the Lord anyone "whose testicles are crushed or whose penis is cut off." Ezekiel 44:9 also decrees that "no foreigner, uncircumcised in heart and flesh, of all the foreigners who are among the people of Israel, shall enter my sanctuary." Access to the temple was evidently a matter of contention in the early postexilic community. The people whose views are reflected in Isaiah 56–66 favored relatively open access and were at odds with those who demanded restrictions (Ezekiel 44). It is apparent that there were bitter divisions within the postexilic community.

The Hope for the Future

The party with which the prophet identifies is described variously as "those who tremble at the word of the Lord" (66:2, 5) and "my servants." The servants are presumably the heirs of "the servant" of Second Isaiah. These people evidently did not enjoy much power in the early postexilic community, but they entertained hopes of a dramatic reversal. Isaiah 65:13 tells the opponents:

Therefore thus says the Lord God:
My servants shall eat, but you shall be
    hungry;
my servants shall drink, but you shall be
    thirsty;
my servants shall rejoice, but you shall be
    put to shame.

The logic of the passage is similar to the Sermon on the Mount in Matthew 5–7: those who hunger and mourn in the present will have plenty and joy in the future.

The expectation of a radical reversal of fortune is one of the key elements in apocalyptic literature (Daniel, Revelation). These chapters of Isaiah anticipate some apocalyptic motifs. The prophet appeals to God to "tear open the heavens and come down, so that the mountains would quake at your presence" (Isa 64:1). There is no hope of salvation by human means, so the hope is for direct divine intervention, in the style of the theophanies of old. Most striking of all is the prophecy of a new heaven and a new earth in 65:17-25. Here the prophet looks forward to a new creation, in which life will be different. No longer shall there be "an infant that lives but a few days or an old person who does not live out a lifetime; for one who dies at a hundred years will be considered a youth, and one who falls short of a hundred will be considered accursed" (v. 20). Life will be longer and better but not essentially different in kind. Third Isaiah does not envision resurrection of the dead or eternal life, as the later apocalyptic writings do. (The new heavens and new earth have a different connotation in Rev 21:1.) His vision of the future remains close to what we found in the mythological utopia of Isaiah 11, where "the wolf and the lamb shall feed together, the lion shall eat straw like the ox" (65:25).

This section of the book of Isaiah ends on a jarring note. We are told that people will look at the dead bodies of the people who have rebelled against God, "for their worm shall not die, their fire shall not be quenched, and they shall be an abhorrence to all flesh" (66:24). This is not the idea of hell, which would emerge some centuries later. There is no suggestion that the wicked are alive to experience unending torment. Rather, the righteous and their descendants will derive satisfaction from the spectacle of the destruction of the bodies of the wicked. This is certainly a step on the road to hell, so to speak, and it appeals to the more vindictive side of human nature. This note, however, is not characteristic of Third Isaiah.

The So-Called Isaiah Apocalypse (Isaiah 24–27)

Cosmic Destruction

The imagery of cosmic destruction and renewal that is associated with apocalyptic writings figures prominently in Isaiah 24–27. For that reason, these chapters have often been singled out and dubbed "the Isaiah Apocalypse." The designation is misleading. These chapters do not have the literary form of an apocalypse (see the comments on the book of Daniel) and are not necessarily a literary unit at all. They are not marked off as a separate section in the text. They do, however, contain a remarkable concentration of images of cosmic destruction.

It is possible that these oracles originally referred to highly specific occasions that we can no longer identify. For example, when Isa 24:10 says that "the city of chaos is broken down," the reference may be to the destruction of Babylon by King Xerxes of Persia in 482 B.C.E., as many scholars believe. But several other occasions have also been proposed, ranging from the eighth to the second centuries, and the text itself provides no specific identification. The reference may not be to one specific city but to a type that represents all cities opposed to God. This type is then contrasted with Jerusalem, in 26:1-2. There is a somewhat similar contrast between Babylon and Jerusalem in the book of Revelation.

It is not possible to relate these chapters to any specific historical crisis with any confidence. Instead, like the ancient myths, they evoke a type of situation that can be applied to various historical crises or can be taken as a foreshadowing of the end of the world. The ancient myths, such as *Enuma Elish* or the Baal myth, were myths of beginnings. These chapters of Isaiah provide myths of ending. In Isaiah 24–27 we recognize several allusions to the old "myths of beginnings," but they are now projected into the future.

Isaiah 24 provides an exceptionally vivid picture of the destruction of the physical world. Already Jeremiah had seen "the earth, and it was waste and void" (Jer 4:23). Isaiah 24:1 uses different language to similar effect. Verse 2 suggests that the cosmic upheaval is a metaphor for social disruption, when roles are overturned. In Isaiah 24 the distress of the earth is attributed to pollution, because its inhabitants have violated "the eternal covenant," the phrase used for God's covenant with Noah in Gen 9:16.

The Defeat of Death

Mythic themes appear again in Isaiah 25. God will prepare a feast for all peoples "on this mountain" (Mount Zion). Mythic conflicts often end with a triumphal feast (cf. Ezekiel 39 and Rev 19:17-21). The banquets in Ezekiel and Revelation have a gruesome character, but the feast in Isaiah 25 is more joyful (rich food, aged wines). The most powerful image in this passage is the statement that God "will swallow up death forever" (25:7-8). In the Ugaritic myths, Death (Mot) swallowed up Baal. The mythological figure of Mot symbolizes here everything that is wrong in human life. It is not apparent from this passage that resurrection or eternal life is envisioned. It may be that the prophet dreamed of a time when death would be no more, but this may be a metaphor for more general relief from the problems of life.

The question of death is raised again in chapter 26. The prophet makes a contrast between other peoples and the people of YHWH:

> O Lord our God,
>> other lords besides you have ruled over us. . . .
> The dead do not live;
>> shades do not rise. . . . (26:13-14)

He continues:

> Your dead shall live, their corpses shall rise.
>> O dwellers in the dust, awake and sing for joy!
> For your dew is a radiant dew,
>> and the earth will give birth to those long dead. (26:19)

Many scholars regard this passage as the first attestation of individual resurrection in the Hebrew Bible. In the context, however, it seems more likely that the resurrection language is metaphorical, as it was in Ezekiel 37, and that the reference is to the restoration of the people. That the prophet speaks of the resurrection of the dead, even metaphorically, is significant. The use of resurrection language would contribute in time to a growing belief that God would exercise his power over death on behalf of his servants. We will find that belief in the book of Daniel.

Leviathan

There is yet another allusion to ancient myth in Isa 27:1: "On that day, the Lord with his cruel and great and strong sword will punish Levia-

than the fleeing serpent, Leviathan the twisting serpent, and he will kill the dragon that is in the sea." There are several allusions in the Hebrew Bible to a battle between God and a monster, in the context of creation. For example, Job 26:12 says, "By his power he stilled the Sea; by his understanding he struck down Rahab." Isaiah 51:9 asks, "Was it not you who cut Rahab in pieces, who pierced the dragon?" In Ps 74:13-14 the monster is called Leviathan. (Leviathan is also mentioned as a primeval monster in Job 3:8; 41:4.) The story of this battle is never told in the Bible, but it is illuminated by the Canaanite myths from Ugarit, where Baal does battle with Yamm, the Sea. Associated with the Sea are monsters called Lotan, the dragon, and the crooked serpent. In the Canaanite myths, this battle is located in the beginnings of history. In Isa 27:1 it is projected into the future to express the hope that "on that day" the Lord will eradicate all the problems in the world.

The Final Edition of Isaiah

Isaiah 24–27 may well be the latest part of the book of Isaiah. At least in one respect it is typical of the book as a whole: a central theme is the reign of YHWH on Mount Zion. The images of cosmic conflict and final victory might have made a fitting culmination to the book, but they were not placed at the end by the editors. Instead, they were associated with the oracles against foreign nations that dominate chapters 13–23.

The book of Isaiah was compiled over several hundred years. The oldest manuscript, in the Dead Sea Scrolls, dates from the third century B.C.E. Some themes run through the book, such as the centrality of Zion and the holy mountain, the references to YHWH as the Holy One of Israel, and the imagery of light.

As the book stands, the historical prophet is relativized. Even his call is moved away from the beginning of the book. Instead, the oracles of judgment with which the book begins stand as a timeless warning not only to Jerusalem but to all who regard themselves as the people of YHWH. Equally, the promises of hope and restoration go beyond the historical context of the return from the Babylonian exile and stand as paradigms of hope for all generations. There is clearly a movement from judgment to restoration in the book as a whole, but it remains a collection of oracles. It is not tightly structured in the manner that we might expect from a modern composition. Nonetheless, it is a book that would speak to many generations long after the time of Isaiah.

Further Reading

Commentaries

Baltzer, Klaus. *Deutero-Isaiah: A Commentary on Isaiah 40–55*. Trans. M. Kohl. Hermeneia. Minneapolis: Fortress Press, 2001.

Blenkinsopp, Joseph. *Isaiah 40–55*. AB 19A. New York: Doubleday, 2002.

———. *Isaiah 56–66*. AB 19B. New York: Doubleday, 2003.

Childs, Brevard S. *Isaiah*. OTL. Louisville: Westminster John Knox, 2001.

Hanson, Paul D. *Isaiah 40–66*. Interpretation. Louisville: Westminster John Knox, 1995.

Seitz, Christopher R. "The Book of Isaiah 40–66." In *NIB* 6:309–552.

Other Studies

Clifford, Richard J. *Fair Spoken and Persuading: An Interpretation of Second Isaiah*. New York: Paulist, 1984.

Hanson, Paul D. *The Dawn of Apocalyptic*, 32–208. Philadelphia: Fortress Press, 1975.

Sommer, Benjamin D. *A Prophet Reads Scripture: Allusion in Isaiah 40–66*. Stanford: Stanford Univ. Press, 1998.

20

Postexilic Prophecy:
Haggai, Zechariah, Malachi, Joel

KEY POINTS

Haggai: prophesied in 520 B.C.E., some 18 years after the first exiles returned.

- Lack of prosperity was due to the failure to rebuild the temple.
- When the foundation did not bring about a change of fortune, it would come **"in a little while."**
- Zerubbabel was God's **signet ring**. Probably expected to restore the kingship.

Zechariah: set of 8 visions in chaps. 1–6.

- High priest Joshua **absolved of all guilt**. His accusers are cast as Satan in a heavenly trial.
- Zerubbabel is the **branch of David** predicted by Jeremiah.
- The restored cult will be supported by **"two sons of oil"** (Zerubbabel and Joshua).

- In Zechariah 6 the prophet mentions "crowns," apparently for Zerubbabel and Joshua. In the end he is told to crown Joshua alone. It seems that Zerubbabel has been erased from the text at this point.

Malachi: sharp **critique of the priesthood**.

- Also seems to reject **divorce**.
- Epilogues to Malachi, which conclude the Minor Prophets, affirm the teaching of Moses and the hope for the **return of Elijah**.

Joel: **Day of the Lord** as day of general judgment on foreign nations.

- Prominence of **eschatology and Day of the Lord** is a unifying theme in the Book of the Twelve.

The prophets Haggai and Zechariah are mentioned in the book of Ezra (5:1; 6:14-15) in connection with the rebuilding of the Jerusalem temple. It is apparent both from the account in Ezra and from the book of Haggai that a considerable time (approximately twenty years) elapsed between the first return, in the reign of Cyrus, and the eventual rebuilding. The exiles returned to an impoverished land, and building a temple was not the highest priority for many of them. The problems are reflected in Haggai 1, which is dated to the second year of Darius (520 B.C.E.).

Haggai

Haggai 1 reports a dispute with people who argued that "the time has not yet come to rebuild the Lord's house." The prophet Jeremiah had prophesied that Jerusalem would be desolate for seventy years (Jer 25:11; 29:10). The actual completion of the temple in 516 B.C.E. came almost exactly seventy years after the destruction. Some people may have believed that any earlier restoration would have been premature. Haggai suggests more mundane reasoning: "Is it a time for you yourselves to live in your paneled houses, while this house lies in ruins?" The returnees were not living in luxury, but they put their own needs first. In a community where resources are scarce, should people attend first to basic human needs, such as housing, or should they devote their resources to worship and a temple? The importance of a temple, even from a purely sociological point of view, should not be underestimated. By devoting their resources to the temple, the people put the community as a whole ahead of individual needs and created an important symbol of their own identity as well as of their religious commitments.

Haggai is unequivocal in his demand that the temple be given the highest priority. His reasoning is not sociological but is grounded in mythological ideas about cult and fertility. In the period since the return from Babylon, the people had planted much but harvested little. The prophet's diagnosis is simple: it is because the house of the Lord is in ruins. This kind of reasoning is completely at odds with modern pragmatism, and it strikes the modern reader as superstitious. More remarkably, it is also at odds with the prophetic tradition reflected in the Hebrew Bible. Prophets like Amos and Micah were extremely skeptical of the value of sacrifice and cultic worship. Jeremiah had derided those who set their hopes on "the temple of the Lord, the temple of the Lord." That tradition was continued in Haggai's own time by the prophet of Isaiah 66, who asked, "What is this house that you would build for me?" Evidently,

Persian Empire

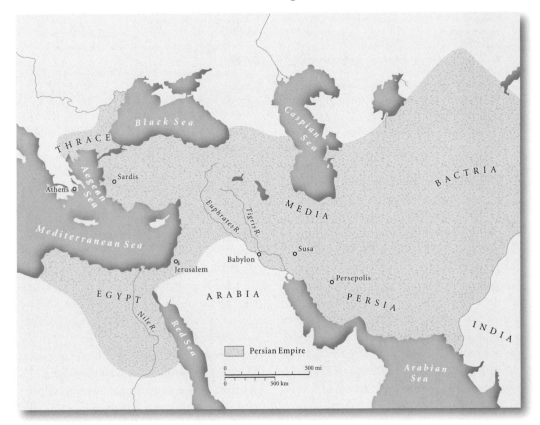

not everyone in Judah shared Haggai's confidence in the efficacy of temple worship.

At the urging of the prophets, the rebuilding of the temple was begun. Haggai 2 describes the rather anticlimactic reaction to the foundations: "Who is left among you that saw this house in its former glory? How does it look to you now? Is it not in your sight as nothing?" Ezra 3:12-13 reports that many old people who remembered the first temple wept when they saw the foundations of the new one. Haggai was unabashed. It was only a matter of time until the glory of the Lord would be revealed.

Haggai's prophecy was not fulfilled. His response is to reaffirm his prediction; it will certainly happen soon, "from this day on." What is remarkable here is that a failed prophecy should still be accepted as inspired and canonical by later generations. Haggai had succeeded in his mission to get the temple rebuilt.

The final oracle in the book of Haggai is especially intriguing. The Lord is about to overthrow the kingdoms of the earth, but he goes further: "On that day, says the Lord of hosts, I will take you, O Zerubbabel my servant, son of Shealtiel, says the Lord, and make you like a signet ring; for I have chosen you, says the Lord of hosts." The royal seal was the means by which deeds were stamped with the authority of the king. To say that Zerubbabel, the governor, was "like a signet ring" was to say that he was the medium by which God's authority was exercised. The designation "my servant" has a similar force.

(Jeremiah said that Nebuchadnezzar was the servant of the Lord; Second Isaiah cast Cyrus of Persia in this role.) Jeremiah 22:23-25 says that even if Coniah (Jehoiachin) king of Judah were YHWH's signet ring, he would be torn off and cast away. The intriguing question here is whether Haggai meant that Zerubbabel would be restored to the kingship, suggesting that he was, in effect, the messiah, the one who would restore the kingdom of David.

Zechariah 1–8

Zechariah is closely associated with Haggai. The opening verse dates the beginning of his career to "the eighth month, in the second year of Darius." The first vision account is dated to the eleventh month of the same year, two months after the last dated oracle of Haggai.

The prophecies that may be attributed to Zechariah are in chapters 1–6, more precisely,

Fig. 20.1. King Darius seated on his throne, from Persepolis (Iran). Photo: © SEF / Art Resource, N.Y.

1:7—6:15. Within this block of material are eight visions and one oracle. These prophecies are framed by sermonic, Deuteronomistic, material in 1:1-6 and chapters 7–8. Chapters 1–8 are often referred to as First Zechariah, and they seem to constitute a coherent book, of which the visions of Zechariah form the core.

The High Priest and the Branch

In Zech 3:1-10, the prophet sees the high priest, Joshua, standing before the angel of the Lord, and "the Satan" standing at his right hand to accuse him. This is one of three cases in the Hebrew Bible where a figure called "Satan" appears. The others are in the prologue of Job and 1 Chron 21:1, where Satan, without the definite article, incites David to take a census. In Job, Satan attends a gathering of "the sons of God" and appears to be a member of the heavenly council. Both in Job and in Zechariah he is the heavenly accuser or adversary.

In Zechariah 3 the scene implies that some people have brought an accusation against the high priest. By setting the accusation in a heavenly tribunal, Zechariah in effect appeals the case to the supreme court. The Lord rebukes the Satan for bringing any accusation against him, because he is "a brand plucked from the fire." In view of the precarious situation of the Jewish community after the exile, the high priest must be affirmed and supported, not criticized. So the Lord invests Joshua with clean garments, thereby forestalling any further accusations.

The investiture is followed by an oracle that makes a twofold promise to Joshua. First, if he observes the Lord's requirements, he will be confirmed in the high priesthood, and given access "among those who are standing here," that is, the divine council. Access to the heavenly council is a privilege granted to prophets in the Hebrew Bible (e.g., Jer 23:18). Here it is extended to the high priest, who becomes the dominant religious functionary in Second Temple Judaism. The access is temporary, as it was in the case of the prophets.

The second promise is that God is about to bring "my servant the Branch." The word "branch" (Hebrew ṣemaḥ) occurs in Jer 23:5 and 33:15, where it refers explicitly to a Davidic king. There is no doubt then that Zechariah is predicting a restoration of the Davidic line. In the context of Zechariah, the branch who is expected can only be Zerubbabel (whose name means "seed of Babylon"). The objection that the Persians would not allow Zerubbabel to become king is beside the point. The prophet is not giving a realistic assessment of Persian policy but expecting a miraculous divine intervention.

Two Sons of Oil

In his fifth vision (4:1-7; 10b-14), Zechariah sees a lampstand or menorah of pure gold, with seven lamps, flanked by two olive trees. The angel's explanation follows in v. 10b. In between, there is another oracle about Zerubbabel, which is an obvious insertion.

The original vision focuses on the menorah, which is well known as part of the furniture of the temple (cf. 1 Kgs 7:49). The lampstand of the tabernacle in Exod 25:31-40 has seven lights. The one in Zechariah's vision has seven lamps with seven lips on each, so forty-nine lights in all. The lights are said to symbolize the eyes of the Lord that range through the whole earth—the heavenly counterpart to the eyes of the king in the Persian imperial system. The choice of the menorah draws attention also to the temple cult. The lampstand symbolizes the presence of the Lord.

The two olive trees are said to symbolize "two sons of oil" (4:14). There is little doubt that the two figures in question are the high priest Joshua and the governor Zerubbabel, both of whom played leading roles in the rebuilding of the temple. (Compare also the roles of the high priest and the "prince" in the New Jerusalem in Ezekiel 40–48.) What is disputed is whether the phrase "two sons of oil" implies that they were anointed (so NRSV: "two anointed ones"). Both the king and the high priest were anointed in ancient Israel. If the governor were anointed, this would imply a claim to royal status. The text does not imply that the anointing actually took place. The reference to oil could hardly fail to suggest anointing when used in connection with a high priest and a Davidic ruler. The functions of these figures are conceived primarily with reference to the temple and its cult, as is also the case in Ezekiel 40–48. They also imply a different kind of community structure from that of the preexilic monarchy. In the new order, high priest and king share power.

The insertion in Zech 4:6-10a sharpens the focus on Zerubbabel. He will rule not by (human) might or power but by the spirit of the Lord. There is no suggestion that rebellion would be necessary. The hope that Zerubbabel would restore the kingship was fueled by his role in the rebuilding of the temple. Since Zerubbabel was performing traditional royal functions in connection with the rebuilding of the temple, it is not surprising that hopes surged that he would restore the monarchy, with or without Persian permission.

A Crown or Crowns?

Chapter 6 concludes with a narrative that relates directly to the messianic hopes of chapters 3 and 4. The prophet is told to collect silver and gold from the exiles who have returned from Babylon. With these precious materials he is told to make crowns. (The plural is usually emended to the singular in English translations.) Then he is told to set it (singular) on the head of the high priest Joshua. The oracle that follows, however, seems much more appropriate for Zerubbabel: "Here is a man whose name is Branch: for he shall branch out in his place, and he shall build the temple of the Lord. It is he that shall build the temple of the Lord; he shall bear royal honor, and shall sit upon his throne and rule. There shall be a priest by his throne, with peaceful understanding between the two of them" (6: 12-13). It is clear from verse 13 that the figure whose name is Branch is not a priest; therefore the oracle cannot refer to Joshua. Like chapter 4, this passage envisions power sharing between king and priest. The anomaly of the passage is that no crown is placed on the head of the royal figure, only on that of the priest.

It seems clear that we no longer have the original form of Zechariah 6. Most probably, the plural "crowns" is correct; the prophet would have made crowns both for Zerubbabel and for Joshua. Zerubbabel, however, was edited out of the text. The idea of crowning the governor was probably too explosive. The crowning of Zerubbabel was either prevented or suppressed, and the text was emended accordingly. We do not know what became of Zerubbabel. The Persian authorities may have realized that he was giving rise to messianic hopes (whether he wished it or not) and may have removed him from the scene.

It is typical of the way that biblical texts were edited that loose ends were allowed to stand. There was no systematic revision of the text to remove all reference to Zerubbabel. This may seem like careless editing from a modern point of view, but it has the advantage of allowing us to see several layers in the text and to reconstruct something of its history.

The Additions to Zechariah

The last six chapters of the book of Zechariah are among the most obscure and difficult passages in the Hebrew Bible. Although they have been classified as part of the book of Zechariah since the Middle Ages, there is no mention of Zechariah in these chapters. They were simply copied after the oracles of Zechariah in ancient manuscripts. Conversely, it is not apparent that the book of Malachi was originally distinguished from the preceding oracles, or that Malachi ("my messenger") was the name of a prophet. All the material in Zechariah 9–14 and Malachi may be regarded as anonymous oracles that were appended to the collection of Minor Prophets.

The End of Prophecy

One of the most intriguing passages in Zechariah 9–14 is 13:2-6, which envisions a time when prophets will be ashamed of their calling and refuse to acknowledge it. Prophecy lost its authority in the Persian period. We do not know the names of any Hebrew prophets after Haggai and Zechariah. In the Hellenistic period, revelatory writings were attributed to ancient worthies such as Enoch or Daniel, not to their real authors. Increasingly in the Second Temple period, religious authority was vested in the scribes who were the authoritative interpreters of the Torah.

Malachi

The oracles attributed to Malachi were probably transmitted anonymously, the name deriving from Mal 3:1, where it means simply "my messenger." In this case, however, we encounter the voice of a distinct prophet. The book consists of six speeches or disputations, with two brief appendices at the end. The units are: 1:2-5; 1:6—2:9; 2:10-16; 2:17—3:5; 3:6-12; and 3:13—4:3 (Hebrew 3:13-21). The appendices are found in 4:4 (3:22) and 4:3 (3:23-24). (The Hebrew text is only divided into three chapters, not four, as in the English translations: Eng. 4:1-5 = MT 3:19-24.)

> See, I am sending my messenger to prepare the way before me, and the LORD whom you seek will suddenly come to his temple. The messenger of the covenant in whom you delight—indeed, he is coming, says the LORD of hosts. But who can endure the day of his coming, and who can stand when he appears?
>
> For he is like a refiner's fire and like fullers' soap; he will sit as a refiner and purifier of silver, and he will purify the descendants of Levi and refine them like gold and silver, until they present offerings to the LORD in righteousness. Then the offering of Judah and Jerusalem will be pleasing to the LORD as in former years.
> —Malachi 3:1-4

A Critique of the Priesthood

The long disputation in 1:6—2:9 is a critique of the Jerusalem priesthood in the Persian period. Unlike preexilic prophets such as Amos or Micah, or even the postexilic prophet of Isaiah 66, Malachi does not question the value or validity of sacrifice. He only demands that it be done properly, arguing that it would be better to close up the temple than to offend the Lord with unworthy offerings. No one would offer a blind or lame animal as a present to the governor. Neither should one use the cult of YHWH to dispose of sick or blemished animals.

Malachi 1:11 makes a remarkable claim: "From the rising of the sun to its setting my name is great among the nations, and in every place incense is offered to my name, and a pure offering." It is possible that the prophet regarded the worship of the highest God in any religion as tantamount to the worship of YHWH. In the book of Ezra, King Cyrus of Persia is said to identify YHWH with "the God of heaven" (Ezra 1:2; in Persian religion the God of heaven was Ahura Mazda). It may be that the prophet took the Persian professions of respect for "the God of heaven" at face value.

The primary concern of the prophet was the integrity of Jewish worship. In Mal 2:4-9 he upbraids the priests of his day by reminding them of "the covenant with Levi." There is no account of such a covenant in the Hebrew Bible. Its existence may have been inferred from the blessing of Levi in Deut 33:9-11. In the Persian period there was believed to be a covenant with Levi, or the Levites, even if it was not explicitly narrated in the Bible. Malachi is insistent that this is a conditional covenant that requires reverence and fidelity on the part of the priests. Here again he is not questioning the importance of the priesthood or the sacrificial cult, but he is holding them to a higher standard than was observed in Jerusalem in his time.

Infidelity and Divorce

The third disputation, 2:10-16, is the most difficult passage in Malachi. Judah, we are told, has profaned the sanctuary of the Lord and "married the daughter of a foreign god." The usual view of commentators is that the passage refers to marriage with foreign women, a problem that figures prominently in the book of Ezra. Those who married foreign women were likely to give some recognition to the religious practices of their wives (cf. the story of Solomon in 1 Kgs 11:1-8). It is clear from the

passage that the offenders had not abandoned the worship of YHWH but were engaging in syncretistic (mixed) worship.

In Mal 2:14 the prophet moves on to a second problem. The Lord "was a witness between you and the wife of your youth, to whom you have been faithless, though she is your companion and your wife by covenant." In view of the reference to the daughter of a foreign god in the previous passage, it is often suggested that Jewish men were divorcing their Jewish wives to marry foreign women, but there is no actual evidence that this was the case. If it were, we should expect that the divorce would be mentioned first, before "the daughter of a foreign god," as the divorce would have cleared the way for the idolatrous marriage. The prophet does not call for the divorce of foreign women or give approval to divorce in any context.

There is explicit mention of divorce in 2:16, but it is obscured by textual difficulties. The word "hate" is commonly used in marriage contracts in connection with divorce; it means to repudiate one's spouse. Accordingly, the phrase should be translated, "for he has hated, sent away . . . and covered his garment with violence." The subject is indefinite. The force of the statement is that to repudiate and divorce (send away) is to commit flagrant injustice. According to Malachi, YHWH disapproves. Divorce was perfectly acceptable in traditional Israelite religion (see Deuteronomy 24), although the right to divorce was restricted to the husband.

Despite a common assumption, there is no indication that Malachi was condemning only the divorce of Jewish wives. The basis for the condemnation is given in 2:15, but the verse is unfortunately corrupt. Literally it reads: "And not one did, and had a remnant of spirit. And what does the one seek? Godly offspring. Guard your spirits, and let no one be faithless to the wife of your youth." The NRSV takes the "one" as God: "Did not one God make her?" This rendering echoes 2:10, "Have we not all one father?" The more usual interpretation takes the "one" as the object: "Did not he [God] make one?" By slight emendation, the word "remnant" *(šᵉʾār)* can be read as "flesh" *(šᵉʾēr)*. The question would then read, "Has he not made one, which has flesh and spirit?" This would be a reference to Gen 2:24, which says that man and wife became "one flesh." The remainder of the verse, "and what does the one seek? Godly offspring," can also be read against the background of Genesis. In Gen 1:28 the only command given to the primal couple is to "be fruitful and fill the earth." On this reading, Malachi sees marriage as a covenant to which God is the witness, and which has as its goal the procreation of godly children. He does not appear to have any place for divorce. The statement in Mal 2:16 can now be read in a new light: "Have we not all one father?" The appeal is to creation and is meant to unify the community, not tear it apart.

The discussion of divorce in Malachi inevitably brings to mind an episode in Ezra 10, which is most probably dated to 458 B.C.E. On his return to Jerusalem, Ezra was horrified to find that Jewish men had married foreign women, and he compelled them to divorce the women and sent them away with their children. We do not know the exact date of Malachi, but it clearly dates from the Persian period. The prophet would have agreed with Ezra in condemning marriage with foreign women because of the potential for idolatry. But he would have disagreed emphatically with Ezra's solution because he saw divorce as contrary to the order of creation in Genesis. The solution was to raise godly children, not send them away.

Malachi's pronouncements on divorce mark a change in traditional Jewish attitudes to marriage. Divorce would still be accepted by mainstream Judaism, but Malachi points to the emergence of a stricter view of marriage as indissoluble. The basis for that view was found in the statement in Genesis that man and wife were one flesh. This stricter view was later developed in the Dead Sea Scrolls, and it receives a famous endorsement in the New Testament in the saying attributed to Jesus: "What God has joined together, let no one separate" (Matt 19:6).

Like a Refiner's Fire

The fifth oracle in Malachi, 2:17—3:5, predicts the coming of the Lord to his temple in judgment in response to the people's complaint, "Where is the God of justice?" The "messenger" or angel sent to prepare the way recalls the angel sent before Israel in the exodus (Exod 23:20) but more directly Isaiah 40, where a figure in the divine council is told to prepare the way in the wilderness. The main issue in dispute is the identity of "the messenger of the covenant." In the context it is difficult to distinguish this messenger from the Lord himself. In Genesis "the angel of the Lord" is similarly difficult to distinguish from the Lord himself. The focus of the passage, in any case, is on the terror and danger associated with the coming of the Lord. The theophany may be understood as a variant of "the Day of the Lord," although the judgment is not on the nations but on the center of the Lord's own cult.

The final oracle, 3:6-12, repeats some of the charges that made the judgment on the cult necessary. Malachi has no objection to sacrifice or offerings. His problem is that people are "cheating God" by not bringing the full offerings and tithes. He also accuses people of cynicism in saying that their worship is for nothing. In 3:16, however, he distinguishes a group of "those who revered the Lord," who seem to be exempt from these charges. As in Isaiah 56–66, so also here we see signs of emerging sectarianism: the elect group that will be saved is not all of Israel or Judah but only the righteous. The tendency to identify such an elect group within Israel becomes fully explicit in the Dead Sea Scrolls.

The Epilogues

The book of Malachi ends with two brief epilogues. The first is a reminder to heed the teaching of "my servant Moses" (Hebrew 3:22; English 4:4), added by an editor, who wanted to affirm the primacy of the Torah. This epilogue may have been intended as a conclusion to the entire Book of the Twelve.

The second epilogue (Hebrew 3:22-23; English 4:5-6) is more specifically related to the oracles of Malachi. It identifies the messenger who would prepare the way of the Lord with Elijah. Elijah had not died but had been taken up alive to heaven. He was therefore available to return and play a part in the end of history. This passage in Malachi is the earliest evidence of the expectation that Elijah would return. It figures prominently in the New Testament, where John the Baptist is identified as Elijah who is to come (Matt 11:14; 17:10-13). In Jewish tradition, a place is set for Elijah at the celebration of the Passover.

Joel

I conclude this survey of the Minor Prophets with the book of Joel. (The book of Jonah is a narrative rather than a collection of oracles and will be discussed in chapter 26.) Here again there is a discrepancy between the Hebrew and English versification. The verses that appear as 2:28-32 in English are designated 3:1-5 in the Hebrew Bible. English chapter 3 corresponds to Hebrew chapter 4.

Joel is placed second in the Book of the Twelve (Minor Prophets) in the Hebrew Bible, between Hosea and Amos, and fourth in the Greek Bible (LXX). The Hebrew arrangement follows a rough chronological order (Hosea, Amos, and Micah occur near the beginning; Haggai, Zechariah, and Malachi at the end). The placement of Joel in the Hebrew Bible, however, is due to thematic contacts with the book of Amos. (The opening couplet of Joel 4:16 [English 3:16] is also found in Amos 1:2. The two books share the theme of the day of the Lord.) Joel provides little internal evidence for its date, but most scholars now agree that it belongs in the postexilic period and is one of the latest books in the collection, if not the latest.

Joel 1:1—2:17 contains a description of a plague of locusts, with exhortations and prayers for deliverance. Joel 2:18-27 gives a reassurance from God. Joel 2:28—3:21 (Hebrew chapters 3 and 4) are concerned with a future time when God will pour out his spirit, save a remnant, and judge the nations.

A striking feature of Joel 1–2 is the motif of "the day of the LORD." This phrase originally referred to a festival day, but it was transformed by Amos into a day of judgment. Joel is exceptional in using the phrase of a plague of locusts, which he describes as an invading army with the Lord at their head (2:11). The impact of such a plague was catastrophic. In the words of 2:3, it transformed the land from a garden of Eden to a desert waste. Such a natural disaster was perceived as a divine judgment no less than a Babylonian invasion.

The "day of the LORD" is used quite differently in Joel 3:14 (Hebrew 4:14). Here it refers to the day of judgment against all peoples in the Valley of Jehoshaphat (which means, "YHWH judged"). Tyre, Sidon, and all the region of Philistia are accused of pillaging Judah. Specifically, they are accused of selling boys and girls as slaves to the Greeks in exchange for prostitutes and wine. We know that there was an active slave trade in the Hellenistic period (third century B.C.E.). The judgment in the Valley of Jehoshaphat, however, is on all nations. This kind of vision of vengeance reappears continually in the later prophetic books: compare Ezekiel 38–39 or Zechariah 14. It reflects the resentment and anger of a people at the mercy of its neighbors.

Joel's vision for the future is not all vengeance. At the end of chapter 2, after the description of the locust plague, the prophet promises the people that "you shall eat in plenty and be satisfied." In chapter 4 he looks for a time when "the mountains shall drip sweet wine, the hills shall flow with milk." In part, his oracles reflect the universal human yearning for peace and plenty. A more specifically Jewish hope is articulated in 3:17: Jerusalem shall be holy and strangers shall never again pass through it.

> Then afterward
>   I will pour out my spirit on all flesh;
> your sons and your daughters shall prophesy,
>   your old men shall dream dreams,
>   and your young men shall see visions.
> Even on the male and female slaves,
>   in those days, I will pour out my spirit.
> —Joel 2:28-29; Acts 2:17-18

In the end of days, the spirit of the Lord will be poured out on all flesh, so that all have the gift of prophecy. This passage is cited in the New Testament in Acts 2 in connection with the outpouring of the spirit at Pentecost.

The Book of the Twelve Minor Prophets

In the preceding chapters I considered several of the Minor Prophets individually. But the Book of the Twelve has also been regarded as a unit from ancient times. Ben Sira refers to "the Twelve Prophets" (Sir 49:10), and the twelve books were copied on a single scroll at Qumran. Originally, these books were grouped together for a practical reason, so that the shorter books, such as Malachi, would not be lost. There is a rough but inexact chronological order. The division of books in the latter part of the corpus is somewhat artificial. The scribes may have decided to distinguish twelve books because of the twelve tribes of Israel. There are, then, some indications of thoughtful arrangement in the Book of the Twelve, but it remains a collection of writings that originated over several centuries, and its unity should not be exaggerated.

The most important common trait running through these books concerns the prominence of eschatology. All the books except Nahum and Jonah refer explicitly to the Day of the Lord, and Nahum refers to a coming divine judgment. The role of eschatology changes, however, in the later books of the collection. Joel reflects a typical pattern, insofar as it starts out with a specific situation and moves to a much wider horizon of cosmic judgment. The same is true of Zechariah. The older prophets were distinguished by their specificity. Think, for example, of Amos upbraiding the rich for selling the poor for a pair of sandals. Already in these books we found some passages that looked to an indefinite future, "at the end of days." In the later prophetic books these passages become more common. When the prophetic oracles were gathered in books and read as Scripture, the original context was often lost from view. Eschatological passages such as Joel 3–4 were not tied to any particular situation. They looked beyond history for a judgment of all nations and a restoration of Israel. None of these oracles, however, envisions the end of the world in the literal sense. Joel is quite different from Daniel, although it is also significantly different from Amos or Jeremiah.

Joel is among the later prophetic books chronologically, but it is placed second in the Book of the Twelve in the Hebrew Bible. The emphasis on the more general kind of eschatology is typical of the editing of the whole collection. It is significant that the Book of the Twelve ends with the prediction of the coming of Elijah before the great and terrible Day of the Lord.

The eschatological focus of the Book of the Twelve receives additional emphasis in the Christian Old Testament, where it is placed at the end of the canon, so that it is taken to point forward directly to the New Testament. In the Hebrew Bible, it simply concludes the works of the Prophets and is followed by the third major section, the "Writings."

Further Reading

Postexilic Prophecy

Cook, Stephen L. *Prophecy and Apocalypticism: The Postexilic Social Setting*. Minneapolis: Fortress Press, 1995.

Hanson, Paul D. *The Dawn of Apocalyptic*. Philadelphia: Fortress Press, 1975.

Haggai, Zechariah, Malachi

Floyd, Michael H. *Minor Prophets, Part 2*, 251–626. FOTL 22. Grand Rapids: Eerdmans, 2000.

Hill, Andrew D. *Malachi*. AB 25D. New York: Doubleday, 1998.

Meyers, Carol L., and Eric M. Meyers. *Haggai, Zechariah 1–8*. AB 25 B. New York: Doubleday, 1987.

———. *Zechariah 9–14*. AB 25C. New York: Doubleday, 1993.

Ollenburger, Ben C. "The Book of Zechariah." In *NIB* 7:735–840.

Petersen, David L. *Haggai and Zechariah 1–8*. OTL. Philadelphia: Westminster, 1985.

———. *Zechariah 9–14 and Malachi*. OTL. Louisville: Westminster, 1995.

Redditt, Paul L. *Haggai, Zechariah, Malachi*. NCB. Grand Rapids: Eerdmans, 1995.

Schuller, Eileen M. "The Book of Malachi." In *NIB* 7:843–77.

Wolff, Hans Walter. *Haggai*. Trans. M. Kohl. CC. Minneapolis: Augsburg, 1988.

Joel

Achtemeier, Elizabeth. "The Book of Joel." In *NIB* 7:301–36.

Crenshaw, James L. *Joel*. AB 24C. New York: Doubleday, 1995.

Wolff, Hans Walter. *Joel and Amos*. Trans. W. Janzen, S. D. McBride, and C. A. Muenchow. Hermeneia. Philadelphia: Fortress Press, 1977.

On the Book of the Twelve

House, Paul R. *The Unity of the Twelve*. JSOT-Sup 97. Sheffield: Sheffield Academic Press, 1990.

Jones, Barry Alan. *The Formation of the Book of the Twelve: A Study in Text and Canon*. SBLDS 149; Atlanta: Scholars Press, 1995.

Petersen, David L. *The Prophetic Literature: An Introduction*, 169–214. Louisville: Westminster John Knox, 2002.

Sweeney, Marvin A. *The Prophetic Literature*, 165–73. Nashville: Abingdon, 2005.

21

Ezra and Nehemiah

KEY POINTS

Ezra-Nehemiah: originally one book. Sometimes thought to be by the same author as Chronicles, but probably not.

- **Ezra 1–6**: return of exiles and building of the temple. Described on the basis of documents. Ezra 4:8—6:18 is in **Aramaic**. Deals with return from exile and building of temple. Material is out of chronological order.
- The **Ezra memoir**: Ezra 7–10 + Nehemiah 8–9.
- The **Nehemiah memoir**: Neh 1:1—7:73a. Nehemiah 11–13 also relates to this.
- Ezra was a **priest** skilled in the **law of Moses**. Sent by Persian

king.

- Law **corresponds substantially to Torah** (including both D and P).
- **Festivals** listed in Nehemiah 8–9 do not correspond exactly to the calendar in Leviticus 23.
- Major incident over **intermarriage**. Ezra forced divorce of foreign wives. No biblical law requires that.
- Nehemiah was concerned with **security** of Jerusalem and **justice**.
- Also concerned for **Judean identity (Sabbath, language)**.

The last section of the Hebrew Bible consists of the Writings *(Ketûbîm)*. This is a catchall category, which includes historical books (Ezra, Nehemiah, Chronicles), poetic compositions (Psalms, Song of Songs, Lamentations), wisdom books (Job, Proverbs, Qoheleth), short stories (Ruth, Esther), and one prophetic or apocalyptic composition (Daniel). The Greek Bible also includes the deuterocanonical or apocryphal books. The order of these books differs in the various Bibles. In the Greek Bible, Lamentations is appended to Jeremiah, and Daniel is also found in the Prophets. Ruth, Esther, Ezra, Nehemiah, and Chronicles are grouped with the historical books (as also are Judith, Tobit, and the books of Maccabees).

Ezra-Nehemiah

The books of Ezra and Nehemiah were originally counted as one book. In modern times, they have often been regarded as part of the Chronicler's History. The concluding verses of 2 Chronicles (36:22-23) are virtually identical with the opening verses of Ezra (Ezra 1:1-3a). There are numerous points of affinity between Chronicles and Ezra-Nehemiah; both show great interest in the temple cult and matters related to it, such as liturgical music and the temple vessels. Some scholars argue that these similarities only reflect the common interests of Second Temple Judaism. It seems best to regard Ezra-Nehemiah as an independent composition.

The content of Ezra-Nehemiah may be outlined as follows.

1. Ezra 1–6, the return of the exiles and the building of the temple. These events took place more than half a century before the time of Ezra and are reported on the basis of source documents. All of 4:8—6:18 is in Aramaic, but this section cannot be regarded as a single source. Rather, it seems that the author cited an Aramaic document and then simply continued in Aramaic. This section is complicated by the fact that the author disrupts the historical sequence to group together related material. At the end of chapter 1 the leader of the Judean community in 539 B.C.E. is named Sheshbazzar. In chapter 3 the rebuilding of the temple is undertaken by the high priest Joshua and Zerubbabel, with no mention of Sheshbazzar. These events can be dated to the reign of King Darius (520 B.C.E.). Yet in 5:16 we are told that Sheshbazzar came and laid the foundations of the temple. In between we find correspondence addressed to King Artaxerxes (486–465) and Darius (522–486). Evidently, the principle governing the composition is thematic rather than chronological.

2. The Ezra memoir. The account of the mission of Ezra is found in Ezra 7–10 and continued in Nehemiah 8–9. This account contains both first- and third-person narratives. Sources incorporated in this account include the commission of King Artaxerxes to Ezra (Ezra 7:12-26), the list of those who returned with Ezra (8:1-14), and the list of those who had been involved in mixed marriages (10:8-43).

3. The Nehemiah memoir. The account of the career of Nehemiah is found in the first person account in Neh 1:1—7:73a. Nehemiah 11–13 also pertains to the career of Nehemiah. These chapters include material from various sources, including a first person memoir (e.g., 12:31-43 and 13:4-31).

It is apparent from this summary that Ezra-Nehemiah reports three sets of events:

Ezra

Several books are associated with the name of Ezra. Adding to the confusion is the use of the Greek form of the name, Esdras. The numbering associated with the name Ezra is different from that associated with Esdras. So we have

Ezra

2 Ezra = Nehemiah

3 Ezra = 1 Esdras. A Greek translation of 2 Chronicles 35–36, Ezra 1–10, and Nehemiah 8:1-3, with some differences in the order of the material and an additional story about three youths at court. This book is included in the Apocrypha.

4 Ezra = 2 Esdras 3–14. This is an important apocalyptic text from the end of the first century C.E., preserved in Latin. It is included in the Apocrypha but not in the Roman Catholic deuterocanonical books.

5 Ezra = 2 Esdras 1–2, and 6 Ezra = 2 Esdras 15–16. These are Christian compositions from the second century C.E. or later.

the initial return and rebuilding of the temple, the career of Ezra, and the career of Nehemiah. It is generally believed that these reports were compiled and edited sometime after the mission of Nehemiah, probably around 400 B.C.E.

The Initial Return

The decree of Cyrus, with which Ezra begins, accords well with what we know of Persian policy toward conquered peoples. An inscription on a clay barrel, known as the Cyrus Cylinder (*ANET*, 315–16; see chapter 19, above), reflects the way the Persian king presented himself to the people of Babylon. Marduk, god of Babylon, he claimed, had grown angry with the Babylonian king Nabonidus for neglecting his cult and had summoned Cyrus to set things right. According to the decree in Ezra 1, he told the Judeans that it was "YHWH the God of heaven" who had given him the kingdoms of the earth and had charged him to build the temple in Jerusalem. Some scholars believe that the Hebrew edict in Ezra 1 is the text of a proclamation by a herald; others suspect that it is the composition of the author of Ezra-Nehemiah, based on the Aramaic edict preserved in Ezra 6:3-5. The latter edict says nothing about Cyrus's indebtedness to YHWH but simply orders that the temple be rebuilt, to certain specifications, and that the vessels taken by Nebuchadnezzar be restored. The authenticity of the Aramaic edict is not in dispute.

A noteworthy feature of the initial restoration is the designation of Sheshbazzar as "Prince of Judah." "Prince" (Hebrew *nāśî*) is the old title for the leader of the tribes in the Priestly

strand of the Pentateuch, and is also the preferred title for the Davidic ruler in Ezekiel (e.g., Ezek 34:23-24; 37:24-25). The use of this title strongly suggests that Sheshbazzar was descended from the line of David and so was a potential heir to the throne. Zerubbabel, who appears to have succeeded Sheshbazzar as governor of Judah, is listed in the Davidic genealogy in 1 Chron 3:19, but Ezra draws no attention to Zerubbabel's Davidic ancestry. The editors of Ezra-Nehemiah were loyal Persian subjects, with no sympathy for messianic dreams.

Sheshbazzar disappears quickly and silently from the stage of history. According to Ezra 5:16, it was he who laid the foundation of the temple. Yet in Ezra 3 it is Joshua and Zerubbabel who take the lead in rebuilding the temple, and the book of Zechariah explicitly credits Zerubbabel with laying the foundation (Zech 4:9). Zerubbabel's activity was in the reign of Darius, nearly two decades after the return. The lapse of time is not noted in Ezra. Any delay in the rebuilding is explained by the opposition of "the adversaries of Judah" (4:1). These people offered to join in the building, "for we worship your God as you do, and we have been sacrificing to him ever since the days of King Esarhaddon of Assyria who brought us here." The implication is that the

Fig. 21.1. The Cyrus Cylinder. British Museum, London. Photo: © HIP / Art Resource, N.Y.

people who were in the land when the exiles returned were the descendants of the settlers brought to northern Israel by the Assyrians (2 Kgs 17:24). The people of Samaria, who had their own governor, hoped to exercise influence over Jerusalem. But there must also have been some people who were native Judeans who had not been deported and who wanted to be included in the community around the Second Temple. The leaders of the exiles, however, took a strictly exclusivist position: "You shall have no part with us" (Ezra 4:3). The exiles regarded themselves as a pure community, which should not be mingled with "the people of the land." This rejection of cooperation, even from fellow Yahwists, was a fateful decision and set the stage for centuries of tensions between the Jewish community and its neighbors.

The correspondence cited to show the opposition to the returnees is out of chronological order. The letter in Ezra 4:11-22 is addressed to King Artaxerxes (probably Artaxerxes I, 465–424 B.C.E.), and is concerned with the rebuilding of the city walls, not with the temple. The city walls are the great preoccupation of Nehemiah, who was active in Jerusalem in the reign of Artaxerxes. This document is inserted into the account of the building of the temple to explain the delay in the construction. According to Ezra 4:17-22, the king ordered that the work be stopped. In contrast, the second letter, in 5:6-17, is addressed to Darius and concerns the rebuilding of the temple. Ezra 6 records the response of Darius, authorizing the continuation of the building of the temple. The impression is given that the Persian authorities vacillated. If the letter to Artaxerxes is restored to its proper context, however, there is no indecision on the part of the Persians with regard to the temple. The rebuilding had been authorized, and the objections were overruled.

The Career of Ezra

In Ezra 7:1 the narrative jumps back to the reign of Artaxerxes. There were three Persian kings with this name: Artaxerxes I (465–424 B.C.E.), Artaxerxes II (405/404–359/358) and Artaxerxes III (359/358–338). Most scholars assume that the reference in Ezra is to Artaxerxes I. The mission of Nehemiah can be dated with confidence to the twentieth year of Artaxerxes I (445), and the biblical record places Ezra before Nehemiah. Nonetheless, there are problems with this dating, and a significant minority of scholars believes that Nehemiah came first, and that Ezra was commissioned by Artaxerxes II in 398. If Ezra came first, then Nehemiah came a mere thirteen years later. Yet he encountered many of the same problems that had occupied Ezra, notably the problem of intermarriage with the neighboring peoples. We should have to assume then that Ezra's reforms were short-lived and, moreover, that he had failed to restore the city walls. But it is likely that his reforms *were* short-lived. Nehemiah complains that his policies were flouted when he returned to the royal court for a time between his two terms as governor. Ezra's policies, which required widespread divorce, must have been resented by many people. Moreover, Ezra was a religious reformer, and so it is not surprising that he failed to concern himself with the city walls. The evidence is not conclusive, but the biblical order of Ezra and Nehemiah remains the more probable.

Ezra is introduced as "a scribe skilled in the law of Moses" (Ezra 7:6). He was also a priest, descended from Zadok and Aaron (7:1-6). He is sent to Jerusalem by the Persian king "to make inquiries about Judah and Jerusalem according to the law of your God, which is in your hand," and also to convey an offering of silver and gold to the temple of YHWH. This mission makes good sense in light of general Persian policy. The Persian king Darius I was widely revered as a legislator in antiquity. The Persian kings had a strong interest in codifying the laws of the various subject peoples in their empire. People might live by their own laws, but it should be clear what those laws were. We know that Darius I appointed a commission of priests and scribes to codify the laws of Egypt. The Persian authorities took a similar interest in Jewish laws, and they may have been responsible for the edition of the Torah, which combined the Priestly and the Deuteronomic legislation. An example of Persian interest in the regulation of Jewish cult has survived in the form of the so-called Passover Papyrus, from 419 B.C.E., which is part of an archive of Aramaic papyri relating to a Jewish community at Elephantine in southern Egypt. This papyrus gives instructions for the observance of the Feast of Unleavened Bread, conveyed to the satrap, by authority of Darius II. The mission of Ezra must be seen in the context of this Persian policy of co-opting loyal subjects and allowing them to regulate their local cults.

The Law of Ezra

In Jewish tradition Ezra is revered as the person who restored the law of Moses, and it is generally assumed that his law was the Torah as we have it. Some modern scholars also credit Ezra with the final edition of the Pentateuch, incorporating the Priestly strand. There are numerous echoes of Deuteronomic law in Ezra and Nehemiah. These are especially prominent in connection with the issue of intermarriage. It is also clear that Ezra knew some form of the Priestly legislation. This appears especially in the regulations for the festivals of Tabernacles (Sukkoth) and Passover. But there are also some details that do not conform either

to Deuteronomic or to Priestly law. The most important example concerns the festivals of the seventh month (Tishri) in Nehemiah 8–9. On the first day of the month, Ezra conducts a solemn reading and explanation of the Torah. This is the date set for Rosh Hashanah, the New Year's Festival, in Lev 23:24. Leviticus speaks of a holy convocation, accompanied by trumpet blasts, but does not mention a reading of the law. There are no trumpet blasts in Nehemiah. In Neh 8:13-17 we are told that on the second day of the month the people discovered the commandment about the Festival of Tabernacles, which they proceeded to observe by making booths and living in them. In Lev 23:34 this festival is supposed to be observed on the fifteenth of the month. Most notable is the discrepancy concerning Yom Kippur, the Day of Atonement, which is legislated for the tenth of the month in Lev 23:27. There is no mention of Yom Kippur in Nehemiah, and there is no observance on the tenth of the month. There is, however, a day of fasting and repentance on the twenty-fourth day of the seventh month in Neh 9:1. The simplest explanation of these discrepancies is that the cultic calendar had not yet taken its final shape when the books of Ezra and Nehemiah were edited. Nonetheless, it remains true that the law of Ezra corresponds substantially to the Torah as we know it, including both Deuteronomy and some form of the Priestly code.

The Problem of Intermarriage

The dominant issue in Ezra, however, is intermarriage. In 9:1-2, Ezra discovers that "the holy seed has mixed itself with the peoples of the lands, and in this faithlessness the officials and leaders have led the way." The "peoples of the lands" are identified in traditional biblical terms (cf. the lists in Gen 15:19-21; Exod 3:8,

17; Deut 7:1; et al.). Some of the names on this list were of immediate relevance (Ammonites, Moabites, Edomites), while others were obsolete (Jebusites, Hittites). We must assume, however, that the primary temptation to intermarriage came from the descendants of the Judeans who had never gone into exile and from the Samaritans. These people were not regarded as members of the Jewish community, at least by purists such as Ezra. The attraction of intermarriage, apart from the normal development of human relations, was compounded by the economic situation. The returning exiles presumably hoped to recover their ancestral property in Judah. Those who had occupied the land in the meantime presumably did not want to cede possession of it now (cf. Ezek 11:15). One way in which the returnees might recover rights of inheritance in Judah was by intermarriage.

> After these things had been done, the officials approached me and said, "The people of Israel, the priests, and the Levites have not separated themselves from the peoples of the lands with the abominations, from the Canaanites, the Hittites, the Perizzites, the Jebusites, the Ammonites, the Moabites, the Egyptians, and the Amorites. For they have taken some of their daughters as wives for themselves and for their sons. Thus the holy seed has mixed itself with the peoples of the lands, and in this faithlessness the officials and leaders have led the way." When I heard this, I tore my garments and my mantle, and pulled hair from my head and beard, and sat appalled. Then all who trembled at the words of the God of Israel, because of the faithlessness of the returned exiles, gathered around me while I sat appalled until the evening sacrifice.
> —Ezra 9:1-4

It is noteworthy that Ezra is only concerned about Jewish men who take foreign wives (note, however, that Nehemiah also objects to intermarriage with foreign men, Neh 13:25). Jewish women who married outside the community did not endanger the patrimony, since they inherited only if there were no male heirs (Numbers 27). Such women were no longer part of the Jewish community. Jewish men who married foreign women, however, brought them into the community and so "mixed the holy seed." An alternative explanation is also possible. In later Judaism a child was recognized as Jewish if his or her mother was Jewish (this is called the "matrilineal principle"). The children of Jewish women would still be Jewish even if the fathers were not, whereas the children of foreign women would not be so.

The prohibition of intermarriage is based on two passages in Deuteronomy, 7:1-3 and 23:3-8. In each case, specific peoples are listed. It is apparent that Ezra's prohibition of intermarriage is broader than either of these, because it includes the Egyptians. The point, then, is not just strict observance of the law, but bespeaks a more extreme fear of contact with outsiders. Moreover, Ezra provides a new rationale for the prohibition. The danger is not just that those who worship other gods might lead the Israelites into idolatry, but that the "holy seed" would be defiled by the union itself. This is quite a novel idea in the Hebrew Bible and presupposes a greater gulf between Jew and Gentile than anything we have seen hitherto.

The solution, allegedly proposed by one Shecaniah was drastic: "Let us make a covenant with our God to send away all these wives and their children" (Ezra 10:3). This action was not taken without coercion. Members of "the congregation of the exiles" were ordered to appear in Jerusalem within three days or have their property forfeited. Then they were made to assemble in the open square before the temple in inclement weather, until they "trembled" not only because of the matter at hand, but also because of the heavy rain. Finally, the people agreed to separate from their foreign wives but pleaded that they not have to stand in the rain. A commission was established to oversee the matter, and within two months all foreign wives had been divorced. Ezra 10 provides a long list of the transgressors. The chapter ends on a chilling note: "All these had married foreign women, and they sent them away with their children" (10:44). We are not told where they went; presumably they returned to their fathers' houses.

Ezra and Nehemiah

We do not know how long Ezra remained in Jerusalem. He and Nehemiah are mentioned together in Neh 8:9; 12:26; and 12:36. It is clear that the editor of Ezra-Nehemiah wanted to give the impression that they were contemporaries. Yet Nehemiah plays no part in Ezra's reform, and Ezra plays no part in Nehemiah's attempt to fortify Jerusalem. Most scholars conclude that the two men were not active in Jerusalem at the same time.

The Nehemiah Memoir

The core of the book of Nehemiah is provided by a first person account, known as the "Nehemiah memoir," which gives a forceful account of Nehemiah's career from his own point of view. This account is largely an attempt to justify himself and his actions. He appeals frequently to God to "remember for my good . . . all that I have done for this people" (Neh 5:19; cf. 13:14, 22, 31). It has been suggested that Nehemiah was required to write a report for

the Persian court in response to the complaints of his enemies. Nehemiah's defense, however, is addressed to God rather than to the king, and so we must assume that such a report, if it existed, was adapted by Nehemiah so as to present his case in the context of the Jewish community.

Nehemiah's account begins in "the twentieth year" of Artaxerxes. Since some of the figures who appear in the account are also known from the Elephantine papyri, there is no doubt that the reference is to Artaxerxes I, and the date is 445 B.C.E. At the outset of the narrative, Nehemiah is a cupbearer to the king. This was a position of considerable importance. The cupbearer had immediate access to the king and was in a position to give him informal advice.

The mission of Nehemiah is undertaken at his own request. His purpose is specifically to rebuild the walls of Jerusalem. He is granted the commission, and also a military escort, because of his personal standing with the king. At first, it seems that a brief mission was envisioned. In Neh 5:14, however, we learn that he was appointed governor of Judah and that he occupied the position for twelve years. Then he returned to the court, but shortly he returned for a second stint (13:6-7).

Nehemiah's great preoccupation on his first visit to Jerusalem was the rebuilding of the city walls. Sanballat, governor of Samaria, and Tobiah, a prominent Ammonite, and their friends express concern that Nehemiah was rebelling against the king (2:19). Later they claimed that Nehemiah wanted to make himself king (6:6-7). They are not said to complain to the Persian court. They appear to have accepted Nehemiah's royal authorization. These people were clearly involved in a power struggle with Nehemiah. His actions can be understood as an attempt to make Jerusalem independent of Samaria and Ammon. He was not attempting to achieve independence from Persia. On the contrary, the distant Persian monarch was the source of his authority.

In addition to political problems, Nehemiah also had to deal with a severe economic crisis caused by a famine. According to Nehemiah 5, there was a great outcry because people had to pledge their fields and houses to get grain. Some were forced to sell sons and daughters as slaves, and some daughters were ravished. The root of the problem (apart from drought) was "the king's tax" (5:4). We do not have much specific information about Persian taxation in Judah, but it was evidently oppressive.

Nehemiah was not about to challenge the king's tax, since his own authority derived from the king. He did, however, challenge the practices of Jews who took pledges from their brethren. The Book of the Covenant (Exod 22:25-27) forbade taking interest from the poor or holding their belongings (cf. Deut 24:10-13). Nonetheless, debt was an endemic problem in ancient Israel and Judah, in both the monarchic and the postexilic periods, sometimes leading to the loss of ancestral property and sometimes to slavery (cf. Amos 8:6; Isa 5:8).

Nehemiah's proposal amounts to a remission of debt and restoration of property, such as was envisioned in the Jubilee Year in Leviticus 25. Such remissions were granted periodically in the ancient Near East, often at the beginning of the reign of a new king. Such reforms tended to be short-lived. We do not know how long Nehemiah's reforms remained in effect. It is unlikely that they outlived his governorship.

The problem of intermarriage appears again in the second term of Nehemiah (Nehemiah 13) This passage serves as an introduction to a confrontation between Nehemiah and "the priest Eliashib" who had given a room in the temple to Tobiah the Ammonite, to whom he was related. The episode illustrates the violent character of Nehemiah: "I threw all the household furniture of Tobiah out of the room" (Neh 13:8). It also shows the difficulty of instituting any lasting reform. Tobiah had been ensconced in the temple when Nehemiah was recalled to the Persian court. We learn in 13:28 that one of the grandsons of Eliashib was the son-in-law of Sanballat of Samaria. The purist policies of Ezra and Nehemiah could not erase the ties that bound the high priesthood in Jerusalem to the upper classes of the neighboring peoples.

In his second term Nehemiah devoted more of his attention to religious problems. In 13:15-22 we read of his attempts to enforce the observance of the Sabbath. The book ends with yet another problem involving intermarriage. "In those days also I saw Jews who had married women of Ashdod, Ammon, and Moab, and half of their children spoke the language of Ashdod, and they could not speak the language of Judah. . . . And I contended with them and cursed them and beat some of them and pulled out their hair" (13:23-25). We can appreciate Nehemiah's concern for the erosion of Jewish identity. His tactics in beating people who did not conform, however, are uncomfortably reminiscent of the behavior of the Taliban when they were in control of Afghanistan.

Nehemiah emerges from his memoir as a person of great integrity. We only have his own account, and it has a clear apologetic character. If Eliashib had left a memoir, he would presumably have shown things in a different light. Nonetheless, we cannot doubt Nehemiah's sincerity. He insists that he sought no personal gain and did not even avail of the allowance traditionally given to the governor (Neh 5:14-19). His legacy was less controversial than that of Ezra. In the words of Ben Sira: "The memory of Nehemiah also is lasting; he raised our fallen walls" (Sir 49:13).

Further Reading

Blenkinsopp, Joseph. *Ezra-Nehemiah*. OTL. Philadelphia: Westminster, 1988.

Clines, David J. A. *Ezra, Nehemiah*. NCB. Grand Rapids: Eerdmans, 1984.

Grabbe, Lester L. *A History of the Jews and Judaism in the Second Temple Period. 1: Yehud: A History of the Persian Province of Judah*. London & New York: T. & T. Clark, 2004.

Klein, Ralph W. "The Books of Ezra and Nehemiah." In *NIB* 3:663–851.

Williamson, H. G. M. *Ezra, Nehemiah*. WBC 16; Waco: Word, 1985.

22

The Books of Chronicles

KEY POINTS

- Alternative account of the history of the kingdoms.
- 1 Chronicles 1–9: Introduction: genealogies.
- 1 Chronicles 10—2 Chron 9: David and Solomon
- 2 Chronicles 10–36: History of Judah after separation from Israel.
- Concludes with restoration from exile.
- David greatly concerned with **cult**.
- Moral problems in David's career are glossed over.

- Solomon also idealized. Model of piety.
- **Construction of temple** emphasized. No forced labor.
- Kings prosper when they follow the Law and fail when they do not.
- **Jehoshaphat** receives more attention than in 1 Kings.
- **Hezekiah** surpasses even Josiah. Keeps **Passover** in Jerusalem.
- Date later than 400 B.C.E.

The books of 1–2 Chronicles constitute an alternative account of the history in 2 Samuel and 1–2 Kings. The secondary character of these books is recognized already in the Septuagint, where they are given the title *Paralipomena*, which means "things omitted" or "passed over." The title in the Hebrew Bible is *dibrê hayyāmîm*, "the events of the days." The title "Chronicles" can be traced back to St. Jerome, who referred to the books as "the chronicle of the complete divine history."

The two books provide a continuous history, which can be divided into three parts:

1 Chronicles 1–9: Introduction
1 Chronicles 10—2 Chronicles 9: the reigns of David and Solomon

2 Chronicles 10–36: the history of Judah from the separation of the northern tribes

Since 2 Chronicles concludes with the restoration after the Babylonian exile (2 Chron 36:22-23 = Ezra 1:1-3a), this account was completed in the postexilic period. The genealogy of the house of David points to a date after 400 B.C.E.

1 Chronicles 1–9

The introductory material in 1 Chronicles 1–9 consists of extensive genealogies, beginning with Adam and continuing down to postexilic times. The lists in the opening chapter derive primarily from the P edition of Genesis. Most interesting here is the continuation of the genealogy after the end of the monarchy. The descendants of Jehoiakim are listed for seven generations, with Zerubbabel as his grandson. The inclusion of the northern tribes shows that the Chronicler conceived Israel as including them and did not equate it with the southern state of Judah.

The genealogical introduction concludes with a list of those who returned to form the postexilic community of Judah (9:1-44). The bulk of the list is made up of priests, Levites, and various temple functionaries. The temple cult is given great prominence in the history that follows.

The Reigns of David and Solomon
(1 Chronicles 10—2 Chronicles 9)

David (1 Chronicles 10–29)

The Chronicler omits David's reaction to the death of Saul but adds his own evaluation: Saul died for his unfaithfulness and because he had consulted a medium. He skips over the civil war between David and the house of Saul and proceeds directly to the anointing of David as king at Hebron and the capture of Jerusalem. The decision to bring the ark up to Jerusalem is reported in more detail than in 2 Samuel 6, with emphasis on the involvement of priests and Levites. The procession with the ark is interrupted when the unfortunate Uzzah touches it and dies (as in 2 Samuel 6–7) and is only resumed in 1 Chronicles 15.

The interruption of the ark narrative allows time for David to prepare a place and pitch a tent for it. David decrees that no one but the Levites are to carry the ark. The Chronicler then provides lists of priests and Levites who

are entrusted with this task, and also of the singers and cultic musicians. The installation of the ark is followed by the singing of praise, illustrated by a medley of passages from the Psalms (cf. Psalms 96; 106).

The report of Nathan's oracle, promising an everlasting dynasty to David, in 1 Chronicles 17 closely follows 2 Samuel 7 but with some differences. There is no mention of punishment in the event of sin, as there was in 2 Sam 7:14. The oracle concludes with an emphatic promise to "confirm him in my house and in my kingdom forever, and his throne shall be established forever" (1 Chron 17:14). "My house," spoken by God, can be understood as the temple. In that case the promise to the Davidic line may be linked to the temple in a way that was not at all the case in 2 Samuel 7.

There follows an account of David's wars in 1 Chronicles 18–20, drawn from 2 Samuel 8; 10; and 19–22. Most notable are the omissions. The entire episode with Bathsheba (2 Samuel 11–12) is passed over, as is the rape of Tamar by Amnon and the subsequent rebellion of Absalom (2 Samuel 13–19). There seems to be a clear tendency to avoid stories that might detract from the portrayal of David as an ideal king.

Chronicles does, however, pick up the story of the census from 2 Samuel 24. Here it is Satan who incites David to count the people. Satan is not yet here the devil, but he is an adversary who puts people to the test. In 2 Sam 24:1, David was incited by "the anger of the LORD." The story has a happy outcome in the purchase of the site for the future temple. In 2 Samuel David got it for 50 shekels of silver. By the time Chronicles was written, inflation had taken its toll. The price now was 600 shekels of gold.

The last days of David in Chronicles have quite a different character from the account in 1 Kings 1–2. There is no intrigue surrounding the succession. Solomon is the only heir apparent. In 1 Kings 2, David's parting instructions had a Machiavellian character, advising his son to eliminate potential enemies such as Joab. In Chronicles his thoughts are entirely on the task of building the temple. The organization of the Levites and of the temple cult occupies chapters 23–26. We are told that 24,000 Levites are given charge of the work in the house of the Lord. There are 6,000 officers and judges, 4,000 gatekeepers, and 4,000 musicians. These numbers seem inflated to the point of absurdity (1 Chron 12:28 says that 4,600 Levites came to make David king at Hebron; in Ezra 8:15-20 fewer than 300 Levites return from Babylon).

Two factors are noteworthy in the organization of the clergy. First, the role of the Levites is to attend the Aaronide priests. The subordination of Levites to priests was a consequence of the centralization of the cult in Jerusalem (see especially Ezekiel 44). Second, the priests are divided into twenty-four courses, to take turns at the temple service—a new development after the Babylonian exile. It was made necessary by the number of priests in Jerusalem in the Second Temple period. It should also be noted that the musicians are said to "prophesy" (25:1). Prophecy seems to be subsumed into liturgy in the Chronicler's vision. In contrast with this elaborate organization of the priests and Levites, the organization of the temporal affairs of the kingdom is described quite briefly in chapter 27.

Solomon (2 Chronicles 1–9)

The account of Solomon's reign is idealized in a way similar to that of David and focuses on the building of the temple. It begins with Solomon's dream at Gibeon, in which he asks for wisdom. Nothing is said of Solomon's elimination of his rivals (1 Kings 2). Solomon is presented in Chronicles as a model of piety, and so his worthiness for building the temple is not jeopardized.

In 2 Chronicles 2, Solomon turns his attention to building the temple. Chronicles makes no mention of forced labor from Israel and has Solomon take a census of aliens before he embarks on the temple building. In Chronicles, then, all the forced labor is imposed on aliens, whatever their origin.

The construction of the temple (2 Chron 3:1—5:1) is the centerpiece of the Chronicler's account of Solomon. Chronicles attaches great importance to the location of the temple. He identifies it with Mount Moriah, scene of the near-sacrifice of Isaac, and with the threshing floor of Ornan the Jebusite, which David had designated as the site for the temple.

The account of the dedication of the temple in 2 Chron 5:2—7:22 proceeds as follows:

1. The introduction of the ark into the temple (5:2—6:2). This section derives largely from 1 Kgs 8:1-13.
2. Solomon's address after this event (6:3-11), blessing the assembly and thanking God for fulfillment of some of the promises to David.
3. Solomon's prayer (6:12-42), closely following 1 Kgs 8:22-53. The temple is not the dwelling place of God, but the place where people may bring their petitions.
4. The conclusion of the ceremonies (7:1-11). Chronicles has fire come down from heaven to consume the sacrifices.
5. Finally, the Lord appears again to Solomon at night, as he had at Gibeon (7:12-22), confirming the choice of the place as a house of sacrifice, and affirming that he will establish Solomon's throne "if you walk before me as your father David walked." This passage follows 1 Kgs 9:1-5.

Second Chronicles 8 summarizes the other building projects of Solomon. Only at this point do we learn incidentally of his marriage to Pharaoh's daughter. Chapter 9 recounts the visit of the Queen of Sheba and emphasizes Solomon's wealth (cf. 1 Kings 10). There is no mention in Chronicles, however, of his love for foreign women or of the multitude of his wives (1 Kings 11).

The History of Judah (2 Chronicles 10–36)

In the older history, the Lord decided to tear the kingdom from Solomon because he had turned away, under the influence of his many wives. This apostasy is not acknowledged in Chronicles. Neither does the Chronicler recount the reason for Jeroboam's original rebellion (the forced labor). He does follow Kings in recounting Rehoboam's refusal to lighten the load of the people. The conclusion, however, places the blame primarily on the northerners who seceded: "So Israel has been in rebellion against the house of David to this day" (10:18). Thereafter Chronicles pays little attention to the northern kingdom, except insofar as it impinges on Judah. It does not share the Deuteronomist's obsession with "the sin of Jeroboam."

Rehoboam

The account of the reign of Rehoboam (11:5—12:16) illustrates the Chronicler's understanding of history. At first the king abides by the law of the Lord, under the influence of the priests and Levites. During this period he prospers (he takes eighteen wives and sixty concubines, and begets twenty-eight sons and sixty daughters). But then he abandons the law of the Lord, and so the Lord sends Shishak of Egypt to punish

him. Then Rehoboam humbles himself, and so the wrath of the Lord turns from him.

In the history of the subsequent kings of Judah, I note only major departures from the account in 1–2 Kings.

Jehoshaphat

In 1 Kings, Jehoshaphat is overshadowed by Ahab of Samaria. He receives much more extensive treatment here (2 Chron 17:1—21:1). Chronicles credits him with extensive reforms. He allegedly sent officials, priests, and Levites to all the cities of Judah "having the book of the law of the LORD with them" (2 Chron 17:9). This would not have been possible in the Deuteronomistic History, since the book was only discovered later, in the reign of King Josiah. Because of this virtuous conduct, the fear of the Lord fell on neighboring kingdoms, and they did not make war on Jehoshaphat.

First Kings 22 reports that Jehoshaphat was allied with Ahab of Samaria in the campaign against Ramoth-gilead. This episode is the occasion of the prophecy of Micaiah ben Imlah, which is repeated in full in 2 Chronicles 18. In Chronicles, when Jehoshaphat returns to Jerusalem, he is met by a seer, who asks, "Should you help the wicked and love those who hate the LORD?" (2 Chron 19:2). Jehoshaphat repeats his mistake later by joining with Ahaziah of Israel (20:35-37). The account of Jehoshaphat also includes a report of a spectacular victory over Moabites and Ammonites that has no parallel in Kings. The story drives home the point that victory in battle is by the power of God, not of human armies. First, Jehoshaphat prays for divine assistance (20:6-12). Then he is reassured by a prophet, Jahaziel son of Zechariah, a Levite. All Jehoshaphat has to do is stand still and see the victory of the Lord on his behalf. Singers go before the army, giving thanks to the Lord. Then the Ammonites and Moabites attack the inhabitants of Mount Seir and end up not only destroying the people of Mount Seir, but themselves as well. Jehoshaphat and his army have only to collect the booty and return to Jerusalem with much fanfare. The emphasis, then, is on ritual, and the battle is entirely miraculous. The story must be regarded as a theological fiction, designed to display the Chronicler's ideas about the proper conduct of a battle. (Compare the highly ritualized story of the fall of Jericho in Joshua 6.)

Jehoram

Chronicles expands the account of Jehoram and portrays him as the first entirely negative figure in the Davidic line. The main embellishment of the account comes in the form of a threatening letter from the prophet Elijah. This is the only mention of Elijah in Chronicles (Elisha is not mentioned at all). The reference to a letter is anachronistic. The use of letters only becomes common in Israel after the Babylonian exile.

Joash

The assassination of Joash is explained by the story that he had murdered a prophet, Zechariah son of Jehoiada (2 Chron 24:25-27).

Hezekiah (2 Chronicles 29–32)

In the Deuteronomistic History, Hezekiah ranks second only to Josiah among the kings of Judah. In Chronicles he surpasses the later ruler. First he repaired the doors of the temple. Then he enlisted the Levites to cleanse the temple. When this was completed, he offered sacrifices and restored the Levites to their liturgical tasks, as prescribed by David. Then "Hezekiah sent word to all Israel and Judah, and wrote letters also to Ephraim and Manasseh, that they should come to the house of the LORD at Jerusalem, to keep the passover to the LORD" (30:1). There is a famous letter from Elephantine in Egypt in the late fifth century B.C.E. regarding the observance of the Passover, but letters are anachronistic in the time of Hezekiah, some 300 years earlier. The fact that emissaries are sent to Ephraim and Manasseh presupposes that the northern kingdom of Israel is no more. Yet, amazingly, the Chronicler has not even mentioned the destruction of Samaria by the Assyrians.

According to 2 Kings, it was Josiah who first celebrated the Passover as a centralized feast in Jerusalem; no such passover had been kept since the days of the judges (2 Kgs 23:22). Chronicles claims that Hezekiah kept the festival in this way and also prolonged the festival for seven days, presumably incorporating the observance of Massoth, or Unleavened Bread. It is unlikely that the Chronicler was drawing on ancient sources here. The tendency to project the full cult of the Second Temple back into earlier history is evident throughout his work.

The account of the invasion of Sennacherib is presented in condensed form. There is no mention of stripping the temple to pay tribute to Sennacherib, as in 2 Kgs 18:13-16. Even the miraculous deliverance by the angel of the Lord is presented in a terse, matter-of-fact way, as a response to the prayers of Hezekiah and Isaiah (2 Chron 32:20).

The glowingly positive account of Hezekiah contains one discordant note. According to 2 Chron 32:24-26, Hezekiah did not respond properly when he was healed from his illness. Therefore "wrath came upon him." When he humbled himself, however, the wrath was deferred to a later time. There is only an indirect basis for this in 2 Kings. There, when Hezekiah shows his treasury to the Babylonian envoys, Isaiah prophesies that all that is in his house will be carried off to Babylon. Hezekiah is not troubled, since there will be peace in his days. In 2 Kings he is guilty at most of imprudence. The Chronicler requires a more theological explanation. The wrath of God must be punishment for a sin—in this case, pride.

Manasseh (2 Chron 33:1-20)

In the Deuteronomistic History (2 Kgs 21:1-18), Manasseh is the bad king par excellence. He is guilty of all sorts of idolatry, and even of human sacrifice. It is specifically because of his sins that Jerusalem is destroyed. Chronicles repeats all the charges against Manasseh but then continues with a surprising narrative. The king is taken captive to Babylon by the king of Assyria. There he is moved to repentance and recognizes the Lord. Accordingly, he is restored to Jerusalem. He proceeds to fortify the city and remove the pagan cults that he himself had installed. The concluding summary (33:19) makes reference to his prayer to God. A composition called "The Prayer of Manasseh" is preserved in Greek and Latin and included in the LXX and in Protestant editions of the Apocrypha, but this is certainly a much later prayer, inspired, no doubt by the references in Chronicles.

Josiah (2 Chronicles 34–35)

The account of Josiah differs from that of Kings in several ways. In Kings the first reforming activity of the young king is dated to his eighteenth year. In Chronicles he begins to seek the Lord already in his eighth year, when he becomes king, and he begins to purge Judah and Jerusalem of the high places in his twelfth year. The repair of the temple, in his eighteenth year, is viewed as part of an ongoing reform. Chronicles, typically, emphasizes the participation of Levites, some of whom were musicians and scribes. The account of the discovery of the book follows 2 Kgs 22:8-20. The novelty of Josiah's Passover has been preempted by Hezekiah in the Chronicler's account, yet the Chronicler echoes Kings in saying that no Passover like Josiah's had been kept since the days of Samuel.

In 2 Kings, the manner of Josiah's death is obscure. We are simply told that when Pharaoh Neco met Josiah at Megiddo, he killed him (2 Kgs 23:29). Chronicles clarifies the situation by saying explicitly that Josiah was fatally wounded in battle. (The account in Kings could be interpreted as an execution.) More surprisingly, Chronicles faults Josiah for fighting against the pharaoh. Neco pleaded with him not to oppose him, because God had commanded him to hurry. But Josiah did not listen to Neco's words, which were from the mouth of God (2 Chron 35:22). Josiah's death, then, is not merely an act of divine mercy, so that he would not see the fall of Jerusalem, but is also in some part a punishment for his own disobedience.

The Conclusion

The desecration and despoliation of the temple provides an appropriate conclusion to the Chronicler's history. Yet the book ends on a hopeful note, pointing forward to the restoration under Cyrus of Persia. The last verse of Chronicles is also the first verse of the book of Ezra.

The Date and Purpose of the Chronicler

The central concerns of Chronicles should be evident from the preceding summary. The covenant with David is foundational, and northern Israel is culpable for failing to respect it. The focus of that covenant is on the temple, at least as much as on the kingship. The proper care of the temple is the responsibility of the priests and Levites, and the Chronicler never tires of emphasizing the roles of the clergy. When the cult is properly maintained and practiced, all is well. There is a strict principle of retribution in history. So the peaceful death of Manasseh must be explained by his conversion, while the violent death of the reformer Josiah betrays disobedience on his part. Prophets figure prominently in the story, but their function is limited to reminding people of what they already know through the Torah. Some of the prophets are identified as Levites. The music of the temple is associated with prophecy, and prophets are credited with compiling historical records. The Chronicler is concerned with "Israel," which includes the northern territory, but he shows little interest in the northern kingdom and does not even bother to report its destruction. Judean kings are faulted for making alliances with their northern counterparts, as these alliances lead only to apostasy.

The purpose of the Chronicler's History depends in part on the date. The concluding reference to Cyrus of Persia requires a postexilic date. The extension of David's genealogy in chapter 3 points to a date after 400 B.C.E. Several scholars, however, have argued for the existence of earlier editions of the Chronicler's History. Some have proposed that a form of the history was drafted in the time of Hezekiah, in view of the prominence accorded to that king. But the portrayal of Hezekiah seems quite anachronistic. In large part the Chronicler seems to have assumed that Hezekiah, as a good king, would have done all the things Josiah is said to have done. The suggestions of earlier editions of the Chronicler's work remain hypothetical. The language of Chronicles is generally regarded as Late Biblical Hebrew—later than P and Ezekiel. There is no trace of Hellenistic influence that would point to a date later than the fourth century B.C.E.

Much of the Chronicler's History can be seen to derive from biblical materials, especially from 2 Samuel and 1–2 Kings. While he may have had occasional access to independent historical information, the great bulk of the cases where he departs from the Deuteronomistic History can be explained by his theological and ideological preferences. Chronicles describes history as the author thought it should have been.

Some suggest that the Chronicler cherished messianic hopes for the restoration of the Davidic kingdom, but the author seems much more interested in the temple cult than in the monarchy. The primary role of the king is to provide for the temple and its cult, whether by building the temple and organizing the cult, in the case of David and Solomon, or by maintaining or restoring it, in the case of later kings (cf. the role of the king in Ezekiel 40–48). No doubt, the author would have welcomed the restoration of the Davidic line, but the proper functioning of the cult was much more important than political independence.

Further Reading

Allen, Leslie C. "The First and Second Books of Chronicles." In *NIB* 3:299–659.

Japhet, Sara. *I and II Chronicles*. OTL. Louisville: Westminster John Knox, 1993.

Klein, Ralph W. *1 Chronicles*. Hermeneia. Minneapolis: Fortress, 2006.

Knoppers, Gary N. *I Chronicles*. AB 12A. New York: Doubleday, 2004.

De Vries, Simon J. *1 and 2 Chronicles*. FOTL 11. Grand Rapids: Eerdmans, 1989.

Williamson, H. G. M. *Israel in the Books of Chronicles*. Cambridge: Cambridge Univ. Press, 1977.

———. *1 and 2 Chronicles*. NCB. Grand Rapids: Eerdmans, 1982.

23

The Psalms and Song of Songs

KEY POINTS

- **Greek psalter** has one extra psalm. Divides some differently.
- **Superscriptions** mention David in 73 psalms. Added later by editors. Eventually all psalms were ascribed to David.
- **5 books in the Psalms**:
  1–41;
  42–72;
  73–89;
  90–106;
  107–50.
  Each ends with a hymn of praise.
  Psalms 42–83 = the Elohistic psalter. (God is called Elohim more often than Yahweh.)
- **Psalms Scroll from Qumran** has different arrangement for last third of psalter.
- **Gunkel**: Different types of Psalms:
  Hymns
  Psalms of Yahweh's enthronement

Individual and communal complaints
Individual and communal thanksgiving
Psalms of ascent
Royal psalms
Wisdom psalms
- **Biblical poetry and parallelism**: repetition with slight variation.
- Human destiny is **Sheol**, the dreary underworld.
- Yet, **trust** in God. **Life** is in God's presence, especially in **temple**.
- **Kingship** of God as creator.
- **Davidic kings as sons of God.**
- God **merciful** but also **vengeful.**
- **Moral problem of vengeance.**
- **Song of Songs: love poetry.** Several changes of speaker.
- **Envisions sexual love outside marriage.**

The Psalms

The book of Psalms (the Psalter) contains 150 psalms in the Hebrew Bible and Christian Old Testament. The name "Psalms" is derived from the Greek *psalmoi*, to sing to the accompaniment of a harp or lyre. In Hebrew the book is called *t^ehillim*, "praises." The Greek Bible (LXX) contains an additional psalm (151), in which David celebrates his victory over Goliath. The Greek psalms are also numbered differently. In two cases consecutive Hebrew psalms (9–10; 114–115) are combined in the Greek (as Psalms 9 and 113), while Hebrew Psalms 116 and 147 are each divided into two (114–115 and 146–147) in the Greek.

Psalms is traditionally attributed to King David. David is depicted as a musician (1 Sam 16:16-23), who composes a lament (for Saul and Jonathan, 2 Sam 1:17), a song of thanksgiving (2 Samuel 22 = Psalm 18), and poetic "last words" (2 Sam 23:1-7). His name appears in the superscriptions of 73 psalms. In thirteen instances (3; 7; 18; 34; 51; 52; 54; 56; 57; 59; 60; 63; 142) the psalm is associated with an event in David's life. One of these, Psalm 18, appears in 2 Samuel 22. These references were added by an editor long after the time of David. Several psalms are associated with other people in the Hebrew text, including Solomon (72; 127), Asaph (50; 73–83), the Korahites (42; 44–49; 84–85; 87–88), and Moses (90). Nonetheless, the association with David was strengthened in the later tradition. In the LXX, eighty-five psalms are ascribed to David. The Psalms Scroll from Qumran claims that David wrote 3,600 psalms. By the first century B.C.E., it was possible to refer to "David" in the same context as Moses and the prophets, to indicate an authoritative body of Scripture. Similarly in the New Testament, citations from Psalms can be introduced as sayings of David (Acts 2:25, 31, 34).

Psalms is divided into five books: 1–41; 42–72; 73–89; 90–106; 107–50. Each book ends with a doxology, a short hymn of praise. Psalm 150 in its entirety is a doxology to mark the end of the Psalter. Several smaller clusters reflect earlier groupings of psalms, such as the Psalms of Asaph and of the Korahites, noted above, or the "Songs of Ascent" (130–34). In the first book (1–41), all but 1, 2, 10, and 33 have superscriptions that mention David. Another cluster of psalms with Davidic superscriptions is found in Psalms 51–70 (of which only 66–67 are exceptions). Moreover, Psalm 72 is followed by an epilogue, which says that the prayers of Jesse, son of David, are ended. This statement would seem to mark the end of an earlier collection. Psalms 42–83 (that is, the second book and most of the third) are sometimes called the Elohistic Psalter, since in these psalms God is called *elohim* more than four times as often as YHWH, whereas the latter

Psalms

Psalms was regarded as a prophetic book in the Dead Sea Scrolls and the New Testament. This is not to say that it was regarded as part of the prophetic corpus: "David" is often mentioned as a third category. But David, too, was regarded as a prophet. In the New Testament, the Psalms are mined for prophecies about the new David, the messiah. This is especially clear in Acts 2. When Psalm 16:10 says "You will not give me up to Sheol, or let your faithful one see the Pit," this is interpreted as a prophecy of the resurrection of the Messiah. Again, Psalm 110 is taken as a prophecy that the messiah would be taken up to heaven: For David did not ascend into the heavens, but he himself says, "The LORD says to my lord, 'Sit at my right hand until I make your enemies your footstool.'"

This way of interpreting the Psalms bears some similarity to the way both Prophets and Psalms are interpreted in the Dead Sea Scrolls. (The form of commentary in the Scrolls is called pesher.) The meaning of the biblical text is unlocked by events, and the events in turn are interpreted by correlating them with the Scriptures.

name predominates in the rest of the Psalter by a ratio of better than two to one. It should be noted that this Elohistic Psalter overlaps the second and third books of the canonical collection.

New light has been shed on the history of the book of Psalms by a Psalms Scroll from Qumran (11Q5). This scroll contains most of the last third of the biblical Psalter, but in an unconventional arrangement (101–103; 109; 118; 104; 147; 105; 146–148; etc.). It also includes a poem identical with 2 Sam 23:1-7 ("the last words of David") and several apocryphal psalms. There is also a prose catalogue of David's compositions placed toward the end of the collection but followed by four psalms. Several other manuscripts of the Psalms found at Qumran also show differences in the order of the psalms. The great majority of the variations are found in the last third of the Psalter. This evidence strongly suggests that the order, and even the content, of the latter part of the Psalter was still fluid in the first century B.C.E. and can only have been settled finally after that time.

The Different Kinds of Psalms

Hermann Gunkel, the founder of "form criticism," argued that the psalms were not the spontaneous prayers of individuals but reflect fixed forms that were transmitted from generation to generation. The truth of this insight is confirmed by the fact that the same forms of religious poetry appear all over the ancient Near East.

The main kinds of psalm are: (1) *Hymns* or songs of praise. These are especially prominent toward the end of the Psalter (the imperative "Hallelujah!" is found in 104–106; 111–113; 115–117; 135; and 146–150). (2) *Psalms of YHWH's Enthronement*. Psalms 93, 97, and 99 begin with the acclamation "YHWH is king!" It has been argued that these psalms were used in a festival of the enthronement of YHWH. There is no other evidence of such a festival, but it may be that the kingship of YHWH was celebrated in connection with the New Year, like the kingship of Marduk in Babylon, or in connection with the Festival of Sukkoth (Tabernacles), which was also known as "the feast of YHWH." (3) *Individual and Communal Complaints*, which Gunkel called "the basic material of the Psalter." These psalms describe a state of distress and appeal to God for help. Some go on to acknowledge a divine response. Their language is often stereotypical, and so they could be appropriated by numerous individuals over the centuries. There are many examples of this kind of psalm from ancient Babylon; some even provide for the person praying the psalm to insert his or her own name. (4) *Individual and Communal Thanksgivings*. These are integrally related to the psalms of complaint. The latter often conclude by giving thanks for deliverance, whether actual or anticipated. These psalms would usually have been accompanied by a thanksgiving sacrifice.

The complaints, thanksgivings, and hymns are the major kinds of cultic poetry in the Psalter. Some psalms that do not fit any of these classifications nonetheless seem designed for ritual occasions. Psalms 15 and 24 are liturgies for people entering the temple. The Psalms of Ascent (Psalms 130–134) are presumably named because they were used by pilgrims, but the individual psalms are of different kinds. Psalm 132 commemorates the bringing of the ark to Jerusalem and may have been associated with a festival. In contrast, Psalm 131 is a simple and beautiful prayer of trust, while Psalm 133 is a meditation on the pleasures of harmonious fellowship.

I have already considered (5) the *royal psalms* in connection with the story of Solomon in 1 Kings. Psalms 2 and 110 are plausibly understood as coronation psalms. Psalm 45 is composed for a royal wedding. Some of the royal psalms fit the categories of complaint or thanksgiving (18; 89; 144).

Finally, (6) the *wisdom psalms* often reflect on the fate of the righteous and the wicked, a typical theme of wisdom literature. Gunkel felt that these poems did not originate in the context of worship. Others hold that they are liturgical pieces and that they reflect the changed character of worship after the Babylonian exile. It is also possible that they originated in the synagogue, where study of the Torah replaced sacrifice as the focal point of worship. The Torah figures prominently in some of these psalms, most obviously in Psalm 119. Similarly in Psalm 1, the righteous are those whose delight is in the law of the Lord. Psalm 19 declares that "the law of the LORD is perfect, reviving the soul." The Torah was not an object of study in the older wisdom literature (Proverbs, Qoheleth). The wisdom psalms that refer to the Torah as the source of wisdom are likely to be relatively late (Hellenistic period).

The inclusion of the wisdom psalms had a significant impact on the shape and character of the Psalter. As the opening psalm in the collection, Psalm 1 sets the tone for what follows, suggesting that the Psalter should be read in light of the Torah as a source for wisdom. Psalm 119 has an impact on the impression made by the Psalter as a whole because of its sheer length (176 verses). These psalms give the Psalter a didactic character. At the same time, they make the point that study is a form of worship in Second Temple Judaism and testify to the growing importance of the Torah for Jewish religious life.

Classification of Psalms in the Hebrew Bible

Hymns: 8; 19; 29; 33; 65; 67; 68; 96; 98; 100; 103–105; 111; 113; 114; 117; 135; 145–150
Psalms of YHWH's Enthronement: 93; 97; 99
Psalms of Individual Complaint: 3; 5–7; 13; 17; 22; 25–28; 32; 38; 39; 42; 43; 51; 54–57; 59; 61; 63; 64; 69–71; 86; 88; 102; 109; 120; 130; 140–143
Psalms of Communal Complaint: 44; 74; 79; 80; 83; 89
Psalms of Thanksgiving: 18; 30; 34; 40:1–11; 41; 66; 92; 116; 118; 138
Royal Psalms: 2; 18; 20; 21; 45; 72; 101; 110; 132; 144:1-11
Wisdom Psalms: 1; 14; 37; 73; 91; 112; 119; 128
(Many psalms are difficult to classify and are omitted from this list.)

The Psalms as Poetry

Most, if not all, of the Psalms were originally meant to be sung. They are written in rhythmic style and are usually regarded as poetry. The most prominent feature of Hebrew poetry is parallelism, the correspondence between the second line of a poetic verse and the first.

The most typical kind of correspondence is *synonymous parallelism*, where both parts of the verse say essentially the same thing. For example, 1:1 declares blessed

> those who do not follow the advice of the wicked,
> or take the path that sinners tread,
> or sit in the seat of scoffers.

But even when there is a very close correspondence, the later part is not necessarily identical with the first. In 1:2 the statement that "on his law they meditate day and night" is not strictly synonymous with the preceding statement that "their delight is in the law of the LORD." The second part of the verse provides some additional information. Hebrew parallelism complements the thought of the first line of a verse, and this may be done in various ways.

A number of other literary devices are exhibited in the Psalms. Several psalms are acrostics, that is, each verse begins with a different letter of the alphabet, in sequence (Psalms 9–10; 25; 34; 37; 111–112; 119; 145). Other common devices include repetition of a word or line to form an *inclusio* (causing the psalm to end in the same way that it began). For example, Psalm 136 begins and ends with the verse: "O give thanks to the Lord for he is good, for his steadfast love endures forever." Chiastic arrangements (ABBA or ABCBA) are also common, both in individual lines and in larger units.

Perhaps the most important poetic characteristic of the Psalter, however, is the use of metaphor and figurative language. Consider, for example, Psalm 69:1-2:

> Save me, O God,
> > for the waters have come up to my
> > > neck.
> I sink in deep mire,
> > where there is no foothold;
> I have come into deep waters,
> > and the flood sweeps over me.

Later in the psalm it becomes clear that certain people hate the psalmist without cause and insult him. The language of drowning is entirely metaphorical and quite evocative. Metaphorical language is especially important in the attempt to speak about God (e.g., 23:1, "The Lord is my shepherd"). In other cases the poets rely on simile, where the analogies are explicit, as when the author of Psalm 131 compares his peace of soul to that of a weaned child with its mother, or as when Psalm 49 says

that human beings are like beasts that perish (49:20).

The Theology of the Psalms

The book of Psalms is not a unified composition in the sense of a modern treatise. It is a loosely edited anthology, in which certain themes are highlighted by the frequency with which they occur and by their placement in the collection. Nonetheless, they provide an ample window on Israelite spirituality.

The Human Situation

As noted above, the most typical kind of psalm in the Psalter is the individual complaint or lament. These psalms, by definition, arise from situations of distress—"out of the depths," in the phrase of Psalm 130. They are often expressed in hyperbolic terms that picture the plaintiff before the jaws of death:

> For my soul is full of troubles,
> > and my life draws near to Sheol.
> I am counted among those who go down
> > to the Pit. . . .
> like those whom you remember no
> > more. . . . (88:3-5)

Sheol and the Pit are the netherworld, where the shade of the person goes after death. (The *nepeš*, or soul, survives after death as a shadowy spirit, like a ghost, but is not really alive). There is no joy or vitality in Sheol.

> The dead do not praise the Lord
> > nor do any that go down into
> > > silence. (115:17; cf. 6:5)

This is the common destiny of all humankind in most of the Hebrew Bible. Even though the psalmist often thanks God for deliverance from death, the reprieve is short-lived.

> O LORD, what are human beings that you
>   regard them,
>   or mortals that you think of them?
> They are like a breath;
>   their days are like a passing shadow.
> (144:3-4; cf. 39:5-6; 90:3-6; 103:15-16)

In light of this rather gloomy prospect, we might expect the Psalms to be depressing, but this is not at all the case. The psalms of complaint do not focus on the ultimacy of death but on more immediate dangers from which deliverance is possible. In Psalm 18 the psalmist confesses that, when "the cords of Sheol entangled me," God "reached down from on high, he took me; he drew me out of mighty waters" (18:5, 16). Consequently, the Psalms as a whole are animated by trust rather than fear.

> Even though I walk through the darkest
>   valley,
>   I fear no evil;
> for you are with me. (23:4)

Despite the inevitability of death and the abject circumstances implied in many complaints, the psalmists seldom indulge in self-abasement. The famous phrase of 22:6, "But I am a worm and not human," is atypical. The confidence of the psalmists is grounded in belief in a benevolent creator God. Psalm 8 marvels at the majesty of the heavens, and asks,

> What are human beings that you are
>   mindful of them,
>   mortals that you care for them?

But he goes on:

> Yet you have made them a little lower
>   than God [or "divine
>   beings," 'elōhim],
> and crowned them with glory and
>   honor.
> You have given them dominion over the
>   works of your hands;
>   you have put all things under their
>   feet. (cf. Genesis 1)

The value of life is ensured by the possibility of a relationship with God. This relationship reaches its fullest potential in connection with the presence of God in the temple. In Psalm 84 the psalmist declares, "My soul longs, indeed it faints for the courts of the LORD," and adds, "a day in your courts is better than a thousand elsewhere." We find here an indication of a transcendent experience that is not negated by human mortality. We find a similar kind of experience in the celebration of human love in the Song of Songs, which declares that "love is strong as death" (Song 8:6).

In some psalms the confidence in divine deliverance seems to suggest that death may not be final after all, at least in special cases. Psalm 16:9-10 affirms:

> Therefore my heart is glad, and my soul
>   rejoices;
>   my body also rests secure.
> For you do not give me up to Sheol
>   or let your faithful one see the Pit.

In the New Testament this passage is taken to refer to the Messiah and is cited as a proof text for the resurrection of Jesus (Acts 2:24-28). In the context of the Hebrew Psalter, the passage may mean only that the psalmist is confident that God will not let him "see the Pit" on this occasion, or before his life has run its natural course. A more intriguing case is provided by

Ps 49:15 (MT 49:16): "But God will ransom my soul from the power of Sheol, for he will receive me." The expression "receive me" recalls the exceptional case of Enoch in Gen 5:24: "Enoch walked with God; then he was no more, because God took him." It was assumed, already in antiquity, that God had taken Enoch up to heaven, granting him an exception to the common human fate. It is possible that the psalmist hoped for a similar exception. The same verb is used in Ps 73:23-26:

> Nevertheless I am continually with you;
>   you hold my right hand.
> You guide me with your counsel,
>   and afterward you will receive me
>   with honor. . . .

Here again the psalmist seems to hope that the relationship with God will not be terminated by death, as would be the case in Sheol. Immortality may also be envisioned in the case of the king. According to 21:4, "He asked you for life; you gave it to him—length of days forever and ever."

It should be emphasized that these cases are exceptional. The normal expectation in the Psalms is that people go to Sheol after death, where they can no longer even praise God. None of the psalms cited here offers any description of what eternal life might be like. They simply express confidence that God will "receive" them. That they entertain such a hope at all is significant, however. Belief in the possibility of eternal life would eventually emerge in Judaism in the Hellenistic period, in the apocalyptic literature and the Dead Sea Scrolls. This belief would be highly important for early Christianity.

The Kingship of God

The central image used to portray God is that of kingship, and the emphasis is on majesty and power. This theology is associated specifically with Zion, the holy mountain in Jerusalem (e.g., 48:1; 97:8; 99:2).

In the psalms celebrating his kingship, YHWH is said to manifest his power by thunder, lightning, and earthquake. This kind of storm language was often used to describe theophanies in the Ugaritic myths, It is associated with Baal, "the rider of the clouds," rather than with El. A classic example is found in Psalm 29. Apart from the name YHWH there is nothing in this psalm that could not have been said of Baal (compare also Psalm 97). Several of these hymns note that YHWH is exalted above the flood and is more majestic than the mighty waters (e.g., Psalm 93). This motif echoes the old Canaanite myth whereby Baal attained the kingship by defeating Yamm, the Sea (cf. 89:9-10). Some psalms use the same imagery in connection with the Exodus (Ps 77:16; 114).

The kingship of YHWH derives from his role as creator and is attested by nature itself: "The heavens are telling the glory of God; and the firmament proclaims his handiwork" (Ps 19:1; cf. 8:3). Consequently, YHWH's kingship is supposed to be universal. The psalmists were surely aware that the kingship of YHWH was not, in fact, universally recognized, so it becomes an eschatological hope. So Psalm 96 calls on all nature to rejoice

> before the Lord; for he is coming,
>   for he is coming to judge the earth.

Psalm 146 affirms:

> The Lord will reign forever,
>   your God, O Zion, for all generations.

We do not find in the Psalms the prophetic critique of present political realities. The Psalter does, however, have an eschatological dimension insofar as it points to an ideal of the universal kingship of YHWH.

The Theology of Human Kingship

The kingship of YHWH has its earthly counterpart in the rule of the Davidic dynasty in Jerusalem. The relationship is pictured vividly in Psalm 2, where the Lord proclaims, "I have set my king on Zion, my holy hill," and in Psalm 110, where the king is invited to sit at the right hand of YHWH. The king is YHWH's son and his vicar on earth. He may even be addressed as 'ĕlōhîm, "god," although he is clearly subordinate to the Most High (45:7). The promise to David, reported in 2 Samuel 7, is reflected in Psalms 89 and 132.

Like his divine counterpart, the king is committed to justice and righteousness. (e.g., Psalm 72). This was the common theology of the ancient Near East. Hammurabi, no less than David or Josiah, proclaimed his purpose "to cause justice to prevail in the land, to destroy the wicked and the evil, that the strong might not oppress the weak" (ANET, 164).

Just as the kingship of YHWH had an eschatological aspect, so too did the rule of the Davidic dynasty. After the Babylonian exile, the eschatological aspect of the royal psalms became more pronounced. When there was no longer a king on the throne, these psalms became monuments to the hope of restoration. Psalm 2, which explicitly uses the Hebrew word māšîaḥ ("anointed one"), would provide a basis for the view that the Messiah is the son of God. This idea plays a central role in Christianity but is also attested in Jewish texts, in the Dead Sea Scrolls (4Q174 = the Florilegium; 4Q246 = the Aramaic Apocalypse or Son of God text), and again in 4 Ezra. Psalm 110 is cited in Acts 2:34 as a proof text for the ascension of Jesus to heaven ("The Lord says to my Lord, 'Sit at my right hand'"). The royal psalms were generally understood as messianic in later Jewish and Christian tradition.

The Character of God

By definition, the God of the psalmists is a God who is expected to answer prayer. Naturally, the psalmists emphasize the mercy of God:

> The Lord is gracious and merciful,
>   slow to anger and abounding in
>   steadfast love. (Ps 145:8)

This is essentially the same characterization of God that is found in Exod 34:6 and repeated several times in the Scriptures (e.g., Ps 103:8). The psalmists praise the faithfulness of God: in the words of the refrain of Psalm 136, "His steadfast love endures forever." The mercy and fidelity of God are the basis for the psalmists' appeals "from the depths" and the subject of profuse thanksgiving.

In many cases, the psalmists pray not only for deliverance, but also for vengeance. So we read in Psalm 94:

> O Lord, you God of vengeance,
>   you God of vengeance, shine forth!
> Rise up, O judge of the earth;
>   give to the proud what they
>   deserve!

The psalmists' idea of what the wicked deserve is sometimes expressed quite vividly:

> O God, break the teeth in their mouths;
>   tear out the fangs of the young lions,
>   O Lord! . . .
> Let them be like the snail that dissolves
>   into slime;
> like an untimely birth that never sees
>   the sun! (Ps 58:6, 8)

The most chilling prayer in the Psalter is found in 137:8-9:

> O daughter Babylon, you devastator!
>> Happy shall they be who pay you
>>> back
>> what you have done to us!
> Happy shall they be who take your little
>> ones
>> and dash them against the rock!

The sentiment is quite understandable, in view of what the Babylonians had done to Jerusalem, but it is none the more edifying for that. Again in 139:19 the psalmist prays: "O that you would kill the wicked, O God," and goes on to plead "Do I not hate those who hate you, O Lord? . . . I hate them with perfect hatred."

These psalms are presented explicitly as expressions of human sentiments, but it is clear that at least some psalmists see God as a God of vengeance, just as surely as they see him as a God of mercy. The two sides of the divine character were stated explicitly in Exod 34:6-7: The same God who is gracious and merciful by no means acquits the guilty but visits the iniquity of the parents on their children even to the third and fourth generation. The justice of God typically entails a threat of violence toward wrongdoers. The Psalms routinely affirm that God will destroy the wicked, even when they are not at all vengeful in tone.

Emotion or Instruction?

The vengeance of God can be a reason for human restraint if it is understood that vengeance is something that should be left to God, not pursued by human beings. It makes a difference here whether we view these psalms as emotive expressions or as moral instructions. There can be little doubt that most of the psalms originated as emotive expressions. Their strength lies precisely in their ability to articulate the full range of human emotions, from anguish to joy. But anger and the desire for vengeance are also basic human emotions that should not be denied or suppressed. For victims of Babylonian terror, or victims of analogous terror in the modern world, Psalm 137 is cathartic. To be sure, it does not express the most noble of sentiments, but it is at least honest and forthright. By providing verbal expression for anger and vengeance, the psalm can act as a kind of safety valve that acknowledges the feelings without necessarily acting on them. If the psalmist took it upon himself to take Babylonian children and dash their heads against the rock, that would be a different matter. The power of the Psalms is that they depict human nature *as it is*, not necessarily as it should be.

Many argue that the editors of the Psalter wished to present it precisely as a book of instruction. This argument derives primarily from the inclusion of the wisdom psalms, and especially from the placement of Psalm 1 at the beginning of the collection and from the sheer length of the Torah psalm, Psalm 119. No doubt there is much to be learned from the Psalms. They teach the majesty of God and the needfulness of humanity, and they encourage people to trust in the mercy and fidelity of God. Yet the prayers for vengeance serve as a reminder that the Psalms must also be read critically. The book of Psalms is not a book of moral instruction. It is primarily a record of ancient Israel and Judah at prayer. Countless generations of Jews and Christians have felt the words of the Psalter appropriate to express their own prayers and feelings. The need to express feelings, however, is no guarantee that those feelings are edifying or that they can serve as moral guidelines.

The Song of Songs

The Song of Songs ("the greatest of songs," often called the Song of Solomon or Canticles in English Bibles) resembles the Psalms only insofar as both are collections of poems. In the Hebrew Bible it is placed among the Writings, after Job, as the first of the five Scrolls or Megillot that are read on major holidays: Song of Songs, Ruth, Lamentations, Qoheleth, Esther. In Christian Bibles, the Song is usually grouped with Proverbs and Qoheleth on the grounds that all three are supposed to be Solomonic compositions. In fact, however, the Song or Canticle is a unique composition, without any close analogy elsewhere in the biblical corpus. It is a collection of love songs, a celebration of erotic love between man and woman.

There was some dispute among the rabbis as to whether the Song should be included in the canon of Scripture. Rabbi Akiba, who died about 135 C.E., is said to have declared that the whole world was not worth the day on which the Song was given to Israel, "for all the scriptures are holy, but the Song of Songs is the Holy of Holies" (Mishnah, *Yadaim* 3:5). But the rabbis preserved the sanctity of the Song by interpreting it as an allegory for the love between YHWH and Israel (despite the fact that the Song never mentions God). According to another Rabbinic saying, anyone who sang the Song in a banquet house, like a profane song, would have no share in the world to come. In Christian tradition the Song was most often read as an allegory for the love between Christ and the church.

The association of the Song with Solomon is due to the fact that his name is mentioned six times (1:5; 3:7, 9, 11; 8:11-12), while there are references to a "king" in 1:4, 12, and 7:5. Opinions vary widely on the actual date of the poems. The appearance of a Persian word, *pardēs*, "garden," in 4:13, requires a postexilic date. Some scholars place it as late as the Hellenistic period, but decisive evidence is lacking.

The crucial factor in appreciating the literary structure of the text is the recognition that there are several changes of speaker. Most often, the speaker is a woman, sometimes addressing the beloved directly, sometimes speaking to "the daughters of Jerusalem." In 1:7—2:7 there is a dialogue between male and female. In 4:1-15 the voice is that of the man, and this is again the case in 6:1-10 and 7:1-9. In view of the changing voices and perspectives, it is difficult to defend the structural unity of the poem. Even those who argue for an overarching unity still distinguish a number of songs within the composition. The number of songs is also a matter of disagreement, ranging from as few as six to more than thirty.

The Song of Songs contains some of the most beautiful poetry in the Bible. It is rich in similes and repeatedly evokes scenes from nature. The beloved is compared to a rose of Sharon, a lily of the valley, a lily among brambles (2:1-2), or to a dove in the clefts of the rock (2:14). The beloved speaks at a time when winter is past, flowers appear on the earth, and the sound of the turtledove is heard in the land (2:10-12). A number of poems are descriptions of the physical beauty of the woman (4:1—5:1; 7:1-9). This kind of poem is called a *wasf* and is typical of Near Eastern love poetry.

Admittedly, some of the similes are startling to the ears of an urban, Western reader: "I compare you, my love, to a mare among Pharaoh's chariots" (1:9). "Your hair is like a flock of goats moving down the slopes of Gilead. Your teeth are like a flock of shorn ewes that have come up from the washing. . . . Your two breasts are like two fawns, twins of a gazelle" (4:1-5). The poetry reflects a bucolic, rural setting with a ready appreciation of the beauty of animal life.

The most striking aspect of the Song, however, is its uninhibited celebration of sexual love. Just how uninhibited it is, is a matter of interpretation. Several passages lend themselves readily to sexual interpretations (e.g., 5:4: "My beloved thrust his hand into the opening, and my inmost being yearned for him"). There is little to indicate that the lovers are married. The poem in 3:6-11 may celebrate a wedding procession, but in most of the poems the lovers evidently do not live together. This is why the woman has to go in search of the man. In 1:7 she asks where he pastures is flock. In 3:2 she rises from her bed and goes around the city to seek him. When she finds him, she brings him to her mother's house. On another occasion she is beaten by the sentinels as she searches for her lover (5:7). In 7:10-13 she urges him to go with her to the vineyards, so that "there I will give you my love." The impropriety of this love is reflected in 8:1: "O that you were like a brother to me, who nursed at my mother's breast! If I met you outside, I would kiss you, and no one would despise me." The love is not protected by the institution of marriage. There is no indication that it is adulterous (that either party is married to anyone else). Most probably, the lovers are young and unmarried.

All of this contrasts sharply with the kind of sexual ethic that we meet elsewhere in the Bible, which imposes penalties (often draconian) for sexual irregularities. The primary concern in the biblical laws is with the institution of marriage. According to Deuteronomy 22, if a man is caught lying with the wife of another, both must die. Also, if a man lies with a woman who is betrothed, both are subject to the death penalty, except that if the incident happens in an isolated area, the woman is not held accountable. In the case of a woman who is neither married nor betrothed, the penalty is much less severe: "The man who lay with her shall give fifty shekels of silver to the young woman's father, and she shall become his wife" (Deut 22:29). The formulation in Deuteronomy implies that the young woman was forced. It does not appear, however, that premarital sex was regarded as a grievous matter so long as a marriage ensued.

The perspective from which the Song of Songs is written, however, differs greatly from that of Deuteronomy. Deuteronomy is concerned with social control. The Song of Songs articulates the viewpoint of the lovers, who find love intoxicating, delightful, and irresistible. From this perspective there can be no question of condemnation, regardless of social disapproval. The Song is unique in the Bible in giving expression to the romantic and erotic feelings of a woman.

The Song is one of only two books in the Hebrew Bible that does not mention God (the other is the book of Esther). Nonetheless, Rabbi Akiba declared it to be "the Holy of Holies." The reason, perhaps, was the purity of the love expressed, which validates itself by its strength and beauty. Love is affirmed as an ultimate value in life. Nowhere is this expressed more powerfully than in 8:6-7: "Set me as a seal upon your heart, as a seal upon your arm; for love is strong as death, passion fierce as the grave. . . . Many waters cannot quench love, neither can floods drown it. If one offered for love all the wealth of one's house, it would be utterly scorned."

Further Reading

Psalms

Commentaries

Clifford, Richard J. *Psalms 1–72*. AOTC. Nashville: Abingdon, 2002.

————. *Psalms 73–150*. AOTC. Nashville: Abingdon, 2003.

Craigie, Peter C. *Psalms 1–50*. WBC 19. Waco: Word, 1983.

Gerstenberger, Erhard S. *Psalms, Part 1; with an Introduction to Cultic Poetry*. FOTL 14. Grand Rapids: Eerdmans, 1988.

————. *Psalms, Part 2; Lamentations*. FOTL 15. Grand Rapids: Eerdmans, 2001.

Kraus, Hans-Joachim. *Psalms*. 2 vols. Trans. H. C. Oswald. CC. Minneapolis: Augsburg, 1988–89.

McCann, J. C. "The Book of Psalms." In *NIB* 4:641–1280.

Other Studies

Brueggemann, Walter. *The Psalms and the Life of Faith*. Minneapolis: Fortress Press, 1995.

Gunkel, Hermann. *An Introduction to the Psalms: The Genres of the Religious Lyric of Israel*. Completed by J. Begrich. Trans. J. D. Nogalski. Macon, Ga.: Mercer Univ. Press, 1998.

McCann, J. C. *A Theological Introduction to the Psalms: The Psalms as Torah*. Nashville: Abingdon, 1993.

Miller, Patrick D. *They Cried to the Lord: The Form and Theology of Israelite Prayer*. Minneapolis: Fortress Press, 1994.

Zenger, Erich. *A God of Vengeance? Understanding the Psalms of Divine Wrath*. Louisville: Westminster John Knox, 1996.

Song of Songs

Commentaries

Murphy, Roland E. *The Song of Songs*. Hermeneia. Minneapolis: Fortress Press, 1990.

Pope, Marvin H. *Song of Songs*. AB 7C. New York: Doubleday, 1977.

Weems, R. J. "The Song of Songs." In *NIB* 5:361–431.

Other Studies

Brenner, Athalya, ed. *A Feminist Companion to the Song of Songs*. FCB 1. Sheffield: Sheffield Academic Press, 1993.

Walsh, Carey Ellen. *Exquisite Desire: Religion, the Erotic, and the Song of Songs*. Minneapolis: Fortress Press, 2000.

24

Proverbs

KEY POINTS

- No references to **history of Israel**.
- **Nature and extent** of wisdom literature.
- Association with **Solomon**. More plausible association of scribal schools with **Hezekiah**.
- **Wisdom instructions** in Egypt.
- **Composition of Proverbs**: 7 collections with superscriptions:
  1:1—9:18: proverbs of Solomon.
  10:1—22:16: proverbs of Solomon.
  22:17—24:22: The words of the wise.
  24:23-34: These also belong to the wise.
  25:1—29:17: Other proverbs of Solomon that the men of Hezekiah collected.

30:1-14: The words of Agur.
31:1-9: The words of King Lemuel.
- Different order in LXX.
- **Proverbial wisdom**:
  Observations.
  Analogies.
  Chain of cause and effect.
  Highly pragmatic.
  Occasional idealism: concern for the poor.
- **Proverbs 1–9: 2 contrasting figures**
  The **strange woman** leads to death.
  Lady Wisdom leads to "life" but not immortality.

The book of Proverbs is quite different from the Torah, Prophets, or historical books. There is no reference to Israel and no interest in history. It is a collection of proverbs or traditional sayings supplemented by instructional literature, presented as the teaching of father to son. This kind of literature is called "wisdom literature" because of the frequency with which words for wisdom and folly occur. While it appears only toward the end of the Hebrew Bible, it was an ancient and widespread form of literature in the Near East, and it may well be more representative of popular thought in ancient Israel than the more dis-

tinctively Israelite books. In the Hebrew Bible, the wisdom literature is represented by Proverbs, Qoheleth (Ecclesiastes), and Job, and by some Psalms, such as Psalm 1. The Apocrypha (deuterocanonical books) includes two major wisdom books, Ben Sira and the Wisdom of Solomon, and there is a hymn to wisdom in the book of Baruch.

Wisdom and Solomon

Proverbs is introduced as "the proverbs of Solomon, the son of David, king of Israel."

Scarcely any scholar now would accept Solomonic authorship for any part of Proverbs. Solomon was the traditional patron of wisdom, as David was the traditional composer of psalms. Qoheleth, which is certainly postexilic and probably Hellenistic in date, also adopts the persona of Solomon, even though it does not use his name. The Wisdom of Solomon, which invokes his name explicitly, was written in Greek around the turn of the era. Proverbs includes some sayings that are not attributed to Solomon: the "words of the wise" in chapters 22–23, the words of Agur in chapter 30, and the words of Lemuel in chapter 31.

Some scholars have supposed that Solomon set up scribal schools in Jerusalem. Such scribal schools are known from other parts of the ancient Near East. In recent years, however, skepticism has grown about the historicity of Solomon's empire because of the lack of archaeological evidence for it. Jerusalem was a small town in Solomon's time, and it expanded significantly only two centuries later, in the time of Hezekiah. Proverbs 25:1 introduces "proverbs of Solomon that the men of Hezekiah copied." Kingship is a prominent theme throughout chapters 10–29 of Proverbs, especially in chapters 28–29. This strengthens the impression that this literature was associated in some way with the royal court, whether this was already the case in the time of Solomon or not.

The Origins
of Wisdom Literature

Proverbs form part of the oral tradition of peoples all over the world. They are essentially oral and are used contextually. A famous example is found in Ezek 18:2: "The parents have eaten sour grapes, and the children's teeth are set on edge." The riddles of Samson, in Judges 14, are similar. In most cases, the individual saying is a unit in itself. Consequently, Proverbs is not a book that lends itself to continuous reading. Wisdom consists in knowing when to use an individual saying aptly in context.

There is a well-attested genre of wisdom instruction, especially in Egypt, that dates back to the third millennium B.C.E. Examples include the teachings of Amenemhet and Ptahhotep (third millennium), those of Amenemope and Ani (second millennium), and numerous others (*ANET*, 412–24; M. Lichtheim, *Ancient Egyptian Literature* 1:58–80; 2:135–63). These instructions were copied in the scribal schools, and new instructions were composed, down to Hellenistic times. They deal with relations between superiors and inferiors, friends and enemies. They often caution about relations with women. They seek to inculcate moral virtues, in the belief that these ultimately lead to success. Self-control is essential. The Instruction of Amenemope is especially noteworthy for its reverence for "the Lord of all" and for the protection of the weak. There are close parallels between this work and Prov 22:17—23:11, which suggest that the Hebrew composition was modeled on the Egyptian. The Egyptian instructions were copied for scribes in schools sponsored by the pharaohs. It is not clear whether such schools existed in Jerusalem before the exile. Nonetheless, the analogy with the Egyptian instructions suggests that this literature was developed under the monarchy to serve the needs of the court. A court setting is also suggested by the Words of the Wise Ahikar (*ANET*, 427–30), an Aramaic wisdom book that circulated very widely in the ancient Near East. Ahikar was supposedly an adviser to the king of Assyria. His name also appears in the book of Tobit.

Popular proverbs and courtly instructions are not mutually exclusive. It may be that the men of Hezekiah made a collection of popular proverbs or incorporated them into their compositions. Proverbs evolved over several centuries. It is usually assumed that the book was finally put together in the postexilic period. By that time the monarchy no longer existed, and the wisdom instructions must have served more general educational purposes. If we may extrapolate from the case of Ben Sira, sages in Jerusalem offered instruction, whether on a tutorial basis or in a more formal school. The book of Proverbs would have provided material for such instruction. This kind of education was distinct from that offered by the Levites, who taught from the Torah (according to 2 Chron 17:7-9). Ben Sira, early in the second century B.C.E., appears to have been the first Jewish wisdom teacher to include the Torah in his curriculum.

The Composition of Proverbs

Within Proverbs, there are seven distinct collections, introduced by distinct headings or superscriptions:

> 1:1—9:18: The proverbs of Solomon, son of David, king of Israel
> 10:1—22:16: The proverbs of Solomon
> 22:17—24:22: The words of the wise
> 24:23-34: These also belong to the wise
> 25:1—29:17: Other proverbs of Solomon that the men of Hezekiah collected
> 30:1-14: The words of Agur, son of Jakeh
> 31:1-9: The words of King Lemuel, with which his mother instructed him

The numerical sayings in 30:15–33 and the poem on the capable woman in 31:10-31 also appear to be distinct units.

These units appear in different order in the Greek translation (LXX), where the sequence is: 22:17—24:22; 30:1-14; 24:23-34; 30:15-33; 31:1-9; 25:1—29:27; 31:10-31. There are also several additional verses in the LXX.

The proverbial core of the book is found in chapters 10–29. Chapters 1–9 contain more developed instructions and more general reflections on the nature of wisdom. Chapters 30–31 contain miscellaneous additions to the book, including the sayings of two individuals who are otherwise unknown and are not evidently Israelites (Agur and Lemuel).

The Nature of Proverbial Wisdom

Several sayings have the character of simple propositional statements. "Anxiety weighs down the human heart, but a good word cheers it up" (12:25). "Hope deferred makes the heart sick" (13:12). The numerical sayings in chapter 30 are likewise attempts to observe and categorize phenomena. Four things are small but exceedingly wise (ants, badgers, locusts, the lizard). Four are stately in their gait (the lion, the rooster, the he-goat, and the king). This latter kind of observation is related to riddles: Name four things that are small and wise, or what do these four things have in common? How is a king like a rooster? There is, of course, also an element of humor in noting the similarity between his majesty and the farmyard fowl.

Observational sayings implicitly appeal to experience. This appeal is only rarely made explicit (e.g., Prov 24:30-34, "I passed by the field of one who was lazy . . ."). In most cases these observations were passed on from father to son, or from teacher to student, and accepted on the authority of tradition. Qoheleth was exceptional in attempting to verify traditional wisdom for himself. Observations are often quite tendentious. They may attempt to preempt discussion by stating that something is simply the case, when it may not be so obvious. Psalm 37:25 claims, "I have been young, and now am old, yet I have never seen the righteous forsaken or their children begging bread." Either the psalmist had not looked very far or he simply assumed that anyone whose children were begging bread was not righteous. Many assertions in Proverbs also are debatable. "Riches do not profit in the day of wrath, but righteousness delivers from death" (11:4; cf. 11:8). But none of these observations claims to derive from revelation or any kind of divine authority. This is human knowledge and open to verification and dispute. It can also be insightful, humorous, and on target. See, for example, the description of the drunkard in 23:29-35.

The observations of traditional wisdom are extended by the use of analogies. Again, comparisons can be tendentious and provide opportunities for biting humor. "Like a gold ring in a pig's snout is a beautiful woman without good sense" (11:22). "Like clouds and wind without rain is one who boasts of a gift never given" (25:14). "Like a dog that returns to its vomit is a fool who reverts to his folly" (26:11).

Another important way in which things are linked together is the chain of cause and effect. "Whoever digs a pit will fall into it, and a stone will come back on the one who starts it rolling" (26:27). Drunkenness leads to "wounds without cause" and "redness of eyes" (23:29). Laziness and idleness lead to poverty (24:30-34). The connection between act and consequence is crucial to the ethics of proverbial wisdom. Virtue is not recommended as an end in itself. Righteousness is ultimately the most profitable course of action. Herein lies

the main problem of wisdom ethics, since the profitability of righteousness is not always in evidence. This problem is treated at length in the book of Job.

The ethical teaching of Proverbs is highly pragmatic. This literature was designed to help the student succeed in life. It was not narrowly religious. Proverbs 23:1-8 (in the section modeled on the Instruction of Amenemope) gives advice on table manners if one is invited to eat with a ruler. There is scarcely a moral issue involved here, but social behavior could have a huge impact on the career of a scribe. Concern for practical results informs the advice of the sages on ethical issues. Even though it is good to help one's neighbor, it is folly to cosign for the debt of another: "If you have nothing with which to pay, why should your bed be taken from under you?" (22:27). "A bribe is like a magic stone in the eyes of those who give it; wherever they turn they prosper" (17:8; cf. 18:16). Advisers to kings and rulers were supposed to be "wise," and their wisdom was no more preoccupied with morality than is the case with political advisers in the modern world. But the opportunism of the wise in the book of Proverbs is always limited by "the fear of the Lord."

We also find moments of idealism in Proverbs, when the conduct recommended cannot easily be identified with self-interest, e.g., concern for the poor. There is some tension within Proverbs on this subject. On the one hand, there is a tendency to blame the poor for their condition and to assume that poverty is the result of laziness (10:4; 13:18). Yet Proverbs also warns frequently against oppressing the poor. This is one of the few occasions where Proverbs appeals to YHWH. "Those who oppress the poor insult their Maker, but those who are kind to the needy honor him" (14:31). "Whoever is kind to the poor lends to the Lord, and will be repaid in full" (19:17; cf. 22:22-23). We find a similar concern in the Egyptian Instruction of Amenemope: "Beware of robbing a wretch, of attacking a cripple; don't stretch out your hand to touch an old man. . . . He who does evil, the shore rejects him, the floodwater carries him away" (Lichtheim, *Ancient Egyptian Literature*, 2:150). The idea that justice required the protection of the needy was recognized throughout the ancient Near East from very early times.

The tension between pragmatism and idealism in Proverbs sometimes results in contradictory advice (contrast Prov 24:11 and 26:17, and 17:23 and 21:14 on bribery). It is of the essence of the wisdom literature, however, that advice that is right for one situation may be wrong for another. As Qoheleth will say, there is a time for everything. Proverbs 26:4-5 juxtaposes two contradictory sayings: "Do not answer fools according to their folly, or you will be a fool yourself. Answer fools according to their folly, or they will be wise in their own eyes." Wisdom is not a matter of knowing a stock of universal truths. It is a matter of knowing the right response on a specific occasion. "To make an apt answer is a joy to anyone, and a word in season, how good it is!" (15:23). Conversely, a proverb in the mouth of a fool is said to hang limp like the legs of a disabled person (26:7).

There is also some tension in Proverbs between the pragmatic, hardheaded wisdom that we have considered and a moralizing tendency that appears in other sayings. Several such sayings appear in chapter 10. "The Lord does not let the righteous go hungry, but he thwarts the craving of the wicked" (10:3; cf. 10:6, 9). The moralizing tendency is often thought to represent a later stage in the wisdom tradition.

The Deity functions in the wisdom literature primarily in two ways. First, God guarantees the cosmic order, which ensures that the chain of cause and effect takes its course. "The eyes of the Lord are in every place, keeping watch on the evil and the good" (15:3). Proverbs has no place for miraculous interventions in history, nor does it encourage prayer for extraordinary deliverance. The role of the Deity in this kind of universe has been compared to that of a midwife. God sees to it that nature takes its course. Second, God is encountered in human affairs as the power that limits human capability. "The plans of the mind belong to mortals, but the answer of the tongue is from the Lord" (16:1; cf. 27:1). Hence, the beginning of wisdom is the fear of the Lord, an attitude of humility and reverence that recognizes our dependent status as creatures.

Proverbs 1–9

In contrast to Proverbs 10–31, chapters 1–9 are made up of lengthy instructions that reflect on the nature of wisdom in a more abstract way.

Two themes predominate in Proverbs 1–9. One consists of repeated warnings against various temptations that beset the young. The other is the praise of wisdom itself. These themes reach a climax in chapters 7–9, where both folly and wisdom are personified in female form.

The "Strange Woman"

The primary image of temptation is "the strange woman" *iššāh zārāh*. This figure is first introduced in 2:16–19, where she is associated with the adulteress (cf. 5:3-4). The most elaborate description is in chapter 7. The author claims to see "a young man without sense" who is accosted by a woman "decked out like a prostitute, wily of heart." She seduces the young man, who goes with her like an ox to the slaughter. The chapter ends on a somber note: "Her house is the way to Sheol, going down to the chambers of death" (7:27). Each of the passages dealing with the strange woman similarly ends with a warning that her ways lead to death (cf. 2:18-19; 5:5).

The "strange woman" of Proverbs has given rise to a multitude of interpretations. The claim that her ways lead down to Sheol leads some commentators to conclude that she is a mythological figure, but it is clear that she is a human figure, not a goddess. She is "decked out like a prostitute" but is not actually one. Many scholars have supposed that the adjective "strange" here refers to foreign women. The warnings against the strange woman might then be related to the crisis over intermarriage in the time of Ezra. Yet Proverbs never indicates that she belongs to a different people. In contrast, a passage from the Egyptian Instruction of Ani warns of "a woman from abroad, who is not known in her (own) town" (Ani iii [13], *ANET*, 420). The woman in Proverbs 7, however, is at home. It is her husband who is out of town.

The most satisfactory explanation of the strange woman is simply that she is the wife of another. This is explicitly the case in chapter 7, which says that her husband has gone on a journey. She is first of all the adulteress. In Proverbs, however, this figure takes on symbolic significance, so that she represents the opposite of wisdom.

The Figure of Wisdom

In contrast to the "strange woman" stands the figure of Lady Wisdom. Wisdom first appears in Prov 1:20, crying out in the street. The thrust of Wisdom's speech is that people need to submit to instruction, and it implies that such instruction is available, whether in a formal school or by individual tutorial. It is not simply a matter of changing one's behavior, although this would surely follow from right understanding. The call of the sage differs from that of the prophet in emphasizing the priority of understanding over action.

According to Prov 2:19, "The LORD by wisdom founded the earth; by understanding he established the heavens." Since the earth was founded with wisdom, nature is rational and admits of understanding. This is the basis for a kind of natural theology, whereby one can arrive at knowledge of the Creator by studying the order of the universe. There is no suggestion here that nature is out of joint or spoiled by sin.

The role of Wisdom in creation is developed at length in the great Wisdom poem in Proverbs 8. Wisdom is again portrayed as crying out at the crossroads and the city gate. She also praises herself. Elsewhere in the Hebrew Bible only the Most High makes such grandiose claims (see especially Isaiah 40–55). This manner of speech has led many scholars to suspect that Wisdom was originally conceived as a goddess. The closest analogies to her speech are found in inscriptions in which the Egyptian goddess Isis sings her own praises (these are called *aretalogies* of Isis). Isis claims, for example, to be the eldest daughter of the sun-god Re, to be the ruler of all lands, to have set down laws for humanity, to control the rise and fall of kings, and many other accomplishments (compare Prov 8:15-16). These aretalogies of Isis are known from Greek inscriptions, which are no earlier than the first century B.C.E., too late to have influenced the book of Proverbs. It may be, however, that similar praises of Isis were known in Egyptian tradition at an earlier date.

> Does not wisdom call,
>   and does not understanding raise her
>   voice?
> On the heights, beside the way,
>   at the crossroads she takes her stand;
> beside the gates in front of the town,
>   at the entrance of the portals she cries out:
> "To you, O people, I call,
>   and my cry is to all that live."
> —Proverbs 8:1-4

Wisdom has also been compared to another Egyptian goddess, Maat, the goddess of truth and justice. Maat was the foundation principle of Egyptian society, and her role in Egyptian religion is somewhat similar to that of Wisdom in Proverbs. But Maat never sings her own praises and is not even portrayed as speaking.

There is no real evidence that Wisdom was regarded as a goddess either in Israel or in Canaan. It is probably true, however, that the way that Wisdom is portrayed is influenced by the depictions of goddesses, especially Isis and Maat. This does not necessarily mean that Wisdom was a goddess herself. She is first of all an attribute of (some) human beings, and also of God in a higher degree. When wisdom is depicted as a female figure, this is the literary device of personification. The Egyptian goddess Maat is to some degree a personification of truth and righteousness. It has been suggested that Wisdom was also a goddess in this way, specifically that she was the patron goddess of wisdom schools.

The role of Wisdom in creation is addressed most explicitly in 8:22-31: "the LORD created me at the beginning of his work, the first of his acts of long ago." The Hebrew word that is translated "created" is *qānāh*, which normally has the meaning "purchase" or "acquire." It is used with reference to human beings acquiring wisdom in 1:5; 4:7; and several other places.

The question then arises whether wisdom was created, or whether it existed independently and was acquired by YHWH. In Job 28 God is said to know where Wisdom can be found but is not said to create her. The later tradition, however, is unanimous in understanding this verse to say that YHWH created Wisdom (this is how the verse is translated in the Greek). Proverbs 8:25 uses birth imagery to speak of how Wisdom was brought forth. Compare Gen 4:1, where Eve says, "I have acquired a man with YHWH." Wisdom is clearly subordinate to YHWH in Proverbs 8 and is used for his purposes.

Wisdom is created, or acquired, before the creation of the world. In Proverbs 8 she is then involved in the work of creation. She forms a bridge between the creator and the created. By acquiring wisdom, human beings can grasp the order of the universe and the purpose of life, but they can also share in the wisdom of God. Wisdom thus provides a rather different model for understanding the relations between God and the universe from what we find in the Torah and the Prophets, where the emphasis is on obedience. This kind of natural theology, or creation theology, is further developed in the deuterocanonical wisdom books of Ben Sira and the Wisdom of Solomon.

Wisdom gives life, just as the "strange woman" leads to death. It is not implied that those who acquire wisdom will enjoy eternal life. The reference is rather to the fullness of life in this world—long life and prosperity (cf. Prov 3:16). Eventually, this promise of fullness of life would be one of the factors that contributed to the rise of a hope for immortality. Among the biblical and deuterocanonical wisdom books, however, this hope is found only in the Wisdom of Solomon.

Proverbs 1–9 concludes by juxtaposing the contrasting figures of Wisdom and "the foolish woman." Wisdom is constructive and nourishing. She builds a house for shelter, and she provides food and drink. (The imagery of food and drink in connection with wisdom will appear again in Ben Sira 24 and plays an important role in the New Testament in the Gospel of John.) The foolish woman resembles Wisdom insofar as she makes her appeal in public places and she also promises nourishment, but her promise is deceptive. Her way leads to death. These contrasting figures sum up the teaching of Proverbs 1–9. There are two ways, but only one delivers what it promises. We are reminded of the story of Adam and Eve, with the false promise of the tree of the knowledge of good and evil.

Proverbs 31

Proverbs ends with a remarkable poem on "the capable wife." This poem is a valuable counterbalance to the picture of the "strange woman" in Proverbs 1–9. It shows that the sages were not misogynistic; they were critical of some female behavior, not of women as such. But for all its professed praise of women, 31:10-31 is unabashedly patriarchal in its perspective. It reflects the crucial contributions of women to agricultural society in antiquity and shows high respect for their competence. In the end, however, much of the glory redounds to the husband, who is a gentleman of leisure because of her labors and can take his place among the elders of the city gates.

Conclusion

Later Jewish tradition would identify the way of Wisdom with obedience to the Torah. There is nothing to indicate, however, that this identification was implied in Proverbs. There is overlap between the commandments of wisdom and those of the Torah, but there is nothing here to correspond to the ritual Torah or the more distinctively Israelite commandments. The instruction was based not on any distinctive revelation to Israel but rather on the common wisdom of the ancient Near East. This tradition of instruction would continue down to the Hellenistic period. Only in the time of Ben Sira was the Torah clearly included in the curriculum.

Further Reading

Commentaries

Clifford, Richard J. *Proverbs*. OTL. Louisville: Westminster, 1999.

Fox, Michael V. *Proverbs 1–9*. AB 18A. New York: Doubleday, 2000.

McKane, William. *Proverbs*. OTL. Philadelphia: Westminster, 1970.

Murphy, Roland E. *Proverbs*. WBC; Dallas: Word, 1998.

Van Leeuwen, Raymond C. "Proverbs." In *NIB* 5:17–264.

General Introductions to Wisdom Literature

Crenshaw, James L. *Old Testament Wisdom: An Introduction*. Rev. ed. Louisville: Westminster John Knox, 1998.

Murphy, Roland E. *The Tree of Life: An Exploration of the Biblical Wisdom Literature*. New York: Doubleday, 1990.

Perdue, Leo G. *Wisdom and Creation: The Theology of the Wisdom Literature*. Nashville: Abingdon, 1994.

Rad, Gerhard von. *Wisdom in Israel*. Trans. J. D. Martin. Nashville: Abingdon, 1972.

25

Job and Qoheleth

The book of Proverbs represents "normal" wisdom in ancient Israel. It is characterized by a positive view of the world and confidence in its order and justice. This worldview was open to criticism, however. The wisdom tradition gave rise to two great works, Job and Qoheleth, which questioned the assumptions on which the world of Proverbs was built.

Job

More than any other book in the Old Testament, the book of Job is recognized as a classic of world literature.

The book consists of a narrative introduction or prologue, followed by a series of poetic dialogues and a narrative conclusion or epilogue. The prologue sets the stage by telling how Job lost everything in a single day because of an arrangement between God and Satan. At first, Job's piety is not shaken. Then three friends, Eliphaz, Bildad, and Zophar, come to visit him. The greater part of the book is taken up with their exchanges with Job. Chapter 28 interrupts the dialogues with a poem on wisdom. Job concludes the dialogue with his friends with a lengthy speech in chapters 29–31.

At this point a new character, Elihu, enters the fray, angry both at Job and at the three friends because of their failure to silence him. Elihu's speech runs to the end of chapter 37, but it adds little or nothing to the arguments of the three friends. Moreover, Elihu is not mentioned in the epilogue to the book. The consensus of scholarship is that Elihu is a secondary addition.

The book reaches its climax in chapters 38–39, when God speaks to Job out of the whirlwind. Job responds submissively in 40:3-5, but God continues with another speech in 40:6—41:34. Again, Job submits with a brief response (42:1-6). The book concludes with a prose epilogue.

The main problem presented by the book is the tension between the dialogues and the prose narratives. In the prologue, Job is a model of patience and resignation (cf. Jas 5:11). At the beginning of the dialogues, however, Job explodes by cursing the day he was born. Throughout the dialogues, the friends defend the justice of God as axiomatic, while Job questions it at every turn. Yet in the epilogue God rebukes the friends, telling them, "You have not spoken of me what is right, as my servant Job has" (42:7). Most scholars assume that the prose frame reflects an older folktale, in which Job was consistently patient. In the book as we have it, however, the introductory story sets up a problem but does not resolve it. Moreover, the epilogue does not quite match the introduction, since it is concerned with the friends rather than with Satan. The traditional story is used as a building block in a new composition, in which both narratives and dialogues play integral parts.

The language of the prose tale points to a date no earlier than the sixth century B.C.E. The language of the dialogues is archaic, but this may be a matter of poetic style. The role of Satan points to postexilic sources (Zechariah, Chronicles). An Aramaic paraphrase, the Targum of Job, from Qumran dates to the third or second century B.C.E., so the biblical book must be older than that. Most scholars date it to the sixth or fifth century. Like the wisdom of Proverbs, Job has a timeless quality that has enabled it to speak directly to people of different eras.

The Prologue (1:1—2:13)

Job is exceptional among the characters in the Hebrew Bible in that he is not an Israelite. He is located in "the land of Uz," which most scholars assume was located south of Israel, in the region of Edom (cf. Gen 36:28; Lam 4:21). The specific location is not important to the story, except insofar as Job is situated in "the east" (1:3), and not in Israel. The international perspective is typical of the older wisdom literature. In Ezek 14:14 Job is linked with Noah and Danel (Daniel) as legendary righteous men. Noah is a biblical figure but prior to Abraham and not properly an Israelite. Danel is known from the legend of King Keret in Ugaritic (Canaanite) lore. The Jewish origin of the book of Job, however, is shown by use of the name YHWH for God.

When we first meet Job, he is "the greatest of all the people of the east." His greatness is shown by his wealth and an ideal family. Even God acknowledges that he is blameless and a model of the fear of the Lord.

Job's life changes because of the intervention of Satan, who is a member of the heavenly council, but who functions as a roving prosecuting attorney, going to and fro upon the earth to ferret out wrongdoing and put humanity to the test.

Satan's attention is drawn to Job by the boast of YHWH: "Have you considered my servant Job?" (1:8). Satan's response cuts to the heart of the popular theology of the ancient world: "Does Job fear God for nothing?" All over the ancient Near East the reigning assumption was that wealth and prosperity went hand in hand with right living. Satan suggests that true righteousness should be disinterested. YHWH, rather chillingly, hands his faithful servant over to Satan to be tested. The first test involves not only the loss of all his property but also the death of his children. Job remains unfazed. Satan, however, is not impressed. He wagers that if God touches Job's person, Job will curse him to his face. The Lord, obligingly, says, "He is in your power; only spare his life." Even his personal affliction, however, does not immediately break down Job's patience, despite the taunting of his wife. Only when he is confronted by his "friends" does his piety crack.

The significance of this opening scene should not be missed. God admits to Satan, "You incited me against him to destroy him for no reason" (2:3). This admission must be kept in mind throughout the dialogues. Job does not know why he is being afflicted. A Hellenistic Jewish writing, called the *Testament of Job*, thought that this was inappropriate and had God reveal to Job in advance what he was going to do. Armed with that knowledge, Job has no problem in maintaining his composure. In the biblical book, however, Job enjoys no such revelation, but the reader is privileged with the "inside story" of what is really going on.

The Dialogues (3:1—27:23)

Job begins the dialogues with a bitter complaint against God. He stops short of fulfilling Satan's prediction that he will curse God to his face. Instead, he curses the day of his birth. His opening salvo belongs to the general tradition of lament literature, although it is exceptional in its bitterness. The closest analogies come from Mesopotamian literature, notably the Babylonian poem "I Will Praise the Lord of Wisdom" (*ANET*, 434–37). These poems are respectful toward the gods and emphasize the need to perform proper cultic acts. The analogy to Job lies in the distress of the poet and in the recognition that the god's ways are inscrutable. The closest parallel to Job is found in the Babylonian Theodicy, from about 1100 B.C.E. (*ANET*, 601–4).

The viewpoint of the friends is grounded in traditional wisdom. "Think now," asks Eliphaz, "who that was innocent ever perished? Or where were the righteous cut off?" (4:7). He appeals to his own experience, but one suspects that his belief is based on dogma rather than on observation. Eliphaz recommends that Job confess his sin and appeal to God's mercy. God's punishment is beneficial in the long run: "Happy is the one whom God reproves" (5:17).

Job reacts with unexpected anger. Eliphaz has assumed Job's guilt without evidence. Job addresses God directly, complaining that God is oppressing him as if he were the Sea or the Dragon, the cosmic enemies of ancient mythology. God should not be affected by human sin and should be able to overlook it. Instead, he is the "watcher of humanity" who targets a human being who will all too soon be dead.

Bildad responds to the challenge in chapter 8: "Does God pervert justice? Or does the Almighty pervert the right?" (8:3). The answer is axiomatic and negative. It is reinforced by the wisdom of the ages: "Inquire now of bygone generations, and consider what their ancestors have found; for we are but of yesterday, and we know nothing" (8:8–9). Bildad affirms the chain of act and consequence that was basic to proverbial wisdom: "Can papyrus grow where there is no marsh?" (8:11). Job must be guilty, and God must be proven right.

Job's reply to Bildad is a pivotal passage, as it anticipates much of what will happen at the end of the book. The problem is that God is both accuser and judge, and so it is impossible to win one's case before him. God prevailed over the Sea and over the mythical monster Rahab. How can a human being hope to withstand him? Where Bildad affirmed the justice of God, Job acknowledges only the raw power of the Creator. At issue is the very nature of justice. Is justice simply the will of the all-powerful Creator? Or can it be measured by standards that humanity can recognize?

Job does not waver in protesting his innocence, but he shows little hope of winning satisfaction: "Though I am innocent, my own mouth would condemn me; though I am blameless; he would prove me perverse" (9:20). This prediction must be borne in mind when we come to the eventual encounter between

---

Satan

When the sons of God assemble in the prologue of Job, Satan also comes among them. While the name connotes "enmity," Satan is evidently an angel of the Lord in good standing, with access to the divine presence. His job is that of public prosecutor. He exercises a similar role in Zechariah 3, where he brings an accusation against the high priest Joshua, although on that occasion he is rebuked. In 1 Chronicles 21, it is Satan who incites David to conduct a census of Israel. In none of these cases is he the devil of later mythology.

The idea of a prince of evil emerges in the apocalyptic literature in the second century B.C.E. The Book of the Watchers, in 1 Enoch, tells of the descent of the sons of God, who beget giants on earth. After the death of the giants, their spirits remain to do evil on earth. In the Book of Jubilees, written some decades after Daniel, a figure named Mastema emerges as the leader of the demons. In the Community Rule, found among the Dead Sea Scrolls at Qumran, we find an instruction concerning Two Spirits, of Light and Darkness. The Spirit of Darkness is known by various names, including Belial and Melchiresha (king of wickedness). The concept of two spirits derives from Persian dualism and is a novelty in the biblical tradition. The first mention of "the devil" is in the Wisdom of Solomon 2:24, in the first century C.E. ("through the devil's envy death entered the world"). By the end of the first century, the various ways of denoting a prince of evil had been combined, as we can see in the New Testament, Rev 12:9: "The great dragon was thrown down, that ancient serpent, who is called the Devil and Satan, the deceiver of the whole world." The "dragon" recall the various chaos monsters of ancient mythology, such as Tiamat in Babylonian myth and Leviathan in Canaanite lore (cf. Isa 27:1).

God and Job at the end of the book. For the present, despair leads to candor: "It is all one; therefore I say, he destroys both the blameless and the wicked. When disaster brings sudden death, he mocks at the calamity of the innocent. The earth is given into the hand of the wicked; he covers the eyes of its judges—if it is not he, who then is it?" (9:24).

The last friend to speak, Zophar, is quite brief. As between God and Job, there can be no contest. "Can you find out the deep things of God? Can you find out the limit of the Almighty?" (11:7). Like Eliphaz, Zophar counsels submission. His argument rests on the unfathomable superiority of the Deity.

Job draws a sharp contrast between himself and his friends. The friends, he claims, are trying "to whitewash with lies" (13:4). They "speak falsely for God, and speak deceitfully for him" (13:7). Job recognizes that they are trying to speak "for God," to defend God's good name, as religious people typically do. If evidence is thought to be damaging to God's good name, it must be explained away, and pious dogma must be maintained. Not only does Job reject that approach, but he claims that God does too: "Will it be well with you when he searches you out? Or can you deceive him, as one person deceives another? He will surely rebuke you if in secret you show partiality" (13:9-10). This claim too will be tested when God finally appears on stage at the end of the book.

Job insists especially on the finality of death. There is hope for a tree that is cut down (14:7), but when mortals expire they are laid low. This denial of resurrection, or of meaningful afterlife, is crucial to the problem of Job. The Hellenistic *Testament of Job* has Job rewarded in heaven for his sufferings on earth. No such easy solution is available to the author of the Hebrew book.

The second and third cycles of dialogue add rhetorical weight to the dispute between Job and his friends, but they add little by way of new argument. Here I highlight only one passage, 19:23-26, which was made famous by its rendition in Handel's *Messiah:* "I know that my redeemer liveth." For traditional Christianity, the redeemer is Christ, but messianic prophecy has no place in the worldview of Job. The Hebrew text of this passage is very difficult and probably corrupt at some points; but the general idea is clear enough. Job expresses his conviction that sooner or later his innocence will be vindicated.

Job's Self-Justification (Chapters 29–31)

The final speech of Job in chapters 29–31 differs from his earlier outbursts. Here he paints a picture of his prime, "when the Almighty was still with me, when my children were around me" (29:5). By his own account, he was a champion of righteousness: "eyes to the blind, and feet to the lame . . . a father to the needy, and I championed the cause of the stranger" (29:15-16). In return, he enjoyed respect: "Young men saw me and withdrew, and the aged rose up and stood" (29:8). Moreover, he thought he had a deal with God: "Then I thought, 'I shall die in my nest, and I shall multiply my days like the phoenix; my roots spread out to the waters, with the dew all night on my branches'" (29:18-20). In chapter 30, however, he expresses his profound disillusionment: "But now they make sport of me, those who are younger than I, whose fathers I would have disdained to set with the dogs of my flock" (30:1). He continues in chapter 31 to set out what might have been fair punishment for various crimes. There is considerable irony in all of this. Job is in no position to bargain with God. Moreover, he comes across as not only righteous but self-righteous. His contempt for the people he would not put with the dogs of his flock is damning. We need not doubt that Job is genuinely righteous in his behavior. He plays by the rules in life. But he also expects life to keep the rules as he understands them.

The Speeches from the Whirlwind (Chapters 38–41)

The book reaches its climax in chapters 38–41, with the speeches from the whirlwind. As both Job and his friends had predicted, YHWH is overpowering. The experience of the theophany, however, surpasses any idea of it that mortals might have entertained and overwhelms Job in a way that no speeches could.

> "Where were you when I laid the foundation of the earth?
>   Tell me, if you have understanding.
> Who determined its measurements—surely you know!
>   Or who stretched the line upon it?
> On what were its bases sunk,
>   or who laid its cornerstone
> when the morning stars sang together
>   and all the heavenly beings shouted for joy?"
> —Job 38:4-7

At no point does YHWH respond to the question raised by Job about his guilt or innocence. How could he? Instead, he hurls at Job a series of impossible questions: "Where were you when I laid the foundation of the earth?" The speeches of God present a catalogue of concerns that are far beyond the reach of humanity but are vital to the running of the universe, from the birth times of mountain goats to the control of the mythical monsters Behemoth and Leviathan. The implication

is clear. God has too many things on his mind to regard Job's fate as of great importance. Job is given a lesson in perspective. Neither he nor humanity in general is as important as he had thought. Job gets the point when he answers meekly: "See, I am of small account" (40:4).

The Epilogue

If the book of Job ended at 42:6, it would be rather depressing. Job had predicted, in chapter 9, that God would make him condemn himself, even though he was innocent. While he does not exactly abandon his plea of innocence, Job repents, at least of speaking of things he did not understand. But essentially Job has been crushed, as if by a thunderbolt. He has been shown that he does not understand the universe, but he has not been given any reassurance that it pays any attention to a moral law, as he had originally assumed.

The book does not end at 42:6, however. Instead, we have a brief, but surprising, prose epilogue. After Job's submission, we might have expected that God would thank the friends for their efforts on his behalf. Instead, he tells Eliphaz, "My wrath is kindled against you and against your two friends; for you have not spoken of me what is right as my servant Job has" (42:7). The friends, we must recall, had insisted that God does not pervert justice. Job, in contrast, had asserted that "he destroys both the blameless and the wicked" (9:22). God agrees with Job. Job had warned the friends that God would not be pleased that they were speaking falsely on his behalf, and in this he was right. We should not necessarily conclude that, in the view of the author, God does pervert justice. Rather, the point is that God does not comply with human conceptions of justice—and is under no obligation to do so.

The friends are not treated harshly, although they have to rely on the intercession of Job. The epilogue provides a happy ending all around, in the manner of comedy rather than tragedy. Job's fortunes are restored. Now all his relatives, who were conspicuous by their absence up to this point, come out of the woodwork to show him sympathy. Each gives him a piece of money and a gold ring. Job's wealth is doubled, and he is given a new family to replace the old one, with the nice touch that the daughters are now given an inheritance with their brothers. (Even the daughters of Zelophehad in Numbers 27 were allowed to inherit only because they had no brothers.)

We might think, initially, that Job was restored to his original state, with some enhancement. But he ought to have learned something from the experience. No great confidence could be placed in people who professed their friendship when he was restored, when they had been absent in his time of need. And he should know from experience that all the newfound wealth and family that he is given at the end could be lost again in one bad day. Never again should Job be so confident that he would grow old in his own nest, or that other people were not worthy to be put with the dogs of his flock.

The book of Job has more than one lesson. As between Job and his friends, Job is vindicated. He was not being punished for any sins, as the reader knew from the beginning. Moreover, his near-blasphemous candor is preferred to the piety of those who would lie for God. His honesty, however, is not tantamount to wisdom. He has to live with the fact that the universe does not revolve around humanity, let alone around Job. The justice of God, if that be the proper term, cannot be measured by human standards.

Qoheleth (Ecclesiastes)

The book of Job may be said to represent a crisis in the wisdom tradition, arising from the realization that some of the most hallowed assumptions are proved false by experience. In traditional wisdom, students are not supposed to rely on their own experience. Rather, as Bildad put it, they should "inquire of bygone generations, and consider what their ancestors have found" (Job 8:8). Consequently, the findings of past generations often hardened into dogma. In a sense, Job was recalling the tradition to its roots by reexamining its basis.

The skeptical questioning of tradition in the biblical corpus reaches its high point in the book of Qoheleth or Ecclesiastes. The inclusion of this book in the canon of Scriptures is remarkable and was a matter of some controversy in antiquity.

The name Qoheleth has never been satisfactorily explained. The Greek form, "Ecclesiastes," "member of an assembly," assumes that the word is derived from *qāhāl*, "assembly." A modern suggestion takes it to mean "gatherer" or "assembler."

The superscription of the book identifies Qoheleth as "the son of David, king in Jerusalem." Qoheleth 1:12 repeats that he was king over Israel. He was traditionally identified as Solomon. (Jewish tradition held that Solomon composed the book in his old age. The attribution may help explain why the book became canonical.) But even if that identification was implied in the opening chapter, it was not maintained consistently. In most of the book, the speaker appears as a teacher who is acutely aware of the injustice of high officials but is unable to do anything about it. At the end of the book we are told that Qoheleth was a wise man who taught the people knowledge.

Qoheleth is exceptionally critical of traditional wisdom, but this need not be incompatible with his role as a teacher.

The language of the book shows that it cannot have been written in the age of Solomon. This is Late Biblical Hebrew, heavily influenced by Aramaic and with many points of affinity with the later Hebrew of the Mishnah. There are two clear Persian loanwords: *pardēs* ("garden," 2:5, the word from which the English "paradise" derives) and *pitgam* ("response, sentence," 8:11). Dates proposed for the book range from the Persian (fifth-fourth century B.C.E.) to the Hellenistic period (third or early second century B.C.E.). There are no Greek loanwords, but then Greek words are very rare in admittedly later writings such as Ben Sira, Daniel, and the Dead Sea Scrolls. Some scholars have held that Qoheleth is influenced by Greek philosophy, especially Epicureanism, but the similarities are superficial. One possible indication of date may be that the author takes issue with belief in life after death: "Who knows whether the human spirit goes upward and the spirit of animals goes downward to the earth?" (3:21). The view that the human spirit goes upward after death is not attested in Judaism before the Hellenistic period, when it appears in the apocalypses of the books of Enoch and Daniel. That this view merits refutation in Qoheleth shows that it must have been current, and this is unlikely before the late third century B.C.E. As in the case of other wisdom books, however, exact dating is not crucial here. Qoheleth is concerned with aspects of life, and death, that are pertinent to all times and places.

Attempts to find a literary structure in the book have not been very successful. There is a clear editorial frame, consisting of a superscription in 1:1 and two epilogues, in 12:9-11 and 12:12-14. Moreover, the book begins and ends with two poems (1:2–11 and 11:7—12:7). The refrain "vanity of vanities" in 12:8 picks up the refrain of the opening poem. One can distinguish roughly between the two halves of the book. The first half is punctuated by the refrain: "all this is vanity and chasing after wind," which marks off sections: 2:1-11; 2:12-17; 2:18-26; 3:1—4:6; and 4:7—6:19. Qoheleth 6:10-12 wraps up the first half by picking up the theme of the opening poem, that there is nothing new under the sun. The second half of the book is marked by the phrases "not find out," "who can find out," and "cannot know." Other refrains are repeated throughout the book: the advice that one should eat, drink, and be merry occurs seven times in all. Concern over the finality of death also runs throughout the book.

Several analogies can be found both for Qoheleth's pessimism and for his advice for the enjoyment of life in wisdom literature of the ancient Near East. Many of these derive from Egypt. The most important are "The Dispute of a Man with His Ba" and the "Songs of the Harpers." In the "Dispute," a man who has become disillusioned with life contemplates suicide. His *ba*, or soul, tries to convince him that life is still preferable to death. The "Harpers' Songs" are tomb inscriptions that reflect on death and call for the enjoyment of life. Qoheleth is also reminiscent of the Epic of Gilgamesh, in which the hero fails in his quest for everlasting life and is advised to enjoy the life that is given to him.

Vanity of Vanities

The first two verses of Qoheleth (1:2-3) introduce two of the basic themes of the book. The first is summed up in the famous phrase "vanity of vanities." The Hebrew word that is traditionally translated as "vanity" here (*hebel*) literally means "vapor." The Midrash, Qoheleth Rabbah, takes it to mean "like the steam from an oven." Some commentators offer "absurd" as a modern equivalent, but while this term captures some of Qoheleth's frustration, it does not convey the key aspect of *hebel,* which is transitoriness. What makes life "vanity" is the finality of death.

The second basic theme has the form of a question: "What profit do people have from all the toil at which they toil under the sun?" (1:2). The idea of "profit" comes from business and perhaps reflects the growing commercialization of Jerusalem in the Hellenistic period. The Hebrew term is *yitrôn,* "that which is left over." The quest for a "profit" from life defines the problem that concerns Qoheleth to a great degree. Again, this problem is impermanence or transitoriness. However much people may seem to gain for a while, in the end it all dissolves like vapor.

The poem in 1:2-11 expresses another aspect of Qoheleth's view of the world: "There is nothing new under the sun." The Hebrew Bible is often said to have a linear view of time, in contrast to the cyclic view of ancient Near Eastern myth; that is, the Bible supposedly allows for a sense of progress and direction in history. This is true of some parts of the biblical corpus, but the wisdom books of Proverbs, Job, and Qoheleth have no sense of a goal in history. The same or similar things happen over and over again. Novelty is an illusion that results from our ignorance of history. The fact that people of long ago are not remembered undermines a common hope in the ancient world that one might live on through one's reputation and good name. Qoheleth insists that there is no transcendence of death and no way out of the cyclical existence in which humanity is trapped.

A Time for Everything

The limits of human wisdom are set out clearly in a famous passage in 3:1-9: "For everything there is a season, and a time for every matter under heaven." The passage goes on to list fourteen pairs of opposites: to be born and to die, to kill and to heal, to love and to hate, and so on. The assertion that there is a time for each of these may seem shocking at first: should there be a time to kill and a time to hate? But in this respect Qoheleth is quite faithful to biblical ethics. As we saw in chapter 6, on the book of Exodus, the absolute prohibitions of the Ten Commandments are relativized in practice in the "book of the covenant" (Exodus 21–24), the casuistic laws that take specific circumstances into account. There are lots of situations where killing is not only permitted but commanded. The psalmist has no qualms about "hating" God's enemies. Where Qoheleth differs from the rest of the biblical tradition is in his lack of confidence that human beings can know the right time. In Proverbs, as we have seen, timing is what distinguishes the wise person from the fool. For Qoheleth, however, this wisdom is beyond the human grasp.

> For the fate of humans and the fate of animals is the same; as one dies, so dies the other. They all have the same breath, and humans have no advantage over the animals; for all is vanity. All go to one place; all are from the dust, and all turn to dust again. Who knows whether the human spirit goes upward and the spirit of animals goes downward to the earth?
> —Qoheleth 3:19-21

Since humanity cannot figure it all out, what are people to do? Qoheleth reiterates the message that one should eat and drink and enjoy the life that is available. He also repeats the key observation that leads to his conclusion: "the fate of humans and the fate of animals is the same. . . . Who knows whether the human spirit goes upward and the spirit of animals goes downward to the earth?" (3:19-21). The traditional Hebrew belief was that the shade of human beings lived on in Sheol. Only in the apocalyptic literature (Daniel and the noncanonical books attributed to Enoch) do we find a belief that the human spirit goes upward after death. Qoheleth is probably taking issue here with beliefs that were just beginning to emerge in his time. His appeal, however, is not to traditional belief but to personal experience. No one knows what happens after death, but the common human experience is that people do not come back. There is no leap of faith here, no wager based on hope without evidence. Qoheleth's philosophy of life is that we should base our lives on the evidence that we have.

Sayings of the Wise

One of the most striking statements in Qoheleth is in 7:16-17: "Do not be too righteous, and do not act too wise. . . . Do not be too wicked, and do not be a fool." Here the Hebrew sage adopts the advice of the Delphic oracle: "nothing too much." In part, the advice may be directed against pretense, against those who are righteous or wise in their own eyes. But Qoheleth's warning must also apply to the kind of zeal that is so often praised in the Hebrew Bible. (The paradigm examples are Phinehas, in Numbers 25, and Elijah.) The comment of Qoheleth is apt: "Surely there is no one on earth so righteous as to do good without ever sinning" (7:20).

Another striking saying in chapter 7 is less enlightened: "One man among a thousand I found, but a woman among all these I have

not found" (7:28). Jewish sages in antiquity (all men) were not especially friendly to the opposite sex. Ben Sira is a much worse offender than Qoheleth in this regard, but the two sages share the prejudices of a male profession in a patriarchal society.

Qoheleth returns to his basic insights in chapter 9. The same fate comes to everyone, righteous and wicked. The conclusion follows: eat your bread with enjoyment, and drink your wine with a merry heart. The wording of this passage is especially reminiscent of the story of Gilgamesh, where the hero fails in his quest for eternal life but is told by the barmaid Siduri that the gods have reserved eternal life for themselves, and that he should enjoy the life that is given to him.

The Concluding Poem

Perhaps the most moving part of Qoheleth is the poem on old age at the end of the book. This poem balances the opening poem in 1:1-11 and shares the same theme: all is vanity or vapor. Qoheleth 12:1-8 is widely recognized as an allegory of old age, although there is no agreement on how the details should be interpreted. Some commentators take the passage as an account of a storm, nightfall, or the ruin of an estate, any of which could serve as a metaphor for old age. The passage is not a sustained allegory but an allusive poem that conveys a cumulative impression of collapse, culminating in the conclusion that all things pass, all is vapor.

The purpose of the poem is stated at the outset: "Remember your creator in the days of your youth." The word for "creator" (*bôrĕkā*) is a wordplay. It is very similar to "pit, grave" (*bôr*), and "well, source" (*b'ēr*). There is a rabbinic saying that one should "know whence you came [your source], whither you are going [your grave], and before whom you are destined to give an accounting [your creator]" (*Abot* 3:1). From the perspective of Qoheleth, the three ideas are closely related. To remember either one's birth or one's death is to remember that one is a creature.

The poem in Qoh 12:1-8 suggests not only the decline of the individual in old age, but also the end of the world, with the failure of the sun and moon and cosmic light. It is interesting to compare the imagery of the poem with a passage from an apocalypse, *Syriac* or *2 Baruch*, written about 100 C.E.: "For the youth of the world is passed and the strength of the creation is already exhausted . . . and the pitcher is near to the cistern and the ship to the port, and the course of the journey to the city and life to its consummation" (*2 Bar.* 85:10). Qoheleth does not expect an end of the world, but he uses the imagery of collapse to convey the sense of an ending. For the present world is always passing away.

The Epilogues

The book of Qoheleth concludes with three epilogues that clearly do not come from the author of the main part of the book. The first, in 12:9-10, describes the author, in the third person, as a teacher of traditional wisdom. The second, in vv. 11-12, comes from an editor who was troubled by the skeptical sayings of the sage. He justifies them by comparing them to goads, but adds quickly: "Of anything beyond these, my child, beware. Of making many books there is no end, and much study is a weariness of the flesh" (as any student can testify). Here we see the canonical impulse at work in the attempt to limit the number of books that can be accepted as authoritative.

The final epilogue, in 12:13-14, does most violence to the spirit of the book. It picks up a verse from 8:17, where the sage says in his heart that God will judge the righteous, but that verse is followed by a passage that explains that human beings and animals have the same fate. There is no irony in the epilogue: all one has to do is fear God and keep his commandments. This is the only time that the commandments are mentioned in Qoheleth. The epilogue practically tells the reader not to pay too much attention to the book. One does not need wisdom; it is sufficient to keep the commandments. Qoheleth never suggested that "the whole duty of everyone" could be identified so simply.

It is not surprising that some scribes found Qoheleth troubling and tried to limit its influence. The greater surprise is surely that it was included in the canon of Scripture at all. Its inclusion may have been due to its supposed Solomonic authorship, but it also testifies to the critical spirit that pervades so much of the Hebrew Scriptures.

Further Reading

Job

Commentaries

Habel, Norman C. *The Book of Job*. OTL. Philadelphia: Westminster, 1985.

Newsom, Carol A. "The Book of Job." In *NIB* 4:319–637.

Pope, Marvin H. *Job*. AB 15. New York: Doubleday, 1979.

Studies

Newsom, Carol A. *The Book of Job: A Contest of Moral Imaginations*. New York: Oxford, 2003.

Perdue, Leo G. *Wisdom in Revolt: Metaphorical Theology in the Book of Job*. JSOTSup 112. Sheffield: JSOT Press, 1991.

Whedbee, J. William. *The Bible and the Comic Vision*, 221–62. Minneapolis: Fortress Press, 2002.

Qoheleth

Commentaries

Crenshaw, James L. *Ecclesiastes*. OTL. Philadelphia: Westminster, 1987.

Lohfink, Norbert. *Qoheleth*. Trans. S. McEvenue. CC. Minneapolis: Fortress, 2003.

Krüger, Thomas. *Qoheleth*. Hermeneia: Minneapolis: Fortress Press, 2004.

Murphy, Roland E. *Ecclesiastes*. WBC 23A. Waco: Word, 1992.

Seow, C. L. *Ecclesiastes*. AB 18C. New York: Doubleday, 1997.

Studies

Fox, Michael. *Qoheleth and His Contradictions*. JSOTSup 71. Sheffield: Almond, 1989.

———. *A Time to Tear Down and a Time to Build Up: A Rereading of Ecclesiastes*. Grand Rapids: Eerdmans, 1999.

26

The Hebrew Short Story:
Ruth, Jonah, Esther

KEY POINTS

- The Hebrew short story.
- Ruth: the good Moabite.
  - —Practical decency and loyalty.
  - —Uncertain date.
- Jonah: the anti-prophet. Ironic view of prophetic righteousness.

- Esther: No explicit mention of God. Loyalty to her people.
  - —Trials and dangers of Diaspora life.
  - —Violence and vengeance.
  - —Additions in Greek translation.

One of the great contributions of the Hebrew Bible to world literature lies in the development of prose fiction, specifically the novella or short story. Many of the quasi-historical narratives in Genesis and Samuel could be viewed as fictional compositions, even if they contain reminiscences of historical events. The story of Joseph is an especially rich and complex narrative that provided a model, to some degree, for the later stories of Esther and Daniel. In addition to these narratives that are imbedded in longer biblical books, there are also several that constitute books in themselves. In this chapter I consider three of these stories: Ruth, Jonah, and Esther. Two others, Tobit and Judith, are preserved in the Apocrypha and recognized as canonical in the Roman Catholic Church.

Ruth

The book of Ruth is exceptional insofar as its heroine is a Moabite woman. Moabites do not usually get good press in the Hebrew Bible. In Numbers 25 the Israelites incite the wrath of YHWH by having sexual relations with Moabite women and joining in the worship of their gods. Deuteronomy 23:3 decrees that no Ammonite or Moabite should be admitted to the assembly of the Lord, even to the tenth generation. Ruth, however, is an exemplary character. Although the story is related to Israelite history at the beginning and at the end, it is primarily the story of family relationships. On this level of interaction between individuals, ethnic origin recedes in importance. Ruth is a story of human action, with little appeal to divine intervention. The occasional references to the Lord, however, are enough to suggest that the entire action is being guided by divine providence.

The story of Ruth is divided into four chapters. The first chapter sets up the situation of crisis. As in some of the stories in Genesis, the action is set in motion by a famine in the land of Israel. In the time of the judges, a man from Bethlehem named Elimelech goes to live in Moab. The man's sons marry Moabite women named Orpah and Ruth. Elimelech dies, and some years afterward his sons die too.

Throughout the ancient Near East the situation of widows and orphans was especially precarious. According to Deut 25:5-10, if a man died without a son, his brother should marry the widow and raise up an heir to the deceased (this is known as the levirate law). This law prevented the widow from marrying outside the family, thereby alienating the family property, but it also was a way of ensuring that the widow would be taken care of. There are only two stories in the Hebrew Bible that illustrate the working of the levirate. One is the story of Judah and Tamar in Genesis, where Judah refuses to honor the practice and Tamar takes matters into her own hands. The other is Ruth.

Naomi tells her daughters-in-law to return to their parents until they should find new husbands. Orpah is persuaded to do this, but Ruth persists in going with Naomi: "Where you go, I will go; and where you lodge, I will lodge; your people shall be my people, and your God my God." Ruth abandons the relative security of staying with her own people, in an act of fidelity to her mother-in-law. The first chapter ends with the return of the two destitute women to Bethlehem (which literally means "house of bread"), and the lament of Naomi that although she went away full the Lord has brought her back empty.

Elimelech has a rich kinsman named Boaz. The levirate law, as formulated in Deuteronomy, applied only to brothers. Boaz would not have been under any legal obligation to help a distant kinswoman, nor do the women claim anything from him as a matter of right. Instead, Ruth proposes to support the women for a while by gathering ears of grain left by the reapers (cf. Lev 19:9-10; 23:22; Deut 24:19-22). When she comes to the field of Boaz, he notices her and protects her. Only at the end of the day does Naomi tell Ruth of her relationship to Boaz and suggest that her meeting Boaz is a sign of the Lord's providential care. Ruth and Naomi are now secure until the end of the barley and wheat harvests, but their long-term future is still precarious.

Chapter 3 brings the story to a climax. Naomi realizes that the best hope for long-term security is to have Boaz marry Ruth. She does not instruct Ruth to ask Boaz to marry her but rather to seduce him. The scene is the threshing floor, where Boaz is winnowing barley. The threshing floor was not only a workplace but also a place of celebration, where men relaxed at the end of the harvest. Hosea accuses Israel of acting like a prostitute on all the threshing floors (Hos 9:1). These were apparently places where prostitutes might expect to find customers. Ruth is told to wash and anoint herself and to put on her best clothes. She waits until Boaz has eaten and drunk and lies down in contentment. There is perhaps an implication that he is slightly drunk. In Gen 19:30-38 the daughters of Lot get their father drunk and then sleep with him. The eldest becomes the mother of Moab. Holofernes becomes drunk in his attempt to seduce Judith. Unlike these figures, however, Boaz is not drunk to the point of unconsciousness. He is merely in a receptive mood.

When the time is right, Ruth "came stealthily and uncovered his feet and lay down"

(Ruth 3:7). The reference to feet is a euphemism. Ruth initiates a sexual encounter. It has been objected that nowhere else in the Hebrew Bible does a woman uncover a man, but herein lies precisely the boldness of Ruth's action. Boaz, naturally, is somewhat startled to find a woman at his "feet," but he is pleased to discover her identity. It is not clear whether the sexual encounter is consummated. Ruth asks him to "spread your cloak over your servant, for you are next-of-kin" (3:9). Spreading the cloak signifies protection. More specifically, in the context, Ruth is requesting that Boaz marry her. Compare Ezek 16:8, where YHWH spreads the edge of his cloak over Israel and covers her nakedness and enters into a covenant with her. We must assume that Boaz lets her stay the night because he finds her attractive, but he handles the question of marriage with all due propriety. There is another man who is more closely related to Naomi, but if he declines to marry Ruth, Boaz will do so as next of kin.

The final chapter provides the resolution. Boaz convenes the elders in the city gate. The closer relative is willing to buy Naomi's field but backs out when he finds that he must take Ruth as part of the bargain. He then formally renounces his right in the matter. Boaz marries Ruth, and the story reaches its happy ending. When Ruth bears a child, Naomi nurses him, and the people say, "A son has been born to Naomi."

The conclusion of chapter 4 attempts to locate Ruth in the context of biblical history. The people pray that she may be like Rachel and Leah, and that the house of Boaz be like the house of Perez, whom Tamar bore to Judah. It is natural enough that Ruth should be linked with Tamar. Both are widows who take bold sexual initiatives so that they can have children. Moreover, we are told that Ruth's child became the father of Jesse, the father of David. Lest

the full significance of this be lost, the book concludes with a genealogy of Perez, who turns out to be a direct ancestor of Boaz. Some scholars argue that this genealogy is the starting point for the story of Ruth. On this reading, the purpose of the book is to put a positive spin on the fact that David's great-grandmother was Moabite, by showing how she won the Lord's favor. But Ruth is not a political story. David is only mentioned at the end, in a virtual appendix. It seems much more likely that the genealogies were added secondarily, to justify the inclusion of a story about a Moabite woman in the Scriptures of Israel. The similarities between Ruth and Tamar would have suggested the link with the genealogy of Perez. Ruth is placed after Judges in the LXX because the story is set in the period of the judges (1:1). In the Hebrew Bible it is placed among the Writings.

The actual date and provenance of the story remain in dispute. Scholars who regard the Davidic genealogy as an intrinsic part of the story tend to date it very early, perhaps in the time of Solomon. At the other extreme, many scholars have assumed a postexilic setting because of its focus on a marriage between an Israelite and a Moabite woman. On this reading, the story was composed as a polemic against the stringent rejection of marriage to foreign women by Ezra. The placement of the book in the Writings lends some support to a postexilic date, since many of the Writings date from this period. Against this view, however, Ruth does not read like a polemic, and the point of the story is not to affirm mixed marriages. Mixed marriage, in fact, is not acknowledged as a problem at all. It seems entirely natural that the sons of a man from Judah who grow up in Moab should marry Moabite women. When the women accept the God of Israel, as Ruth does, there is no problem whatsoever. The viewpoint of Ruth is entirely different from that of Ezra, but it does not necessarily follow that Ruth was composed as a polemic against Ezra.

Ruth presupposes an agrarian society where people moved easily between Judah and Moab. It is written in classical Hebrew prose. It seems somewhat more likely that such a story would have been written before the exile rather than after, but the date remains quite uncertain. The practice of levirate marriage was presumably traditional, and the action of Boaz is not constrained by legal obligation but is motivated by kindness toward a destitute kinswoman, who also happens to be attractive and adventuresome.

The message of the story should not be tied too closely to any hypothesis about its date. The view that it is political propaganda, whether for David or against Ezra, does not do justice to this gentle and humane story. The message is simply that people who act with fidelity and compassion are ultimately blessed by God, even if they have to endure difficult circumstances for a while.

Jonah

Our second Hebrew short story is located among the prophets, but the book is unlike any other in the prophetic corpus. It is not a collection of oracles but a story about a prophet. The subject, Jonah son of Amittai, is presumably the individual mentioned in 2 Kgs 14:25, who is said to have prophesied in the reign of King Jeroboam II of Israel in the eighth century B.C.E. From the passage in 2 Kings we may infer that this Jonah was a prophet of hope, who prophesied the restoration of the boundaries of Israel. The prophet described in the book of Jonah has nothing in common with this figure except his name. He is almost certainly a fictional character, invented several centuries later.

Jonah is something of an anti-prophet. When the word of the Lord comes to him, bidding him go to Nineveh, he goes instead in the opposite direction, to Tarshish (Spain), to flee from the presence of the Lord. His adventures are the stuff of comic legend. When a storm rises at sea, the sailors cry, each to his own deity. Ecumenical to a fault, they urge Jonah also to pray to his god. This cacophony of prayer fails to produce the desired result, so they resort to lots to determine the cause of the storm. The lot falls on Jonah, who confesses that he is fleeing from his God. He urges the sailors to cast him overboard as a human sacrifice to appease the deity. They are reluctant to do so, but eventually they comply, out of desperation. The storm is calmed. Such an extreme sacrifice might be expected to be efficacious. Compare the story of the king of Moab, who turned the tide of battle by sacrificing his son (2 Kgs 3:27). Moreover, the miraculous result has the added effect of inducing the sailors to fear YHWH and worship him.

Jonah, however, does not die as might be expected. A large fish swallows him, and he remains in its belly for three days and three nights. Inevitably, this story was taken by early Christians as prefiguring the resurrection of Christ on the third day (see Matt 12:39-41). More generally, Jonah became a symbol of resurrection in early Christian art. Jonah's resurrection, however, is rather ignominious: the fish vomits him out on the dry land.

While in the belly of the fish, Jonah prays to the Lord. His prayer takes the form of a psalm of thanksgiving, which is scarcely appropriate to Jonah's situation. He has not been driven away from YHWH's sight—he has deliberately fled from it. His life has not yet been brought up from the Pit. Most probably, the psalm was added by a later editor. There are several clear examples of inserted prayers in the books of Esther and Daniel, where the prayers are found only in the Greek translations. The prayer allows for a pause in the narrative between Jonah's descent into the fish and his reemergence and so helps the pace of the story. This particular psalm was chosen because of its imagery: "The waters closed in over me; the deep surrounded me."

Fig. 26.1. Jonah. Catacomb of S. Callisto, Rome. Photo: Alinari / Art Resource, N.Y.

His deliverance from the fish allows Jonah a new beginning. Chapter 3 resumes the narrative by having the word of the Lord come to Jonah a second time. This time, Jonah obeys and goes to Nineveh. The size of the city is exaggerated. The ruins of Nineveh are roughly three miles across, certainly not three days' walk. The Ninevites immediately believe the prophet and repent with sackcloth and fasting. Never in the history of prophecy had a proclamation produced such a dramatic response. Even the animals fast and are clothed with sackcloth. The text does not say explicitly that the God to whom the Ninevites cried was the God of Israel, although that may be implied, since this was the God in whose name Jonah spoke. Needless to say, there is no historical record of any such repentance by any Assyrian city.

There is yet another ironic twist in the story. Jonah is not happy about the conversion of Nineveh. It should have been destroyed, as it deserved. The Lord is too merciful. That is why Jonah tried to run away. So now he goes out of the city. At first the Lord provides him with a bush for shelter, but then it withers. At this point Jonah prays for death, as Elijah had done in the wilderness in 1 Kings 19. The destruction of the bush provides a final parable: If Jonah is concerned for the bush that withered, should he not be more concerned for Nineveh, "that great city in which there are more than a hundred and twenty thousand persons who do not know their right hand from their left, and also many animals?" (4:11).

The biblical prophets are often critical of the traditions and beliefs of Israel and Judah, and the tendency of "the chosen people" to be complacent and self-righteous (Amos is an obvious example). In most cases, however, they maintain a sharp distinction between Israel and the other nations and often call down the wrath of God on Israel's enemies. The book of Jonah is exceptional in its compassion for the Ninevites, who are human beings like any others, and most of whom have little knowledge of the schemes of their rulers. It is even more exceptional in treating a prophet as a figure of fun. (Admittedly, Jonah is never actually called a prophet, but he is called to speak in the name of the Lord.) The author is suggesting, gently, that Hebrew prophets should not take themselves quite so seriously.

The universalistic message of the book, which makes little if any distinction between Jew and Gentile, is generally thought to point to a date in the postexilic period. The statement that Nineveh *was* a great city has been taken as a clue that it no longer existed—that is, that the book was written after 612 B.C.E. when Nineveh was destroyed. None of this is conclusive, by any means. More significant, perhaps, is the impression that this is "belated" literature, written in reaction to the stereotypes of the Torah and the Prophets. It can hardly be later than the Persian period, since it was included in the collection of prophetic writings.

Esther

The book of Esther differs from Ruth and Jonah insofar as its heroine is located in the Diaspora, at the Persian court. In this respect it resembles the stories of Joseph (at the Egyptian court) and Daniel (Babylonian and Persian courts), and the apocryphal book of 3 Maccabees (Ptolemaic Egyptian court). The "court tale" is often distinguished as a subgenre. A rich fund of stories set at the Persian court can be found in the Greek historian Herodotus. The stories of Joseph, Esther, and Daniel are especially closely related, although each has its own distinctive emphases.

The Greek (LXX) translation contains six extended passages (107 verses) that have no counterpart in the Hebrew. These passages are regarded as part of the canonical text in the Roman Catholic tradition, but they are clearly secondary additions to the MT. There is also another Greek recension (or edition) of Esther known as the Greek Alpha Text (AT). This recension is found in five medieval manuscripts, but many scholars believe that it contains a form of the text that is older than the MT.

The book of Esther is divided into ten chapters. The first chapter locates the story "in the days of Ahasuerus, the same Ahasuerus who ruled over 127 provinces from India to Ethiopia." The king in question is better known as Xerxes. Xerxes I (485–465 B.C.E.) did in fact rule from India to Ethiopia, but there were only 120 provinces, or satrapies, in his empire (the correct number is given in Dan

6:2). Ahasuerus is said to give two banquets, one for all his officials and ministers lasting 180 days, and one for all the people of Susa, the capital, lasting 7 days. The queen, Vashti, gives a banquet for the women at the same time. Persian kings were famous for their banquets, but the description given in Esther is clearly hyperbolic. In all, Esther describes no fewer than seven banquets at the royal court. Banquets become, in effect, a major structuring device of the story.

The king orders the queen to appear before him "wearing the royal crown, in order to show the peoples and the officials her beauty" (1:11). Vashti refuses. The king's desire to put his wife on display recalls a story in Herodotus about a Lydian king, Candaules, who was so proud of the beauty of his wife that he insisted that his bodyguard, Gyges, should see her naked (Herodotus 1.8–12). The queen was enraged when she discovered the plot and insisted that Gyges murder Candaules. In Esther, the honor of the queen required that she refuse, but by so doing she slighted the honor of the king.

Vashti's refusal is elevated into an issue of imperial concern: If the queen can disobey her husband with impunity, so might any wife disobey her husband. So Vashti is banished from the king's presence by a law of the Medes and the Persians that cannot be altered (a folkloric motif found also in Daniel). The removal of Vashti sets the story of Esther in motion by creating the vacancy at the royal court that she would fill.

The second chapter explains how Esther was chosen to be a member of the royal harem and then crowned as queen in place of Vashti. Esther has no qualms about being taken into the royal harem. Unlike Judith, she shows no concern for observing distinctive Jewish practices. In fact, she conceals her Jewish identity, on the advice of her cousin and mentor,

Mordecai, a loyal subject of the king. Mordecai uncovers a plot against the king's person.

Chapter 3 introduces Haman, who is appointed over all other officials. Conflict develops when Mordecai refuses to prostrate himself before Haman in the Persian manner. It is apparent from Esth 3:4 that prostration was not in accordance with Jewish custom. Again, the honor of both characters is at stake. Haman attributes the slight to the fact that Mordecai is a Jew and resolves to destroy all the Jews in the kingdom. The excessive character of this reaction is typical of the hyperbolic style of Esther. Haman appeals to the king but does not mention the Jews by name. Instead, he characterizes them as "a certain people . . . whose laws are different from those of every other people, and who do not keep the king's laws" (2:8). These people are evidently not assimilated but retain their distinct identity within the empire. As typically happens in stories of this sort, the king is entirely gullible and gives his assent without question. A decree is issued for the destruction of all the Jews.

The crisis facing the Jewish people presents a special dilemma for Esther. Mordecai asks her to go to the king to intercede. She responds that no one may enter the presence of the king without being summoned. Mordecai's reply goes to the heart of the predicament: "Do not think that in the king's palace you will escape any more than all the other Jews. For if you keep silence at such a time as this, relief and deliverance will arise for the Jews from another quarter, but you and your father's family will perish. Who knows? Perhaps you have come to royal dignity for just such a time as this" (4:14).

The danger to Esther's life is quickly dispelled in chapter 5. The king offers to grant anything she might ask. At first she requests only that the king and Haman join her in a banquet. Haman is elated, but he is still galled by the insubordination of Mordecai, so he gives orders that a gallows be prepared for him. From this point forward, the story is marked by the repeated reversal of expectations. By the king's order, Haman has to attire Mordecai with robes and lead him on horseback around the city. But a worse fate awaits him. In chapter 7, when the king and Haman come to her banquet, Esther tells the king about the plot against the Jews, whom she now identifies as "my people." When the king asks who is responsible, she identifies Haman. When the king storms out in anger, Haman throws himself on Esther to beg for his life, but the king returns and thinks it is a sexual assault. Haman is hanged on the gallows he had prepared for Mordecai.

The story now moves to its conclusion. In chapter 8 Esther asks the king to revoke the decree against the Jews. The king tells her and Mordecai that they may write as they please and seal it with his seal. The letters, written by Mordecai, give the Jews permission to kill any people who might attack them, throughout the provinces. So on the very day on which the Jews were to be destroyed, they slaughtered their enemies by the thousand, with the knowledge and permission of the king (chap. 9). They instituted the Festival of Purim to commemorate the occasion.

Esther and History

Several details in the book are historically problematic. Mordecai was supposedly among the exiles taken to Babylon by Nebuchadnezzar. Yet he is active in the reign of Xerxes, a century later. The number of provinces, or satrapies, is inaccurate. There is no historical evidence for the deposition of a Persian queen, and so forth. But the fictional character of Esther should be quite clear from the style of the book, which is full of hyperbole and stock characters, such as the gullible king and the wicked courtier. The idea that a Persian king would give the Jews in his kingdom unlimited authority to slaughter their enemies is simply incredible.

As presented in the Hebrew Bible, the book appears to be a festal legend told to explain why Purim is celebrated. The actual origin of this festival is unclear. It is not a religious festival. No prayers or sacrifices are prescribed, but drinking to inebriation is permitted by the Babylonian Talmud (*Megillah* 7b). The name Purim is explained in Esth 3:7 as referring to the casting of lots (cf. 9:26). It may be that Purim was a pagan festival before it became a Jewish one. The first attestation of the festival is in 2 Macc 15:36, where it is called Mordecai's day. The idea of a festival commemorating a slaughter has a parallel in Herodotus, who says that the Persians celebrated a festival called Magophonia, to commemorate the slaughter of the Magi who seized power after the death of King Cambyses (Herodotus 3.79).

The reference in 2 Maccabees is also the earliest attestation of the story of Esther. No trace of the book has been found in the Dead Sea Scrolls. One fragmentary Aramaic document, 4Q550, is a tale set at the court of Xerxes, which was dubbed "Proto-Esther" by its editor. It has no specific links with Esther that would justify that label, but it appears to be a tale of the same general type. The reference in 2 Maccabees shows that the book was known in Israel before the turn of the era, but it was probably not yet widely accepted as Scripture. Its status was still disputed in rabbinic times (b. *Megillah* 7), and it is missing from many Christian lists of canonical books. The book was probably composed somewhere in the eastern Diaspora around the fourth century B.C.E.

Esther is the earliest known narrative of an attempt to wipe out a Jewish community in a Gentile environment. In later history such stories become all too familiar, down to the Holocaust in the twentieth century. We do not, however, have any evidence for attacks on the Jewish communities in Persia or Babylonia in the Persian or early Hellenistic periods. Persian kings are generally depicted as protectors of the Jews, and indeed the king in Esther is also benign. Why then should the author of Esther have conjured up the nightmarish fantasy?

The reason given by Haman for his plot against the Jews is that "their laws are different from those of every other people, and they do not keep the king's laws" (3:8). The latter part of this charge is a calumny: Mordecai is a loyal subject of the king. But the perception that the Jews were a people set apart, who refused to assimilate fully into the Gentile culture, is a constant factor in conflicts between Jews and Gentiles in later times, beginning in the Hellenistic era. Most fundamentally, Jews, with relatively few exceptions, refused to worship the same deities as other people. They also had peculiar customs in the matter of food, which inhibited social relations. Because they were "a people set apart," they felt, and were, especially vulnerable, even in a relatively tolerant culture such as that of Persia. If conflicts arose, such as that between Haman and Mordecai, the distinctive, alien character of the Jews made them an easy target for resentment and suspicion. Hence the fear of attack by Gentiles was present even before it became a reality.

The Religious Character of Esther

The reason for Esther's silence about God is much debated. To describe the book as secular would be anachronistic. The hand of the God of Israel may be hidden, but it is nonetheless present. Mordecai tells Esther that if she does not act, "deliverance will rise for the

Jews from another quarter" (4:14) and suggests that Esther's royal rank was providential. Later, Haman's friends advise him that he cannot hope to prevail against the Jewish people. These statements can hardly be explained without the tacit acknowledgment of the God of Israel. Yet it is striking that the Jews are not even said to thank the Lord for their deliverance. The silence of Esther on this subject can only be explained by the theology of the author, which bears some analogy to the wisdom literature, where God acts behind the scenes of history. The stories of Joseph and Ruth are also somewhat reticent about divine intervention, although neither is entirely silent on the subject. Esther differs from the wisdom literature, however, in its unabashed focus on the Jewish people and defense of their interests.

The absence of the Deity from the narrative of Esther has given offense to some scholars over the centuries. Even more problematic, however, is the conclusion of the book, where the Jews slaughter their enemies and then establish a festival to celebrate the occasion. The slaughter is a fantasy, but that hardly makes the vengefulness less distasteful. The glorification of violence is not exceptional in the Hebrew Bible. At least in Esther, the Jews are attacking people who wanted to attack them, although their actions go well beyond the bounds of self-defense. But Esther cannot be held up as a model for relations between ethnic groups. There is no attempt at reconciliation. This is all the more remarkable since Esther shows no desire for Jewish independence. The sovereignty of the Persian king is not questioned. The ideal situation is one where the king can be manipulated to advance the interests of the Jews. In the fantasy of Esther, the Jews are triumphant. The politics of ethnic antagonism, however, seldom yield such a clear-cut result.

Violence, and even the fantasy of violence, most often begets just more violence.

Further Reading

General

Brenner, Athalya. *A Feminist Companion to Esther, Judith and Susanna.* FCB 1/7. Sheffield: Sheffield Academic Press, 1995.

Lacocque, André. *The Feminine Unconventional: Four Subversive Figures in Israel's Tradition.* OBT. Minneapolis: Fortress Press, 1990.

Wills, Lawrence M. *The Jewish Novel in the Ancient World.* Ithaca: Cornell Univ. Press, 1995.

Ruth

Campbell, Edward F. *Ruth.* AB 7. Garden City, N.Y.: Doubleday, 1975.

Fewell, Danna Nolan, and David M. Gunn. *Compromising Redemption: Relating Characters in the Book of Ruth.* Louisville: Westminster John Knox, 1990.

Nielsen, Kirsten. *Ruth.* Trans. E. Broadbridge. OTL. Louisville: Westminster John Knox, 1997.

Trible, Phyllis. "Ruth, Book of." In *ABD* 5: 842–47.

———. *God and the Rhetoric of Sexuality*, 166–99. OBT. Philadelphia: Fortress Press, 1978.

Jonah

Limburg, James. *Jonah.* OTL. Louisville: Westminster John Knox, 1993.

Sasson, Jack M. *Jonah.* AB 24B. New York: Doubleday, 1990.

Sherwood, Yvonne. *A Biblical Text and Its After-life: The Survival of Jonah in Western Culture.* Cambridge: Cambridge Univ. Press, 2000.

Trible, Phyllis. "Jonah." In *NIB* 7:463–529.

———. *Rhetorical Criticism: Context, Method, and the Book of Jonah.* GBS. Minneapolis: Fortress Press, 1994.

Wolff, Hans Walter. *Obadiah and Jonah.* Trans. M. Kohl. CC. Minneapolis: Augsburg, 1977.

Esther

Berlin, Adele. *Esther: The Traditional Hebrew Text with the New JPS Translation.* Philadelphia: Jewish Publication Society, 2001.

Crawford, S. White. "The Book of Esther." In *NIB* 3:853–972.

Fox, Michael V. *Character and Ideology in the Book of Esther.* Columbia: Univ. of South Carolina Press, 1991.

Levenson, Jon D. *Esther.* OTL. Louisville: Westminster John Knox, 1997.

Moore, Carey A. *Esther.* AB 7B. New York: Doubleday, 1971.

27

Daniel, 1–2 Maccabees

aniel is probably the latest composition in the Hebrew Bible. Like Ezra, it is written partly in Hebrew and partly in Aramaic. The Greek edition of the book includes passages and whole stories that are not attested in the Hebrew Bible. Moreover, it contains the only example in the Hebrew Bible of a genre, apocalypse, that was of great importance for ancient Judaism and also for early Christianity. In Christian tradition, Daniel is regarded as the fourth of the major prophets, and the book follows those of Isaiah, Jeremiah, and Ezekiel. In the Hebrew Bible, however, Daniel is placed among the Writings. It may be that the canon of prophetic writings was already closed when Daniel was written. It may also be that the rabbis saw the book as having more in common with the Writings than with the Prophets.

As found in the Hebrew Bible, the book falls into two sections. The first six chapters are stories about Daniel and his friends, who were allegedly among the exiles deported from Jerusalem by Nebuchadnezzar. The second half of the book, chapters 7–12, consists of a series of revelations to Daniel, which are explained to him by an angel. Strictly speaking, only the second half of the book is an apocalypse, but the stories in chapters 1–6 form an introduction that sets the scene. One of the oddities of the book is that the division by language does not fully coincide with the division by genre. Chapters 2:4b—7:28 are in Aramaic. Chapter 1 and chapters 8–12 are in Hebrew. It seems clear that the book was written in stages. The Aramaic stories in chapters 2–6 originally circulated independently. Chapter 1 was written as an introduction to these stories, presumably in Aramaic. The first of the visions, in chapter 7, was composed in Aramaic for continuity with the tales. The remaining chapters were added in Hebrew, presumably because of patri-

otic fervor at the time of the Maccabean revolt. The opening chapter was then translated into Hebrew, so that the beginning and end of the book would be in Hebrew, forming an *inclusio.* This explanation is, of course, hypothetical, but it gives a plausible account of the way the book took shape.

The Greek Additions to the book are of two kinds. Two poetic compositions, the Prayer of Azariah and the Song of the Three Young Men, are inserted into chapter 3. The stories of Bel and the Dragon and of Susanna are freestanding stories analogous to the stories in chapters 1–6.

Greek Empire

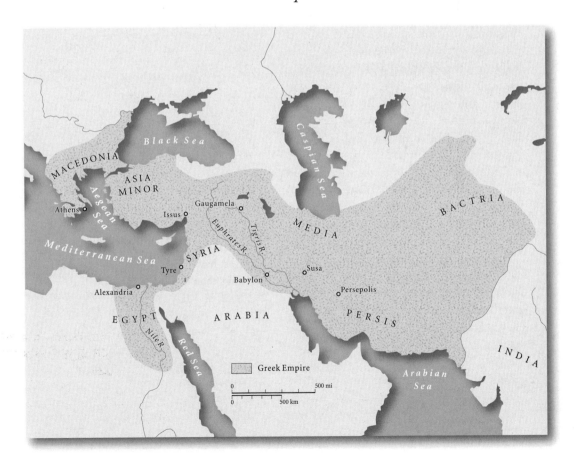

The Court Tales

The stories in Daniel 1–6 have much in common with the short stories in the Hebrew Bible, especially those of Joseph and Esther. Like these stories, they are "court tales": stories about Jews at the court of a foreign king. Like Esther, the stories in Daniel are set in the eastern Diaspora and most probably originated there. Unlike Esther, however, Daniel is overtly pious, and the stories are punctuated with prayer and praise. Nonetheless, they share with Esther the concern about maintaining Jewish identity in a foreign land, in the service of a foreign king.

The tales tell the story of a group of young Judeans who were deported after the conquest of Jerusalem. Any attempt to derive historical information from these stories encounters insuperable problems. The opening verse dates the siege of Jerusalem to the third year of King Jehoiakim (606 B.C.E.). We know from other sources, both biblical and Babylonian, that Nebuchadnezzar did not besiege Jerusalem until 598/597, and Jehoiakim died before the siege began. Chapter 2 is set in the second year of the reign of Nebuchadnezzar, which would require that he had conquered Jerusalem in his first year. Later chapters present problems that are even more glaring. Daniel 4 claims that Nebuchadnezzar was transformed into a beast for seven years. Chapter 5 presents a king of Babylon named Belshazzar. Belshazzar was a son of the last king of Babylon, Nabonidus, and governed Babylon in the absence of his father. He was never king, however. Daniel goes on to say that after the death of Belshazzar, "Darius the Mede" received the kingdom. No such figure is known to history. Attempts to read these tales as history are misdirected. They are legends, full of miraculous elements (the fiery furnace, the lions' den). They are meant to inspire awe and wonder and are not to be taken as factual accounts. It is unlikely that Daniel ever existed. A Daniel is mentioned in Ezek 14:14, 20, in conjunction with Noah and Job, as a legendary righteous person. He is also mentioned in Ezek 28:3 as a paradigmatic wise man ("are you wiser than Daniel?"). The Daniel of the book of Daniel, however, would have been a younger contemporary of Ezekiel. It is likely that the biblical author borrowed the name of the legendary hero and assigned it to a fictional Judean in the Babylonian exile.

The story of Daniel, then, is not historical. It is meant to be exemplary. Daniel is an exceptional Jew, who does things that the ordinary person cannot hope to imitate, but he models a lifestyle for Jews in the Diaspora. He strikes a fine balance between loyalty to his pagan rulers and fidelity to his God and to his religious tradition.

Daniel 2

By way of illustration of the court tales, I will consider chapter 2. The king has a dream and summons the Chaldeans (Babylonian diviners). He does not tell them the dream but demands that they tell both dream and interpretation. The demand is, in human terms, impossible, and can only be satisfied by divine intervention.

The king flies into a rage and orders that all the wise men be killed. This kind of hyperbolic reaction is typical of these stories. The king is a stock figure, like a character in a fairy tale. The execution order applies even to Daniel and his companions, who have not been consulted at all up to this point. Daniel, however, manages to get a stay of execution so that he can attempt to resolve the problem.

The Chaldean wise men are helpless in the face of the king's demand. Daniel, however, has a resource on which he can draw. He and his companions pray to the God of heaven, and the mystery is revealed to him in a dream or "vision of the night."

Nebuchadnezzar's dream concerns a giant statue composed of different metals: gold, silver, bronze, and iron mixed with clay. These are interpreted as representing a series of kingdoms. Nebuchadnezzar's Babylonian kingdom is the head of gold—the golden age. Each of the succeeding kingdoms is inferior to the one that precedes it. The fourth kingdom is strong as iron and crushes everything, but it is mixed with clay and so has a fatal weakness. In the end the entire statue is destroyed by a stone that becomes a mountain. Daniel interprets this to mean that "the God of heaven will set up a kingdom that will never be destroyed, nor shall this kingdom be left to another people" (2:44).

There are ancient parallels for the representation of history by a sequence of metals of declining value in the Greek poet Hesiod, who wrote about 700 B.C.E., and in a Persian text,

---

Daniel

The Book of Daniel had a profound influence on Western history in many ways. The most fateful, perhaps, was that Daniel is the only book in the Bible that predicts "the end" in a specific number of days. Daniel chapter 9 divides history after the Babylonian exile into seventy weeks of years, or 490 years. Since Daniel took Jeremiah's prophecy of seventy years as symbolic, however, there was no reason why the 490 years should not be taken as symbolic, too. Again, at the end of the book, Daniel is given two further calculations of the time until the end, 1,290 days and 1,335 days. These numbers have provided fertile ground for apocalyptic speculation down through the centuries. Each day could be understood as a year, but the numbers could also be interpreted in more ingenious ways and could proceed from various starting points.

One of the most famous attempts to calculate the end on the basis of Daniel was that of William Miller, a farmer from upstate New York (1782–1849). He based his calculation on Dan 8:43: "For two thousand three hundred evenings and mornings, then the sanctuary will be restored." Taking one day = one year, and starting from the return of Ezra, which he dated to 458 B.C.E., Miller arrived at 1843 as the year of the end. When that year passed, some of his followers settled on a new date of October 22, 1844. The failure of the end to materialize on that day became known as "The Great Disappointment." One Millerite recalled: "We wept and wept until the day dawn." The Seventh-day Adventist Church arose out of the Millerite movement.

In recent years there have been many attempts to reinterpret Daniel's prophecy on the assumption that either the founding of the state of Israel, or the occupation of the West Bank in the 1967 war, was a crucial date in the final week of years.

the Bahman Yasht, chapter 1. The schema by which ages or kingdoms were represented by metals was known in the ancient Near East.

Daniel's interpretation of the statue draws on another widely known pattern: the idea that a sequence of four kingdoms would be followed by a lasting fifth one. Several Greek and Roman sources describe the sequence as follows: first Assyria, second Media, third Persia, fourth Greece, and finally Rome. Daniel does not identify the four kingdoms, but their identity becomes clear as the book progresses. When the Babylonian kingdom falls at the end of chapter 5, the new ruler is called Darius the Mede. He is followed by Cyrus of Persia (6:28). The sequence starts over in chapter 7, which is dated to the first year of Belshazzar of Babylon. He is followed by Darius the Mede (9:1) and Cyrus of Persia (10:1), and Daniel is told that after the prince of Persia, the prince of Greece will come (10:20). The four kingdoms, then, are Babylon, Media, Persia, and Greece. Babylon replaces Assyria, because it was the Babylonians who conquered Jerusalem. The presence of Media, however, can be explained only by reference to the schema of the four kingdoms. Media never ruled over the Jews, and no such person as Darius the Mede ever existed. (There were three Persian kings called Darius, all after Cyrus.) Darius the Mede is invented to fit the traditional pattern of the sequence of kingdoms.

It is somewhat surprising in a Jewish text to find the reign of Nebuchadnezzar, the king who had destroyed Jerusalem, depicted as a golden age. Nebuchadnezzar is Daniel's king, and some flattery is in order. He does not tell Nebuchadnezzar that the final kingdom will be Jewish; the king is free to think that it will be a Babylonian restoration. But Jewish readers know better. The mountain that develops out of the stone is Mount Zion, and the God of

heaven is sure to favor his own people. Moreover, the whole statue, representing all Gentile sovereignty, will be brought crashing down. Nonetheless, Daniel is not suggesting rebellion. The promised kingdom will only come about long after the reign of Nebuchadnezzar. Eschatology is deferred. For the present, the Jews in Babylon are quite content in the service of the Gentile king.

Nebuchadnezzar expresses admiration for Daniel's god, and he appoints Daniel ruler over the whole province of Babylon. He does not seem to perceive the threatening character of the prophecy. The exaltation of the hero is part of the genre, a stock ending to a tale such as this. The ending of the story of Belshazzar in chapter 5 is even more incongruous. Belshazzar honors Daniel, even though he has predicted his imminent death.

The Purpose of the Tales

The tales in Daniel 1–6 have been aptly said to present "a lifestyle for the Diaspora." Their message to the Jews in exile is twofold: participate in the life of the Gentile world and be loyal to the king, but realize that your ultimate success depends on your fidelity to your God and his laws.

In the context of the book, the tales in chapters 1–6 establish the identity of Daniel, who presents his own visions in chapters 7–12. The way Daniel is described may provide a clue to the kind of people who produced this literature. He is a wise man who does some of the same things as the Chaldeans but relies on the power of his God to reveal mysteries. He is not a prophet, and he only rarely strikes a prophetic note in addressing the Gentile kings. Neither is he the kind of wise man portrayed in Proverbs or Qoheleth. His wisdom consists in his ability to interpret dreams and other mysteries such as the writing on the wall (compare the story of Joseph). He has no quarrel with Gentile rule as such, for the present, although the interpretation of Nebuchadnezzar's dream in chapter 2 expresses the hope that the Gentile kingdoms will eventually be overthrown.

The Visions (Daniel 7–12)

The visions in the second half of the book of Daniel differ from the tales in chapters 1–6 both in genre and in setting. Chapters 7 and 8 are symbolic visions in the prophetic tradition (cf. especially the visions of Zechariah). In each case the visions are interpreted to Daniel by an angel. In chapter 9 the revelation takes the form of the interpretation of an older prophecy from Jeremiah, but again the interpretation is given by an angel. In chapters 10–12 Daniel has a vision of an angel, who then narrates the revelation to him. In each case the revelation is eschatological in the sense that it concerns the end of history. The final revelation ends with a prediction of resurrection and judgment. This is the only passage in the Hebrew Bible that speaks unambiguously of individual resurrection. This hope is also expressed in 2 Maccabees and the Wisdom of Solomon, which are part of the Old Testament in the Roman Catholic tradition but are not included in the Hebrew Bible, since they were written in Greek.

The Genre Apocalypse

While angelic interpreters are also found in the prophetic visions of Zechariah, the combination of angelic revelation and transcendent eschatology (involving the judgment of individuals after death) constitutes a new genre in biblical literature. This genre, apocalypse, takes its name from the book of Revelation in the New Testament. There is an extensive apocalyptic literature from Judaism in the Hellenistic and Roman periods. The book of *1 Enoch* contains no fewer than five apocalypses, all attributed to Enoch, who supposedly lived before the flood. Some of the Enoch apocalypses are older than Daniel, some roughly contemporary, and one, known as the *Similitudes of Enoch,* is later, most probably from the first century C.E. Another cluster of apocalypses, *4 Ezra* and *2 and 3 Baruch,* were composed at the end of the first century C.E., at about the same time as the book of Revelation. Several of these apocalypses, especially the *Similitudes of Enoch, 4 Ezra,* and Revelation, were directly influenced by Daniel. All the Jewish apocalypses are pseudepigraphic: their real authors are not named, but the works are attributed to famous people who had lived centuries earlier (or in the case of Enoch, thousands of years earlier). This device presumably added to the authority of the compositions. It also allowed the seer to "predict" many things that had actually happened by the time that the book was written and thereby to strengthen confidence in the real predictions.

The Setting of the Visions

The setting of Daniel 7–12 also differs from that of chapters 1–6. The tales are set in the Diaspora and generally reflect an acceptance of Gentile rule. The visions, in contrast, are focused on events in Jerusalem and reflect a time of persecution. While no names are mentioned, they point quite clearly to the persecution by the Syrian king Antiochus IV Epiphanes in 168–164 B.C.E., which provoked the Maccabean revolt and which is described in 1 and 2 Maccabees. At that time Syrian forces occupied the Jerusalem temple and installed a pagan altar there. The pagan altar becomes known as "the desolating abomination" or "abomination of desolation" both in Dan 11:31 and in 1 Macc 1:54. Some Jews were put to death for observing the law of Moses (e.g., by having their sons circumcised) or for refusing to participate in pagan sacrifices. According to Deuteronomy, those who kept the law should prosper and live long lives. Now Jews were confronted with a situation in which those who broke the law prospered and those who observed it risked losing their lives. It is against this backdrop that the visions of Daniel must be read.

Daniel 7

In chapter 7 Daniel has a terrifying dream, which is really a nightmare. He sees four great beasts rising from the sea. The fourth is especially terrifying. It grows horns, including one final upstart horn that is especially offensive. Then the scene changes to a heavenly throne room, where a judgment is held and the beasts are condemned. Then Daniel sees "one like a son of man," that is, one like a human being, coming on the clouds of heaven. This figure is given dominion and a kingdom that will never pass away.

This vision resembles Daniel 2 in some respects. Both visions involve four kingdoms and a final kingdom that will not pass away. But the imagery is very different. The first kingdom in chapter 2 was represented by a head of gold and so could be thought to be a golden age. In chapter 7 all the kingdoms are beasts that arise from the sea.

This imagery draws on old mythic traditions that can be traced back to the Canaanite texts from Ugarit but that are also often reflected in the Hebrew Bible. In the Ugaritic myths, the Sea, Yamm, is a monster who challenges the authority of the god Baal and is crushed by him. In ancient Israel, YHWH, not Baal, is the God of life, and there are numerous allusions to a battle between him and the Sea and a monster that is called Rahab or Leviathan (Job 26:12-13; Isa 51:9-11). In Isa 27:1 the battle is projected into the future: "On that day the LORD with his cruel and great and strong sword will punish Leviathan the fleeing serpent, Leviathan the twisting serpent, and he will kill the dragon that is in the sea." In this myth, which is quite different from the account of creation in Genesis but very similar to creation myths of the ancient Near East, the work of creation involves subduing the sea and killing its monsters. In Daniel 7 the beasts rise up again. The four kingdoms are portrayed as manifestations of primeval anarchy let loose upon the world.

In Dan 7:9 thrones are set up and a white-haired "Ancient of Days" appears, surrounded by thousands of servants. This figure is evidently God. It is surprising, then, when another figure appears "with the clouds of heaven." In the Hebrew Bible, the figure who rides on the clouds is always YHWH, the God of Israel (cf. Pss 68:5; 104:3). Yet in Daniel 7 this figure is clearly subordinate to the Ancient of Days. The juxtaposition of two divine figures can be understood against the background of the Canaanite myth. There the high god was El, a venerable figure with a white beard. The young fertility god was Baal, who is called the "rider of the clouds" in the Ugaritic texts. In the Hebrew Bible, YHWH usually combines the roles of El and Baal. In Daniel 7, however, they are separated. The influence of the Canaanite mythic tradition is clearly evident in the relationships between the Ancient of Days, the rider of the clouds, and the beasts from the sea. We do not know in what form the author of Daniel 7 knew this tradition.

Some of it is reflected in biblical poetry, but the author probably had sources that are no longer available to us. Of course he adapted the tradition. The rider of the clouds does not attack the Sea as Baal had attacked Yamm. The conflict is resolved by a divine judgment. And of course the Jewish author would not have identified the Ancient One and the rider of the clouds as El and Baal.

The identity of the "one like a son of man" (7:13, RSV) in its Jewish context is the most controversial issue in the book of Daniel. Traditional Christian exegesis assumed that this figure was Jesus Christ because of the way the phrase "Son of Man" is used in the Gospels. This understanding of the figure could not have been available to Jews before the Christian era. Daniel's son of man was identified as the Messiah in both Jewish and Christian exegesis for many centuries. But there is no other reference in Daniel to a messiah (a king who would restore the kingdom of David). Over the last century or so, there have been two main interpretations of the "one like a son of man." Many scholars assume that this figure is simply a symbol for the Jewish people. The alternative, and more satisfactory, interpretation is that he is an angel, most probably the archangel Michael, who represents the Jewish people on the heavenly level.

The argument that the "one like a son of man" is the Jewish people takes the angel's interpretation as the point of departure. According to the interpretation, the four beasts are four kings or kingdoms. Then, "the holy ones of the Most High" will receive the kingdom. Some scholars assume that the "one like a son of man" is a symbol for the holy ones, who are then identified with the Jewish people. In the literature of this period, however, holy ones are nearly always angels. (Compare the "watcher and holy one" who announced Nebuchadnezzar's fate in

Daniel 4.) Whenever else Daniel sees a "man" in his vision, the figure turns out to be an angel (see Dan 8:15; 9:21; 12:6-7). In Daniel 10, each people has a heavenly "prince" or protector. The "prince" of Israel was the archangel Michael. Most probably, it is Michael who is depicted as "one like a son of man" coming with the clouds of heaven.

Daniel 7 addresses the situation of the Jewish people under Antiochus Epiphanes. The offensive "little horn" is Epiphanes. The Jews are given into his power for "a time, two times, and half a time," or three and a half years. But eventually Israel's heavenly allies, the holy ones, prevail. The Jewish people are "the people of the holy ones of the Most High" who receive the lasting kingdom in 7:27.

Daniel's vision dramatizes the conflict in which the Jews found themselves in the time of Antiochus Epiphanes. This crisis is worse than might be thought: it is nothing less than an eruption of primordial chaos. But it is also reassuring, for the end of the story is known. The holy ones will eventually prevail, and the Most High will pronounce judgment. The appropriate response on the part of the Jewish people is not to take up arms in its own defense but to wait for the deliverance from heaven. All of this will be spelled out more clearly in the last revelation of the book.

Daniel 10–12

The final revelation of the book spans chapters 10–12. Daniel 10:2-9 describes how Daniel has his vision—by fasting for three weeks. Whether the author of the book actually had visions in this way is something we cannot be sure of, but it seems plausible. Other apocalypses describe other techniques for inducing visions. For example, in *4 Ezra*, Ezra eats "the flower that is in the field" (2 Esd 9:24).

Daniel's vision in this case resembles that of Ezekiel in Ezek 8:2: a wonderful gleaming man who turns out to be an angel. He is dressed in linen like a priest. He explains to Daniel the real nature of conflicts on earth. He is engaged in combat with the "prince of Persia," and after that the "prince of Greece" will come. Nobody helps him except "Michael your prince." Michael, prince of Israel, is the archangel. The princes of Persia and Greece are presumably the patron angels of those peoples. In earlier times they would be called simply "gods." Conflicts on earth are decided not just by human actions but by the actions of the gods or patron angels.

The angel proceeds to tell Daniel what is written in "the book of truth," a heavenly writing that is analogous to the tablets of destiny in Babylonian mythology. The course of history is predetermined. The history in question begins with the last kings of Persia and extends down to the second century B.C.E. No names are mentioned, in accordance with prophetic style, so the impression is given that the future is perceived dimly. Kings of Syria (the Seleucids, in the Hellenistic period) are called "the king of the north." Kings of Egypt (the Ptolemies) are called "the king of the south." In 11:21 "a contemptible person" will arise. This is Antiochus Epiphanes. Verses 25-28 describe Epiphanes' first invasion of Egypt, which took place in 170 B.C.E. and was relatively successful. Verse 29 describes his second invasion of Egypt, in 168,

which was a disaster. He was confronted by the Romans (the Kittim) and ordered to withdraw. He obeyed. Daniel implies that he took out his frustration on Jerusalem. While the king was in Egypt, civil war had broken out in Jerusalem between the former high priest, Jason, and the current one, Menelaus (see 2 Macc 5:5-14). The king took it that Judea was in revolt and sent in the troops.

After this, for reasons that remain controversial, Antiochus attempted to suppress the Jewish cult. Some Jews collaborated. Daniel says, "He shall seduce with intrigue those who violate the covenant" (11:32). The people who know their God, however, stand firm. The real heroes, from the viewpoint of Daniel, are the "wise" (Hebrew *maskilim*) who instruct the common people, even though some of them do so at the cost of their lives.

It is reasonable to suppose that the authors of Daniel belonged to the circle of "the wise." The instruction they gave to the masses presumably corresponded to the revelations of Daniel: that the human conflicts were only a reflection of conflicts on the supernatural level, and that the outcome was assured. Some scholars have argued that "the wise" should be identified with a party known as the Hasidim, who are mentioned three times in the books of Maccabees (1 Macc 2:42; 7:12-13; 2 Macc 14:6). We know very little about these people, except that they were militant supporters of the Maccabees. Daniel 11:34 says that the wise shall receive little help. This has often

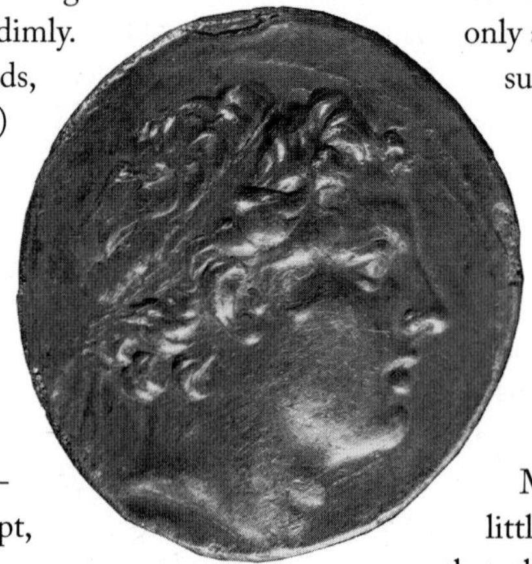

Fig. 27.1. Tetradrachma of Antiochus IV Epiphanes (175–163 B.C.E.), Seleucid king of Syria who, by his persecution in Judea, provoked the Macabean revolt (167 B.C.E.). Israel Museum (IDAM), Jerusalem. Photo: © Erich Lessing / Art Resource, N.Y.

been interpreted as a slighting reference to the Maccabees. It is not clear, however, that Daniel would have regarded the Maccabees as any help at all. In his view, the battle would be won by the archangel Michael. The role of the Jews was to keep themselves pure and not do anything to obstruct their heavenly deliverer.

Daniel 11:40-45 describes the downfall of the king. Verse 45 claims that he would meet his death between the sea and the holy mountain, that is, in the land of Israel. This prophecy was not fulfilled. Antiochus Epiphanes died in Persia from wounds received in an attempt to rob a temple late in 164 B.C.E. The unfulfilled prophecy reveals the date of the composition of Daniel. All the "predictions" are correct down to the persecution. This part of the prophecy was presumably written after the fact and served to inspire confidence in the real prediction of the end of the story, which was yet to come. The prophecy must have been written before the news of Antiochus's death reached Jerusalem.

The death of the king is not the climax of the prophecy. According to Dan 12:1-3, "At that time Michael, the great prince, the protector of your people, shall arise." Then all those written in the book of life would be delivered. Some would rise to everlasting life and some to everlasting contempt. The wise would shine like the stars forever. We know from a passage in *1 Enoch* 104 that "to shine like the stars" means "to become companions of the angels." The idea of astral immortality, that some souls ascend to the stars after death, was well known in the Greek world. Daniel does not say that everyone will be raised, only the righteous and the wicked. Neither does he say that the resurrection will involve a body of flesh and blood. Daniel 12:2, which is usually taken to refer to "the dust of the earth," can better be translated as "the land of dust," or Sheol. The idea then is

that the wise, at least, are lifted up from Sheol to heaven.

> "At that time Michael, the great prince, the protector of your people, shall arise. There shall be a time of anguish, such as has never occurred since nations first came into existence. But at that time your people shall be delivered, everyone who is found written in the book. Many of those who sleep in the land of dust shall awake, some to everlasting life, and some to shame and everlasting contempt. Those who are wise shall shine like the brightness of the sky, and those who lead many to righteousness, like the stars forever and ever."
> —Daniel 12:1-3

The hope for resurrection explains why the wise could let themselves be killed in the time of persecution. The traditional hope in ancient Israel was for a long life and to see one's children's children. This hope was changed radically by the idea of resurrection to a glorious afterlife. The goal of life would henceforth be to become like the angels, so that one could live with them forever. This new hope is central to the apocalyptic literature. It figures prominently in the Dead Sea Scrolls, and it was essential to the rise of Christianity. Of course, the transition in the nature of Jewish hope was not instantaneous and complete. Some Jews (e.g., the Sadducees) did not accept the idea of resurrection. Those who did believe in resurrection did not necessarily give up their old ideas about fulfillment on earth. But the idea of individual resurrection, which occurs in the Hebrew Bible for the first time in Daniel, introduced a kind of hope for the future that was radically new in the context of Jewish tradition, and that would have far-reaching consequences for the development of religion in the Western world.

Two final points from Daniel 10–12 require comment. In 12:4 Daniel is told to "keep the words secret and the book sealed until the time of the end." We should not infer that the book of Daniel was to be kept secret. The time of the end was the time when the book was actually written. The command to keep it secret explained why these visions had not been known before the Maccabean period.

The second point concerns the calculation of the time of the end in 12:11-12. The first of these verses says happy are those who persevere and attain the 1,290 days. The second says happy are those who persevere and attain the 1,335 days. Two different numbers are placed side by side. A third number, 1,150, was given in chapter 8, and in that case it was clear that the number was counted from the time that the temple was profaned. The simplest explanation of the different numbers is that when the shorter number passed, a new calculation was made. This phenomenon is well known from the case of the Millerites in nineteenth-century America, who recalculated the end

---

Dates in the Hellenistic Period (B.C.E.)

336–323	Campaigns of Alexander the Great
320–198	Judea ruled by Ptolemies of Egypt.
198–164	Judea conquered by Seleucids of Syria
175–164	Antiochus IV Epiphanes
175–168	Hellenistic reform in Jerusalem
168–167	Profanation of temple; Maccabean revolt
164	Rededication of temple by Judas Maccabee
164–63	Judea independent under Hasmoneans (descendants of Maccabees)
63	Conquest of Jerusalem by Pompey, Roman general

---

several times. In the case of Daniel, however, there is a further complication. All the figures given amount to more than three years and may be taken as approximations of the time, times and half a time, or three and a half years mentioned elsewhere in the book. But according to 1 Maccabees, the temple was restored by Judas Maccabee exactly three years after it was profaned. It would seem that the author of Daniel's visions did not regard the Maccabean restoration as the "end." Most probably, he still awaited the resurrection of the dead.

1 and 2 Maccabees

The events in the time of Antiochus Epiphanes (175–164 B.C.E.), which form the backdrop of the visions of Daniel, are described in 1 and 2 Maccabees. First Maccabees was most probably written in Hebrew but is extant only in Greek and other translations. Second Maccabees was composed in Greek and was an abridgment of a longer history by Jason of Cyrene. It is somewhat ironic that these stories of Jewish liberation are not represented in the Hebrew Bible and owe their preservation to the Christian churches. Both books are canonical in the Roman Catholic tradition and are included in the Protestant Apocrypha.

First Maccabees

First Maccabees tells the story of the Maccabee family and their immediate descendants, the Hasmonean dynasty, who ruled Judea for approximately a century, down to the conquest of Jerusalem by the Roman general Pompey in 63 B.C.E. The history in 1 Maccabees extends as far as the accession of John Hyrcanus in 135 B.C.E.

The events leading up to the Maccabean revolt are described rapidly in the opening chapter. Only brief notice is given to the "Hellenistic reform" by which "certain renegades" got permission from the king to follow the Gentile way of life. They then built a gymnasium in Jerusalem and "removed the marks of circumcision," presumably because they exercised nude, in the Greek fashion (1:11-15). First Maccabees, however, pays little further attention to these people. In this account the trouble results from unprovoked aggression by the Syrian king, Antiochus Epiphanes. First he pillaged Jerusalem. Two years later he sent a tax collector, who again plundered the city and established a citadel, in which he installed "a sinful people, men who were renegades" (1:34). Finally, "the king wrote to his whole kingdom that all should be one people and that all should give up their particular customs" (1:41-42). Consequently, a violent attempt was made to suppress the Jewish religion. Copies of the law were destroyed, people were put to death for having their sons circumcised, and the temple was profaned by the installation of the "profaning sacrilege," an altar on which pagan sacrifices were offered. The claim of 1 Maccabees, that the king tried to impose uniformity on his whole kingdom, cannot be sustained. Antiochus Epiphanes was known to celebrate the multiplicity of deities worshiped in his kingdom. His repressive measures were directed only against the Jews.

According to 1 Maccabees, the revolt that broke out was inspired by fidelity to the covenant. It was initiated by Mattathias, the father of the Maccabees, who refused to offer pagan sacrifice and killed a Jew who came forward to do so. Thus we are told, "He burned with zeal for the law as Phinehas did against Zimri the son of Salu" (2:26). (Cf. Numbers 25, where Phinehas, grandson of Aaron, kills an Israelite in the act of intercourse with a Midianite woman.)

The Maccabees, however, were prepared to qualify their adherence to the law. First Maccabees 2:29-38 tells of a group of pious Jews who withdrew to the wilderness to avoid the persecution. They were attacked on the Sabbath day. They refused to violate the Sabbath by defending themselves, and so they were slaughtered, calling on heaven and earth to witness that they were being killed unjustly. The invocation of heaven and earth is an allusion to Deuteronomy 32, which goes on to say, "Vengeance is mine, [says the LORD]" (Deut 32:35). Those who died on the Sabbath may have hoped that God would avenge them. Their mentality may have been similar to that of the "wise" in Daniel 11, who lay down their lives but are assured of vindication in the hereafter. When Mattathias and his friends heard of the slaughter on the Sabbath, they mourned for the victims, but they resolved that they would defend themselves on the Sabbath, lest the whole Jewish people be wiped from the earth. In doing so, they resolved to break the law for the greater good of the people. Not all pious Jews agreed with this decision. The dilemma, however, is one that has continued to confront Judaism down to modern times.

The remainder of 1 Maccabees recounts the heroic exploits of the Maccabean family.

Second Maccabees

The book of 2 Maccabees offers a different perspective on the same events. The book begins with two letters to the Jews in Egypt, urging them to join in the celebration of the purification of the temple (Hanukkah). These letters are prefixed to the book proper, which begins at 2:19. Second Maccabees differs from 1 Maccabees in several respects:

1. It gives a much fuller account of the events leading up to the persecution, especially of the so-called Hellenistic reform.

2. It makes no mention of Mattathias and focuses on Judas Maccabee, rather than on the whole family.

3. Much of the credit for the success of the rebellion is given to the deaths of the martyrs, which may be regarded as the centerpiece of the book.

4. The story ends before the death of Judas, after one of his greatest victories, over the general Nicanor. (This victory is reported in 1 Macc 7:43-50.)

Chapter 4 provides an extensive account of the Hellenistic reform, which was described in a few verses in 1 Maccabees. A man named Jason, brother of the high priest Onias, obtained the high priesthood by bribing the king, and proceeded to build a gymnasium and introduce the Greek way of life in Jerusalem. (The word "Hellenism" is used here for the first time to refer to the Greek way of life.) Then a man named Menelaus, who was not of the high priestly family, outbid Jason and became high priest. Menelaus also contrived to have the legitimate high priest, Onias, murdered. When Antiochus Epiphanes invaded Egypt for the second time (in 168 B.C.E.), Jason attempted unsuccessfully to stage a coup. When the king heard of fighting in Jerusalem, he thought that the city was in revolt and sent in the troops. Shortly after this he took measures to suppress the Jewish religion. According to 2 Maccabees, the temple became a place where prostitutes had intercourse with Gentiles, and Jews were compelled to celebrate a festival in honor of the Greek god Dionysus.

The account of these events in 2 Maccabees is generally more satisfactory than that of 1 Maccabees. It becomes clear that the king's

Fig. 27.2. Qumran, where the Dead Sea Scrolls were found. Photo: John J. Collins.

Fig. 27.3. Scale model of Herod's temple. Holy Land Hotel, Jerusalem. Photo: © Erich Lessing / Art Resource, N.Y.

actions were not entirely unprovoked but were a response to what he perceived as rebellion on the part of the Jews. Nonetheless, the attempt to suppress the Jewish religion is extraordinary in antiquity. Some scholars suspect that the persecution may have been the idea of the renegade Menelaus, as a way of crushing the opposition of traditional Jews. All the ancient accounts, however, place the responsibility on the king. It may be, as some ancient authors suggest, that the king regarded the Jewish religion as barbaric. It was certainly highly distinctive in the ancient world, in its insistence on monotheism and rejection of idolatry. On this account, the king would have been trying to make it like a Greek cult, in effect, to "normalize" it. But there was no precedent in the Greek world for an attempt to suppress a cult in this manner. Better precedents, in fact, can be found in the biblical tradition, notably in the reform of King Josiah (2 Kings 22–23), which suppressed the cults of the Israelite high places.

In placing so much emphasis on the Hellenistic reform, 2 Maccabees represents the basic conflict as one between Hellenism and Judaism. Yet the "reforms" of Jason and the building of the gymnasium encountered no significant opposition. It was only when the king attempted to suppress the traditional forms of Jewish worship that a revolt broke out. The essential conflict, then, was not over broad cultural issues but over the freedom of the Jewish people to practice their traditional religion as they saw fit.

Second Maccabees dwells at length on the deaths of the martyrs and tells in gruesome detail the story of a mother and seven sons (chapter 7). The second brother says that "the king of the universe will raise us up to an everlasting renewal of life, because we have died for his laws" (2 Macc 7:9). The faith of the brothers, then, is essentially the same as that of the "wise" in Daniel: they give up their lives in this world in the hope of exaltation after death. In 2 Maccabees, however, the resurrection has a distinctly physical character. One brother offers his hands to be cut off because he is confident that he will get them back again (7:11). The emphasis on bodily resurrection seems to be inspired by the circumstances of the story, where the bodies of the young men are subjected to torture.

In general, 2 Maccabees places much more emphasis on divine assistance than was the case in 1 Maccabees. This is why the deaths of the martyrs are effective. Angelic horsemen appear to assist the Jews in battle (11:8). There is much less emphasis here on the human achievements of the Maccabees.

Perhaps the greatest legacy of 2 Maccabees, however, lies in the stories of the martyrs. These stories served as blueprints for numerous similar tales in later Judaism and especially in Christianity. An early example is found in the book of 4 Maccabees, which is sometimes included in the Apocrypha, although it is not part of the Roman Catholic Bible. It is typical of these stories that the tyrant confronts the martyrs in person, and that the latter have an opportunity to affirm the beliefs for which they die. Second Maccabees 7 is also typical insofar as the conviction of the martyrs is grounded in the hope of resurrection.

———, ed. *The Encyclopedia of Apocalypticism.* Vol. 1: *The Origins of Apocalypticism in Judaism and Christianity.* New York: Continuum, 1998.

Daniel

Collins, John J. *Daniel.* Hermeneia. Minneapolis: Fortress Press, 1993.

———. *Daniel, with an Introduction to Apocalyptic Literature.* FOTL 20. Grand Rapids: Eerdmans, 1984.

Goldingay, John E. *Daniel.* WBC 30. Dallas: Word, 1989.

Lacocque, André. *The Book of Daniel.* Atlanta: John Knox, 1979.

Montgomery, James A. *A Critical and Exegetical Commentary on the Book of Daniel.* ICC. Edinburgh: T. & T. Clark, 1927.

Seow, C. L. *Daniel.* Westminster Bible Companion. Louisville: Westminster John Knox, 2003.

Smith-Christopher, Daniel L. "Daniel." In *NIB* 7:17–194.

1 and 2 Maccabees

deSilva, David A. *Introducing the Apocrypha*, 244–79. Grand Rapids: Baker, 2002.

Doran, Robert. "1 Maccabees," "2 Maccabees." In *NIB* 4:1–299.

Harrington, Daniel J. *The Maccabean Revolt: Anatomy of a Biblical Revolution.* Wilmington, Del.: Glazier, 1988.

Further Reading

Apocalyptic Literature

Collins, John J. *The Apocalyptic Imagination.* 2nd ed. Grand Rapids: Eerdmans, 1998.

28

The Deuterocanonical Wisdom Books:
Ben Sira, Wisdom of Solomon

```
KEY POINTS

Ben Sira: early second century B.C.E. Before Daniel, but written in      • Problem of theodicy: affirms omnipotent creator.
   his own name.                                                         • Role of scribe.
• Evidence for emerging canon.                                          Wisdom of Solomon: first century C.E., Alexandria. Written in
• Practical instructions in chaps. 1–23, punctuated by praise of          Greek.
   wisdom.                                                               • 3 parts: book of eschatology, book of wisdom, book of history.
• Hymn to wisdom in chap. 24.                                           • Affirms immortality of soul as solution for theodicy.
• Hymns to creator in chaps. 39–43.                                     • Wisdom modeled on Stoic Logos: spirit that holds all things
• Praise of the fathers in chaps. 44–50.                                  together.
• Negative view of women.                                              • Affirms possibility of knowledge of God from observation of
• Wisdom identified with Torah. But use of Torah is still allusive.        nature.
• Rejects judgment after death.
```

The books that make the greatest theological difference between the Roman Catholic Old Testament and the Protestant and Hebrew Bibles are Ben Sira and the Wisdom of Solomon. These books increase the prominence of wisdom literature in the Catholic Bible, and this material is congenial to Catholic interest in natural theology. The Wisdom of Solomon is indebted to Greek philosophy more than any other book of the Old Testament. It is also the only book of the Old Testament that professes a belief in the immortality of the soul, an idea that would have enormous importance in the history of the Christian West.

The Wisdom of Ben Sira (Ecclesiasticus)

The book of Ben Sira was written in Hebrew, in Jerusalem, in the first quarter of the second century B.C.E. It is the only book of the Apocrypha that is cited in rabbinic sources. Ben Sira (Sirach in Greek) is identified in a preface written by his grandson, who translated the book into Greek. According to the preface, Ben Sira had devoted himself to reading the Law and the Prophets and the other books of the ancestors. This shows that the Law and the Prophets were recognized categories at this time. The other writings of the ancestors, however, constituted an open-ended category, and Ben Sira's book resembled them in kind.

The book is not fully preserved in Hebrew. Fragments of six medieval manuscripts were recovered from the Cairo Geniza in the late nineteenth century. These cover most of chapters 3–16 and fragments of chapters 18–36. Much older fragments were found among the Dead Sea Scrolls. Some of these are very small fragments, but the poem in 51:13-20 is included in the Psalms Scroll from Qumran Cave 11. Finally, twenty-six leather fragments were found at Masada, the stronghold by the Dead Sea where the Jewish revolutionaries made their last stand against the Romans in 73 C.E. These fragments contain much of chapters 39–44. In all, about 68 percent of the book is now available in Hebrew. The full text is preserved in Greek, Latin, and Syriac. The book enjoyed considerable popularity in Christianity, so that it became known as "the church book," *Liber Ecclesiasticus.*

As in Proverbs, literary structure is difficult to discern in Ben Sira. The book is divided in two by the hymn to Wisdom in chapter 24. Much of the first half of the book is taken up with practical instructions, punctuated by poetic passages in praise of wisdom. The second half of the book contains longer, more theological reflections. The instructional part of the book is brought to conclusion with hymns to the Creator in 39:12-35 and 42:15—43:33. The "Praise of the Fathers," a long poem in praise of biblical heroes, follows as a kind of epilogue (chaps. 44–50). The book concludes with two poems in chapter 51.

Ben Sira on Women

The practical instruction deals with matters familiar from ancient wisdom litera-ture: honor of parents, friendship, treatment of children and slaves, and so on. The most controversial part of this is Ben Sira's view of women. The sage extols the good wife in 26:1-4, 13-18. She is praised for silence and modesty. There is no mention of business activity on the part of the wife, such as we find in Proverbs 31. A more significant difference from Proverbs, however, is that Ben Sira also discourses on the wickedness of women (Sir 25:13-26; 26:6-12, 19-27). One might compare the portrayal of the "strange woman" in Proverbs 7, but Ben Sira is speaking of wives and daughters, not strangers or prostitutes, and his rhetoric is much more extreme. "Any iniquity," he declares, "is small compared to a woman's iniquity" (25:19). In 42:14 he goes further: "Better is the wickedness of a man than a woman who does good; it is a woman who brings shame and disgrace."

Much of Ben Sira's negative comment on women arises from a fear of being put to shame (see his discussion of daughters in 42:9-14). In 22:3 he declares bluntly, "The birth of a daughter is a loss." Such sentiments were not unknown in ancient Judaism (or elsewhere in the ancient world). According to the Babylonian Talmud: "without both male and female children the world could not exist, but blessed is he whose children are male and woe to him whose children are female" (*Baba Bathra* 16b). Yet Ben Sira is exceptional in his vehemence.

One of the sage's statements about women is especially unfortunate. In 25:24 he declares: "From a woman sin had its beginning, and because of her we all die." There can be little doubt that this is a reference to Eve. Elsewhere Ben Sira ignores the fall and suggests that God created humanity mortal from the start. This is the only time in Jewish literature before the

Christian era that the woman is blamed for the origin of sin and death. Even the responsibility of Adam emerges only in the literature of the first century c.e. (Rom 5:12-21; 1 Cor 15:22; Wis 2:23-24; etc.). For another expression of the view that the woman was more culpable than the man in the garden of Eden we have to wait until the Pastoral Epistles, where we read in 1 Tim 2:14 that "Adam was not deceived, but the woman was deceived and became a transgressor." This view had a long and unfortunate history in Christianity.

Wisdom and the Law

Ben Sira, however, makes other, more positive, contributions to the tradition. He personifies the figure of Wisdom as a female intermediary between God and the world. In chapter 24, "Wisdom praises herself" in the assembly of the Most High. She is a heavenly figure, in the company of the heavenly hosts. The self-praise resembles a series of inscriptions (called "aretalogies") in which the Egyptian goddess Isis recites her own accomplishments. The claims made by Wisdom are extraordinary. She came forth from the mouth of the Most High. That which comes forth from the mouth is either breath (spirit) or word. We are reminded of Genesis 1, where God creates the world by speaking. As we shall find in the Wisdom of Solomon, the Word (Greek *Logos*) was a very important concept in Hellenistic philosophy. The statement that Wisdom came forth from the mouth of God lays the foundation for the identification of Wisdom with the Word or Logos. Again, the statement that Wisdom covered the earth like a mist recalls the spirit of God hovering over the deep in Genesis 1, and suggests a close association between Wisdom and the spirit.

Wisdom praises herself,
  and tells of her glory in the midst of her people.
In the assembly of the Most High she opens her
      mouth,
    and in the presence of his hosts she tells
        of her glory:
"I came forth from the mouth of the Most High,
    and covered the earth like a mist.
I dwelt in the highest heavens,
    and my throne was in a pillar of cloud.
Alone I compassed the vault of heaven
    and traversed the depths of the abyss.
Over waves of the sea, over all the earth,
    and over every people and nation have I
      held sway.
Among all these I sought a resting place;
    in whose territory should I abide?
Then the Creator of all things gave me a
      command,
    and my Creator chose the place for my tent.
He said, 'Make your dwelling in Jacob,
    and in Israel receive your inheritance.'"
—Ben Sira 24:1-8

The statements in 24:4-5 are even more startling: "I dwelt in the highest heavens, and my throne was in a pillar of cloud. Alone I compassed the vault of heaven and traversed the depths of the abyss." In the Hebrew Bible, only YHWH could make such claims. The pillar of cloud was famously associated with the divine presence at the exodus. In Sirach 24, the presence of God in the world is mediated by Wisdom.

Wisdom held sway over all peoples and places (this was also one of the claims of Isis). But she sought a resting place. The Creator commands her to "make your dwelling in Jacob, and in Israel receive your inheritance" (Sir 24:8). So she took root in the holy tent and was established in Zion, in the Jerusalem temple, the place where God had made his name to dwell according to Deuteronomy 12. The idea of Wisdom finding a home on earth is important background for the prologue of the Gospel of John, which speaks of the Word becoming flesh and dwelling among us. Wisdom in Ben Sira does not become flesh. But it does find a particular dwelling place on earth.

In vv. 19-22 Wisdom invites people to eat of her fruits and promises that those who partake of her will hunger and thirst for more. Here again we have language that is later taken up in the Gospel of John. In John 6:35 Jesus says, "I am the bread of life. Whoever comes to me will never be hungry, and whoever believes in me will never be thirsty." Although one text speaks of hungering for more and the other of never being hungry again, the idea is basically the same. Both Wisdom in Ben Sira and Jesus in the gospel offer a kind of food that is unlike any other.

The most surprising statement of all, however, is found in Sir 24:23: "All this is the book of the covenant of the Most High God, the law that Moses commanded us." Wisdom, in short, is nothing other than the Torah of Moses.

The identification of Wisdom and the Torah can be understood in two different ways. On the one hand, it can be taken to mean that the Torah is the exclusive source of wisdom; on the other, it may mean that the Torah is one privileged formulation of wisdom that in principle can be found anywhere. Ben Sira recognized that the Torah was not the exclusive source of wisdom. In 39:4 he says that the scribe who devotes himself to the study of the law of the Most High "travels to foreign lands and learns what is good and evil in the human lot." The Torah is one valid source of wisdom, but it is not the only one.

The importance of Ben Sira in the development of the Jewish wisdom tradition lies precisely in the fact that he included the Torah of Moses among the sources of wisdom. The earlier wisdom books, Proverbs, Qoheleth, and Job, are distinguished by their lack of any explicit reference to the Torah. Wisdom represented an educational tradition in Israel that was quite distinct from the teaching associated with the cult. Ben Sira was the first wisdom teacher to include the Torah in his curriculum.

Theodicy

Ben Sira reflects at length on the problem of evil. He tries out various answers, and they are not all compatible with each other. Creation is characterized by pairs of opposites: "Good is the opposite of evil and life is the opposite of death; so the sinner is the opposite of the godly. Look at all the works of the Most High; they come in pairs, one the opposite of the other" (33:14-15; cf. 42:24-25). The idea that evil has to exist because good must have its opposite derives from Stoic philosophy. The Stoic Chrysippus, who lived a little earlier than Ben Sira, wrote that there is nothing more foolish than those who think that good can exist without evil. This idea, however, does not sit easily with Ben Sira's insistence elsewhere (especially chapter 15) on human free will.

Ben Sira also borrows from the Stoics the idea of teleology: everything is created for a purpose, to meet some need. Everything is good in its appointed time. Storms and natural disasters are created to give vent to God's anger. Ben Sira rather blithely claims that "all these are good for the godly, but for sinners they turn into evils" (39:27). This idea can hardly withstand serious reflection. The book of Job had already shown that disasters can strike the good and the bad without distinction.

The problem of evil was acute for Ben Sira, because he resolutely resisted the idea of reward or punishment after death. Death is simply the Lord's decree for all flesh. Whether life is for ten or a hundred or a thousand years there is no inquiry about it in Hades (41:1-4). In this respect, his view of life resembles that of Qoheleth. Unlike Qoheleth, however, Ben Sira still wants to insist that there is justice in the world. So he suggests that while all creatures are troubled by anxiety, this affects sinners seven times more. Death and destruction were created for the wicked. He does not find a satisfactory explanation, however, for the fact that these things also befall the just.

Ben Sira remains convinced that the world is in the power of a benevolent and all-powerful Deity. At the end of the hymn to the Creator in chapter 43, he declares, "He is the all" (43:27). Taken at face value, the phrase sounds pantheistic. The Stoics believed that the world (*cosmos*) was the body of God and was animated by a Spirit or Logos. Ben Sira, however, hardly meant this rhetorical flourish to be taken literally. He clearly maintains a distinction between the Creator and creation. The more typical phrase is "God of all" (36:1). He does, however, see a very close relation between God and nature or creation. In this he is typical of the wisdom tradition.

The Role of the Scribe

Ben Sira gives us a clearer picture of his role in society than do most biblical writers, and certainly more than any other wisdom writer. In 38:24—39:11 he discusses the vocation of the scribe in contrast to other professions. This kind of contrast is modeled on a famous Egyptian composition from the second millennium, the Instruction of Duauf, also known as "The Satire on the Trades" (*ANET*, 432–34). Ben Sira is not as derisive of other professions as the Egyptian sage was, but he leaves no doubt about the superiority of the life of the scribe. After all, "How can one become wise who handles the plough . . . and whose talk is about bulls?" (38:25). Since he is not independently wealthy, he aspires to serve great men (39:4). He belongs to the class of retainers, who depend on the rich and powerful for their livelihood. It is not surprising, then, that he takes a conservative position on social ethics and seldom strikes a prophetic note, although he sometimes claims to be inspired (e.g., 24:33).

Ben Sira depicts the scribe as one who is devoted to the study of the Torah but also seeks out wisdom in all its forms and even travels to foreign lands to seek it out. He is pious and prays to the Most High (prayer is seldom mentioned in the earlier wisdom books). His goal is to win honor in his lifetime and leave a glorious name after his death.

It seems likely that Ben Sira earned his living by teaching. In the final poem he calls on the uneducated to come to him "and lodge in my house of instruction" (51:23; the Hebrew phrase is *beth midrash*). This is the earliest reference to a school in Jewish tradition. Ben Sira's school was probably based on a tutorial system. Sirach 6:34-36 advises the aspiring student to find a wise teacher, attach oneself to him, and wear out his doorstep. Formal education in Judaism was still in its infancy. Ben Sira represents a milestone in the development, not only by the fact that he mentions a house of instruction, but also by the fact that he combines the teaching of Torah with traditional wisdom.

The Wisdom of Solomon

The Wisdom of Solomon is a very different kind of wisdom book from Ben Sira. It was composed in Greek, in Alexandria, Egypt, most probably in the early first century C.E. The author had evidently had a good Greek education and knew a great deal more about Greek philosophy than Ben Sira. Wisdom is not a philosophical tract; it is rather a rhetorical piece that draws on philosophical ideas. One of these ideas is the immortality of the soul, a concept that was quite alien to Ben Sira and the older wisdom tradition, and that makes a profound difference in the worldview of Wisdom.

The book falls into three sections: the "book of eschatology," 1:1—6:21; the "book of wisdom," 6:22—10:21; and the "book of history," chapters 11—19. The author drew on different kinds of source material in the various sections, but the book is held together by the central role of wisdom, which is most fully expressed in the second section.

The Book of Eschatology

The opening section of the book is presented as an address to the rulers of the earth, but it is essentially an argument that justice ultimately prevails. The core of the argument is found in chapter 2. Here the philosophy of the unrighteous is laid out in a long speech. They reason that life is short and sorrowful, and that no one has been known to return from Hades. Thus far Qoheleth and even Ben Sira would agree. The wicked, however, draw an extreme inference. Not only do they resolve to enjoy the good things of creation, but they also resolve to "let our might be our law of right, for what is weak proves itself to be useless" (2:11). They plot against the righteous man and resolve to put him to the test, "for if the righteous man is God's child, he will help him, and will deliver him from the hand of his adversaries" (2:18). So they condemn the righteous to a shameful death. But, says the author of Wisdom, they

reasoned wrongly, for they did not know the mysteries of God. God "created us for incorruption, and made us in the image of his own eternity" (2:23). The souls of the righteous are in the hand of God, and no torment touches them. In the eyes of the wicked they seemed to die, but they are at peace (3:3). The contrasting fates of the righteous and the wicked are further dramatized in chapter 5, in a judgment scene. The unrighteous learn that they have been mistaken, and find that the righteous, whom they had held in derision, are numbered among the sons of God.

For the Wisdom of Solomon the vindication of the righteous is awaited after death. In this respect, Wisdom breaks with Proverbs, Qoheleth, and Ben Sira. The author was familiar with, and influenced by, apocalyptic literature. Daniel similarly hoped for vindication after death (Dan 12:3). Even closer parallels to Wisdom can be found in the noncanonical Epistle of Enoch (*1 Enoch* 91–105). The language in Wisdom 5, which refers to the angelic host as sons of God and holy ones, also has many parallels in the Dead Sea Scrolls.

Wisdom was also influenced by the Greek philosopher Plato, who provided a famous discussion of justice in his dialogue, the *Republic*. In the second book of the *Republic*, Glaucon argues that injustice is more profitable that justice. He further argues that in order to compare the just and the unjust, we must imagine them in their pure states. The unjust man must not be recognized as such, while the just must be a good person who is thought to be bad: "The just man who is thought unjust will be scourged, racked, bound—will have his eyes burnt out, and at last, after suffering every kind of evil, he will be impaled" (*Republic* 361). There is a similar separation of pure types in the Wisdom of Solomon. The wicked enjoy prosperity on earth, while the righteous are condemned to a shameful death. The analogy with Plato suggests that the author of Wisdom, too, is constructing a philosophical argument. The passage need not be taken to reflect any actual historical persecution of the righteous.

The most important influence of Platonic philosophy is found in the understanding of immortality. The hope is not for resurrection but for the continued life of the soul, which is untouched by torment or death. According to the prayer of Solomon in Wis 9:15, "A perishable body weighs down the soul, and this tent of clay encumbers a mind full of cares." Plato had written that "so long as we have the body, and the soul is contaminated by such an evil, we shall never attain completely what we desire" (*Phaedo* 66B). Similar ideas can be found in the Jewish philosopher Philo. For Plato the soul was preexistent. Wisdom seems to play with that notion in 8:19-20: "I was indeed a child well-endowed, having had a noble soul fall to my lot, or rather being noble I entered an undefiled body." But Wisdom attaches no importance to the preexistence of the soul. Rather, the soul is immortal because it is made in the image of God (2:23), and it maintains that immortality through righteousness. Wisdom even goes so far as to say that God did not make death. Death entered the world through "the envy of the devil" (2:24; this may be the earliest attestation of the identification of the snake in the Garden of Eden as the devil). Those who belong to the lot of the devil bring death on themselves by their conduct. Wisdom differs from Plato, then, in making the immortality of the soul dependent on righteousness. Nonetheless, the idea of the immortal soul is clearly derived from Platonic philosophy.

The righteous man claims to be the child of God, and so the wicked taunt him, "If the righteous man is God's child, he will help him and deliver him" (2:18). The Greek word translated "child" in the inclusive translation of the NRSV is *huios*, son. In the Gospel of Matthew, during the crucifixion, the chief priests and elders mock Jesus, saying, "He trusts in God; let God deliver him now, if he wants to; for he said, 'I am God's Son'" (27:43). Jesus is identified as the righteous one of whom Wisdom spoke. Wisdom 3:1, "The souls of the righteous are in the hand of God," has traditionally been sung or recited as part of the liturgy of burial in the Roman Catholic Church.

But the souls of the righteous are in the hand of God,
and no torment will ever touch them.
In the eyes of the foolish they seemed to have died,
and their departure was thought to be a disaster,
and their going from us to be their destruction;
but they are at peace.
—Wisdom 3:1-3

The Book of Wisdom

In the opening chapter of the book we are told that wisdom is a holy spirit (1:5). It is identical with "the spirit of the LORD," which fills the world and holds all things together (1:7). The concept of wisdom in the Wisdom of Solomon is indebted to such passages as Proverbs 8 and Sirach 24, but it is also influenced by Stoic philosophy. The Stoics conceived of the spirit *(pneuma)* as the soul of the universe. It was a fine, fiery substance that spread through all reality and brought it to life. It was identified with the Logos (Word or Reason) that was the rational principle in the universe. It could sometimes be called God. The description of wisdom in Wis 7:22—8:1 is heavily indebted to Stoic descriptions of the Logos. It is portrayed as a fine, pure substance that can penetrate all things and bring order to the universe. Wisdom differs from the Stoic Logos insofar as it is not itself an immanent God but is rather the link between a transcendent God and the universe. It is a breath of the power of God and a pure emanation of his glory. This combination of the Stoic Logos with a transcendent God was not unusual in Hellenistic philosophy around the turn of the era, when Stoics and Platonists borrowed freely from each other's ideas.

In the Wisdom of Solomon, wisdom is conceived as a power that transforms people: "In every age she passes into holy souls and makes them friends of God and prophets" (7:27). Wisdom is a spirit, but it is also a fine substance that can actually enter into people and transform them. Later Christian theology would adapt this understanding of wisdom to develop the notion of grace as a spiritual substance that connects humanity with God. The idea of wisdom was also taken up and adapted in the Christian doctrine of the Trinity. On the one hand, wisdom is the Logos or Word, with which Jesus is identified in John 1. On the other hand, wisdom is the spirit of the Lord that fills the whole world. Wisdom 1:7, "The spirit of the Lord has filled the world," is traditionally sung at the beginning of the Roman Catholic Mass for Pentecost, the primary celebration of the Holy Spirit in the Christian liturgical calendar.

The Book of History

Much of the discussion in the third section of the book has to do with idolatry. The author is scathing in his contempt for the Egyptians, who worshiped "irrational serpents and worthless animals" (11:15). He is much more sympathetic toward philosophers, who thought that the elements of nature were the gods who rule the universe. These people, he suggests, "are little to be blamed, for perhaps they go astray while seeking God and desiring to find him" (13:6). Yet they are not to be excused, for if they were able to know so much why did they not arrive at knowledge of God? Underlying this critique is the author's own view of the relation between God and the universe: "From the greatness and beauty of created things comes a corresponding perception of their creator" (13:5). This kind of argument for the existence of God, on the basis of the regularity of nature, became a cornerstone of the kind of Christian theology that is called "natural theology." Natural theology was widely accepted in the Middle Ages and remains characteristic of the Roman Catholic tradition.

Further Reading

Ben Sira

Camp, Claudia. "Understanding a Patriarchy: Women in Second-Century Jerusalem Through the Eyes of Ben Sira." In *"Women Like This": New Perspectives on Jewish Women in the Greco-Roman World*, ed. A. J. Levine, 1–39. SBLEJL 1. Atlanta: Scholars Press, 1991.

Collins, John J. *Jewish Wisdom in the Hellenistic Age*, 21–111. OTL. Louisville: Westminster, 1997.

Crenshaw, James L. "The Book of Sirach." In *NIB* 5:603–867.

Skehan, Patrick W., and Alexander A. Di Lella. *The Wisdom of Ben Sira*. AB 39. Garden City, N.Y.: Doubleday, 1987.

Wisdom of Solomon

Collins, John J. *Jewish Wisdom in the Hellenistic Age*, 178–221. OTL. Louisville: Westminster, 1997.

Kolarcik, M. "The Book of Wisdom." In *NIB* 5:435–600.

Winston, David. *The Wisdom of Solomon*. AB 43. Garden City, N.Y.: Doubleday, 1979.

29

From Tradition to Canon

KEY POINTS

- The nature of this collection.
- How would we recognize **inspiration**? **Revelation**?
- What is meant by a **canon**?
- **Gradual formation** of authoritative collection.

- **Enduring value** of biblical literature.
- Passion for **justice**.
- Prose fiction.
- **Abuse of Bible** in modern world.

The writings that make up the Hebrew Bible and Old Testament are the literary heritage of ancient Israel and Judah. These writings were composed and copied and revised over several hundred years. They are diverse in content as well as in literary form. Themes that are central to some books (e.g., the covenant, in Deuteronomy) are absent from others (Proverbs, Qoheleth). Rather than impose uniformity on this literature, we should recognize its inherent diversity.

The Bible does not preserve all the literature of ancient Judah. We know from the Dead Sea Scrolls and from some of the Pseudepigrapha that there were many other writings in circulation. We should like to know more of the principles of selection of the canon. The Torah had been accepted as authoritative since the Persian period, and the Prophets since the beginning of the second century B.C.E. The only area where there was room for debate in the final selection was the Writings. Sectarian writings, such as the books of Enoch or some of the Dead Sea Scrolls, were not widely enough accepted to warrant inclusion. The books included were those that were cherished by the rabbis who laid the foundations of Judaism after the revolt against Rome in 66–70 C.E. The larger collection found in the Greek Bible reflects the more extensive corpus of writings that circulated in the Greek-speaking Diaspora.

The editors who gathered these books together made only very modest efforts to impose a meaningful shape on the collection. The different order of the Greek and Hebrew Bibles is a case in point. The fact that the

Prophets are placed at the end of the Septuagint version supports the Christian view of the Old Testament as an essentially prophetic collection that points forward to the fulfillment of revelation in the New Testament. But the editing of the biblical books, like their composition, was a gradual process that went on over several hundred years. The "canonical shape of the text" is largely in the eye of the modern interpreter. The Bible consists of a collection of diverse writings that can be, and always has been, interpreted in various ways.

Sacred Scripture

On one level, the Hebrew Bible and Old Testament are collections of documents pertinent to the religious history of ancient Israel and Judah. For Jews and Christians over the centuries they are more than that; they are also sacred scriptures, which are in some way authoritative, even in the modern world. The understanding of these writings as sacred scripture is bound up with claims of inspiration or revelation and with the status of "canon," which is ascribed to the collection.

Inspiration and Revelation

Claims of inspiration and revelation can scarcely be discussed profitably in an academic context. It is possible, however, to say something about the way in which such claims arose and what they might entail.

Such claims are made in some biblical books but by no means all. The laws of the Pentateuch supposedly originated in the revelation to Moses on Mount Sinai, although many of them are transparently later. The prophets spoke their oracles in the name of the Lord. There is no claim of divine inspiration in the narrative and historical books, however, and the wisdom literature makes no pretense of being anything but human. Nonetheless, the claim of inspiration was gradually extended to the whole corpus, by analogy with the Law and the Prophets.

It is often assumed that an inspired text must be historically accurate, whereas modern scholarship has repeatedly cast doubt on the veracity of biblical stories. (Think, for example, of the book of Joshua.) But the assumption begs questions of genre and intention. Joshua is not an exercise in historiography in the modern sense of the term. There is no reason, in principle, why a work of fiction should not be inspired as easily as a historical chronicle. Again, it is commonly assumed that an inspired text must be morally edifying. Many biblical texts most certainly are not, by any civilized measure. (Think, again, of Joshua and the alleged wholesale slaughter of Canaanites with divine approval.) But again, there is no reason in principle why a text that is shocking might not be inspired. Such a text can raise our moral consciousness by forcing us to confront the fact that immoral actions are often carried out in the name of religion. Claims of inspiration and revelation often carry with them assumptions and presuppositions that turn out to be inappropriate to the texts. For this reason, they are problematic. Rather than ask whether a text is revealed (and by what criteria could we possibly decide?) it is better to ask whether a text is revelatory, whether we learn something from it about human nature or about the way the world works. A text that is neither historically reliable nor morally edifying, such as the book of Joshua, may be all too revelatory about human nature.

People who approach the Bible with strong presuppositions about its inspired or revealed character are often at pains to save the appearances of the text and explain away anything that might conflict with their presuppositions. In the ancient world, this was often done by means of allegory, the interpretation of a text as meaning something other than what it actually says. This method was originally developed by Greek scholars in Alexandria to explain away the scandalous behavior of the gods in Homer's epics. It was adapted by Jewish scholars in Alexandria around the turn of the era, most notably Philo, who wrote extensive commentaries on the Torah, interpreting it in terms of Platonic philosophy. Later this method was used by the Christian church fathers, and it was widely accepted as a legitimate method of interpretation in late antiquity. An allegorical interpretation might, for example, explain the commands to eradicate the Canaanites as commands to root out vice from the soul. Such interpretations have little credibility in the modern world, however, and often seem to smack of dishonesty. (We are reminded of Job's charge that his friends would "lie for God" or distort the evidence to try to make God look good.) It is better to come to terms with the text in its own terms than to allegorize it so that it conforms to our ideas of propriety.

Canon

The term "canon" means "measuring stick," and it was used in the Hellenistic world for the standard or norm by which things were evaluated. It was adapted in early Christianity to refer to "the rule of faith." To speak of the Bible as canon implies that the Bible is the standard by which everything else is judged. This idea has a more central place in Protestant Christianity than in Judaism or in Catholicism. The status of "canon" is not something that is inherent in the biblical text but reflects the kind of authority conferred on the text by a particular community.

The idea of a canon has become fashionable in secular literary criticism in recent years to denote the corpus of classic works that stand as benchmarks of excellence in a field. So one might say that Homer was canonical in ancient Greece, or Shakespeare in English literature. Canonical works are copied over and over again, and they become the standard reference works of their particular field. The biblical books can be said to be canonical in this sense for Judaism and Christianity. They provide a fund of stories and sayings that are the basis for a common discourse. They provide analogies by which new experiences can be understood and problems addressed. The biblical books are not necessarily benchmarks of literary excellence, although some of them may be, but they provide case studies in moral and religious reasoning. The case of the Bible, however, is somewhat different from that of a literary canon because of the claim of divine inspiration and the religious authority that it implies.

The ways in which the Bible has functioned as canon have varied widely among religious communities. Biblical texts are not always laws to be obeyed or examples to be imitated. There are many more subtle ways in which people may be informed by a canonical book. Some modern approaches to the canon have celebrated that diversity. In the phrase of James A. Sanders, the canon is "adaptable for life." It is not a tightly coherent, systematic collection that imposes one orthodox view of life. Rather, it is a smorgasbord of resources, some of which may be helpful at one time, others at another. From this perspective, what is important about the canon is the process whereby old texts are constantly used to address new situations. From this perspective, the canon is a resource rather than a norm, but the need to refer constantly to the canonical text inevitably places some restraints on the interpreter.

Enduring Values

The importance that the Bible has enjoyed in the Western world is due in large part to its canonical status in Judaism and Christianity and to the widespread belief in its inspiration. The influence of these books on Western culture is enormous. Knowledge of biblical stories is indispensable for the appreciation of Western art and culture. Think, for example, of the Sistine Chapel paintings of Michelangelo, or of Milton's *Paradise Lost*. Even apart from its importance as a cultural aid, however, the Old Testament remains vital and engaging literature even from a purely humanistic perspective. Here it may suffice to mention two factors that render the Bible an important resource for humanistic education.

First, no other collection of documents from the ancient world, and scarcely any other documents at all, speak with such passionate urgency on the subject of social justice. The primary voices in this respect are those of the Hebrew prophets, but the law codes of the Pentateuch are also important. Biblical laws are not always satisfactory by modern standards. Biblical attitudes to slaves, women, and foreigners are all mired in the cultural assumptions of the ancient world, with only occasional flickers of enlightenment. Nonetheless, the concern for the unfortunate of society in these books is remarkable and often stands as a reproach to the modern Western world.

Second, it has been claimed that the biblical authors were the pioneers of prose fiction. Whatever the historical merits of this claim, and it is not without substance, the achievements of the biblical writers are not just a matter of literary form. The biblical narratives offer a warts-and-all picture of human nature that has seldom been surpassed. When the Bible is read without moralistic presuppositions, it gives a picture of human nature that is not comforting but may well be said to be revelatory.

In the modern world, the Bible, and especially the Old Testament, is often viewed with suspicion because of its association with religious fundamentalism. There are laws in the Bible that can only be described as narrow-minded and intolerant, but the collection as a whole cannot be characterized in this way. This is a collection of writings marked by lively internal debate and by a remarkable spirit of self-criticism, directed not only at the people of Israel but sometimes at the myths and certainties of the tradition. Think, for example of Job, or of Jonah's ironic portrayal of prophecy. It is somewhat ironic, then, that fundamentalistic readings of the Bible treat it so often as a bedrock of certainty. The portrayal of the Bible as a source of infallible truth does not arise from a reading of the Bible itself, but is a monstrous imposition upon it.

One of the most persistent themes of the Hebrew Bible is the critique of idolatry. This applies not only to carved or molten statues but also to the human tendency to absolutize things that are merely part of the created order. Perhaps the greatest irony in the history of the Bible is that it itself has so often been treated as an idol and venerated with a reverential attitude while its message is ignored. Biblical figures from Abraham to Job do not hesitate to argue with the Almighty. The least that might be expected of readers of the Bible is that they bring the same critical spirit to bear on the biblical text.

Further Reading

Barr, James. *Holy Scripture: Canon, Authority, Criticism*. Philadelphia: Westminster, 1983.

Barton, John. *Holy Writings, Sacred Text: The Canon in Early Christianity*. Louisville: Westminster John Knox, 1997.

Sanders, James A. "Adaptable for Life: The Nature and Function of Canon." In *Magnalia Dei, The Mighty Acts of God: Essays on the Bible and Archaeology in Memory of G. E. Wright*, ed. F. M. Cross et al., 531–60. New York: Doubleday, 1976.

Glossary

Achaemenid—Dynasty of Persian kings (559–333 B.C.E.).

Acrostic—A poem in which lines begin with the letters of the alphabet in sequence.

Ahikar—Legendary Assyrian sage.

Akhenaten—Pharaoh Amenophis IV (c. 1350 B.C.E.), whose devotion to the god Aten (the solar disk) was the closest thing to monotheism before the rise of Israel.

Akiba—Rabbi, early second century C.E.

Akitu—Babylonian New Year's festival.

Akkadian—The language of ancient Babylon and Assyria.

Amarna—The place where Akhenaten had his court.

Amarna letters—Letters from vassals in Canaan to the Egyptian court, in the time of Akhenaten.

Amenemope—Name associated with Egyptian wisdom book that is thought to have influenced Proverbs.

Amphictyony—League of tribes around a central shrine.

Anat—Canaanite goddess.

Apocalypse—Literary genre of revelations about the end.

Apocrypha—Books that are included in the Catholic Bible but are not found in the Hebrew Bible or in the Protestant canon.

Apodictic law—Absolute, declarative law. No ifs or buts.

Aram—Syria.

Aramaic—Language of Syria. Closely related to Hebrew. Standard language of diplomacy under the Persians.

Arameans—People from ancient Syria.

Aretalogies—Inscriptions in which a goddess recites her own accomplishments.

Asherah—Canaanite goddess, also worshiped in Israel. Also the name for a sacred pole at cult sites.

Astarte—Canaanite goddess also worshiped in Israel.

Aten heresy—The exclusive worship of Aten, the solar disk, by Akhenaten.

Athtar—God in Ugaritic myth. Morning star.

Atrahasis—One of the Babylonian accounts of creation.

Baal—Canaanite storm-god.

Bahman Yasht—Persian apocalyptic text with vision of four kingdoms.

Ban (ḥerem)—The custom of slaughtering the enemy as a sacrifice to the god of the victors.

Bar Kokhba—Leader of Jewish revolt against Rome in 132–135 B.C.E.

Book of the Covenant—Laws in Exodus 20–23 that follow the Decalogue.

Canaan—Area including Palestine, Lebanon, and part of Syria in the second millennium B.C.E.

Canon—The corpus of biblical books, viewed as sacred scripture.

Canonical approach—Theological approach to the Old Testament as Scripture, regarding the final form of the text as authoritative.

Casuistic law—Case law, based on specific situations.

Centralization of cult—Prohibition of sacrifice outside of Jerusalem by King Josiah, 621 B.C.E.

Chaldeans—Babylonian diviners.

Chemosh—God of Moab.

Cherubim—Mythical winged creatures, portrayed in Jerusalem temple.

Chronicler's History—1–2 Chronicles.

Collar-rimmed jars—Type of pottery associated with early Israel.

Corvée—Forced labor.

Cosmogony—Story about the origin of the world.

Court narrative—Account of intrigues at David's court, 2 Sam 9—1 Kings 2 (= Succession Document).

Covenant—A solemn agreement. Used especially of agreements between God and Israel.

Covenant, Book of—Exodus, chapters 21–23.

Covenant form—Structure of covenant, understood on the model of ancient treaties.

Credo—"I believe." Profession of faith.

D—The Deuteronomic source in the Pentateuch.

Dagon—God of Philistines.

Day of the Lord—Day of divine intervention in prophetic texts.

Dead Sea Scrolls—Texts found near Qumran by the Dead Sea, beginning in 1947.

Decalogue—The Ten Commandments.

Demiurge—Maker of the world; creator.

Deuterocanonical—Books included in the Roman Catholic canon but relegated to the Apocrypha in Protestant Bibles.

Deutero-Isaiah, Trito-Isaiah—see "Isaiah, Second" and "Isaiah, Third."

Deuteronomic reform—Reform of King Josiah, 621 B.C.E. Centralized the cult in accordance with Deuteronomy 12.

Deuteronomistic History—The books of Joshua, Judges, Samuel, and Kings.

Diaspora—Settlements of people living apart from their ancestral homeland, especially Jews after the Babylonian exile.

Divided monarchy—The division of the Israelite kingdom at the death of Solomon into Judah in the south and Israel in the north.

Divination—Means of consulting the gods.

Documentary Hypothesis—The theory that the Pentateuch was composed by combining four main strands or documents (J, E, D, P).

E (Elohist)—Narrative source in the Pentateuch.

El—Canaanite high god. The word *El* is a generic name for "god" in Biblical Hebrew.

Elephantine papyri—Aramaic documents from Jewish garrison in south of Egypt in the fifth century B.C.E.

Elohim—The Hebrew word for God. Can be understood as either singular or plural.

Enuma Elish—Babylonian account of creation.

Ephraim—Tribe named for son of Joseph, in

central hill country of Israel. Often used as a name for Israel.

Epic—Story of human heroes, involving actions of the gods.

Epicureanism—A school of Greek philosophy that advocated the (sober) enjoyment of the present.

Eschatology—Discussion of the last things.

Etiology—A story that explains the cause of something.

Etymology—A story that explains the origin of a word or name.

Form criticism—Analysis of small units of biblical literature, with attention to genre and setting.

Former Prophets—The books of Joshua, Judges, Samuel, Kings (= the Deuteronomistic History).

Four-room house—Style of house typical of early Israel.

Gerizim—Mountain near Shechem. Site of Samaritan temple in Hellenistic period.

Gilgamesh—Hero of popular Mesopotamian epic.

Grundschrift—German for "basic document." Used in the nineteenth century for what was later called the Priestly Writing (P).

Habiru—People on the fringes of society in the second millennium B.C.E. Possibly related to Hebrews.

Hadad—Another name for Baal.

Hades—Greek name for the netherworld.

Hanukkah—The celebration of the purification of the temple by the Maccabees in 165 of 164 B.C.E.

Hasidim—Party of Jewish pietists during Maccabean revolt.

Hellenistic—Adjective referring to the Greek-speaking world after the conquests of Alexander the Great (died 323 B.C.E.).

Hellenistic reform—Introduction of Greek customs into Jerusalem, 175–168 B.C.E.

Ḥerem (ban)—The custom of slaughtering the enemy as a sacrifice to the god of the victors.

Hexateuch—First six books of the Bible (Pentateuch plus Joshua).

High places—Open-air places of worship.

Hittites—People of Asia Minor (modern Turkey) in the second millennium B.C.E.

Holiness Code (H)—Leviticus 17–26. Closely related to the Priestly source.

Horeb—Mountain of revelation in E and D traditions (instead of Sinai). The name means wilderness.

Hyksos—People from Syria who ruled Egypt for about a century (1650–1550 B.C.E.).

Immanuel—"God with us." Name of child foretold in Isaiah 7.

Inclusio—Literary device whereby the ending corresponds to the beginning.

Isaiah, First—Isaiah 1–39, or portions thereof.

Isaiah, Second—Isaiah 40–55.

Isaiah, Third—Isaiah 56–66.

J (Yahwist)—Narrative source in the Pentateuch.

Jebusites—Inhabitants of Jerusalem before Israelites.

Jeroboam, sin of—Erection of cult sites in northern Israel, at Bethel and Dan, contrary to Deuteronomic law.

Joseph, tribes of—Ephraim and Manasseh.

Josephus—Jewish historian, late first century C.E.

Ketûbîm/Writings—Third part of canon of Hebrew Scriptures.

Levirate law—Law requiring the brother of a deceased man to marry his widow.

Levites—Priests descended from Levi. Subordinated to Zadokite priests in Jerusalem after the exile.

Literary criticism—A variety of approaches that examine a text as literature.

LXX (Septuagint)—The Greek translation of the Old Testament.

Marduk—Main god of Babylon.

Mari—Place on the Euphrates where important texts from the second millennium were discovered.

Marzeah—Feasting, related to the cult of the dead.

Mashal—Literary form involving analogy. Can refer to proverb, parable, or taunt song.

Masoretic text (MT)—The traditional text of the Hebrew Bible, as fixed in the Middle Ages.

Masseba—Sacred pillar or standing stone.

Midbar—Hebrew for wilderness.

Middle Platonism—A form of Greek philosophy that combined elements of Platonism and Stoicism.

Midrash—Rabbinic commentaries on biblical texts.

Milcom—God of the Ammonites.

Mishnah—Compilation of rabbinic law from the second century C.E.

Moabite Stone—Inscription of King Mesha of Moab from the ninth century B.C.E., commemorating victory over Israel.

Mot—Death. A god in Ugaritic myth.

Myth—Sacred story.

Nābî—Hebrew word for prophet.

Natural theology—Knowledge of God derived from the created order. Typical of wisdom literature.

Nazirite—Person consecrated to God by a vow (see Numbers 6).

Nebi'im/Prophets—Second part of canon of Hebrew Scriptures.

Negev/Negeb—Area south of the hill country of Judah.

Nehushtan—Bronze serpent associated with Moses.

New Criticism—A formalistic movement according to which the meaning of a text can be found through close examination of the text itself, without extensive research into social, historical, and literary questions.

Old Greek—The original Greek translation of the Bible, which is different in some cases from that preserved in the Septuagint.

Oracle—An utterance attributed to God or the gods.

P—Priestly strand in the Pentateuch.

Patriarchal—Relating to the patriarchs (Abraham, Isaac, and Jacob).

Pentateuch (Torah)—The first five books of the Bible, also called "the books of Moses."

Philistines—see "Sea Peoples."

Philo—Jewish philosopher in Alexandria, early first century C.E.

Pit—A term for the netherworld (Sheol).

Platonism—Greek philosophy influenced by the teachings of Plato.

Postexilic—The period after 539 B.C.E. when Cyrus allowed the exiles in Babylon to return to Judea.

Primeval history—Narratives concerning the origins of human life, e.g., Genesis 1–11.

Pseudepigrapha—Books that are attributed to famous ancient people (such as Enoch) who did not actually write them.

Qoheleth—The book of Ecclesiastes.

Qumran—Site where Dead Sea Scrolls were discovered.

Rabbinic—Judaism in the period c. 150–650 C.E.

Redaction criticism—The study of how books or blocks of material such as the source documents of the Pentateuch were edited.

Restoration—Return of Judean exiles from Babylon to Jerusalem after the Babylonian exile.

Rib—Accusation or lawsuit.

Samaria—Capital of northern Israel.

Samaritans—People who lived around Shechem in Second Temple period. Had temple on Mount Gerizim. Rejected by Jerusalem as descendants of Assyrian settlers but worshiped God of Israel.

Satrapies—Persian provinces.

Sea Peoples—People who invaded the area of Palestine around 1200 B.C.E. and became the Philistines.

Second Temple period—The period after the Babylonian exile down to the first century C.E. (539 B.C.E.–70 C.E.).

Septuagint (LXX)—The Greek translation of the Old Testament.

Shamash—The sun or sun-god.

Sheol—Hebrew name for the netherworld. Like Greek Hades.

Sitz im Leben—German for "setting in life." Technical term in form criticism.

Solomonic enlightenment—Supposed flowering of culture in reign of Solomon. Now doubted.

Source criticism—Attempt to distinguish different sources in the biblical text, especially in the Pentateuch.

Stoicism—A school of Greek philosophy that emphasized the role of reason in the world.

Succession document—Account of intrigues at David's court, 2 Sam 9—1 Kings 2 (= Court narrative).

Suffering Servant—Figure described in Isaiah 53, whose suffering and death saves others. Probably meant to describe Israel in the exile.

Sukkoth—Festival of Booths or Tabernacles.

Sumer—The earliest great culture in Mesopotamia, where the first known writing system was developed around 3200 B.C.E.

Suzerainty treaty—A treaty in which one party is subordinate to the other.

Talmud—Rabbinic compilation of commentaries on the Mishnah. There are two Talmuds, the Jerusalem Talmud (Yerushalmi), which dates from the fifth century C.E., and the Babylonian (Bavli) from the sixth.

Targum—Paraphrastic Aramaic translation of biblical texts.

Tel Dan inscription—Inscription from the ninth century B.C.E., mentioning "house of David."

Tetragrammaton—The divine name YHWH, so called because it has four letters.

Theodicy—A theological justification of the goodness of God in the face of suffering or evil.

Theogony—Story about the birth of the gods.

Theophany—Manifestation of a god.

Tiamat—The mother goddess in the Babylonian creation story, *Enuma Elish*.

Torah (Pentateuch)—The first five books of the Bible, also called "the books of Moses."

Tosefta—Collection of rabbinic laws that supplement the Mishnah.

Transjordan—Area east of the Jordan River.

Twelve, Book of the—Minor Prophets, Hosea to Malachi.

Ugarit—Modern Ras Shamra, in northern Syria, where important tablets were discovered in 1929.

Vassal treaty—A treaty in which one party is subordinate to the other.

Vulgate—Latin translation of the Bible by Jerome ca. 400 C.E.

Wisdom literature—Texts that give advice on morals and manners or reflect on the meaning of life, e.g., Proverbs, Job, and Qoheleth.

Yahwist (J)—Narrative source in the Pentateuch.

YHWH—The God of Israel, pronounced Yahweh. Traditionally, Jews do not pronounce the divine name and do not insert the vowels. Instead, they say Adonai (the Lord) or ha-Shem (the name).

Yamm—Sea. A god in Ugaritic myth.

Yom Kippur—The Day of Atonement.

Zadokites—Priests descended from Zadok (priest under David and Solomon). High priests in the Second Temple period were Zadokite, down to the Maccabean revolt.

Zaphon—North. Name of mountain in Syria, sacred to Baal.

Zion—Hill in Jerusalem. City of David.

Zion theology—Belief that God had chosen Zion and would protect it.

Zoroastrianism—Persian religion based on teachings of Zoroaster (Zarathustra).

Index of Names and Subjects